Also by Wil Haygood

In Black and White:
The Life of Sammy Davis, Jr.

Two on the River (photographs by Stan Grossfeld)

King of the Cats: The Life and Times of
Adam Clayton Powell, Jr.

The Haygoods of Columbus:
A Family Memoir

LEE COUNTY LIBRARY
107 Hawkins Ave.
Sanford. NC 27330

sweet thunder

Watertown, NY, 1937: Sixteen-year-old Walker Smith Jr. so dazzled the audience that Jack Case, the legendary local sports editor (holding cigar) became an instant admirer. Case saw to it that Smith left town with a new name: Sugar Ray Robinson.

sweet thunder

the
life
and
times
of

Sugar Ray Robinson

**Wil
Haygood**

Alfred A. Knopf
New York · 2009

THIS IS A BORZOI BOOK
PUBLISHED BY ALFRED A. KNOPF

Copyright © 2009 by Wil Haygood

www.aaknopf.com
Knopf, Borzoi Books, and the
colophon are registered trademarks
of Random House, Inc.

Grateful acknowledgment is made
to Harold Ober Associates, Inc.
for permission to reprint an excerpt
from *The Sweet Flypaper of Life* by
Roy DeCarava and Langston Hughes,
copyright © 1955 by Langston Hughes.
Reprinted by permission of Harold Ober
Associates, Inc.

Library of Congress
Cataloging-in-Publication Data
Haygood, Wil.
Sweet thunder : the life and times of
Sugar Ray Robinson / by Wil
Haygood.—1st ed.
p. cm.
"A Borzoi book."
Includes bibliographical references and
index.
ISBN 978-1-4000-4497-9
1. Robinson, Sugar Ray, 1920–1989.
2. Boxers (Sports)—United States—
Biography. I. Title.
GV1132.R6H39 2009
796.83092—dc22
[B]   2009005534

Manufactured in
the United States of America
First Edition

for Phil Bennett, Peter Guralnick, and Greg Moore—
cornermen supreme

contents

illustrations

sweet thunder

All his life the great prizefighter would stare with deep wonder and searching upon this constantly moving cavalcade. It was that world outside the ring that snared Sugar Ray Robinson, the world where beauty and grace held a potent sway. He leaned into Lena's voice and studied Langston's poems. He tried explaining to Miles that their respective artistries had much in common, believing that the trumpet and fighting gloves shared similar mysteries.

As the American calendar kept rolling over the emotional headlines of the forties and the dangerously quiet fifties, a part of the world was spinning in a singular rhythm all its own. From private home to nightclub, from lodge to auditorium, there was a gathering of caramelized and brown and black faces. Sepia dreams—lovely, spilling forth at night—were everywhere, thousands captured in their net. These dreams could not escape segregation, or the laws of the land. But still, art poured from their conditional existence, like music lyrics written on a windowpane.

That would be Billy Eckstine ("the sepia Sinatra," they called him) sitting in the chair at Sugar Ray's hair salon. The salon sat next to the prizefighter's Harlem nightspot, called *Sugar Ray's.* His name glowed in red neon cursive lettering atop the awning. The long mahogany bar hosted the famous—starlets, comics, jazzmen, politicians, crooners. The gangsters behaved themselves. And Sugar Ray loved every minute of it. Tapping his feet, fingering his money clip. Why, he loved this world so much there were times he wondered if it just might overtake his primary line of work. Which was delivering pain and causing blood to flow.

prologue

round midnight

HE IS SUCH A NOCTURNAL FIGURE. Rarely does he rush about—moving, instead, as if in some kind of ether. Even on those days when thousands upon thousands leave their Manhattan homes for Madison Square Garden to see him under the klieg lights or for Yankee Stadium to watch him beneath moonlight, the great Sugar Ray Robinson stirs gently. His work evenings begin around nine o'clock. By midnight he is finished with his work inside the ring, though sometimes, of course, it ends much sooner—a first- or second-round knockout. In Boston in 1950, at the end of the fifth round in a fight with Joe Rindone, Robinson turned to Nat Hentoff, a young reporter at ringside, and mentioned that he hoped the TV audience was enjoying the fight.

"This fight isn't on TV," Hentoff told Robinson.

"What?" Robinson snapped, disappointed.

"And so," recalls Hentoff, "he went and knocked the guy out the next round."

Time to stir.

Huge crowds gather to see him after the fights—after yet another great battle with Jake LaMotta, Carmen Basilio, Gene Fullmer. But he is known for lingering in the dressing room. He travels with a personal valet. Appearance is everything to him: His suits are hand-stitched on Broadway by tailor Sy Martin. (Sy does tailoring for Duke Ellington and a lot of Hollywood stars.) Finally, there he is, and the members of the crowd reach out to him—newsmen, autograph seekers, gangsters. Only after he has satisfied them is he free to take to the night, authoring a style—cosmopolitan, jazz-touched, elegant—unique to the midcentury fight game. In France they respect his power, but truly love his style.

Scores of admirers—many of them habitués of Broadway and Manhattan literary salons—will trek to his rural training camp at Greenwood Lake, New York. He often runs alone, mountains in the distance, a solitary figure sweeping across land once trod by the Iroquois. He looks good in the morning light. Vermeer would have loved him. His nightclub was on 124th Street in Manhattan. That boozy and golden Hollywood couple, Elizabeth Taylor and Richard Burton, would sit for hours sipping champagne, devouring heaps of collard greens. (In 1968 Burton starred in a movie, *Candy,* a sexual satire noted for nothing in cinema history save its eccentric cast: Burton, Marlon Brando, Walter Matthau, James Coburn, and a cameo by Robinson. Burton cast Robinson because he respected legends; Robinson did it for the money.)

Those who have watched him in the ring get as much pleasure, it seems, watching him outside of it—alighting from his flamingo-colored Cadillac down at the Manhattan pier, embarking for Europe on the *Liberté* ocean liner, smiling from the pages of *Life* magazine in white tie and tails. Because it is America, and he is a black man, and it is a time of fierce segregation and racial polarization, there are always two drama-laden ghosts—Jack Johnson and Joe Louis—looming up at him. The public acclaim for heavyweight champions Jack Johnson and Joe Louis had often been seen through the splintering and consuming twentieth-century prism of race, but it was not so with Robinson. He declined that war and enlisted in cultural enlightenment, laying claim to a different piece of cultural terrain. He sought to force a new sensibility in the way we view athletic accomplishment and society. He was the first black athlete to largely own his own fighting rights, and the first to challenge radio and TV station owners about financial receipts. Unlike Johnson and Louis, he negotiated his own independence, constantly battering back the belief that the athlete—especially the Negro athlete—was an uninformed machine. He simply wished the world to see him as larger than the contours of the ring. So while the champagne slid down his throat, he measured the barriers he'd slip through and plotted his entrée into high society.

He believed business acumen would make him whole. But there was something else—style. His name pops up on best-dressed lists; he is a pal to jazzmen—Dizzy Gillespie, Count Basie, Nat King Cole, Billy Eckstine among them. In the autumn of 1952, he will abandon boxing and turn to the world of entertainment. He will headline his own stage show, traveling with the likes of Count Basie and Cootie Williams; Cootie is an old Ellington standby. Sugar Ray plays piano and drums, and practices his tap dancing until drenched in perspiration. Style is as much a mystery as the cosmos.

Sugar Ray Robinson was the first modern prizefighter to take culture—music and grace and dance—into the ring with him. He had convinced himself that style was as much a discipline as boxing. That he dominated both, for so long, causes the world to marvel. Before the headlines of Selma and Montgomery and Little Rock—he followed the Little Rock crisis that day in 1957, full of pain at reports of the little Negro children being verbally assaulted and pelted with rocks; he'd suffer a rare loss that very night—before all the marches, before it seemed as if a new America had just dropped from the sky right onto the old one's front porch, there was another America and it swirled in its own lovely mist. And a good amount of that swirling could be seen in the long glass mirror of Sugar Ray Robinson's nightclub. A jazz-age architect designed the place. Its red neon lettering out front allowed the name of the club—*Sugar Ray's*—to fall, at night, right onto the hoods of the long automobiles. It was hard to imagine the proprietor did not plan it that way.

But stare into that mirror and there they are too—songstress Lena Horne, poet Langston Hughes, and trumpeter Miles Davis—habitués of the place. They were becoming seminal figures in their own right, and they swayed as a kind of cultural chorus of the 1940s and 1950s alongside Robinson. Their lives intersected; but more than that, they were Robinson allies, themselves in the vanguard of a certain kind of style. The singer, trumpeter, and poet were not unlike cultural attachés, swooning their music and prose out into the world with elegant defiance, commiserating or celebrating at one of Robinson's dining tables inside his club. They all wished to push back the curtain onto mainstream America. Robinson long feared being trapped in the ring, being webbed in the American imagination merely as an athlete. He would tell acquaintances, at the height of his worldwide fistic accomplishments, that the sport actually bored him, that there were other venues to challenge his creative prowess. He marched and listened as a Renaissance man might. Art enveloped and seduced him. So, as we follow him in and out of the ring, in and out of his midnight sonatas, across America, to and from Europe, we will intermittently follow the poet, trumpeter, and songstress, watching the spells they weave, the battles they fight, against the backdrop of Sugar Ray Robinson's times.

For so many years he has stood as the golden figurine of boxing. Newspapermen and promoters were bewildered by him, believing him uppity and arrogant. He simply would not bend or yield his stature. After leaving the ring, he refused to do boxing commentary, leaving many to wonder if he thought the sport foolish—or sacred. But his image glowed in the fantastical ruminations of children, and they scampered after him, truly feeling his generosity. His link to them was deep. Because this saga begins like that of so many who fight for food and glory—in the eyes of a desperate and hungry child.

Sitting in their church pews gave them time to ponder. They knew that one of the greatest battles they'd have to wage—plotting a way to beat the devil who worked hard to capture the attentions of many in their flock—was upon them. The streets of Manhattan and Harlem were shadowy and menacing; the Depression of the 1930s was unforgiving and could cause young minds to totter in misdirection. The city's tabloids, playing up the morbid crime sagas, told the price of inattention to juvenile vices.

So the ministers and deacons of Salem Methodist Episcopal Church—with the important support of their wives—listened up when they heard of an unusual manner in which to fight back. This mix of Bibles and boxing made sense to them: It required energy to fight sin. They agreed to the creation of the Salem Crescent Athletic Club—a boxing team.

When young Walker Smith Jr., with his long arms and sweet smile, joined the crusade, he proceeded to deliver the church's name and image into a different realm of appreciation. They found themselves saluted, admired, and envied for reasons other than the strictly biblical. Old has-been fighters slipped into the basement to watch the boy, their heads rolling like hurt plums. The boy was special and the ministers knew it. Told from the pulpit of his near-mythical exploits, which had been achieved in small towns up and down the Eastern seaboard, the congregation would utter the same word over and over: Amen. And then they would drop coins and small bills into a basket, so that the Walker Smith–led club might continue its crusade.

1921–1942

say goodbye to Walker Smith Jr.

THE CITY OF DETROIT was founded by French slaveholders. They suffered a political rebuke in 1837 when the Michigan legislature opted to join the United States. State officeholders then rose up and outlawed the so-called peculiar institution of slavery.

In the coming years, escaped slaves would rush into the city. Many were delivered by daring operatives of the Underground Railroad. Northern-based organizations, many on job recruiting missions, also sent representatives into the Deep South—preachers prominent among them—to urge the disenfranchised to come North. Negro newspapers displayed flashy advertisements—"The Flight out of Egypt" one slogan trumpeted—telling of jobs in factories and steel plants. Pullman porters slyly handed out leaflets on train platforms and inside rail stations, with curious passengers folding the material into their purses and wallets. A representative of a Detroit organization, preparing to go South on a recruiting mission, certainly felt the emotion in a letter from a semiliterate man who wished to escape Georgia: "I am Sick of the South and always has been, but the opertunity has just come our way so by God healp and you I will soon be out of the South. I was just reading in the morning Beaumont Enterprise Paper where thay Burn one of the Race to Stake for God sack please help to get me out of the South."

In time, the flow of migration into Detroit seemed unstoppable. Germans were joined by Irish, who were joined by the French. Few, however, were as starved for social acceptance as the Negro. Between 1910 and 1930, the number of Negroes in Detroit swelled from 5,000 to 120,000. The population jump gave the impression that the metropolis was a kind of mecca. In addition to its progressive mind-set, there was a constant motion and energy about 1920s

Detroit. And Henry Ford's mechanical machines played a huge role in the bustle.

Auto magnate Ford, who said his ideas often came to him while rocking in a rocking chair, had unveiled his Model T back in 1908. He constantly pondered ways to speed up production. He knew he had hit upon something with the idea of an assembly line: Workers placed at one end of the plant would pass an assembled chassis up the line; axles would be added, then wheels, then the body. In 1913 the process could be completed in twelve hours, thirty minutes. Ford wasn't satisfied, though; the following year the time was down to ninety-six minutes. It was taxing work, but the jobs were coveted. The carmaker—himself of Irish immigrant stock—offered a forty-hour workweek at $5 a day. It was a handsome wage. And Negroes were hired in appreciable numbers at the Ford plant. Mindful of the social dynamics, Ford even employed a couple of Negro personnel officers. The legend of Henry Ford quickly grew; it could be heard in a 1920s ditty: "I'm goin' to Detroit, get myself a good job,/Tried to stay around here with the starvation mob./I'm goin' to get me a job, up there in Mr. Ford's place,/Stop these eatless days from starin' me in the face."

Walker Smith Sr. was a farmer in rural Georgia. He toiled raising peanuts, corn, and of course cotton. He was small in stature—five feet seven—and possessed a powerful work ethic. He imagined, however, that the $10 a week he was averaging would keep him and his family swallowed in poverty forever. In 1920 relatives in Detroit boasted of "good salaries" there, coaxing him to join the great exodus and come North. Smith announced to his family—wife, Leila, daughters, Marie and Evelyn—that he would venture there alone first, and if the city was to his liking, he'd send for them. There was immediate concern among family members: They'd be alone; the Southern rural darkness could be full of foreboding to a lone woman and her daughters. Smith tried to stifle his family's concerns. He was determined to go.

Once in Detroit, it took Walker Smith little time to find employment. He found a job in construction; he began bringing home $60 a week—six times his income as a farmer! The Georgia immigrant could only smile at his good fortune. The clothing stores in downtown Detroit dazzled Smith; he purchased new clothing—tweeds, two-tone shoes, straw hats. Because of Prohibition, the city was dry. But Walker Smith knew just where to go to get himself a drink—

the darkened speakeasies in the heavily populated Negro area of the city, along Hastings Street, an area known, coarsely, as Black Bottom, though its social milieu in fact included various ethnic groups in addition to numberless Negroes. (Rumrunners also slipped into the city from Canada and sold their home brew from glass jars. The rum-running was abetted by illegal gambling and prostitution, giving the city, come nightfall, a rather dangerous vibe. A feared police unit known as the Black Hand Squad patrolled the area.) Confronted with the teeming nights, Walker Smith rubbed his hands together and proceeded to shuck off his country upbringing: A construction worker by day, maybe, but by night a wiry dandy who had already made enough to purchase himself one of Henry Ford's Model T's. Walker Smith didn't miss the Georgia fields at all.

Months after his arrival in Detroit, he had saved enough money to send for his family to join him. Leila Smith and her daughters boarded a train, and as it chugged forward—their own family's flight out of Egypt—they bid rural Georgia farewell. Leila Smith was happy.

Upon their arrival in Detroit, Leila reconnected with husband Walker. He was delighted to see his family together again. He ushered them into a modest home on McComb Avenue, and Leila's daughters began helping around the house as much as they could. Walker hoped for a son.

In the ensuing weeks, Leila and her daughters—like so many newcomers—were simply stunned by the pace of Detroit: booming construction cranes; Model T's swerving around corners; police officers with pinched faces wielding billy clubs upon the homeless. Reinhold Niebuhr—whose writings would later become influential reading for the seminary student Martin Luther King Jr.—was a young minister living in Detroit at the time. Niebuhr also found the city bewildering: "A city which is built around a productive process . . . is really a kind of hell," he felt. "Thousands in this town are really living in torment while the rest of us eat, drink, and make merry. What a civilization!"

Walker Smith, Jr.—born May 3, 1921—would spend his youngest years in this Northern environment. He was proudly named Walker, after his father. They called him Junior. (Robinson's birthplace would come, in later years, to be claimed by both the citizens of Michigan and Georgia, although Sugar Ray himself preferred Detroit.) The infant child barely saw his father, however, as Walker Sr. was now working two jobs, his second on a sewer line. After her son's birth Leila went back to work as a maid at the city's Statler Hotel. The young child was left, for the most part, in the care of his two sisters, Marie and Evelyn. The sisters spoiled the boy by rocking him, giving him sweets, fussing over him in the cold weather. Little Walker, however, would retain vivid impressions of his father from sweet and slow Sunday afternoons: The father would get dressed up, stand in front of the mirror, cackle with confidence in Junior's direction. "He was a good dresser," the son would recall of his father, and his description might have summed up the evolution of his own future sartorial bent. "Conservative, but stylish. He liked dark suits—blues, grays, and browns. And I can remember that in the summer he wore two-tone shoes and a white Panama hat." The father's Model T entranced little Walker. He furtively explored the machine, once playing the part of stowaway: "One time I hid in the rumble seat of his Ford. When I hopped out, he had to drive me home. He didn't like that because he had to use more gas. And that meant he was wasting money."

Few if any Southern migrant families could foresee what was about to happen inside the borders of Detroit in the mid-1920s. The combustion of Henry Ford's automobiles was one thing; human combustion quite another. The crowding of migrants—and foreign immigrants—meant a housing squeeze. There was an unstoppable flow of families seeking opportunities, seen hustling daily from the trains down at Michigan's Central Terminal—and it started to cause painful ruptures.

Many residents of the Black Bottom area suffered from high rents, inadequate medical care, and brutish police tactics. "Black because we lived there, Bottom because that's where we were at," Walker Sr.'s only son would later lament about the Black Bottom district. And what slowly began to creep into the city's soul was Henry Ford's xenophobia.

In the summer of 1921, Ford—whose genius seemed strictly business-oriented—had approximately five hundred thousand copies of *The Protocols of the Elders of Zion* printed for local reading pleasure. It was a thinly veiled treatise attacking Jews, full of anti-Semitic vitriol. Bigots were the only ones who got pleasure from reading it. Ford's narrow racial views on social matters—at variance from the needs of his labor-hungry auto plants—were hardly unexpected, since they echoed much of the national discourse. President Woodrow Wilson had brought a nasty segregationist attitude with him to the White House: Negro civil servants lost hundreds of jobs with little or no explanation; the color line in social venues in the nation's capital was tightened even more. Actions—or inaction—from the top tiers of the government had a way of filtering downward. There were newspaper accounts of racial hatred across the country.

In May of 1921 in Tulsa, Oklahoma, a Negro youth, Dick Rowland, went into a downtown building to use the bathroom. A white seventeen-year-old girl claimed he attacked her. Rowland denied guilt but was quickly arrested and taken to jail. A group of local blacks armed themselves to help the sheriff protect Rowland from a possible lynching. Enraged, local whites went on a rampage, galloping through the Greenwood section of the city—known as "the Negro Wall Street of America"—firing weapons at random and setting fire to buildings. Some of the fleeing blacks were gunned down from behind. A. C. Jackson was a physician who bravely stayed to give medical care to the wounded that first night. On the second day, with his home surrounded by a sneering mob, Jackson stepped outside, the smell of ash still in the air. "Here I am," the frightened man said. "Take me." Two bullets then ripped into his chest, killing him. Before it was over, at least one hundred blacks had been killed (some accounts cite three times that number), and over a thousand homes and businesses torched. An investigation eventually exonerated shoeshine man Rowland of all charges. Not a single white person was ever arrested. Eighteen months later came another horror down South: Believing a Negro had raped a white woman in Sumner, Florida, white residents sought vengeance in nearby Rosewood, an all-black town. At least seventeen blacks were murdered. Those who saved themselves had fled with a few meager possessions into nearby woods.

In Detroit, little Walker Smith and his family soon found themselves living in a cauldron of social unease. On Christmas Eve of 1923 the Ku Klux Klan held a rally around Detroit's City Hall. They sang carols holding the hands of their children while flames from a burning cross licked at the night air. They warned of more rallies and marches.

It is little wonder that dinnertime conversation at the Smiths often reflected concerns about the city's dangers: Leila fretted about

Black Bottom and the crime; she worried about the strangers who sidled up to her two lovely daughters, whispering sweet nothings; she lamented that Walker Sr. didn't spend more time with their little son. And she feared the presence of the Klan. Walker Sr., in his Panama hat, was not worrying about the social order: He was intent on playing the role of Detroit hepcat, not Georgia rube.

It was finally the actions of a Black Bottom neighbor that would justify the fears of Leila Smith and many other local blacks—fears that left Leila painfully missing quiet afternoons in the countryside she had left behind.

Ossian Sweet was one of the few Negro doctors living and working in Detroit's Black Bottom district. Born in Florida, he had obtained his medical degree from Howard University in the nation's capital. He settled in Detroit in 1921. He and his wife, Gladys, had a daughter, Iva, and with his practice doing well, they wished to purchase a home away from Black Bottom, someplace in the city that was safe and might herald their middle-class stature. They bought a home on Garland Street, sold to them by a white couple. The neighborhood was all white. The couple who sold the Sweets the house told them—disingenuously—that while they would be integrating the neighborhood, they would not face any danger in doing so. But even before the Sweets moved in, posters appeared around the neighborhood advertising their arrival, and calling for protests. Threats against the Negro family were uttered at community meetings.

On move-in day—September 8, 1925—the good doctor surrounded himself with protection, calling on his brother Henry and a group of Negro friends. Inside the house, they were well armed with guns. The first night passed with relative quiet, in spite of curious onlookers outside the windows. Before nightfall on the second day, however, more than three hundred whites had gathered near the house, all of them watched by police. Hurled stones and chunks of coal crashed onto the porch, shattering windows, causing the police to bolt into action. Ossian Sweet was determined to protect his family and property. Firing began from inside the house. With bullets whizzing, folk ducked and scattered. Voices howled. Two men—white—were hit. They were quickly taken to a nearby hospital. Eric Houghberg would survive his wound, but Leon Breiner would not. Eleven Negroes were arrested, including Ossian's wife, Gladys.

Within days the national press picked up the story of a Negro doctor bent on defending his family—and of a man who lay dead. The Klan threatened reprisals.

James Weldon Johnson, the poet and literary figure, was executive secretary of the NAACP. The case of the Sweets touched him, and he decided to throw the weight of the civil rights organization behind the accused. Negro lawyers would be fine as part of the legal team, but Johnson feared they wouldn't be able to maneuver around the politics of the case, given the entrenched racism in the legal structure of Detroit. He wanted a white lawyer—an outsider—on the team, and someone with a national reputation. After much wooing, Clarence Darrow, famous from the Scopes monkey trial and renowned for championing the oppressed, joined the defense team just two weeks before the trial's beginning. The Sweet brothers and their codefendants—save for his wife, Gladys, who was released on bail—remained behind bars. Ossian was defiant. "I am willing to stay indefinitely in the cell and be punished," he said. "I feel sure by the demonstration made by my people that they have confidence in me as a law-abiding citizen. I denounce the theory of Ku Kluxism and uphold the theory of manhood with a wife and tiny baby to protect."

Negro newspapers jumped into the fray from their editorial pages. "The heroic defense of their homes exhibited by those brave and fearless Detroiters," came a salvo from a Negro publication in Philadelphia, "makes every Negro in this country their debtor." When white liberal publications chimed in, defending Ossian Sweet's right to protect his family, the NAACP knew it had backing beyond the Negro hallways of the nation. "The law in America is presumably broad enough to cover the Negro as well as the white man," the New York *World* opined—if a touch dreamily.

Clarence Darrow and his legal team went to work. "I realized that defending [N]egros, even in the [N]orth, was no boy's job," Darrow had said. As the trial got under way, the aging, white-haired lawyer showed dramatic flourishes in the courtroom, clipping away at eyewitness testimony offered by whites.

It all ended in a mistrial, which meant the Sweets and their cohorts might still go to prison, as there would be a second trial. And for that second trial, Darrow enlisted the services of Thomas Chawke, a shrewd local attorney who had made a reputation defending gangsters. In facing the jury, Chawke talked about the city, its reputation, its politics, and its future. But the crowd awaited the big man in suspenders with the dramatic face: Darrow. He also talked of community, of safety, of man's right to defend hearth and home. But he took the jurors into the very source of Ossian Sweet's American ambitions; into the very heart of the pursuit of freedom: "Prejudices have burned men at the stake, broken them on the rack, torn every joint apart, destroyed people by the million," he thundered. "Men have done this on account of some terrible prejudice which even now is reaching out to undermine this republic of ours and to destroy the freedom that has been the most cherished part of our institutions. These witnesses honestly believe that it is their duty to keep colored people out." He talked of slavery, of blood, of the long nights endured by black Americans. Summing up his argument to the jury, he said: "I ask you, gentlemen, on behalf of this defendant, on behalf of these helpless ones who turn to you, and more than that—on behalf of this great state, and this great city which must face this problem, and face it fairly—I ask you in the name of progress and the human race, to return a verdict of not guilty in this case!"

And the jury did so. Supporters of the defendants surrounded Darrow and the other lawyers. The Sweets were finally free to go home. The NAACP celebrated the case, and invited Dr. Sweet to appear before audiences.

It was not quite enough, however, to assuage the fear that continued to grip blacks in the city. If a Negro doctor such as Ossian Sweet could have his life hanging in the balance, what might befall a common family from the South with no high connections or fancy college degrees? What calamity might befall the Smiths?

In March of 1927, Leila Smith, along with her two daughters and five-year-old Walker Jr., fled both her husband and Detroit. A train delivered them all back to Georgia. Leila Smith took the children to the home of her mother. With the children—in her mind—out of harm's way, she returned to Detroit. The South was still the South, and she needed money now, being the sole breadwinner for the family. She remained in Detroit a whole year, saving her earnings.

In Georgia, little Walker Smith walked barefoot. He went hunting with uncles. "We ate well," he would recall. "We had fresh milk from a big cow named Duck." He witnessed the slaughtering of livestock, which shocked him. He missed his mother. Within a year

Leila Smith returned to retrieve her children. In her absence, little Walker had grown extremely close to his sisters, grateful for their attempts at mothering. It was an attachment he would joyfully honor his entire life. Leila told them she was taking them back to Detroit. They wanted to know about their father, but Leila made no promises that he would be a constant part of their life. The children were surprised—and little Walker especially bewildered—but all happily boarded the train because they wanted to be with their mother.

Upon coming back to Detroit, little Walker felt a sense of déjà vu: "The gray of winter was in the sky. The paint was peeling on most of the houses. The yards and alleys were muddy with melting snow."

But this time Leila Smith had a plan for her son: He'd join the Brewster Recreation Center. (Membership was twenty-five cents a month.) With luck that would keep him away from the ravages of Black Bottom.

As soon as little Walker pushed his way through the doors of the center, he fell in love with it: He could swim, he could play basketball. He could paint and draw and play checkers. He came to see a kind of symphony at work: children running about who were just like him, many desperately poor like him, all uplifted by camaraderie and good times. He started seeing a big light-skinned youth around the center. Men uttered his name. The young man had won trophies while fighting in the ranks of the Amateur Athletic Union (AAU). Every other month, it seemed, Joe Louis Barrow—whose name would later be shortened to Joe Louis—won yet another trophy for the Brewster rec center. There were news clippings on the walls at Brewster about him, and every little boy and girl saw those clippings. In time, little Walker became entranced. He followed Joe Louis Barrow around like an itchy kitten. Louis's family also lived in Black Bottom, and his stepfather was yet one more laborer in Henry Ford's employ. (John Roxborough, a Black Bottom numbers runner, financed Joe's early Detroit training and led him into the professional ranks.) It was at Brewster that little Walker himself first put on a pair of boxing gloves. No one thought much about it, though the little tyke did seem unnaturally quick—it was the way his arm would shoot out from his shoulder. But he'd as soon zip off to play basketball as box: He simply wanted to play.

A weariness, however, had already set in upon Leila Smith's life in Detroit. She couldn't make ends meet. No sooner would she consider a reconciliation with her husband than news of yet another infidelity on his part would stop her. He had turned into a cad and ne'er-do-well. There was that unyielding racial antagonism in the air—and the Depression was gnawing at many Black Bottom families barely holding-on. A female acquaintance told Leila to come to New York City, suggesting she could start anew there. For a single woman with three children, the decision to make such a move took uncommon bravery.

In the late autumn of 1932, Leila—a woman possessed of a stout and no-nonsense character—gathered up her family and their belongings. They went downtown and climbed aboard a bus bound for New York City. Years earlier Leila Smith had joined so many others in the flight out of Egypt; now came her flight out of Detroit. She had made up her mind she was finally going to divorce her husband, and mother and children had conspired to keep Walker Sr. unaware of the plan. Upon visiting the house and realizing they had packed and left, he quickly rolled around Black Bottom in his Model T, trying to catch a glimpse of them—of his family, his estranged wife, daughters, his only son. But no matter how fast he drove, which corners he turned, the Model T was useless. They were gone.

Little Walker Smith and his family settled into Manhattan. Their first home, a three-room flat in midtown, was temporary quarters. Leila found work as a seamstress. Little Walker—eleven years old in 1932—busied himself in those early months by hanging out in front of the Broadway theatres in and around Times Square. He had acquired a fondness for tap dancing and jitterbugging. Along with new friends, he showed off impromptu dance steps beneath the neon-spilling theatre marquees. They were vagabond performances. When he wasn't being shooed away, passersby dropped money at his feet: "Sometimes we'd make a couple dollars apiece on a good night," Walker Jr. would remember of the dancing. But he missed Detroit—especially the Brewster Recreation Center—and he missed his father. He sometimes journeyed down to the docks of the Manhattan waterfront and stared out at the great hulking ships. He dreamed out into the rhythm of their horns and over the open waters. He had no manly defenders and trusted no one save his mother and sisters. He was a fatherless child in an unknown city, a place bigger and even more mysterious than Detroit.

And when he barreled through the door of his home, complaining about yet another neighborhood scuffle—which he invariably got the worst of—Leila Smith showed no mercy. He was new to the community, he was going to be tested; she insisted he stand his ground. She harangued Walker Jr. about cowardice; she pushed him out the door to face his foes time and time again. His sisters fretted after him, but Leila instructed them against coddling. Her eyes seemed to bore right through Walker as he stood staring at her, his very own mother, who was pushing him back out toward the direction of danger.

Leila Smith had been a field hand in the South. She did not have a fragile psyche; she was coarse and blunt and aggressive with her language. She argued with grocery store clerks over bills and she argued with rent collectors. She had lived under a roof with one man— Walker Sr.—whom she could not trust, who did not listen to her. She would not suffer such a fate again. When little Walker seemed to need a hug, he often received more tough words from his mother, stinging language about standing up, about pride. "She'd give you a fucking beating if you got smart with her," recalls newspaperman Jimmy Breslin, who got to know the family in later years and befriended Leila. "She had been a field hand in the South. Now she could be fun. But she was a tough woman."

Economic miseries were everywhere. In 1932, millions of Americans were losing jobs by the month. Wages were down 40 percent compared to just three years earlier. Impoverished children were especially vulnerable. Little Walker, who always seemed to be hungry, took free lunches at the local Salvation Army—"hot dogs and beans," he would sadly remember.

By the time the family moved uptown, into Harlem, Franklin D. Roosevelt had settled into the White House: His first day on the job was March 6, 1933. The patrician and former New York governor was determined to lift the country from the jaws of misery. "This nation asks for action, and action now," he proclaimed. First there was an emergency session of Congress and following that, one hundred thrilling days of groundbreaking legislation. The president came to the aid of the banking industry. The rail system was bailed out of financial trouble; stock exchanges were regulated. He put money behind his soothing radio speeches: $500 million flowed into every state to help the downtrodden. The Civilian Conservation Corps was established. Flooding in the Tennessee Valley was brought under control by the Tennessee Valley Authority. Unemployed men were hired for public works projects across the country: Mammoth bridges went up over San Francisco Bay and the Florida Keys.

Looking around Harlem, little Walker Smith refused to pity himself. As he knew, it would draw no sympathy from his mother. Rather, he kept himself busy. He swiped candy; he snatched fruit from vendor stands, dashing around curbsides, his chest heaving as faceless grocers yelled after him. He sold scrap wood, cans, bottles. He shot dice for nickels—earnings from the odds and ends he sold—with tough-looking kids. More and more he fought back against street foes, the better to elicit smiles from his mother. (The recollections of desperate children like himself leaning into waywardness would play a powerful role in his later years.) Leila Smith saw and heard much that worried her in her new surroundings: constant sirens, the ragged children running about—all part of the unpredictable vibe of urban street life. She feared a years-long descent by her son into that dreaded state that any parent abhorred: juvenile delinquency.

What Leila Smith also noticed in her new community was the array of churches it featured. Those churches served the highbrow and the less cultured. They fed the hungry, sent masses into the streets for protest rallies, demanded better attention from Manhattan politicos. They calmed the masses during spasms of rioting. Their ministers became notable community figures, quoted in newspapers, on the radio, in national church publications. They were men like Adam Clayton Powell (Senior and Junior) of the Abyssinian Baptist Church; J. W. Brown of Mother A.M.E. Zion; Hutchens C. Bishop of St. Philip's Protestant Episcopal; George Sims of Union Baptist; W. W. Brown of Metropolitan Baptist; William Lloyd Imes of St. James Presbyterian; and Frederick A. Cullen of Salem Methodist Episcopal. From their pulpits these ministers preached against vice and sloth; they abhorred the devil's presence but hardly denied it. They spoke of their congregation's young members, and the need for the adults to guide and offer instruction, to lead by example.

But there existed two Harlems: In one Harlem there were poetry readings and social teas; there were gatherings that featured notable speakers who talked about national affairs and the doings they were privy to in the Roosevelt White House. In this Harlem, the collegiate sons and daughters of prominent families, home on school break, talked of their studies at Fisk, Howard, and Lincoln universities. In this Harlem there was music by the Harlem Symphony; there were NAACP galas and fraternity soirees. Paul Robeson and Ethel Waters stepped about this Harlem, and one might shake the hand of writers Wallace Thurman or Countee Cullen—the latter the adopted son of Frederick A. Cullen of Salem Methodist. One might even see a youthful Langston Hughes standing outside the Harlem Y, a parrot atop his shoulder. This was a sweet place where a Renaissance spirit blossomed like flowers, where Negro couples strolled about in raccoon coats. "A blue haze descended at night and with it strings of fairy lights on the broad avenues," a cultural critic and resident of that Harlem would remember. That was the bright side of the two-sided coin of Harlem.

The other side was darker and unforgiving—and it was that side that dominated the lives of little Walker Smith and his sisters and mother. Their Harlem was a rough place, a lower-class enclave of broken families, of flophouses and boardinghouses. Of racketeers and gangsters, of big crime and petty crime. Of handouts and hand-me-down clothing, of little boys often scampering about like lambs being hunted. This Harlem had curt and exacting landlords aplenty: "Send it, and send it damn quick" was one famous landlord's consistent advice to those who were late with rent money. Little Walker Smith would recall: "Mom really had a time trying to feed us." The Smiths had no family references, no entrée into a more elevated society. They were invited to no formal events. They blurred into all the other anonymous faces in the community; they were scraping by in the harsh Harlem. But now and then, galloping along with his buddies up and down busy Seventh Avenue, young Walker would get glimpses of that gilded Harlem—a dashing Negro couple in furs; glittering silverware behind a glass window in the hands of diners; a lone dandy leaning against a lamppost; a crowd alighting from the neon-lit Lafayette Theatre, the gleaming Model T's–like exclamation points announcing certain lifestyles; the gorgeous sepia-tinted photographs in the window of famed photographer James Van Der Zee. ("In Harlem he is called upon to capture the tragedy as well as the happiness in life, turning his camera on death and marriage with the same detachment," Cecil Beaton would say of the gifted Van Der Zee.) The unfolding scenes—the kaleidoscope of an elegant life beyond his reach—would all give pause to the young Walker Smith. And now that he knew this world existed, he would be unable to unshackle its dynamism from his boyish mind.

What FDR's government couldn't do fast enough—tackling the woes of urban communities—churches and church leaders had to do instead. In Harlem this meant the intervention of the clergy in the children's play hours. It became their mission, in any congregation where the church had enough muscle, to create activities that might fill an afternoon or evening for wayward souls. It was easy to hear the near singsong lament of mothers whose children were getting into trouble, who were losing focus. Those mothers, more often than not, showed no hesitancy in turning to local churches for help.

"Harlem in those days didn't have much in terms of recreational outlets," recalls Robert Royal, who was a young boy in the community then and who would come to befriend the adult Robinson in later years.

Given such a reality, the more a minister seemed attuned to the community's needs, the more renowned he became. The big churches pooled their resources, recruiting adults who possessed some particular expertise in an area of athletics. And before long, many of the churches had basketball teams, softball teams. But one church, Salem Methodist Episcopal, distinguished itself in a rather untraditional arena—its boxing team. "They recognized the influence of Henry Armstrong and Joe Louis," Royal says of the Salem church officials.

Rev. Cullen, the influential leader of Salem Methodist—he lived in a lovely fourteen-room manse on Seventh Avenue—had listened raptly when members of his staff brought the idea of the boxing team to him. It was Roy Morse who had originally suggested the idea to those staff members.

Morse, born in New York City, had been a star sprinter on the track field in the city during his junior-high and high-school years, getting mentions in the press in 1910 for winning major titles. He went on to Buffalo City College in 1911, also excelling in athletics before financial hardships cut his studies short. Back in New York, sitting in the pews at Salem Methodist, Morse conferred with some of his boyhood friends who had taken up boxing and then floated the idea of a boxing club at the church. Congregants quickly approved the plan—anything to get a jump on the lurking machinery of the devil—and it was a done deal with Rev. Cullen's approving nod.

Certain churches began to distinguish themselves by their specialties in after-school programs. "St. Philips was known then for basketball," recalls Arthur Barnes, who grew up in Harlem. "And Salem Crescent had the fighters. If you were interested in boxing, that's where you went to train." Morse recruited onetime boxer and manager George Gainford to the staff. In time, Salem Crescent Athletic Club acquired a certain cachet, and it went beyond the borders of Manhattan. As Robert Royal remembers, "Salem Crescent was one of the top boxing programs in the country. If you came out of Salem Crescent, you were a proven warrior."

Leila Smith couldn't find a Brewster Recreation Center in Harlem, but she was desperate for her son to get involved in some type of after-school activity. Walker seemed completely indifferent to his studies at Cooper Junior High School. The boy walked the halls with a street swagger, rolling his shoulders, lingering in those hallways too long. He was late with homework assignments; school officials warned him about shooting dice. Schoolgirls dismissed him as cocky and even arrogant, his whiffs of charm not enough—not yet—to assuage concerns about his demeanor.

A neighborhood friend dragged Walker along to Salem Methodist one afternoon to show him its boxing facilities. (Young Walker knew the church because he had shot dice in the alleyway behind its ornate walls.) Walker had bragged to friends about having some boxing skills—and about having met Joe Louis. Louis would not become champion until 1937, and so in 1934 many of his friends knew nothing of the Joe Louis that Walker talked about. Those who had heard of the fighter didn't believe him.

Salem Methodist sat at 129th Street and Seventh Avenue. It had shiny pews and lovely windows; Salem officials had paid $258,000 for the chapel in 1923, during a year when Negro congregations were buying properties throughout Harlem to show their business acumen. Thirteen-year-old Walker Jr. descended the stairs to the Salem church basement, where the boxing facilities were set up.

Boys his age and older were sparring, skipping rope, grunting, tying on gloves. His lit eyes jumped from scene to scene. That smell of sweat—"a strange perfume to me," he would call it—was everywhere. Because of his limited introduction to the sport in Detroit—and because he had already overstated his prowess to friends—he had convinced himself that to retreat now was to lose face. In his mind, he was right where he belonged.

This setting, he quickly concluded, might serve as an extra shield against the mean streets. His modus vivendi within his new surroundings was simple—he would have to hold on, just as he had been doing all his short life. He was a skinny youth who had heard of the terrors that circled his Black Bottom neighborhood in Detroit and survived them. He had been whisked away from his father and did not become morose or depressed. He had committed petty acts of thievery—showing youthful courage, however misplaced—and yet had not been caught and thrown in detention. Survival was all. Now he found himself in a neighborhood rough at the best of times and now battered by the Depression, a place that could gobble him up, but he wouldn't let it. The two-sided coin of Harlem had now rolled right up to young Walker Smith. That descent into a church basement offered a kind of clarity he had never felt before. The boy—whose independent mind seems to have sprung directly from his strong-willed mother—could not allow a moment's worth of fear down where the fists were flying. Underground, he realized, for the first time in his life, he could unburden himself of little-boy worries. The officials explained to him what was expected of a member of the Salem Crescent Athletic Club, the name the young pugilists fought under. He listened—not in that unfocused way he listened to teachers at Cooper Junior High—but with genuine raptness.

He told his mother about Salem Crescent and its vaunted boxing program. He wanted to join, and his enthusiasm filled Leila Smith with joy. He would fight, just as she had long told him to, just as she herself did whenever she had to.

"Sugar Ray had a nickname for my grandmother. It was 'Punch.' That's how tough she was," says Ken Bristow, Robinson's nephew.

Leila Smith delighted in knowing that her son would have authority figures watching over him and teaching him, a mission his own father had abandoned. The Smiths were not a churchgoing clan, but Leila thought that a place that might welcome and protect her son was a divine blessing indeed.

George Gainford had been shifting around the world of amateur boxing for years. He had tried boxing in his own youth, but had been an undistinguished prospect. Upon realizing his own career had no future, he turned to managing. The few fighters he managed, however, proved unremarkable. The world of managing excited him more than anything, but opportunities for Negro managers were limited. Unlike the Negro managers behind Joe Louis's rising career, he did not have access to the ready money it took to manage one fighter, let alone several. So he went about picking up points of wisdom about training fighters. He quizzed other high-profile trainers, such as New York City's Ray Arcel. "You're only as good as the fighter you work with," Arcel once said, full of simple but potent insight. "I don't care how much you know, if your fighter can't fight, you're another bum in the park." Gainford visited other gyms, particularly Stillman's in midtown Manhattan, and watched trainers putting their fighters through workouts. He made mental notes of all that he saw. He pulled out rolled-up copies of *Ring* magazine from his back pocket and sat down to read and reread stories about trainers and fighters and why certain fighters won titles while others vanished. In his early years at Salem Crescent, he was the trainer as dreamer: In his garrulous moments he spoke of his dream that one of his little warriors might rise up and become a king, a champion; he hoped that as he turned toward yet another set of footsteps coming down the stairs there might be another champ-in-the-making like Jack Johnson, another titleholder like Henry Armstrong, gliding into view. The fight game relied on a mixture of hunger and timing— and a trainer's ability to pick talent.

George Gainford stood at ring's edge and watched Walker Smith's maiden workout. He had seen neophytes work out hundreds of times. He was always looking for something that might hold his interest: the way an inexperienced fighter moved his feet, the quickness of a jab, a naturalness and comfort in the ring. A trainer had to make snap judgments as he imagined into the future on behalf of a young novice fighter. It was not a sport to be taken on as a hobby; a young fighter must want something, must desire to take a certain road to a certain place. Gainford looked at the boy, and as the minutes passed, a look of comfort crossed his face: "You got good moves," he confided to young Walker. The other young fighters looking on—always hungry for any praise from Gainford—knew it was a high compliment he had given to this newcomer. Walker beamed. It was enough of a compliment to get him a spot on the Salem Crescent team. He would start low; he would have to work his way up; he would have to show dedication and discipline. In the days and weeks that followed, Gainford warned him—brushing off the boy's incessant questions about opportunities to fight—that it was the road trips that so often told the tale. Those AAU and Golden Gloves bouts were the ones that drew the attention of the press, and where the Salem boys had first cemented their reputation.

Gainford liked the adulation heaped upon him by Salem church members, elderly women and deacons patting him on the back on his strolls about the church premises, praising the accomplishments of his young charges. His girth was widened by the delicacies laid out by churchwomen—dinners of chicken dumplings and collard greens, black-eyed peas and sweet potatoes. Gainford and his boys would often wrap leftover food in napkins for a post-workout snack.

The trainer drove a 1931 Model T, and there were few things that delighted him as much as loading his young fighters into his car—young Walker always sat in the back, on the so-called rumble seat, unable to muscle his way past the bigger team members—and taking off up or down the East Coast, into New York, Pennsylvania, Connecticut. (Gainford had spent a great deal of time on the church phone, talking to amateur promoters, lining up bouts.) On the day they took off, church members would often gather to bid them farewell, one of the deacons offering a prayer, the chorus of onlookers nodding and shaking the fighters' hands. Then they vanished through the gritty streets of Manhattan.

They stopped in towns large and small, a Depression-era caravan with a big Pied Piper instructing them, upon reaching their destination, to grab their bags from the car (careful with the satin robes!), to be respectful to elders they came across while making their way to the locker room, to remember they were representing a highly respected Manhattan church. When his fighters had stacked up wins that he thought were particularly impressive, Gainford would make his way to the nearest phone booth and get in touch with the reporters he knew in New York—especially at the *Amsterdam News,* the *New York Herald Tribune,* the *New York Daily Mirror*—and try to get their accomplishments written up. The young fighters loved seeing their names in print.

But Walker Smith was not seeing his name written anywhere. He grew petulant because Gainford would not allow him to fight yet. Gainford, like most trainers, was truly interested in bringing along a promising heavyweight, and the fighter on his team who fit that bill was Buddy Moore, upon whom he lavished attention. Gainford urged young Walker to be patient. "Smitty, you gonna get killed, you can't beat nobody," he once chided him, trying to temper the boy's impatience. The words would sting, just as the challenges made to him by his very own mother—to get back outside and fight!—had stung.

Young Walker Smith was tall for his age, and rangy. In the Salem basement, Gainford, his attention seemingly always on another fighter, began to gaze over at young Walker. He was becoming impressed with the manner in which the boy worked out, the way he attacked the punching bag; the look of quickness in his hands. "At first he didn't look like much [of a] fighter," Gainford would come to reflect. "All he did was hit and run, but he had one thing. He wanted to learn. He was the first kid in the gym and the last one to leave. He'd say to me, 'Suppose I do this, what the other guy do?' I'd tell him and then he'd say, 'And then suppose I do this and this? Then what happens?' "

The novice figured he needed a mental understanding of boxing, of strategies and defensive postures. He'd ask Gainford questions in the basement gym, and questions when they got back out on the road; there were more questions whenever Walker watched another Salem fighter in the ring. Then he would scoot up alongside the fighter and ask him still more questions—no matter if he won or lost—about the fight just finished.

In little time, young Walker realized he had found something unique. A traditional school setting couldn't hold his attention, but a boxing ring could. He was hyperactive and dreamy. With his father still in Detroit, the boy also seemed starved for a male adult figure, and Gainford and the church deacons at Salem gave him a sense of being looked after. For the first time in his life, he knew the constancy of mature male voices. These were churchmen, proud and unbent. Some had been robbed of their own childhood dreams, and now, with the chance to pour those dreams into others, they puffed themselves up with measurable pride. They leaned on Scripture, promising the first shall be last, the last first; they slipped quarters to the Salem boys who looked particularly hungry; they introduced those same boys to Harlem police officers, a not-so-sly warning about the ramifications of mischief. They built a cocoon around the boys because, with the odds so heavily against them, this church setting—the dreams inside a boxing ring—echoed a financial reality: One of the few ways for a black man in America to approximate a version of being rich was to fight professionally and win. A black man wearing a pair of maroon gloves inside a boxing ring could excite the blood rush of others without getting himself killed. And pocket the kind of money Negroes only dreamt about. The great Jack Johnson had commanded $30,000 for some fights—a figure that exceeded the salary of every U.S. senator during his reign. Young Walker was a willing listener.

On the AAU circuit the Salem team traveled, there were trainers who were not beyond bending rules and even outright trickery. Gainford believed he was as nimble of mind as any of his fellow trainers. There were plenty of moments where eyebrows were raised in the back rooms of small fight venues: Some fighters appeared too old; others were so skilled it was believed they must have fought for money—a violation of AAU rules—in unknown places. It sometimes appeared that fighters had been switched, with a new fighter borrowing the identity of an injured one at the last minute. Trainers would justify the ethical lapses to themselves because they wanted to get their fighters experience. Gainford always had a handful of AAU cards stowed in his back pocket; he wisely kept more cards than fighters, because fighters sometimes simply didn't show up at the church for the out-of-town journeys, giving him the chance to promote a second- or third-string fighter right on the spot.

One evening in Kingston, New York, Gainford and his fighters had been impressing the crowd, displaying their typical prowess. The bout's organizer had a flyweight he wanted to match up against one of Gainford's fighters, but Gainford informed him he had no flyweight on his roster. Then Walker Smith—his voice had almost become a constant echo in Gainford's ear—quickly pleaded with Gainford to give him a chance to fight the opposing flyweight. Gainford thought for a moment, huddling briefly with Smith. He couldn't ignore the eagerness in the boy's eyes, the same boy who was always pummeling him with questions about fighters and strategies down in the Salem basement. Gainford made up his mind then and there: "Here's my flyweight," he told the organizer, pointing to Walker. The organizer needed the kid's AAU card, which George didn't have, because he'd not yet thought of getting Walker Smith—untested and unproven—an AAU card. But Gainford did still have a card for another one of his former fighters, Ray Robinson, a Virginia-born boxer who had become bored with the sport and left the team. Thinking on his feet, Gainford told the organizer that his young flyweight's name was Ray Robinson.

The quick name-shifting was just fine with Walker Smith: He was going to fight, on this night, away from family, and adrenaline was rushing through him. He was going to have the chance to prove he'd been listening to Gainford when the trainer took time to answer his incessant questions. Gainford told the boy to hustle off to the dressing room and get dressed. (George always carried a couple of extra satin robes.)

"Ray Robinson"—né Walker Smith—was surrounded by other fighters in the dressing room, all waiting to take their place in the ring when summoned. Sitting alone after getting dressed, he fretted but tried to conceal his nerves. No one moved when the name Ray Robinson was called, fighters looking all about. Finally, he snapped to attention. Minutes later, he found himself in the ring, surrounded by noise and lights and the whispering which suddenly seemed loud and George Gainford standing over him and his Salem Crescent boxing mates cheering him on. "As scared as I was," he would recall, "I was happy." He swung; some of his punches were wild, but more often than not he connected. Gainford yelled from the corner; his boxing mates yelled; the lights got in his eyes, but he moved about the ring with a quickness that surprised even Gainford. He was antsy between rounds, like someone who had been wound up. In the third round he let loose with a barrage of jabs that excited the gathered boxing fans. The judge had seen enough; "Robinson" was declared, at the end of the third, a unanimous winner. Gainford was happily surprised, grabbing his fighter, wrapping a towel around his neck, grinning wide.

It is that first amateur victory that the prizefighter remembers with nostalgic rapture. And it is that victory in which the living element of fear—a thing that Gainford and the old Harlem fight trainers were so practiced in spotting—vanishes, as if shot down with a lethal arrow. In its place something else takes over, an even more profound sense of invincibility than any young street ruffian might possess, and with it a soaring hunger. And it is not a hunger that can be sated by heaps of hot food. It is the kind of hunger that can only be satisfied beneath the lights, by widening eyes and the smiles of old men and while standing over yet another defeated foe. With each victory, the winner reduces his world of rivals by one, believing that the universe now sits in a more manageable state of affairs. The hunger becomes a heady mixture of need and pride—and also a sensation extremely difficult to escape. And now the teenage Robinson was possessed by it. He had done something solid and enviable with his hands; he was flush with talent and knew it. He did not know exactly how he had done it, for his fists had been flying so fast, and it was all removed from mathematics or any type of diagramming. That was the magic and sweetness of it: It was almost beyond explanation. For years and years afterward, Robinson would regale writers with the story of this fight in Kingston, as if it were the beginning of his realization of being on earth.

In the days and weeks afterward, Gainford began taking "Ray Robinson" more seriously. Other team members noticed. The Robinson-Gainford conversations, in and out of the ring, were now longer, intense one-on-one sessions. Gainford lectured about defensive strategies, about how to navigate space in the ring. (To stave off any scandal, they both decided to keep the name Ray Robinson for the time being.)

That night in Kingston would prove to be no aberration. Gainford's newly discovered fighter would do the same thing in the following months: Again and again, he would step into a ring and outperform his opponents. Now, when he reminded fellow Salem pugilists that he had known Joe Louis, they began to believe him. And he got a better seat in Gainford's Model T as it rambled over the rural roads of eastern America.

Back home in Manhattan the young fighter would run through Central Park, then run right back into the Salem gym, where he'd pepper Gainford with yet more questions—questions that had come to him while running. All through 1936 he won—knocking out some opponents with vicious left hooks that stunned the closely watching Gainford and becoming, just like heavyweight team member Buddy Moore, a Salem mainstay. He won wristwatches for his victories; church members at Salem, who knew of his family's struggles with poverty, slipped him dollar bills; predictions were made that he'd someday make the local Golden Gloves team. He felt confident enough that he began visiting the famed Grupp's Gym in Harlem, standing around and staring. He skipped school to go to boxing exhibitions around Manhattan, finally dropping out of DeWitt Clinton High. His mother, Leila, did not protest, not with her son having stashed away over $900 in earnings from being out on the road. Now he could help with family bills. Leila began to help her son prepare for fights—washing his satin robes, rubbing his muscles. He worked on his balance, his speed in the ring; he worked on moving backward while punching. All of his daily pleasures seemed derived from grappling with the mysteries of boxing.

He no longer feared neighborhood bullies or ruffians. Old men in Harlem restaurants began nodding in his direction as he strolled by. Leila and his sisters recognized a deepening of his voice. His new maturity kept him away from back-alley games of tossing dice. New members on the Salem Crescent team now looked at him with measured respect. Gainford's trust in him grew as well, so much so that he chose him as Salem's team captain. Gainford would often make a few hundred dollars on his outings, delivering fighters to these amateur contests, and he'd share some of the money with his protégés, Robinson and Buddy Moore, often receiving the biggest share. The crowning delighted Robinson, and he now alighted from Gainford's automobile with a little more authority in his step, pushing through the doors of small-town arenas as if his victories were all but assured.

Sometimes, out on the road, they slept in abandoned barns, fighters spread-eagled on heaps of hay. Other times they slept in Gainford's car. They were too proud to complain, believing in the dreams that turn young fighters into contenders. Their comings and goings kept church members intrigued, and their exploits were occasionally broadcast from Rev. Cullen's pulpit.

Jack Case was sports editor and a writer at the *Watertown Daily Times.* He had joined the staff in 1920, becoming sports editor nine years later. He seemed to have contacts all across the upstate New York region. Watertown was a small town that sat thirty miles from the Canadian border and had once been a main way station for those on the Underground Railroad. In the 1930s—despite the harsh economic times haunting much of the country—it had a reputation as a kind of millionaires' row. Men who ran companies lived and prospered there. Its bucolic charm was partly cultivated; Frederick Law Olmstead, who had designed Central Park in New York City, designed one of Watertown's parks. But the town still delighted in its small-town virtues and could even remind visitors of the tenderness of Thorton Wilder's *Our Town,* which had opened on Broadway in 1938.

The local newspaper was full of intimate little stories about who was coming and going down at the train depot, about the pie festival and the celebrated county fair. And sometimes stories about the Negro boxers who traveled through town. They were an unusual sight, fit-looking Negro youths in a town with very few Negroes among its own population. In the beginning, the locals stared at the fighters but finally became accustomed to their pilgrimages and offered them friendly and welcoming gestures. Jack Case—stout of body, often seen with a cigar in his right hand, fond of three-piece suits—was fascinated by boxing. He covered as many of the local events held at the Starbuck Avenue Arena as he could for the newspaper. The arena was a converted downtown building that had once served as a cafeteria for munitions workers during World War I. With the rise of amateur boxing, townsfolk were eager to find a large enough venue to showcase regional fighters as well as fighters from Canada, and the Starbuck fit the requirements. Jack Belden, a local Watertown promoter, listened on the phone that first week of January 1939 as Gainford bragged about his Salem boxing team, particularly Ray Robinson. Belden had heard many such proclamations about fighters; but Gainford was unwavering in his praise, telling Belden he wouldn't have to pay his team's expenses if Robinson proved to be a bust.

The Robinson-led Salem Crescent team arrived in Watertown on January 5 for scheduled bouts that evening. Robinson's opponent was Dom Perfetti, an Eastern states champion known to be a rugged brawler. Perfetti was the highest-ranked foe he had faced. The small press contingent, Case among them, was seated ringside: "Cauliflower Row" they called that section, owing to its close proximity to the fighters' bruised faces.

Shortly after the bell rang for Robinson and Perfetti, Case realized he might be witnessing a special arrival in Robinson. The fighters had started out in the first "at top speed, showing some clever boxing and hefty punching," Case would report. A volley of punches in the second round had fans on their feet as the fighters "tossed leather with reckless abandon," landing blows to the head and body. Robinson exhibited some dazzling moves that kept the fans riveted: "He tossed his right hand in a peculiar style, seeming to 'cook it' momentarily before delivering his blow," Case recounted. "The motion apparently threw Perfetti off guard and time after time the bantamweight king would absorb two telling blows without being able to strike one in return." Perfetti wasn't just any local fighter; he was the Eastern states champion. Robinson would be his undoing. "The little Negro," Case wrote, "traveled at top pace from the opening gong until the final bell sounded. He not only outboxed the rugged eastern champion, but he also outpunched him whenever the two collided in the center of the ring to swap leather." Case—and all the others at ringside, including Belden, the promoter—flinched throughout the bout as they watched the punches land. It was over in the fifth, the champion Perfetti beaten. There were murmurs throughout the crowd, long gazes focused on Robinson. Gainford had become accustomed to seeing his young fighter's quick dispatch of opponents and simply moved into the ring with a towel to drape around Robinson's neck as he offered congratulations. Audience members crowded toward the aisle as fans tried to get a closer look at Robinson. They chattered and whispered within earshot of him and Gainford; there were compliments and disbelieving eyes. A gaggle had formed as Robinson descended from the ring. Case rose up to greet him.

"That's a sweet fighter you've got there, a real sweet fighter," Case said to Gainford as they paused next to him.

A nearby woman piped up: "As sweet as sugar."

Case looked out over the gathering before leaving the arena and sensed an awe still hanging in the air from the Robinson bout.

As Jack Case excitedly made his way back to the newsroom to write up his story that night—passing the brick buildings and the Fords and Packards parked along the street—all the boxers he had seen swirled in his mind. Robinson clearly stood out. Case was a writer, and newspaper writers remembered little details, phrasings that the uninitiated might miss. The anonymous woman's "sweet as sugar" comment stayed with him, and he used it as he typed out his story for the next day's morning edition. It began: "Sugar Robinson, clever little New York mittman, proved to be everything his nickname implied at the Starbuck avenue arena Wednesday night where he boxed his way to a five round decision over Dom Perfetti . . . eastern states champion. Those who watched Robinson perform [declared] he was one of the 'sweetest' pieces of fighting machinery that has been seen here in many months." Case saw no need to inform readers that it was he—Case—who had slipped the moniker Sugar on Robinson during the very writing of his article. The *Watertown Daily Times* headline writer picked up on the emotion in Case's story. It was a one-column article, but it had four headlines stacked atop one another: RAYMOND SCORES WIN OVER CHAMP, it began. Then, below: NEW YORK NEGRO MITTMAN TRIUMPHS OVER DOM PERFETTI HERE. Below that: GOTHAM SCRAPPER PROVES SENSATION AT LOCAL CLUB. And below that: OUTCLASSES AMSTERDAM BOXER IN FIVE ROUND MAIN BOUT AT ARENA.

It was an effusive tribute to young Robinson, and he hoarded some of the newspapers. His fellow Salem fighters teased him about the "Sugar"—not to mention the use of "Raymond" in the headline, a name no one actually called him. But he liked Sugar, very much. It quickly caught on. The rhythm of it, the near-musical quality of it, was what delighted him so much: Sugar Ray Robinson. It rolled almost liltingly from the lips, as if the three names were a stitched-together appellation of something elegant and athletic. He said the name to himself over and over again. His father had seemingly forgotten him, so he felt he owed nothing to the name he'd been given at birth. He was his own man now. His mother, Leila, no longer mocked him, questioning his courage on the streets. The kid in the mirror, the kid who had tramped along the streets of Black Bottom in Detroit, the kid who had sat staring out over Manhattan's East River wondering about his fate, began to feel as if he had reinvented himself. Boxing program profiles would claim he had been "born in Virginia"—due to his AAU card and the birthplace it specified for the real Ray Robinson—but he didn't mind. The name was his now and it made him smile when he heard it uttered. "Walker Smith Jr. was a forgotten man," the young fighter would declare.

Neither Case nor promoter Belden could forget Sugar Ray Robinson, and they went about turning him into a local marquee sensation. Case even took to the local radio airwaves, trumpeting

Robinson's skills. Two weeks after his debut there, Sugar Ray was back in Watertown to face another opponent. He beat Harvey Lacelle. It was a victory that could hardly go unnoticed: Lacelle had been a Canadian contender. After the bout, Lacelle praised Robinson and said he had never faced a tougher foe. Four months later—on May 3, Robinson's eighteenth birthday—Robinson squared off in Watertown again, this time against Larry Zavelitch, another Canadian. It was a rough and challenging first four rounds. But the fight was called in the fifth when Robinson unspooled a bolo punch that sent Zavelitch reeling. That night Case and Belden cornered Gainford, inquiring about plans for Robinson's future. Gainford kept mum, exchanging pleasantries without revealing plans of any kind. The locals would see Robinson one more time, in June of 1939, when he would defeat a fighter from Binghamton, New York. The string of victories had cemented a feeling of confidence within Robinson. Gainford shared his young fighter's emotions: "Ray's going to be world's champion some day," he predicted while in Watertown.

It was after his riveting march through a string of amateur opponents in Watertown that Sugar Ray Robinson really began to sense his own star quality. Winsome girls back in Manhattan began to stop him, angling for conversation. They badgered his sisters about his comings and goings. He could afford better clothing and favored loud-colored shirts, two-toned shoes, fedoras. He strolled about Times Square, the Bowery, Greenwich Village, imagining himself set apart from other boys in the city his age because he had money and car keys. He had newspaper clippings that told of his victories. He got hold of an old Victrola record player and began toting it on the road with him. He had a stack of records—Fats Waller, Duke Ellington, Jelly Roll Morton, Scott Joplin—that he packed up carefully. In small but discernible ways, Gainford began to bend to the will of his budding pupil: Robinson wanted music as he was preparing to leave the dressing room for his bouts. Gainford would put the music on and as the Fats Waller tune circled the dressing room, Robinson would begin dancing to it. Gainford could only smile as Robinson stepped out into whatever local arena, the jazz melodies wafting in the air, his fighter bobbing and weaving, guided by the jazz in his head and the beckoning lights.

That Robinson now had money—a few $20 bills in those Depression years seemed like a small fortune—gave him a sense of accomplishment at home as well. He climbed the stairs to the family apartment with bags of groceries purchased with his money. He helped his mother with her overdue bills. George loaned him a 1928 Ford to tool around town, and he found plenty of girls willing to hop in the front seat with a rising young fighter. "I didn't have a license but I had money for gas, and that was better than a license," Robinson would recall. He took his dates out to Coney Island, swooping up and away on the roller coaster through the night air. The neighborhood juvenile delinquents—sashaying around with their folded pocketknives and razor blades—steered clear of him. It was his reputation.

Her name was Marjorie, and she was pretty, with darkly hued skin, and an aggressive manner about her. He escorted her to dances on Lenox Avenue. They talked of his out-of-town journeys, of music and movies. He splurged, taking her to ice cream parlors, up and down the aisles of department stores. Other girls followed his comings and goings in the neighborhood, but he was bewitched by Marjorie and their sexual chemistry. When she became pregnant in 1938, he panicked, fleeing to his sisters for advice. They could only remind him of the importance of sharing the news with their mother, Leila. And that no-nonsense woman wasted little time in marching to the home of Marjorie's parents. Leila Smith worried about scandal, her son's future, and she promised them that her son would marry Marjorie. Marjorie's parents, however, objected—while the girl remained silent under her father's gaze. There were heated back-and-forth discussions, until Marjorie's parents relented. The couple married in a ceremony at a local church—but not Salem Methodist. Ronnie Robinson was born in the fall of 1939. Shortly afterward, Sugar Ray and Marjorie had their marriage annulled. They had been nothing but teenage lovers and both came to believe it the best course. Robinson had financial responsibility for a child, but it did not derail him as it might have another young father. There were more fights, more money slipped to him by Gainford. It was, to him, an indication of what money could genuinely do. For the rest of his life, Sugar Ray would have just a minimal paternal relationship with his firstborn son.

Beginning in 1922, the New York *Daily News* inaugurated a speed-skating event, dubbed the Silver Skates Derby. It was one of several activities and sporting events the newspaper promoted in hopes of boosting circulation and attracting new readers. Over the next few years the event became a public relations bonanza, talked about on the subways and praised in the executive suites of the newspaper itself. Paul Gallico, the *Daily News* sports editor, was surprised at the success of the annual event. Gallico happened to be enamored of amateur boxing, and had long dreamed of a local boxing tournament. He figured that such a tournament would be as successful as the skating derby if the newspaper got behind the idea. He decided to ask Joseph Patterson, the newspaper's publisher, for a meeting. A group of newspaper officials, Patterson among them, listened to Gallico's pitch over dinner at a restaurant in Little Italy. Patterson, himself dizzied by the success of the skating tournament, quickly agreed. (Anything that might boost circulation!) Patterson told Gallico he wanted it done in a topflight fashion, with nothing spared in terms of promotion. Gallico said he already had a name, a takeoff of Silver Skates: Golden Gloves. Sensing possibilities, the newspapermen made quite a merry party of it.

Gallico and others set about scouring the city and outer boroughs, informing amateur coaches of the planned competition. There would be elimination rounds in the city and outlying areas, they explained; there would be safeguards against fixes and the type of skullduggery long associated with the sport; there would be a round of championship bouts staged at Madison Square Garden to declare weight-class champions. Gallico worried, wondering if the feverishness of the preparations would be matched by the number of entrants. Some of the organizers of local boxing events considered themselves lucky if they got a hundred entrants in amateur tournaments. In one of his columns prior to the event, Gallico wrote that he hoped the competition would "unearth some unknown with a bland and modest smile and a kick like a navy smokeless, who will blast his way through" to the championship rounds. He was stunned when the entry forms began piling up on his desk; he had to cut off the submissions when the number of applications topped a thousand.

The elimination rounds began in Brooklyn on March 11, 1927, and spread to all of the boroughs. The finals were held at Madison Square Garden before an audience of more than 21,000—while another 8,000, huffing with disappointment, were turned away. Soon, a similar event was staged in Chicago and, sensing a potential rivalry, New York and Chicago officials combined the two competitions, bringing together the Golden Gloves champions from each city. The popular event became known as the Inter-city championships. Flashbulbs went off at train stations in both cities as the young pugilists leaned over the railings, whistling and waving their fedoras and grinning their world-beating grins. By the mid-1930s the event had become a sensation, even adding foreigners to the mix. In 1937 an international competition featuring U.S. boxers against the Italian team was staged outdoors, at Yankee Stadium, with a crowd of more than 52,000. A tough and gritty team from Mussolini's Italy—boasting the presence of 1936 bantamweight Olympian Ulderico Sergo—won the event, 6–5. (There would be no international contest the following year, owing to the specter of war in Europe.) In 1937 the organizers staged a one-day quarterfinal round at Madison Square Garden. Thousands of Golden Gloves fans peered down, over and across three boxing rings, as simultaneous fights took place throughout afternoon and evening sessions. A total of 107 bouts were held, with the arena in constant motion. *Daily News* newsboys hawked fresh editions outside the Garden, barking in staccato rhythms the results of many of the fights. Paul Gallico, the energetic force behind the Golden Gloves, had gone off to write novels and screenplays—but his event had made Manhattan an undisputed amateur boxing mecca.

Broadway and Hollywood stars were always spotted among the throngs inside the Garden on Golden Gloves nights. (Outside, police officers on horseback struggled mightily to control the crowds.) Champion fighters—Gene Tunney, Joe Louis, and Max Baer among them—were also spotted, thick-shouldered men in sharp suits adding luster, waving and pointing, sometimes even doing radio play-by-play. George Gainford's young fighters at Salem Crescent were excited about the thrilling extravaganzas taking place at the Garden.

In 1938 Sugar Ray Robinson began dreaming of getting his own shot at a Golden Gloves title. Several members of the team harbored such ambitions. Robinson's dream consumed him: All through the year he trained harder than ever; he asked Gainford more questions about fighters he might be fighting; he thumbed through Chicago newspapers, gleaning what he could about fighters he might face there if he made it far enough in the competition. Robinson also worried that Gainford might pay more attention to Buddy Moore, the Salem heavyweight prospect, than to him. And that fear made him train harder still. There was a severe intensity in his eyes, owing to the regimen he set for himself. He ran long stretches along the pathways of Central Park as the sun set behind the trees. He watched his diet, he reminded wayward friends he could not keep company with them any longer because of his fight preparations.

Salem churchgoers realized what was taking place down in their basement in the months prior to the 1939 Golden Gloves elimination trials: George Gainford and Harry Wiley, another coach, getting their boys ready for the intense battles that lay ahead. And when the 1939 trials began, three Salem fighters—Robinson, Buddy Moore, and Spider Valentine—quickly stood out. They kept eliminating their foes. And the more Robinson fought, the louder the murmurings became about his lethal left hook, the swiftness with which he danced around the ring.

Arthur Mercante was a Golden Gloves referee during the 1939 preliminary events. He knew how much the city looked forward to the affair. "It was a very depressed period of our lives," he would recall decades later. "The event really helped the New York *Daily News* stay on its feet, because they were having difficulty surviving. Everybody looked forward to going to the Golden Gloves." Mercante had gotten to know certain fighters in the semifinals leading up to the finals night. Robinson struck him as having special talents. "I'd be watching him from my corner. He'd come into the ring looking absolutely beautiful. He textured his skin by putting some kind of ointment all over his body. And he was always well-coiffed. He would say he wanted to leave the ring exactly as he entered it— looking beautiful."

And as Robinson started defeating his foes on his way to finals night, Mercante, witnessing some of those bouts, recoiled at the power of his punches. He couldn't remember seeing a fighter with such a combination of speed and brutal power. Golden Gloves attendees would stop Mercante in the hallways, heatedly inquiring about the kid from the church in Harlem.

By early March, Robinson had garnered enough preliminary victories that he began attracting a real following. On March 6, more than eighteen thousand fans made their way into Madison Square Garden to watch the young fighters; many were looking for the fighter from Salem Crescent. He did not disappoint. "Among the more impressive youths," *The New York Times* would note a day later, "was Ray Robinson . . . who gained the 126 pound open championship. Flooring his opponent for a count of eight in the second, Robinson proceeded to batter him at will and easily earned the decision." Within the narrative of the *Times* article, Robinson received a small headline above the section lauding his exploits: ROBINSON FINE BOXER, it proclaimed. It was his first such recognition. The *Times* article added: "Robinson took the fancy of the crowd with his defensive skill as well as a punishing long right uppercut that invariably found the mark." On the finals night of his 1939 Golden Gloves tournament, Robinson emerged from the bowels of the arena, ready for his bout, with more than fifteen thousand spectators hovering. The lights caught his shimmering satin robe as he came into view, and fans began yelping and pointing. One of those pointing toward him that night happened to be actress Mae West. West, daughter of a heavyweight boxer, was enamored of the sport. (She was also secretly linked to several Negro fighters, liaisons that provided scandal sheets with juicy material.) On Robinson's big night, West—seated ringside between two older men in black tuxedoes—was swathed in white fur and a floor-length satin dress. She wore a bejeweled hairnet atop her blonde locks; a flowery adornment could be seen on the shoulder of her fur coat. The actress, who had started out in burlesque, billed as "The Baby Vamp," looked every bit the grown-up now. Robinson would remember "a roar of applause" as he came into view. He happened to be matched against a familiar figure: Salem Crescent teammate Spider Valentine. The two fighters had won enough contests to be pitted against each other. Robinson wanted to make an especially good showing, the better to steal some of the Salem spotlight from heavyweight Buddy Moore, who had brutally vanquished several opponents on his way to finals night.

It mattered little that Spider Valentine knew Robinson's moves, having seen them so often in the Salem gym. Robinson was too swift a puncher; Valentine fell early from a Robinson blow. He took more punishment in the second round, unable to dodge Robinson's punches, which rose and fell like the tentacles of an octopus. By the end of the third—the noise from the crowd rising—the referee had seen enough. It was all over.

And all just beginning for Sugar Ray Robinson.

The flashbulbs went off; there were shouts, and fans rose up, saluting Robinson's victory. He stood in the ring, gazing, squinting, raising his gloved fist, bathed in the fluorescent glow. The boy from Black Bottom—by way of Salem Crescent—was now a champion. Buddy Moore was also a champion, but Robinson's feat had been accomplished with what many concluded was rare artistry. The memory of the evening would mean so very much to him. "The greatest thrill I ever got," he would say, "was when I won the Golden Gloves and they streamed that light down on me in the Garden and said, 'The Golden Gloves featherweight champion, Sugar Ray Robinson!' " Newspaper writers made note of him. Predictions now floated all about him. The next morning Robinson scoured the city, ignoring the cold weather, grabbing as many newspapers as he could. His Golden Gloves win boosted his confidence tremendously, as had his triumphs in Watertown, New York.

Many fighters, of course, have good stretches, reaching beyond their trainer's expectations for them. There were onetime Golden Gloves winners walking around the Bowery in 1939, destitute and out of the game. The has-beens were often spotted in the shadows at gyms around the city, dodging questions about what went wrong. The winner's pair of miniature bronzed Golden Gloves—valued at $65—carried no guarantee of future success.

If there were any one-shot-wonder doubts about Robinson's gifts, though, they were dispelled when he returned to the Golden Gloves event twelve months later and offered a furious—and more lethal— display of his talent. He marched toward finals night like a man possessed: He knocked out Howard Hettich of Charlotte, North Carolina, in the first round. Andy Nonella didn't fare much better. Sixty seconds, and Mr. Robinson's work was finished. *The New York Times* allowed that Robinson had offered "the best showing of the night" in his victory. Robinson had flattened Nonella before the sixty-point mark, only to see Nonella rise. "He gamely made for his foe," the *Times* reported of Nonella, "but was unable to reach the elusive Robinson, who sprayed a steady stream of lefts to the face." Robinson squared off with Joseph Vidulich days later. Only forty-six seconds into round one, Vidulich went blank: another knockout. The *Times* called the deposing of Vidulich "a spectacular knockout" on Robinson's part. "With a terrific right to the jaw, Robinson sent Joseph Vidulich of New Jersey sprawling over the lower rope." At

1:41 of their first-round matchup, Jimmy Butler of Atlanta, Georgia, joined Robinson's other victims after another knockout. Robinson had the reporters squirming in their seats. Photographers captured him—taller than most of his challengers—pounding into the heads of crouching opponents, who were desperately trying to defend themselves against the fusillade.

Gainford was now witnessing a fighter withdrawing inside himself, blocking out the world, and unleashing scintillating gifts. Gainford could only wrap the white towel around Robinson's neck and whisper into his ear about the fine job he had done. The applause was deafening. This is what Madison Square Garden fight fans loved—the maturation of a fighter right before their eyes. The Manhattan press did not at first accept Robinson's moniker "Sugar" and began referring to him as "Death Ray," an appropriate nickname, in their minds, given what they were witnessing. Robinson practiced a ring etiquette that some found odd, though women liked it: He moved gingerly toward his flattened opponents, helping to lift them from the canvas, even at times motioning for medical help. He possessed traits of magnanimity as well as vengefulness. The Salem Crescent fighter, it was agreed, had "set the standard for sportsmanship" in the Golden Gloves event.

Aware that future financial backers were watching, Robinson had badly wanted to pull the spotlight from Salem heavyweight Buddy Moore. Now he had done it. He had had admirers uttering his name as they rushed through the doors of the Garden; he had made his own headlines. He wanted George Gainford to see only one Salem Crescent fighter in his mirror—Sugar Ray Robinson. He had now become, in a span of twelve months, a Manhattan sensation. The old fighters at Stillman's Gym would try to find comparisons, mentioning the likes of Henry Armstrong, the bolo-punching Missourian, and Kid Chocolate, the great Cuban-born fighter who was New York world featherweight champ from 1932 to 1934. They would spin their comparisons out all day long, giving them new angles, until Gainford and Harry Wiley would tell them—and anyone else who would listen—that Sugar Ray Robinson was unlike any boxer they had ever seen on the local or national fight scene. "Robinson never has lost," Gainford reminded them, time and time again.

And now, when Sugar Ray Robinson rose from the basement of Salem Methodist Episcopal Church, gliding out into the sunshine, there was an unmistakable glow about him. Other team members allowed him to make decisions about where to eat, what movies to go see, which music to go listen to. Older team members liked his discipline and focus. He walked like a champion.

For his back-to-back Golden Gloves victories, Robinson received plaudits from the Salem Methodist church hierarchy. On some Sundays parishioners would spot him, his mother, Leila, and his two sisters sitting among them. They were a family in repose, the commingling of boxing and Bibles now making welcome sense to Leila Smith.

It caught few by surprise when the young Sugar Ray, having conquered the amateur ranks, now eagerly wished to turn professional. The Smith family was still strapped for cash, and Leila could often be heard lamenting in the confines of their home about another bill she was late paying. The prospect of turning pro excited Gainford: Sugar Ray was indeed the most valued fighter in his group. But if it excited Gainford, it also worried him: The New York professional fight game could seem a Byzantine operation. Men operated in the shadows; fighters seemed to be managed and owned by different entities; many fighters were beholden to the Mob. A Negro fight manager stepped into that game with many questions that no one would answer, and with little true security for his fighter. It was Curt Horrmann who offered a plan.

Horrmann had been born into a well-off Staten Island family, owners of a beer brewery. One New York columnist would note, "His family is wealthy enough to keep him in crepes suzette for life." As he grew into manhood—he had a well-appointed Manhattan apartment at 64 East Seventy-eighth Street—his patrician air become more pronounced: Tall and dark-haired, he carried himself with a sense of authority. Horrmann was also a familiar face at the downtown Stork Club, whispering among the beautiful Manhattanites as he consumed his favorite meal—a steak dinner. His maroon Packard sat parked outside, gleaming. With family money in his pockets and time on his hands, Horrmann looked about for activities in the Manhattan area that might occupy and also excite him. At various times throughout 1938 and 1939, however, he had been bedeviled with an array of illnesses; at one point it was pneumonia and his family feared for his life. But he recovered and went back to finding an occupation. He started to ponder the fight game, with the idea of finding a rising young fighter to invest in. His advisers suggested he take a look at Buddy Moore, the Salem Crescent heavyweight. At Madison Square Garden during the 1940 Golden Gloves, Horrmann found himself fascinated not by Moore, but by the new Manhattan sensation—Sugar Ray Robinson.

Gainford realized Horrmann could offer Robinson what he couldn't: money. Money to train and set up a training camp; money to bring in talented sparring mates; money that would keep Robinson from having to work—as he sometimes did—as a grocery clerk. "He can come up with a hundred-dollar bill faster than any man alive," Gainford told his young fighter.

In mid-1940, Sugar Ray Robinson, George Gainford, and Curt Horrmann all signed an agreement, granting Horrmann the right to manage Robinson. Horrmann would get 33 percent of the future pro's earnings; Gainford would get 10 percent; and Robinson the rest.

The troika of Robinson, Gainford, and Horrmann started to assemble in the summer of 1940, and both trainer and manager watched Robinson intently during training sessions. There were some in Manhattan fight circles who wondered if Robinson and Gainford had made the right decision in bringing the inexperienced Horrmann into their camp. But Gainford realized the necessity of financial backing. Robinson recorded his first professional win on October 4, 1940, in Manhattan against Joe Echevarria in a two-round technical knockout. Robinson mowed down all six of his opponents to close out the year, and just thirteen days into 1941, he had already registered two knockouts. His fighting style depended a great deal on balance and lightning speed. At times whirling around the ring—as if moving from rock to rock across a shallow lake—he seemed the epitome of lightness and balance, until he stopped to unload a series of punches that drew gasps from onlookers.

If Herman Taylor, a Philadelphia-based fight promoter, had had his way, Robinson and Gainford would have adopted that city as a base of operations. Taylor was the first big-time promoter to imagine greatness for Robinson. Between the winter of 1940 and the summer of 1941, Taylor set up seven fights for Robinson in Philadelphia. Sugar Ray defeated every foe, five by vicious knockouts. While some of those fights had been on under cards—warm-up bouts leading to the main attraction—they served their purpose: Robinson became a celebrity in the city. Men showed up at his fights wearing blue jackets and white pants—blue and white being Robinson's robe colors—and women searched their closets for blue and white ensembles. Taylor introduced him to Main Line movers and shakers; society ladies beamed around him. Children began recognizing him.

Robinson returned to the city for a July 21, 1941, fight with Sammy Angott. Angott had been a lightweight champion, and while it was a non-title fight, the stakes were huge for Robinson. It was a main attraction; now other fighters were on his main card. In the second, Robinson caught the tough Angott with a right, crumpling him to the canvas. Gainford watched as the referee began a count; Robinson glared at the fallen Angott, who finally lifted himself up. But Angott—six years older than Robinson and several inches shorter—never regained any equilibrium in the ring. Robinson won the ten-rounder in a decision. There was much joy during the train ride back to Manhattan. Robinson had received his largest purse to date—$6,000. He was flush and giddy, and he told his mother, Leila, to quit her job at the linen factory. She did. Marie and Evelyn were told to pick out new wardrobes. Sugar Ray insisted his mother find a larger apartment, and they quickly relocated to 940 St. Nicholas Avenue, on one of the nicer blocks in Harlem. New furniture arrived—he had selected the parlor set himself. Fresh drapes were hung. There were family tears at the newfound wealth.

Robinson's travels in 1941 and early 1942 took him twice to Detroit for fights, both of which he won with little trouble. Shortly before that first fight in Detroit, a middle-aged man came looking for Robinson, and when he found him, both hugged: Walker Smith Sr. was happy to see his son after a nearly decade-long estrangement. They talked about his budding fight career, and about his sisters Marie and Evelyn. Robinson sensed, however, his father was suffering financially, and before leaving the city, slipped him money. Robinson had a far more sentimental streak toward his father than did other family members, and for the next few years his father would pop up at some of his fights up and down the East Coast.

On September 19, 1941, Robinson faced Maxie Shapiro in New York City. It was Robinson's debut as a pro at Madison Square Garden. Squealing with delight, he and Gainford rode around the block, staring up at the marquee over and over: BOXING TONIGHT—SUGAR RAY ROBINSON VS. MAXIE SHAPIRO. Robinson would remember the night out for its sentimental value. Shapiro never forgot the encounter for other reasons: "I moved out in the first round and went into a crouch. All of a sudden—*whsst!* This blur went past my head. Then—*whsst!* Another blur. It must have been something like that in the foxholes. The second round I didn't get low enough. I felt like I got hit in the forehead with a baseball bat. I was on the floor twice, and in the third round I was being careful, but he was too fast. *Whsst!* Here it comes again, and I'm on the floor again, and I said to myself, 'The hell with it. I've got a bellyful of this guy,' " At the end of the third round, the referee thought so too, and called it for Robinson.

More knockouts followed; Robinson seemed a man in a hurry. He and Gainford and Horrmann were seen rolling through Manhattan in Horrmann's maroon Packard; they looked easy and confident, all three full of smiles. Robinson purchased new suits, new wide-brimmed hats, casting silhouettes against the dusk. Horrmann was careful to avoid segregated venues like his revered Stork Club, so they dined in Harlem and at fine restaurants in the Bronx with gleaming china and silverware. They wanted a training camp—just as Joe Louis had a training camp. Horrmann's money financed the site at Greenwood Lake, outside New York City, where Joe had also trained. Horrmann determined they must have nothing but the best and so he outfitted the camp—all for Robinson—with a tutor (who doubled as a secretary), a dietician, an assistant trainer to help Gainford, and an assortment of crack sparring partners, most of whom were former Golden Gloves champions themselves. Bob Considine, the great sports columnist for *The Washington Post,* turned his attention to Robinson in 1942 as the young fighter kept piling up victories. Considine—who felt that many a Negro fighter had been left on the scrap heap by unscrupulous managers—hoped that Horrmann's presence in Robinson's corner might usher in a new era of financial solvency for Negro fighters, if others took the cue. Considine believed that, with Horrmann, Robinson was now a beneficiary "of superb handling." Considine added: "In another era he might already be on his way back to his shoeshine box."

Sugar Ray Robinson had totaled twenty-eight victories within two years of turning professional. One month after defeating Maxie Berger, he stepped into the ring—again in Manhattan—against Norman Rubio. Rubio was known as a "tough, two-fisted clouter," and there were those who thought Robinson might suffer his first defeat. Nat Fleischer, founder of the venerable *Ring* magazine—the boxing bible—did not. Fleischer was in attendance that night and came away so astonished that he put the young Robinson on the cover of the June 1942 issue of *Ring*. It was Robinson's first national cover: "Ray Robinson—Colored Welterweight Champion of the World," the headline said. It was misleading, since Robinson held no championship as of yet, but few argued with the prediction. On that cover he is shown in a picture-book pose, the left arm extended and the right close to his chest. His hair is close-cropped and his boyish look belies the lethal impact of his fists. Fleischer, who wrote the accompanying article, gushed. He was already among those who were proclaiming that Robinson "rates among the welters as does Joe Louis among the heavyweights." He added of Robinson's gifts arrayed against Rubio: "Speed to burn, hitting power that pounded his man into a state of helplessness, aim that landed punches with sharp-shooting accuracy, blocking that enabled him to pick off punches that looked dangerous—he had all these in addition to contempt for his opponent that went a wee bit too far." Robinson, who defeated Rubio in an eighth-round TKO, had acquired a habit of turning his back on his felled opponents—walking swiftly toward his corner as if he were late for an engagement beyond the arena. It unnerved the likes of Fleischer. "In order to achieve the greatness of [George] Dixon and [Joe] Gans," Fleischer wrote, "Robinson must put his entire mind on the technique of fighting and forget the gallery."

Yet such gestures were musical flourishes that Robinson took into the ring, and they moved those in the gallery. His success depended on an allegiance to technique, a point Fleischer missed. The technique fed the flourishes, and Robinson often left center ring accused of being cocky—or original. Horrmann and Gainford believed in the latter label.

Robinson was actually loath to relinquish so much of his potential income to Horrmann and thought Horrmann took too much of his earnings. In moments heightened by hubris, Sugar Ray Robinson thought he could manage himself. He worried incessantly about fight contracts, percentages; he sought to arrange meetings with radio executives to determine their station's cut of his fights. The executives were perplexed by his demands, which they ignored. Gainford could not corral his young fighter. Robinson remembered the simplicity of the bootleg fights of his younger days: The money—after Gainford's shavings—went directly to him, the winner, from Gainford's palm. There were no middlemen. What he saw up close in his youth he could not now forget. "I had learned," he would remark, "that if I had to get punished, I was going to get as much money as I could for it." Robinson also thought Horrmann acquiesced too much when dealing with fight promoters; Horrmann, however, felt he had to bend in favor of the opposition—not only to stop fighters from fleeing possible matchups with the dangerous Robinson, but also to ensure Robinson of a consistent fight schedule. There were times when Horrmann, in dealing with managers of the likes of Fritzie Zivic—many fighters had found themselves battling Zivic's arsenal of dirty tactics—sounded naive and unprepared for hard negotiating. "Robinson is a comparative novice in there," Horrmann said a year into Robinson's pro career, when negotiating the Zivic bout, "but he can be as rough as Zivic." (Robinson defeated Zivic in blistering back-to-back contests, each of which went ten rounds.) If Horrmann seemed a little too silk-stocking for the grubby world of boxing, it was not his only problem: His family members wondered what he was up to, investing money in a Negro fighter who resided in Harlem, a world away from their New York. They wondered about Horrmann's long stretches away from home, on the road with Robinson and Gainford. They worried about his health. But Horrmann loved all of it. He grinned like the men who owned baseball teams, like racehorse owners, like tycoons even: He owned something; he was proving his investment had been shrewd; his fighter was winning, bout after bout. His daddy had founded a brewery; he had discovered a fighter, a fighter who had already jumped onto the cover of *Ring* magazine! But then Sugar Ray Robinson—blinded by Horrmann's old-money wealth, the kind of deep wealth he wanted, and that he believed promoters were keeping him from attaining—wished to be rid of his manager. The contretemps caught Horrmann by surprise. He tried reasoning, but Robinson was determined: He wanted independence; he believed he and Gainford could handle his career, and Gainford bent to his wishes. He had to pay Horrmann $10,000 to buy back his contract.

Sugar Ray Robinson had said goodbye to Walker Smith Jr.—and to Curt Horrmann. It was now just him and Gainford. And, of course, Leila and Evelyn and Marie—he would always trust women more than men. Already he had been mentioned in the same breath as Henry Armstrong and Joe Gans. Many expected the young fighter to hone the greatness he already possessed. It was the arc of mystery behind all great athletes: The truly gifted found their greatness within; they were almost beyond teaching. Babe Ruth was simply powerful with a bat; Jesse Owens's legs churned in a blur; Joe Louis's punch from ten inches out packed frightening strength upon impact. The great ones reveled in the flaws and inconsistencies of others. Managers could do the expected things on their behalf—travel arrangements, providing comfortable surroundings, demanding rest. But the great athlete was full of singular will, forging ahead against the open space where new records might be set, where new foes might be beaten. George Gainford, for the first time in his life, now had a superior athlete in his keeping. As long as he had him, he knew, he would not end up a bum in anyone's park.

But there were few things that made the young Sugar Ray Robinson feel as triumphant as being invited to work out with Joe Louis at his training camp outside Manhattan. Louis and his managers sensed something special about Robinson. Welterweights did not command the kind of attention heavyweights did—but this fighter, Robinson, was unique, and they hardly had to read *Ring* magazine to realize it. At the camp, for the most part, the young Robinson rowed the boat out on Greenwood Lake while Louis or one of his managers fished. He was the young knight—beneath the king, Louis, and his men. He listened but also watched how they lived. He first saw the lovely Lena Horne there—she had come to visit Joe, whom she was dating. The young Sugar Ray acquired a sense of what real fame could be like. He slept in the cabin at night and dreamed of it for himself.

As 1942 came to a close, Sugar Ray Robinson was a mere twenty-two years old. He had already—and with riveting quickness—reached a height that was awe-inspiring to many. But he saw only the glitter of championship belts, and he did not own one yet. His hunger for competition seemed insatiable. Now removed from poverty, he was happy. He was free to go at the world.

But the world had gone to war. And Joe Louis and Sugar Ray Robinson were about to find themselves on the battlefield—albeit stateside.

Theirs was a tricky relationship, and it ran, for the most part, quite smoothly. That's what gave it its mystery. It was so free of competition. At Joe's big fights, Sugar Ray would glide down the aisles, nodding, his hair glistening as he turned like a politician. Joe, spotting him from inside the ring, would raise his big chin in the young fighter's direction.

Both were estranged from their fathers and were not above seeking out father figures.

Joe was older by six years, and it struck many that at times there was something of a big brother–little brother rapport between them. Sugar let onlookers think what they wished. Children scampered after both.

As they strolled side by side in fedora and tweed, there glowed about them something rich and magical: they were two of the freest Negroes in America in 1942.

Inside the ring, both liked the short jab. Outside of it, each liked long-legged, mulatto-colored women.

Joe's favorite band was Duke Ellington's. An Ellington tune on the airwaves at the time—"Sepia Panorama"—was sweet and lively, and Joe and Sugar jumped to it.

Joe was hitched to the troika of Jack Blackburn, Julian Black, and John Roxborough, his trainer and two managers. Among those three, there had been prison time, unsavory friendships, numbers running. Joe's country grin wasn't able to keep up with their slipperiness. Sugar watched it all, licking at the air until he understood that the fame had some darkness to it, some furtive underpinnings. Sugar convinced himself he could match wits with any city slicker—a class of human being not unknown to him.

As Sugar was rising—and Joe falling into the aging smoke that catches all prizefighters—war cannons sounded. They found themselves in the Army, side by side.

The children would miss running after them.

1943–1944

Sugar Ray's uniform

WHILE LEADING TROOPS into battle in 1775—and with time to assess his setbacks while shifting and plotting new strategies during the American Revolution—George Washington came to a conclusion about sartorial affairs and his colonial militias: His soldiers were badly dressed. In the field, their clothing consisted of com-

The communiqués had reached the highest levels of the White House. The U.S. military, worried about resentment in the ranks because of discriminatory practices against Negroes, needed to show a unified front in battling the Nazis. Two big sensations in Negro America—Joe Louis and Sugar Ray Robinson—suddenly found themselves in the Army.

mon apparel: shirts and pants and shoes they managed to grab from cabin or tent. Spotting them from yards away, one was hard pressed to distinguish a private from an officer. The slipshod dress—soldiers had no uniforms at the Battle of Bunker Hill—often created confusion in the ranks. Soon enough Gen. Washington insisted on uniforms for all his men. The standards of military dress would be elevated even more in succeeding American engagements.

It was World War II that marked the first time military dress was lent the sheen of celebrity. From Broadway to Hollywood, men and women from the entertainment ranks would be featured in newsreels and on magazine covers wearing their military attire. *Life* and *Photoplay* magazines were particularly adept at placing uniformed stars on their covers and throughout their pages. Jimmy Stewart and Clark Gable looked as genuine in uniform on a military base as they had on celluloid.

Nothing created more of a high-wire act for American officialdom, however, than the combination of blacks and war. It was a segregated country, and Secretary of War Henry L. Stimson remained opposed to integration of the armed forces. But Washington officials were aware of the sporadic outbursts of Negro activism around the country in recent years, protesting the failure of antilynching and antidiscrimination legislation. Some notable figures from the black community—Paul Robeson, W. E. B. DuBois—had uttered rather romantic sentiments about the Communist Party, a circumstance that made Washington twitchy, the more so after the blood began to spill upon the sand following the bombing of Pearl Harbor on December 7, 1941.

Might blacks sour on patriotism? Might America be unable to showcase a unified front across racial lines? Labor leader John L. Lewis, in a nationwide radio address delivered before the attack on Pearl Harbor, minced no words about what he saw as the state of war and jobs and equal rights. "Labor in America wants no war nor any part of war. Labor in America wants the right to work and live—not the privilege of dying by gunshot or poison gas to sustain the mental errors of current statesmen."

Could a populace—black men and women—be gathered up and set down on military bases and all the while be expected to heed the same imprisoning rules that applied in outside society?

There were no Negro Hollywood stars for the War Department to woo. No figure from the Negro community in Tinseltown whose weekly movements were followed and marveled at by the larger public, giving them the aura of celebrity and creating a public relations boon.

Having no one from Hollywood to turn to, the War Department reached into the Negro world of sports. And that meant Joe Louis and Sugar Ray Robinson.

Robinson was clearly rising in boxing circles, and quite rapidly. In 1941, in an Associated Press sports editors' poll ranking athletes, Robinson received 29 points to Joe Louis's 14. That positioned Robinson in sixth place to Louis's tenth. Frank Sinkwich, the University of Georgia's galloping halfback, was named the nation's number-one male athlete that year; Boston Red Sox slugger Ted Williams was right behind Sinkwich. (Before he had officially entered the military, Robinson participated in a celebrity boxing event at Camp Upton, on Long Island, with the main draw being an exhibition bout between Joe Louis and his sparring mate George Nicholson. It was a mixture of boxing and entertainment watched by a crowd of seven thousand, and both Sugar Ray Robinson and Bill "Bojangles" Robinson were there and whispered about.)

On the streets of Harlem, Sugar Ray Robinson was beginning to carry a special cachet. The reporters had begun referring to him as "the Harlem Dandy." Whereas Joe Louis struck many as severe, Robinson was as light and chipper as a dancer. In addition, Robinson lived in Harlem; Louis was a visitor to that cultural stomping ground, waltzing about after his big bouts and on social occasions. The height of Joe's power had been in the mid- and late thirties.

"If you'd see both of them on the street," recalls the influential congressman Charlie Rangel, who was raised in Harlem and would see Louis and Robinson side by side and gawk at them as a kid, "you'd want to run over to Sugar Ray. If both of them were walking into a bar, you'd get a wave from Joe. But Sugar Ray would stop and be rapping. Joe was very self-conscious. If there was an opposite of that, it was Sugar Ray."

But poll standings aside, Sugar Ray wasn't about to overtake Joe Louis's popularity in the early months of wartime as the government waged a battle for the hearts and minds of black folk. Joe was legend; Joe was lore; Joe was going to have a poem ("Joe Louis Named the War") written about him and the war.

Joe Louis had given black America an emancipation right into the sports world when he became heavyweight champion in June 1937 by knocking out Jim Braddock at Comiskey Park in Chicago.

Braddock, a Depression-era hero—the Cinderella Man—had overcome poverty to stage a ring comeback in the early 1930s; his defeat of champion Max Baer on June 13, 1935, was considered a seismic upset. The victory set up his bout with Louis. Louis was a native of rural Alabama, and on the day of the Braddock match, some of his relatives living in the Bukalew Mountains near Lafayette, Alabama, got themselves into town so they could press ears to the radio. Louis had trained in near-isolation in Wisconsin for the Braddock title match. There was so very much at stake, and there were also worries from many quarters about the measure of Louis's gifts: He had been knocked out in June 1936 by the German Max Schmeling at Yankee Stadium. As that bout deepened, and Schmeling—who looked on his way to defeat—began staging something of a comeback, whites, soaked with emotion now, began to root for the German, a noise that caused those in Louis's corner to wonder about national loyalty. (An ocean away, Adolf Hitler, chancellor of the Third Reich, was goose-stepping his Nazi armies around Europe, killing and plotting war.) It was in the eighth round of that 1937 Chicago bout when, with the world listening, Louis's fierce right caught Braddock. "I laid it solid," Louis would recall, "with all my body, on the right side of his face, and his face split open. He fell in a face-down dive." Louis had become the first black champion since Jack Johnson. Johnson was so mercurial, there were even those in the Louis camp who considered the retired champ unpredictable and belligerent. Johnson was still displaying a lavish appetite for white women, agitating many blacks as he complained that black women had taken advantage of his financial largesse. Joe Louis left no doubt about his cultural pride. Upon his victory over Braddock there were celebrations in mud-strewn Negro hamlets, in gin joints, in houses of ill repute in Detroit, in dressing rooms of Negro League ballplayers barnstorming through the South, in hair salons, on rooftops where garden parties were held in Harlem, beneath the hanging lights of the fine homes that Negroes had purchased in the Georgetown section of the nation's capital. Joe had made sure that—as William Nunn, the sports editor of *The Pittsburgh Courier* put it—"all the fondest dreams of the 12,000,000 racial brethren of the new champion have come true. He has been a credit to them and now he rides the 'Glory Road.' He has taken them up with him. He is theirs." The aura of Joe Louis spread like honey. A Harlem columnist felt obliged to remind his readers: "For the benefit of some Harlem lovelies, Joe Louis is due in Harlem next week."

When Louis felled Schmeling in June 1938 in their ballyhooed rematch—against the smoke of war in Europe and the attendant rise of Naziism—he had produced the final line needed in a narrative arc that could be felt from Sugar Ray's Harlem to the offices of the War Department: The nation needed to be unified on the home front.

In 1942 Louis's musings about patriotism had an undeniable psychological weight for the American Negro. The military printed up Army posters showing Louis in uniform—helmet, khakis, canteen on belt loop, his face grim and a bayonet in hands—with some words he had uttered at a rally enlarged beneath the photo: "We're going to do our part . . . and we'll win because we're on God's side." Suddenly, he was the Negro basso profundo that sounded through the political worries of the nation. Sugar Ray Robinson—inducted into the Army in February 1943, thirteen months after Louis—was the keening alto sax in the corner. He looked strikingly handsome in his pressed Ike jacket, his creased slacks, and his corporal's stripes. (Official military records would list him as Corp. Walker Smith, his birth name.)

It would, however, be the last time that Robinson would seem to shrink in the presence and aura of a fellow prizefighter. He had yet to gain his first belt title; his welterweight size made him look thin as a fashion model. Even though he had had some tough battles in the ring already, he still retained a boyish look. But he was certainly positioning himself as the one figure—with his athletic prowess and rhythmic style—who was ready to burst right through the curtains of racial witchery that both Jack Johnson and Joe Louis had had to part.

It seemed that entertainers and movie stars were everywhere in the military seasons of 1943 and 1944. If they were not in uniform, they were performing on military bases. Actresses such as Hedy Lamarr, Bette Davis, Gene Tierney, and Carole Lombard were involved in the effort, their beauty and verve helping to sell war bonds and bring smiles to the troops. Jimmy Stewart—who had been a huge hit in Frank Capra's *Mr. Smith Goes to Washington* in 1939—joined up and became a bomber pilot. The matinee idol Tyrone Power would end up in the South Pacific. Fellow actor Ronald Reagan reported to Fort March in San Francisco. (Hollywood hummed into action with its patriotic-themed films. *This Is the Army* starred Kate Smith, Irving Berlin, and, among others, Lt. Ronald Reagan and Sgt. Joe Louis. The film was full of skits and songs; Joe's role was a speech-making cameo. He appeared in a swaying all-black musical number, in which some lovely black dancers cavort about, pointing out the cut of military uniforms and crooning—about the uniforms specifi-cally—"That's What the Well-Dressed Man in Harlem Will Wear." The film was directed by Michael Curtiz.)

Not long after, Carole Lombard's plane, a TWA DC-3, went down in the Nevada mountains, killing her and the crew—she had been out selling war bonds, blowing kisses—her husband, a heartsick Clark Gable, joined the military. Gable and Lombard had nicknames for each other: Ma and Pa.

"Why Ma?" Gable asked, over and over, until it began to sound like an echo.

The American GIs needed laughter, so the comics packed their bags too. Jack Benny cracked wise, though he thought it smart to leave his black sidekick, Eddie "Rochester" Anderson, behind, given the racial setup of military life. The champion of the comics, how-ever, was a jovial-looking jokester who had been born in England but raised in Cleveland. Bob Hope—who had boxed as a teenager before abruptly leaving that sport behind—took to war shows like a starlet to Sunset Boulevard. Hope had made a name for himself in vaudeville. Then came Broadway and comedy shorts. Hollywood summoned him and he garnered attention in *The Cat and the Canary* in 1939. But his early "road" pictures with crooner Bing Crosby—*Road to Singapore* in 1940 and *Road to Morocco* in 1942—set new stan-dards for that kind of hilarity. The war shows seemed to have been dreamed up for a man such as Hope: Some days he did four perfor-mances, yuk-yuking it with the troops, tossing out silly lines about his cowardice, about his Hollywood friends. At a performance in Tunisia, a wiseacre in uniform popped off at Hope.

"Draft dodger! Why aren't you in uniform," came the voice, stun-ning Hope.

"Don't you know there's a war on?" Hope answered, his vaudeville timing smooth as ever. "A guy could get hurt!"

Sugar Ray Robinson and Joe Louis—paired up in the military—were not on the road to Morocco. They were, however, soon on the road to Alabama.

A Brooklyn-born singer and aspiring chanteuse took her dreams to Los Angeles in 1941. She was looking for beauty—the kind shared by others—and grace and acceptance. Lena Horne settled into a Hollywood apartment, in a neighborhood where Negroes were not welcome; neighbors apparently believed she was "Latin"; no one bothered her. Duke Ellington and others had convinced her to go West; there was talk from an acquaintance of a new nightclub opening. Then came the haunting news of war—and the nightclub dream faded. "Everything's over," Horne imagined upon hearing news of Pearl Harbor humming over the radio. Only it wasn't, of course. She soon befriended others who believed in beauty and grace, among them Billy Strayhorn, a composer and arranger who worked closely with Ellington; and Katherine Dunham, an iconoclastic Negro dancer—she had done doctoral work in anthropology at the University of Chicago—who had formed a dance company, the Dunham Dancers, and who now had engagements in Los Angeles with her troupe. Ellington was already on the ground in Los Angeles. He was in town with a show called *Jump for Joy.* (Among its cast was Dorothy Dandridge, another ethereal young beauty, this one from Cleveland, Ohio. Dandridge had made her screen debut—a tiny part—in *A Day at the Races,* a 1937 Marx Brothers film.) It was at a *Jump for Joy* performance that Horne met the gifted Strayhorn. Horne had a manner of quickly delighting those she met. There was laughter, the sharing of home-cooked food and good wine, gossip, the jangled wartime nerves, which they all defeated with their bonhomie and togetherness and the music spilling out of the record player. Together with the willowy Dunham Dancers, Horne opened in a nightclub act at the Little Troc, a new club on Sunset Strip. Strayhorn, who was as fixated with Horne—in a platonic way; he was gay—as she was with him, did a version of "Honeysuckle Rose," among other songs, for the young singer. It was wartime; she sang at the nightclub as if there might be no tomorrow. It was beautiful and sweet and suggestive, and word spread. On Sunset Boulevard, when it came to new and sensational acts, word traveled like blown dandelions. Movie stars—those not snatched up by the military—came to hear her sing. A newspaper critic would conclude that the Little Troc nightclub was suddenly on everyone's lips because "Lena Horne, a singer from the Downtown Café Society in New York, is being hailed as another Florence Mills. She has knocked the movie population bowlegged and is up to her ears in offers. She came out here unknown . . ." Greta Garbo caught her act. So did Cole Porter; so did Marlene Dietrich; so did Lauren Bacall. Strayhorn, who wore owlish glasses and resembled a boyish professor, gleamed when he heard the words he wrote sail from her lovely lips. (Cole Porter invited Horne to a cast party for *This Is the Army.*) With the lavish publicity and attention, MGM elbowed their way into Horne's orbit and quickly signed her up to a movie contract. It was huge news, and the Negro press reported on it happily. The studio needed to find a vehicle for Horne. They came up with *Cabin in the Sky,* a Broadway musical that they felt sure would transfer quite well to the screen.

While awaiting the start of filming on *Cabin,* Horne settled in at another Sunset Boulevard nightclub, the Mocambo. The gushing trailed her there; newsmen filed reports about cops having to fight back the crowds. Ted Le Berthon, a Los Angeles *Daily News* writer, caught her Mocambo act: "And, well, who is Lena Horne? . . . An exquisite olive skinned, 22-year-old beauty of the Negro race whom anyone might mistake for an aristocratic and exciting Latin American seniorita, with inkily dark gleaming eyes. She wore a sea green evening gown and stood there with a powerful smile of quiet affection. And then she began to sing. And before the evening was over, all of us . . . had seen and heard the greatest artist in her field in our time in history . . . No appeal to innuendo. Just the high mystery of art, of the more complete individual."

Lena Horne was ready for the big screen.

MGM hired Vincente Minnelli to direct the movie version of *Cabin in the Sky.* Chicago-born, he was young, vivacious, and always had ideas popping out of his head. It helped the studio's confidence in him that he had directed *Ziegfeld Follies* on Broadway. And before that, he had served a stint as art director at Radio City Music Hall; he was no stranger to drama and constant movement on a stage. *Cabin* was indeed a movie of its time, with grave stereotypical shortcomings. But there is no denying its buoyancy, its sparkling light, its unforgettable costumes and orchestral arrangements. It also, in addition to featuring Horne, drew upon a scintillating ensemble—Duke Ellington, Eddie "Rochester" Anderson (finding work without Mr. Benny), Louis Armstrong, Butterfly McQueen, Ethel Waters, and Rex Ingram. It is a heaven-glancing fable: the Hollywood imagination at the time seemed taken with transporting Negroes to heaven—or having Negroes ponder the route there while engaging in all manner of shenanigans and conniving. (*Green Pastures,* another all-Negro musical, released in 1936, had a similar setting, although a gentler tone.) The *Cabin* plot revolves around Little Joe, a gambler (played by Rochester) who suffers a gunshot wound. Of course the shooting unnerves his wife, Petunia, played by Ethel Waters, who receives top billing in the film. Petunia prays mightily that he will recover. The movie being a fable, Little Joe is granted a reprieve from certain death, but he must stop gambling. The devil lurks, setting off a test of wills between himself and emissaries from Heaven over the direction of Little Joe's soul. The devil has extra help, a handmaiden, Georgia Brown, played by Horne. Georgia sidles up next to Little Joe, bewitching him, slinking about. She shows up in his backyard, primping, swaying her hips. Moviegoers had gone to the theatre to see *Cabin* because they were enamored of Ethel Waters. By the movie's end, they found themselves talking about Horne.

Hollywood glitter aside, there was still a war going on. Horne—when she couldn't personally reach Joe Louis—depended on friends and contacts for news about both Louis and Robinson and Negro involvement in the Army. Negro soldiers, however, needed no reminding to keep tabs on Lena Horne. As one wrote in a missive to MGM: "Now we have someone we can pin on our lockers."

It was a geographical reality that the majority of military bases were located in the Deep South. This often meant that Negro soldiers from the South, many of whom had left the region because of the stinging racial climate, were now returning to familiar scenes—peering from train and bus windows across cotton fields in Alabama, peanut farms in Georgia, darkening woods in Mississippi; staring into the faces of old Negro men and women in their eighties who had lived long enough to remember the last breaths of slavery. The soldiers found there was little difference between the outside world and the cocoon of an Army base: They still had to sit in the back at base movie theatres; they still had separate living quarters. It was a painful conundrum: the word "democracy" was hollered everywhere, but second-class treatment was meted out to them daily. Many of the soldiers and their family members wrote heartbreaking letters to First Lady Eleanor Roosevelt, complaining of their mistreatment. She appealed to President Roosevelt, who appealed to Secretary of War Stimson, who said he would not be conducting any social experiments—such as integration—during wartime. Still, the Army could not ignore its Negro troops, and Army officials came up with the idea of creating a separate office that would take Negro concerns under consideration.

Thus the War Department on Negro Affairs was born. It rather bizarrely consisted of just one official, and that official was given just one secretary. One of the department's earliest ideas was to send Joe Louis on a tour of Army bases to stage exhibitions. The aim of the tour would be to promote troop morale; the underlying mission was to foster racial unity. Louis, who traveled to Washington to discuss the plan, was told to handpick his traveling mates. He quickly decided on Sugar Ray. Then his sparring mate George Nicholson was chosen. Sugar Ray—shrewd in such matters—suggested another fighter for the contingent, a smoothie from Los Angeles. As Sugar Ray knew, "California" Jackie Wilson had a nifty biographical flourish: He'd participated in the 1936 Berlin Olympics, taking a silver medal. Of Louis's traveling crew, Wilson was the only one who had seen and sniffed the dangerous Nazi air up close. At those 1936 games, Hitler had risen—his face frozen in anger but the eyes dark as bullets—and abruptly left the stadium rather than witness the triumph of the black sprinter Jesse Owens. West Coast fight fans had begun clamoring for a Robinson-Wilson bout back in May 1942, following Robinson's tough victory against Marty Servo. Jimmy Nelson, who operated the Dunbar, a Negro hotel in Los Angeles, liked spinning out to reporters the possibilities of certain matchups that he just knew would draw large crowds. In 1942 both Robinson and Wilson were rated top-five contenders. Nelson imagined that a Wilson-Robinson bout—Wilson being local—would be great business not only for the Hollywood crowd, but for the out-of-town Negro fight fans who would book rooms at his establishment. Sugar Ray was no "superman," the hotelier Nelson huffed. He talked about the blows Robinson had taken in the Servo bout. He warned that Robinson would face an even nastier challenge in Wilson: "Anyone Jackie Wilson can hit can be hurt," Nelson said.

The drumbeat would be answered; the bout was announced for February 1943.

On the other side of the country, in a column on the eve of the announced Robinson-Wilson match, something struck Arthur Daley, sports columnist of *The New York Times,* about the specter of war bumping up against the grace of the gifted athlete. Daley lamented the perils of three figures—Joe DiMaggio, the Yankee hitter, Jackie Wilson, and Robinson. In Daley's mind, time and war would now conspire to rob these men of precious gifts; it was as if a movie screen would go blank, darkening further imagination of what they might do and become. Daley seemed to realize that each had a quality that set him off beyond the sporting arena; each was lit by a unique style that made his accomplishments far more than sweat and brawn. And now this: Hitler moving across Europe, the headlines claimed by reports of troop movements, and ordinary citizens keeping watch for foreign submarines along coastlines. It all meant a need for baseball bats and boxing gloves to be put aside. And a deep accompanying reality: War was war. Men became heroes, and heroes died.

The Robinson-Wilson matchup didn't take place in Los Angeles but in New York City on February 19, 1943, with twenty thousand watching: Sugar Ray bested the Olympian in the tenth round of a frenetic bout. Ten days later, Sugar Ray reported for Army duty. Joe DiMaggio had reported for duty February 24 at the Santa Ana Air Base near Los Angeles. (Wilson was already enlisted and had been on furlough for the Robinson bout.) The three athletes had shouldered so many dreams—including the dreams of others—and now in the minds of their followers there was so much uncertainty surrounding their continued grace. "It may seem odd at first glance to group Robinson, Wilson and DiMaggio together," Daley of the *Times* wrote. "Yet the entire story of America at war is told by these three athletes."

George Nicholson was the kind of fighter who made a living giving his body over to the blows delivered by truly great fighters: He had been sparring partner to both Louis and Jim Braddock. Champions look for sparring partners who might challenge them; the sparring partner, however, must possess a nimble mind, ever conscious of the vagaries of a champion's mood and daily disposition. Nicholson possessed not only bravery but humility and on fight night was content enough to simply recede into the shadows with his little bankroll and the belief he had been both teacher and peer to the fighter in the ring.

As for Sugar Ray, he was that well-dressed soldier of Harlem that they were singing about. *Ring* magazine would feature him in full uniform on its September 1943 cover. His right palm rests on the brim of his military hat in a salute; the uniform looks crisp and elegant; the eyes are focused into the distance. "Corp. Ray Robinson, World's Outstanding Welterweight, now in Army Air Force at Mitchel Field," it says in the bottom left corner of the cover. There is a bit of an advertisement too: BUY UNITED STATES WAR BONDS AND STAMPS. (Corporal Robinson looks as handsome and coolly brave as any other wartime figure—Jimmy Stewart, Clark Gable—who would grace magazines in uniform.)

This was the first time that the American military had backed anything like the Robinson-Louis tour. It reflected a larger shift in the way the military treated Negro soldiers. During World War I, nearly 90 percent of Negro troops were assigned to labor duty. Black soldiers finally got their chance to fight in World War II, but their numbers were small and the units were mostly segregated. The Army was not shy about showcasing the Negro boxers and their show of patriotism and sent photographers attached to the U.S. Army Signal Corps to snap away.

In the late August heat of 1943 at Fort Devens, Massachusetts, Joe and Sugar Ray and their traveling Army companions began what was announced as a hundred-day tour. As Joe signed the base arrival book, Sugar Ray—looking snappy in uniform—stood staring over his shoulder, a knot of admiring soldiers surrounding both. Joe assumed his usual demeanor of seriousness. Cornered by reporters, he'd talk about patriotism and would offer short, clipped utterances about the need for good troop morale. Sugar Ray was far more jovial. Although the tour was barely under way, it was already being billed as "[t]he world's greatest boxing show." As they made their way around the Massachusetts base, word spread quickly. Negro soldiers—attached to the all-Negro 366th Regiment—were surprised at the sight of the traveling contingent and set about slapping palms, whistling, pointing, getting up close. The scheduled morale-boosting events consisted of boxing exhibitions and chatter. At one Fort Devens event, upwards of seven thousand soldiers whooped and hollered at the sight of the group. "Hail, Hail, the Gang's All Here," an Army band let loose as the boxers made their way toward the exhibition ring. The group had great leeway, and their days involved a lot of improvisation. Sometimes Sugar would even warble out a tune. In the ring set up outdoors at the rural military camp—GIs piled on jeeps, tall pine trees rising in the distance—Joe and George went at it for a few rounds, then Sugar Ray and California Jackie took a turn. The GIs on the ground, as if inside a fevered arena, howled and whistled as the fighters landed punches. The scenes revealed a summer-camp tableau full of vigorous activity. The group got a lot of questions about their weight, their past opponents. Joe and Sugar Ray signed autographs at the Fort Devens Army hospital. Many of the patients were arrivals from battles in North Africa. The fighters scrawled their names on the plaster arm and leg casts of soldiers. Standing side by side outdoors one morning, Joe and Sugar Ray previewed an all-white contingent of Army nurses stepping lively in formation.

It was no accident that the Army began Joe and Sugar Ray's tour in the state of Massachusetts. The New England state had a long and liberal military history. The Fifty-fourth Massachusetts Volunteers was a celebrated black regiment that had distinguished itself during the Civil War. Still, by 1942 the American military was far from leaving racial separation behind, as Eleanor Roosevelt—considered such an ally to the Negro populace—was being reminded almost daily. At Fort Devens, however, the racial interaction was easy. And there was an undeniable warmth between Joe and Sugar Ray and the Negro soldiers on base who made up the 366th Regiment. The fighters huddled as the soldiers shared confidences with them. At a service club dance for the Negro unit, Joe and Sugar Ray swayed to the music and mingled with the musicians. Off base, they'd buy soldiers meals; they'd listen as GIs regaled them with stories of listening to their fights back home on radio—against Sammy Angott, against Braddock, against the German Schmeling, against Freddie Cabral, against Billy Conn, against Ralph Zannelli. Sometimes it seemed that between them—and in the eyes of the soldiers—Louis and Robinson had knocked out the whole damn world. There were salutes and hearty handshakes as they prepared to depart the base. *Life* magazine believed that the Fort Devens appearance by Joe and Sugar Ray presented "a quiet parable in racial good will." But Robinson was bemused and bewildered by such optimism. The Army, on one hand, had indeed made him feel patriotic: He stared at himself in mirrors in his dress uniform, admiring how he had suddenly become a part of the American armed forces—a single soul, but a part of the mass maneuvering and march of machinery. And he quickly came to admire the sense of order and regimentation that went with military life. But this social experiment left him with a kind of nervousness. He remembered the racial nightmares in Detroit, and all those social activists in Harlem who told of lynchings throughout the South. Beneath the public relations façade, he was dubious about this so-called goodwill effort. He deferred to Louis—the big wheel in the Army's PR machinery—while keeping a sharp sensibility about his surroundings.

They rolled on like a caravan: Fort Meade in Maryland (ten thousand saw them and cheered); Camp McCoy in Wisconsin; Camp Grant in Illinois; Sioux City Army Air Base in Iowa; Fort Riley in Kansas. Often following the exhibitions, Louis and Robinson and the others would pose with Negro soldiers—buffed and shirtless— who had taken part in the boxing shows. The amateur pugilists were dubbed "Brown Bombers." The Brown Bombers complained— quietly, away from their superiors—to Louis and Robinson that they were tired of being assigned to sanitation crews. The two marquee names on the tour vowed to get the complaints back to Washington. Both Louis and Robinson were in the headlines: RAY ROBINSON BOXES FOR SOLDIER BOYS; JOE LOUIS SIGNS IN AT FORT DEVENS. They kept signing autographs. They gave away pairs of boxing gloves to smiling soldiers. They guffawed onto each other's shoulders. Away from the military bases, they patrolled the Negro bars in those Northern and Midwestern cities, unrolling ten- and twenty-dollar bills at the bar, buying drinks. They took weekend furloughs and hightailed it back to Manhattan. They were seen at the swank Savoy Club together; they were seen in the lobby of the Hotel Theresa, where the out-of-town jazzmen often stayed when visiting

Harlem. They were seen with wrapped gifts under their arms for female admirers. They cackled with fight promoter Mike Jacobs, who lent both money. They knew they'd pay Jacobs back the only way that mattered to him: by agreeing to the bouts he would arrange for them. (A photographer had followed Robinson into Jacobs's Brill Building office on one of those forays. Jacobs—always quick to inquire about how "the war" was going—was wearing a three-piece wool suit, white shirt, printed tie. He looked suave. But Sugar Ray, in his dark military dress uniform, his corporal's hat, looked far more elegant.)

And there was the scene on the beach, at Atlantic City, the breeze coming in sweetly off the ocean: Edward Allen—destined to spend time with Sugar Ray in later years, when he would become dentist to Miles Davis, Sugar Ray's pal—was in that boardwalk city as a Navy ensign. He was walking toward the beach, and he saw a horde of black faces. He heard shrieking as he got closer. "I turned to a friend," he would recall years later, "and said, 'What's going on?' And he said, 'Sugar Ray's down there.' " Allen kept walking, and there, true enough, was Sugar Ray. "He was just going to the beach," says Allen. "The people were really fascinated. It was like girls hollering behind Frank Sinatra."

Even when Joe and Sugar Ray were on duty, Army brass were astonished at their rather loose and sometimes instantaneous rescheduling. There were missed trains and bus trips, a hurry-hurry effort to catch up and get to the troops when they were running late. Some officers huffed, complained to Washington. But with star power—even Negro star power—came allowances. It could not be dismissed either that the traveling show had the backing of the War Department, which meant it had the backing of the Roosevelt White House.

Angelo Dundee, whose fame would come in the 1960s as Muhammad Ali's valued trainer, was in the Army during the war. He boxed on occasion, but mostly he trained fighters for exhibition bouts. He heard of the Louis-Robinson tour, news of it spreading fast on the homefront grapevine. "It was a tremendous thing because Louis and Robinson were so popular," he would recall.

Before autumn's end, in their crisp uniforms and shiny shoes, Sugar Ray and Joe Louis would find themselves stepping onto military bases in the Deep South.

Between them—and prior to 1943, when Robinson joined the

military—Joe Louis and Sugar Ray Robinson had fought dozens of pro fights. But fewer than five of all of their combined bouts had taken place below the Mason-Dixon line. Joe Louis hadn't felt the sting of daily Southern racism since his Alabama childhood; Sugar Ray's family had Georgia roots, but he had come of age in a freer Detroit. While Joe Louis retained traces of a country demeanor, there was little doubt that New York City, Chicago, and Detroit—places of urban sophistication and the cities he was most fond of—had rubbed off on him. As for Sugar Ray, he had taken naturally to the spin of the city, bouncing up off the pavement of New York City and Harlem poverty like a man to the wicked and hustling environs born. Boxing topped off the stature of both men. Its money- and headline-making victories and attendant glory had propelled them into a sphere of living—Sugar Ray in 1943 was relatively new to it—that kept nasty and brutish racial insults at a remove. These were not men who shuffled in their gait. They drank champagne with actors and actresses and singers; they shopped for clothes at fine tailors on Broadway. They were mystical; Joe Louis and Sugar Ray Robinson were two Negroes who made others curious. When their feet hit the ground, they knew exactly which direction they were going.

The South that Louis and Robinson descended upon in late 1943 was still very much a bruised land. The Depression had been a long and painful song, but it was the Civil War and the way it pitted South against North, slavery against freedom, black against white, that remained the visceral touchstone in the area. Down where those battles had been fought, their economic and cultural echoes were far from silent, the land far from healed.

White soldiers in World War II Southern Army camps came from households where the Confederate flag still blew in the outdoor breeze; where Gen. Robert E. Lee and Jefferson Davis were epic heroes; where states' rights remained the last gasp of proof that the South had done something right and fruitful in its bid at state-by-state secession. Many of the soldiers in the World War II Army camps across the Carolinas, across Georgia and Mississippi and Alabama, were the great-grandsons of Civil War veterans. They lived in homes that held Civil War–era keepsakes: pistols, caps, swords, sepia-tinted photographs.

In 1908 after Jack Johnson had entered the boxing ring in Sydney, Australia—"Come on and fight, nigger!" champion Tommy Burns had unwisely yelled to Jack—and walked out of it as the crowned champ, Negroes in America celebrated. They celebrated all over—in Georgia, in Mississippi, in Alabama. Not long after Johnson's history-making bout, the deacon of a white Baptist church in Birmingham, Alabama, was startled that his Negro carriage driver dared challenge him on the amount of the fee. The carriage driver did not wish to be underpaid. An argument ensued; the white deacon shot the carriage driver dead. Friends of the driver hoped for justice and gathered in the courtroom for the beginning of legal proceedings. The judge released the deacon. He then turned to the gathering of Negroes with an admonishment: "You Niggers are getting beside yourselves since Jack Johnson won the fight from a white man. I want you to mind what you do in this town. Remember, you are in the South, and remember further that when you speak to white gentlemen you should speak in a way that is best becoming a Nigger. This act will be repeated daily by the white gentlemen of this city if you Niggers don't find your places."

The Louis and Robinson contingent, traveling by military plane, arrived first in Mississippi. They landed at Keesler Field, an air base in the Magnolia State. Some Negro troops had heard about their arrival, and as soon as they spotted them, moved toward them for handshakes, then autographs. Glancing about, taking in the surroundings, Sugar Ray told the soldiers he'd see them at that night's show. (Sugar Ray was calling the exhibitions "shows," because sometimes he'd do stand-up comedy; he'd tell stories; he wanted to allow for improvisation, which made him happy and seemed to loosen Joe up.)

"[W]e wanted to see Joe and you now because we won't be able to see the show," one of the soldiers said.

"Why not? You on guard duty?" Sugar Ray wondered, Joe waiting for the soldier's answer.

"No," said the soldier, "the Negro troops aren't allowed to mix with the white on this base. Only the white troops will be at the show."

"Isn't this the United States?" Sugar Ray snapped. "Isn't this America?"

"No, man," another soldier answered, "this is Mississippi."

At the base, after the formalities of signing in, Sugar Ray—

sporting corporal's stripes and proud of it—sought out a Special Services officer.

"Is it true that the Negro troops won't be allowed to see our show?" Sugar Ray inquired.

The Army officer seemed annoyed by Sugar Ray's line of questioning. He simply told him it was a decision that had been made by a general on base.

"Well, tell the general that unless there's a Negro section in there tonight, there won't be a show," Sugar Ray said.

The officer, speechless, strode away.

Sugar Ray retreated to his barracks, bragging to Joe about what he had just told the officer. (Joe had contacts inside the War Department, and he told them of the egregious slights the troupe endured. Like a diplomat, he preferred working through the chain of command. Sugar Ray, far more emotional, meant to put his impatience to use on the ground; he imagined immediate solutions. Joe Louis would himself realize he had no power over young Sugar Ray's emotional and improvisational streak.)

A siren hummed in the Mississippi air outside their barracks; Sugar Ray whispered to Joe that it was the base general himself. A door opened and the general marched right over to Sugar Ray. Joe turned ever so slightly to watch.

"I understand that you are giving orders on my base," the general said to Sugar Ray. "I want you to know that you are supposed to take orders, not give them."

"I beg your pardon, sir," Sugar Ray said, but not in the tone of a man who meant to leave it there.

Joe instantly felt that Sugar Ray had gone too far. "Easy, Ray," the world champ whispered.

It was too late.

With the general's jeep idling, soldiers hovered outside to get a glimpse of the unfolding drama.

Sugar Ray told the general that he and Louis and the others were "under orders" from the War Department itself—making it seem as if they were outside the general's command—and that if Negro troops couldn't see the show, they would not perform. Joe was stunned. Sugar Ray was surely inching up on some kind of disciplinary action, if not outright court-martial.

When the general pointed his finger at Sugar Ray, admonishing him, the young fighter blurted out that he'd call the War Department. The general snapped back that if there were any calls to be made to the War Department, he'd make them himself. Then he marched out. Joe half-circled in front of Sugar Ray and called him "crazy" for doing what he had just done.

They both sat and stewed, joined by Nicholson and Jackie Wilson, anticipating the worst. As word spread, fellow Negro soldiers felt proud of them.

Not long after, Sugar Ray, who had convinced himself he would not back down, was ordered to the general's headquarters. The summons drew grunts and wide-eyed stares from nearby soldiers; it elicited under-the-breath predictions of doom.

The general—his mood surprisingly calmer, his tone more relaxed—told Sugar Ray that he had indeed called Washington and had actually gotten permission for the Negro and white troops to mix. So the show would go on. The general sought to absolve himself personally of the segregation: "When you complained about the situation, it gave me ammunition to have something to call Washington about, so I did," he offered. A happy Sugar Ray smiled, and saluted.

That evening the racially integrated group of soldiers whooped loud, watching and gyrating as the quartet of boxers showed their skills. Sugar Ray grinned a lot and nodded at the Negro soldiers particularly—as if to offer affirmation that his course of challenging the general had been nervy but right.

Unlike in Massachusetts, however, Sugar Ray and Joe would not be welcomed to "review" any contingent of marching female nurses. The mix of Negro eyes upon white females in the South was a losing proposition. The large numbers of missives from Southern politicians that arrived on the desk of Secretary of War Stimson—lashing out at him for allowing some military brass leeway around segregation on bases—happened to be full of vile accusations about black men, all wrapped around rather flowery language praising white womanhood. In Alabama, whites—and especially Negroes—had hardly forgotten the Scottsboro incident: On March 25, 1931, nine young Negroes had been in a boxcar on a Southern Railroad freight train that rolled out of Tennessee into northern Alabama. They were hoboing, looking for work. There was a scuffle with some white hoboes; the Negroes had gotten the better of them in the confrontation. The roughed-up whites reported the incident to Alabama authorities. A posse stopped the train and arrested the nine black youths. At the Scottsboro jailhouse, they were stunned to find out they had been accused of rape by Ruby Bates and Victoria Price, two young white women who had also been hoboing on the train. A mob threatened lynching until the governor summoned the National Guard. There was a trial and the meting out of lengthy prison sentences and death sentences. (A young Langston Hughes was touring the South, giving readings. The trial proceedings so unnerved him that he wrote a poem, "Christ in Alabama.") The trial had sparked national and international outrage; the white women had recanted the charges, and appeals made all the way to the Supreme Court had ended in victories. Still, the retrials only offered up new indictments. All nine would end up serving long prison sentences. Some of the nine would issue ghostwritten memoirs after their release from prison. The books told of prison beatings, rapes, tear-gassing, escape attempts. The father of Clarence Norris, one of the nine, had been born a slave. Amidst the dogwood trees and Confederate flags of Alabama, the Scottsboro Boys had been dropped into a Southern-spiced version of Dante's Hell.

The conundrum of race was not an easy thing for Sugar Ray Robinson to digest. He had come of age in the world of Northern amateur boxing; its participants were a willing mixture of white, black, and Hispanic. Beyond that world he had been surrounded by the church elders of Salem Methodist in Harlem, men and women who did as much as possible to keep their young congregants shielded from the lash of racism. And even beyond that stood his fearsome mother, Leila, who often and boldly engaged in public arguments with white store owners and bill collectors. Sugar Ray mostly took racial disrespect on a case-by-case basis—as if the perpetrator were but another foolish sap in the ring with him—and not as a cause. Louis, however, was a symbol and knew it—because of both his boxing and the color of his skin. Whereas Louis began to feel a kind of hurt for the entire lot of Negroes, Robinson's hurt went only as far as his individual emotions would take it.

Whenever they could, Louis and Robinson would get off base and go visit one of the local Negro colleges that dotted the South. They'd strut around in their uniforms, smiling, cadging phone numbers from attractive coeds and female administrators. Robinson particularly liked corralling traveling jazzmen to join him and Louis for meals and soulful bonhomie. They spent money without thinking about it—on soldiers, women, the barhopping strangers who crossed their paths. Sugar Ray would come to estimate that between them, he and Louis had spent around $30,000 during their traveling together on behalf of Uncle Sam: "Picking up tabs, buying presents for chicks, tipping big" is how he put it. They carried hundred-dollar bills in money clips. It was the Army, but inside of themselves they waltzed to the high life. "[W]e knew there was more money where that had come from," Robinson said later. That money had come from victories, which had made them a kind of royalty, which is why they were on assignment from the White House itself.

Jimmy Stewart had movie roles and movie money awaiting him when his Army hitch was over. Joe DiMaggio, who was swinging his bat in the California sunshine, playing on an Army team—JOE DIMAGGIO SLAMS FIRST ARMY HOMER, said one headline—had the Yankees waiting on him. Robinson and Louis had men awaiting them who wanted to drive gloved fists into their faces and rib cages. And they would have to take on those challenges—because that was where more of the money would be coming from.

The caravan of the world's greatest boxing show had a calmer visit to Fort Benning, Georgia. Getting there they had passed turpentine camps and chain gangs; shacks where Negro sharecroppers lived, shacks where white sharecroppers lived. They saw children with slack faces who looked hungry. Joe was yanked back to his past, his childhood; Sugar Ray had no spiritual connection with the landscape. He missed the North, he missed home; he missed the way the jazz music floated into him when he pushed open the door to one of those Harlem jazz spots on 125th and the way the red lipstick on the faces of the pretty women shimmered and how the cool cats offered him their hand for a shake.

Edward Peeks—who would go on to a career as a respected journalist—was one of the black soldiers in Georgia who witnessed the Louis-Robinson visit: "We'd congregate," he says. "Sugar Ray was quite the joke teller. They were the Hollywood soldiers, him and Joe."

If the white soldiers' reaction was sometimes more muted toward Joe and Sugar Ray than the reaction of Negro soldiers, it could be understood. There had been no pictures of Jack Johnson in the homes of the white soldiers who sat looking at Robinson and Louis in these jerry-built outdoor boxing rings. To have a quartet of Negro boxers standing before them in the Southern sunshine—and walking by them afterwards with stripes on their uniforms—was a startling and unexpected scene.

Reception was coolish when, after a brief respite, they arrived in Alabama.

Camp Siebert was an Air Force base near Gadsden. The base itself had been so crowded that Army officials found residential housing for Louis and Robinson and the others in Gadsden. Neither Louis nor Robinson had any complaints about the rather liberal setup.

The white bus drivers who ferried soldiers in Alabama and many other parts of the South had been deputized during the war. The distinction meant they could carry pistols, and they had been instructed they had the right to draw those pistols on Negro troops who refused to move to the back of their buses.

Alabama may have been the Deep South, but Tuskegee, Alabama—not far from Gadsden—held historic joys for the American Negro: Booker T. Washington's Tuskegee Institute had trained many of the nation's black educators. The school, opened in 1881, would achieve widespread attention under Washington.

Born a slave, educated at Hampton Institute in Virginia—he had arrived at Hampton with fifty cents in his pockets and a powerful plea that he be allowed to stay—Washington had been given the opportunity to head Tuskegee from its beginnings. He oversaw construction, kept Alabama politicians and educational officials pacified, and cashed the checks sent to him by steel magnates and philanthropists from up North to keep the Negro school going. He rode about the campus on horseback, his hazel eyes scanning the premises. At times haunted-looking figures—aging men and women—appeared at the school grounds. Some had come to see their children who were enrolled; others, Negroes in droopy attire, had simply ambled onto the premises, lost, figures still gripped by slavery's vicious imprint, carrying a look that Washington himself had once known: bewilderment and wonder at the sight of so many of their own brethren carrying books. Washington, in time, became famous, courted by national figures and U.S. presidents alike. In life, Booker Taliaferro Washington was a man who smiled when there was reason, and rarely otherwise. (His reputation was that of a stern and conservative leader, but he was amiable enough to allow students to have a telegraph line installed in 1910 so they could follow the Jack Johnson–Jim Jeffries battle as it unfolded. The students had had to chip in to a campus kitty, however, to help defray the costs of setting the line up.) By the time of Washington's death in 1915, Tuskegee had become an important and nearly hallowed landmark of black achievement and aspiration.

It was at an airfield in Tuskegee, in the early stages of the war effort, that the U.S. military agreed to train black pilots to fly bombing missions over Hitler's Germany. The soldiers, who had gone through a battery of tests, who were screened and then screened again, were seen by some as a pet project of First Lady Eleanor Roosevelt, and sometimes were referred to as ENs— "Eleanor's Niggers." (The Tuskegee Airmen were hardly anyone's pets; they distinguished themselves during World War II, earning an array of medals and honors.)

Albert Murray, a Tuskegee graduate, had joined the Tuskegee English faculty in 1941. On visits after college he had gotten out of the South, going all the way to exotic Harlem, visiting bookstores, finding clubs where he could listen to jazz. He had met Sugar Ray at the Hotel Theresa and came to a quick conclusion about him: "Sugar had the same effect on people that movie stars had on people." Murray was born in Nokomis, Alabama, in 1916, a year after Booker T. Washington's death. His mother, Sudie, had attended Tuskegee. Murray himself got a scholarship in 1935 to attend the institution. He was an erudite individual and carried himself both seriously and whimsically. He had befriended writer Ralph Ellison, who also attended Tuskegee—though the great novelist never got around to graduating. Murray considered himself and Ellison "the heirs and continuators of the most indigenous mythic prefiguration of the most fundamental existential assumption underlying the human proposition as stated in the Declaration of Independence, which led to the social contract known as the Constitution and as specified by the Emancipation Proclamation and encapsulated in the Gettysburg Address and further particularized in the Thirteenth, Fourteenth, and Fifteenth amendments."

Sugar Ray Robinson and Joe Louis, Jackie Wilson and George Nicholson—all four inside the social contract known as wartime, a period echoed so hauntingly in the Gettysburg Address—were staring out onto the new year of 1944 now.

As days and weeks passed, news came in of mounting Allied victories against Hitler, and there was hope in the air. Army officials had also begun hinting that the boxing troupe would likely be ordered to take their show overseas, into the European theatre. Both Louis and Robinson—especially Robinson—grumbled about their boxing careers being put on hold. But there was no way to maneuver around orders. (Boxing rankings did remain intact, an acknowledgment of the fighters who were at war and unable to defend titles.)

On the base at Camp Siebert, the troupe resumed their duties, a pattern set by habit now: chatting with military officials, then breaking away to joke and bond with the enlisted GIs. They joined the GIs for chow. They looked at pictures of girlfriends back home and complimented them. They told stories of New York City, of Detroit and Chicago. They made predictions about who they might fight after the war. Louis thought of Billy Conn; Sugar Ray of Jake LaMotta. (It was boxing promoter Mike Jacobs, in New York City, who had planted such possibilities in their minds.)

Tuskegee officials invited Robinson and Louis to a campus football game. Students tried to get glimpses of the group.

No matter how optimistic the Louis- and Robinson-led group became while on Southern military bases, there was an undeniable reality outside the gates.

First Lady Eleanor Roosevelt had touched upon something profound in one of her newspaper columns six months earlier when she fretted about the prospects for racial harmony during wartime. "The domestic scene is anything but encouraging and one would like not to think about it, because it gives one a feeling that, as a whole, we are not really prepared for democracy."

Alabama had been seething for months, and a lot of that anger had settled in Mobile. Mobile was the site of the huge Addsco shipyard. A shipyard during wartime meant jobs. In 1940 the city's population had been 79,000; three years later it had exploded to 125,000, thanks to the lure of employment. Selden Menefee was a journalist who set off on a reporting tour in early 1943. The journey took him to Mobile. "Here is an historic town that slept for 230 years, then woke up in two," he would report, referring to the wartime population explosion.

It didn't take Menefee long at all to sense a combustible rivalry in the making between desperate whites and blacks who had either gotten jobs or were still vying for them at the Mobile shipyard. "If these 'poor whites' are full of anti-Negro prejudices, as they are, it is because the whiteness of their skins is the one thing that gives them a degree of social status," Menefee observed.

In one of those well-intentioned moves on the part of management, Negro welders were upgraded. The upgrade put them side by side with white workers. There was a war on; machinery needed to be produced, and the quicker the better. But the new work assignment for Negroes flouted the time-honored pact of segregation. White workers rebelled. One white worker fired off a letter to the local newspaper: "We realize the fact that they are human beings," the letter offered; however, "we don't any more want to work or want our women to work alongside a Negro than you would want to take one into your dining room and sit him down between your wife and mother to eat dinner, or for your wife to invite the cook in for a game of bridge, or take her to the movies."

One morning whites armed with bricks and metal bars charged a group of Negro welders. Their voices rose with the raising of their weapons: "No nigger is goin' to join iron in these yards," one shouted. There was blood, fear, confusion, and anguished cries. When the melee finally ended, eleven blacks would need hospital care. Several days of important productivity were lost. Company leaders had to regroup. They decided to separate the workers, giving the segregationists a victory.

The Army boxers' existence in Alabama had seesawed between the city of Gadsden and the base itself. Off base, there were the rules of segregation and four Negroes holding their tongues. It was on base that their freedom existed, bolstered by the Army stripes they wore with such pride. (Robinson had recently been promoted to sergeant). But even on base, there were stark reminders of the twilight world of separation. Soldiers lined up to take buses into Gadsden for social outings. There were two buses for white soldiers, but only a single bus for Negro soldiers. The disparity forced the Negro soldiers to wait until their crowded bus made its trip into town and then circled back for another. While waiting one afternoon, fidgeting, scanning the road for the Negro bus, Joe Louis grew impatient. Ever since fame had found him as a fighter, he had been used to being catered to. Sugar Ray was comfortable, quite easy, refusing to become agitated.

Then Louis suddenly turned to Sugar Ray. "No use standin' round here," he said. "I'm goin' to call us a cab."

Sugar Ray nodded as Joe turned away, walking off toward a knot of white soldiers and in the direction of the phone booth, which was near them but in a whites-only area. Yards from the phone booth stood an MP. He had a billy club in his hand. Louis dialed for a cab while Sugar Ray waited. The MP fixed his eyes on Sugar Ray, then on the phone booth, claimed by Joe Louis. That visible and invisible line—of demarcation, of Negro soldier and white soldier—had been crossed. Outside the phone booth, in the open air, soldiers stood smoking and chatting. The strong Southern accents were running together like the voices of a posse of men idling at an Alabama card table. But the relaxed air began to tighten. The MP came over to Louis as he stepped out of the booth. The MP was unsmiling and ordered Louis back over to the Negro side. Louis's expression darkened; he asked the MP exactly what he meant. "Soldier," the MP began—not "Sgt." Joe Louis, as his rank would have demanded— "your color belongs in the other bus station."

Louis launched into a spiel that took on a tone of morality and military togetherness: "What's my color got to do with it? I'm wearing a uniform like you."

Other soldiers were now turning around, their attention caught by the rising voices, the white MP and the Negro soldier going toe to toe.

"Down here you do as you're told," the MP sharply offered, and in one of those half-conscious motions, laid his billy club against Louis's rib cage in a threatening manner.

"Don't touch me with that stick," the Alabama-born Louis shouted at the MP.

Now everyone was watching. Sugar Ray's eyes widened as he inched closer. The MP drew himself up, a man suddenly becoming taller.

"I'll do more than touch you," the MP said.

And then came the reflexive raising of his billy club. At that moment—and before it touched any piece of Joe Louis's flesh— Sugar Ray leaped upon the MP, his arms around the MP's neck. Both fell—this was fortunate for the MP, since it prevented Sugar Ray from unleashing a left hook—and they tumbled onto the grass. Other MPs came running. Sugar Ray and the MP were wrapped around each other, clawing and scratching, the MP's eyes gone red with fury. And before the other MPs had a chance to swing their billy clubs at Louis and Robinson, a cacophony of shouting rose from other Negro soldiers nearby: "That's Joe Louis, that's Joe Louis." With the champ's name coursing through the air, with Sugar Ray and his opponent staring hard, with Sugar Ray's hands twitchy and ready to be balled up, turned into fists—the way they'd be in the dressing room with manager George Gainford standing by him—the MP stepped back. He and his fellow MPs needed to digest this bizarre and heated scene. Chests were heaving in and out.

"Call the lieutenant," one of the MPs ordered.

It didn't take long before Sugar Ray Robinson and Joe Louis found themselves riding in a jeep, headed to jail. Sugar Ray had struck a military policeman! Sgt. Joe Louis certainly knew how serious this could be. George Nicholson and Jackie Wilson had rushed to telephones. They had to get help. Joe was figuring out how he'd get permission to call Washington; he'd have to explain this to the War Department, to his contacts. He had contacts in the black press; he was particularly close to Billy Rowe of *The Pittsburgh Courier*. And he'd call upon those contacts if need be.

But by the time they reached the jail, Army officials on the base had decided that neither Robinson nor Louis would be locked up. They realized the publicity would be awful: two Negro fighters sent to promote racial solidarity behind bars in the state of Alabama. War was on everyone's mind, but race had jumped into the headlines as well. The sporadic rioting and protests by blacks that had erupted in parts of the country over the issue of jobs and equality was not something the U.S. government wanted to supplant the issue of patriotism. Not now; not in Alabama, which had already experienced the eruptions in Mobile. A decision was quickly made at the jailhouse that both Robinson and Louis would be free to go; that no charges of any kind would be filed. It all had come down on orders from the provost marshal himself. Dropping the case did not, however, quell murmurs and rumors amongst the Negro troops about the duo and their fate. Ominously, one of the Army officials had heard that Negro soldiers were saying Louis and Robinson had been beaten and bloodied by MPs. Sugar Ray was asked to tell the troops it wasn't so, that he and Louis were fine.

Outside, in the free air, Sugar Ray gave Joe a smile; Joe gave Sugar Ray a smile. Then the two fighters went to tell fellow Negro soldiers they were all right. And the Negro troops, after looking them over, smiled too.

Louis had been reminded yet again of the limits of his diplomacy when in the company of the feral Sugar Ray. He was simply no match for Sugar Ray's edge and spontaneity. Robinson had never learned the patience it took to survive in a segregated society. He hailed from Harlem, a revolutionary place. His fists had become his politics. The event served to mark the beginning of Robinson's changed attitude toward the war. He wanted no part of it anymore. He complained to female acquaintances by telephone about the unfair treatment. He worried about injury, imagining that a physical attack could derail his boxing dreams and his goal of a championship belt. Sugar Ray Robinson had come into the military watching the way Louis moved and operated around white officers; now Louis watched the way Robinson moved around them.

That evening on base, some of the Negro GIs pulled out paper and pencil. Letters would be written home about Sugar Ray Robinson and Joe Louis, about the lightning-quick battle they had fought in the state of Alabama; how the military jeep had raced them to lockup and how they had emerged from inside the jail headquarters with such an easy and beguiling countenance about them. "If I was just an average G.I., I would have wound up in the stockades," Louis would later remark of the Alabama affair. But Sugar Ray Robinson and Joe Louis were men who had been battling and winning all their lives. There was nothing—nothing at all—average about either one of them. (When news broke of the fracas in the Northern press, military officials were quick to play it down. The affair was just the kind of uneven press the military did not need in its effort to promote a unified home front.)

The cross-country tour continued.

Soon they were in Jacksonville, Florida, where more soldiers gently slapped their backsides, where they sparred with one another. Where, come nightfall, they only had to turn on their heels and walk a few steps for good music and fine drink: In Jacksonville, they were allowed again to take roomier accommodations off base, lodging above a Negro nightclub called the Two Spot. And this was suddenly young Sugar Ray Robinson's idea of the Army: Ellington and trumpeter Cootie Williams on a jukebox; women in his line of vision wearing silk skirts; an environment where his grin carried currency, the way it did in Harlem. He and Louis cavorting about the Two Spot were a sight to behold. They were the Negro answer to Hollywood, the home-front equivalent of cinematic stars at war.

In Jacksonville, old men who spotted them did double takes, squinting, wondering if that was the champ, Joe Louis himself. And then there'd be Louis and Sugar Ray—the latter far less well known than Louis, though many recognized his name—sidling up to them. Women smiled as they glided by, smiled more flamboyantly when the fighters gave them their undivided attention: "Joe and I had a few laughs in the South, too" is how Sugar Ray would remember Jacksonville.

But Sugar Ray would eventually be slowed in his activities. He threw his elbow out of joint. Then, during some horseplay with Louis, he cut his foot on a piece of broken glass. Comedian Bob Hope had certainly been right: A guy could get hurt in the war! (Throughout Robinson's military service, he was constantly coming down with an assortment of ailments—colds, sore throat. They were the type of ailments other soldiers might have kept quiet about and plowed through, but he was quick to get himself to infirmaries. It gave him the air of a hypochondriac—all of it was a prelude to a larger plot he had in his mind.)

Army officials decided to send Robinson back East to heal, to a base in New York State.

But the tour had been so successful, had impressed Army brass so much—despite the incidents in Mississippi and Alabama—that the War Department proceeded with the plan to send the troupe to Europe to continue spreading the gospel of patriotism and racial tolerance.

The second year of World War II was a good year for the lovely Lena Horne. Music critics at national publications began to gush over her. She had arrived like a phoenix. Marshall Field, a smooth and big-hearted philanthropist, was also publisher of *PM,* an evening news-paper. The publication featured Horne on the cover of its magazine: "How a girl from Brooklyn became this season's biggest nightclub hit," it said, heralding her rising popularity. "And how she's quietly using her unrehearsed success to win respect for her people." *Time* magazine weighed in with rapture: "Unlike most Negro chanteuses, Lena Horne eschews the barrel house manner . . . conducts herself with the seductive reserve of a Hildegarde. But when Lena sings at dinner and supper, forks are halted in mid-career. Flashing one of the most magnificent sets of teeth outside a store she seethes her songs with the air of a bashful volcano. As she reaches the end of 'Honeysuckle Rose' . . . her audience is gasping."

She appeared in another movie, *Stormy Weather,* released in 1943. She got major billing in the musical extravaganza that featured Bill "Bojangles" Robinson, Fats Waller, and Cab Calloway among others. The costumes were wicked and the feline dancers exotic. Calloway's creamy zoot suit was offset with an extravagantly brimmed hat. Horne wore silky dresses and a flower-bedecked headdress. She looked like an Egyptian beauty queen. The film was a romance that revolved around Horne and Robinson. The Robinson character had been drawn from the life of musical sensation James Reese Europe. (Europe was born in Mobile, Alabama, to musically gifted parents. He became a conductor and composer. In the summer of 1912 he staged an event at Carnegie Hall, a "Symphony of Negro Music"— the first large-scale Negro musical event ever to take place there. Europe volunteered for World War I, enlisting with the Fifteenth Infantry Regiment of the New York National Guard. The black regiment found little but hostility while training in South Carolina, and the U.S. government wisely dispatched them directly to France. Overseas, the regiment won medals and adulation. They were mentioned in the French press. James Reese Europe fought at the front, a machine gun in hand. Away from the battlefield he picked up a baton, conducted orchestral musicians. After the war, back in the states, the Negro regiment to which James Reese Europe belonged was honored in a parade down New York's Fifth Avenue. Europe died tragically in 1919 in Boston, where he had taken his celebrated orchestra; during intermission one night, a mentally disturbed band member stabbed him.)

In 1943 Lena Horne stood on the deck of the liberty ship, *George Washington Carver,* and christened it. Dignitaries behind her whooped and hollered and celebrated in the sunshine. At the Hollywood Canteen—it was integrated; actress Bette Davis kept the place jumping—Horne wore a red, white, and blue apron. She went to Tuskegee, arriving on a Jim Crow train, and posed with the Negro combat pilots there. Someone had helped her into a brown leather bomber jacket. She looked divine. But the mood changed on those military bases when she was asked to sing before segregated groups of soldiers. She'd glide down from the stage toward the Negro troops in the back, her Hollywood-borrowed costumes dazzling and causing necks to crane, and sing directly to them. The Negro soldiers were astonished—and delighted. The USO was not happy; in fact, her disobedience angered them. The organization suggested she stop performing; then they censured her. The Army didn't want drama on the home front; but Lena—like Sugar Ray, like Joe Louis—couldn't help herself.

Before the war, before those Japanese planes came floating over Pearl Harbor and doing their bloody damage, a kid in East St. Louis had been down in a basement practicing his trumpet. He borrowed what he could from those whom he idolized: bandleader Harry James wore velvet collars, so young Miles Davis started wearing them. Young Miles liked the way Clark Terry played trumpet—especially his speed—so he began playing fast. (Terry, who lived in the city, would take young Miles to local nightspots; they'd play beyond moonlight into the next morning.) Young Miles stood under trees in city parks, watching older musicians give concerts. He tapped his feet, nodded his head, and dreamed. Son of a dentist—and raised on good manners—he was shy. In 1943 he tried out for Eddie Randle's Blue Devils band in St. Louis and was jubilant when he won a spot. The Randle band was the house band at Rhumboogie, a local club. They called the kid Little Davis. Eddie Randle himself would recall of Miles's St. Louis beginnings: "He was growing out of this world. He was good and he didn't know it. He had a beautiful sound." Older musicians would chat with Little Davis, complimenting him. (Ellington himself came through one night—tall, sturdy, smiling, famous. Noise hummed around him like bees, but he heard, clearer than anything, the bass player, Jimmy Blanton. Like that—a snap of the finger—Ellington hired Blanton. Miles saw it all and was stunned at the sheer electricity of it: Ellington hearing someone, hiring the musicians, then leaving town. Like a ghost. Miles told other kids; those kids told other kids; between them all, it added up to a wonderful pocketful of dreams.)

Little Davis wore suits, kept late hours, had the keys to his daddy's car. When his parents split up, he lived with his mother. There were arguments. He wanted to be a musician, which, to her, sounded like someone—her child!—paving the way to becoming nothing more than a bohemian. He heard only himself, his dream within, and the music wailing from other musicians. He became musical director of Randle's band: It was by default, inasmuch as the other band members worked during the day, but it gave him the chance to arrange rehearsals and oversee them as well. He met musicians coming through St. Louis, the same musicians whose records he listened to at home—Sonny Stitt, Fats Navarro, Benny Carter—and he heard them perform at the speakeasies he slipped into. He met an Oklahoman by the name of Alonzo Pettiford: "Man, could that motherfucker play fast—his fingers were a blur. He played that real fast, hip, slick Oklahoma style."

Even though he sat in with Billy Eckstine's band in St. Louis, he wanted things to happen faster. He thought of joining the Navy. What fascinated him was that so many musicians were in the Navy, and were playing in a band in the Great Lakes. He'd heard about some members of Lionel Hampton's band being there; his friend Clark Terry was there. But finally, young Davis decided on another route. His idols, Charlie "Bird" Parker and Dizzy Gillespie, were in New York City. When the leaves began to fall, when the air began to grow crisp, when Hitler was on the run in Germany, he boarded a train for Manhattan. He had the kind of confidence that a young New York City boxer had to have; that a young Brooklyn chanteuse had to have. "I thought I could play the trumpet with anybody" is how Miles Davis would put it.

The poet was flat broke during the war. Langston Hughes was complaining to friends in 1943 about a $126 IRS bill. Money from Hughes's 1935 Broadway play, *Mulatto,* had all but vanished. Some acquaintances—fellow playwrights, lyricists, bar-stool poets—also worried that the poet Hughes might have to go off to war himself. Hughes hardly had the aura of a war-starved personality, though he certainly looked both fit and debonair as he gallivanted around Harlem. He was a darling of high society; he was an artist. He was brave in words—if a bit effete in reality. Langston at war? His friends started to fret. His longtime ally, Carl Van Vechten—their friendship stretched back to the Harlem Renaissance, Van Vechten the white patron saint, Hughes the young surveyor of that 1920s milieu—cautioned Hughes that if he should be hauled off to the military, he should first offer Yale University the honor of having his papers and other important personal items. A shawl that had been worn by Sheridan Leary, the first husband of Hughes's grandmother, was especially prized by Van Vechten: Leary had accompanied John Brown on his messianic Harpers Ferry raid with that shawl draped around his shoulders. It may have been a rather grim dose of reality for Hughes, the poet, but Van Vechten was thinking of posterity, which required sober decision making. Alas, Hughes was never drafted into the military. But when the Selective Service board sent him a questionnaire, he sat down and dutifully answered: "I wish to register herewith . . . my complete disapproval of the segregating of the armed forces of the United States into White and Negro units, thus making the colored citizens the only American group so singled out for Jim Crow treatment, which seems to me contrary to the letter and spirit of the Constitution and damaging to the morale and well-being of not only the colored citizens of this country but millions of our darker allies as well."

Hughes was living the life of an American writer—penury and all—during the war. He was desperately trying to line up lecture invitations. He was working on a second volume of autobiography, which he had titled *I Wonder as I Wander*. The book might be published, he confided to a friend, "if I did not wander even more than I wonder." (His first autobiography was titled *The Big Sea* and spoke of his youth, his cold father, his busboy poet days in the nation's capital, and his first lunge at prose and poetry as he swam with the artistic tide of the Harlem Renaissance.) In 1943 he was working with the Writers' War Board; he wrote a song about equality for a Negro Freedom Rally and a dramatic presentation—"For This We Fight." Then luck struck for the writer: He got a return invitation to Yaddo, the artists colony in Saratoga Springs, New York, which he had first visited in 1942, at a time when his fame was rapidly spreading beyond just Negro admiration.

Yaddo—green, quiet, remote—had charmed Hughes. He loved the woods, strolling narrow roadways, listening to the sounds of nature, joining the other guest artists for dinner by candlelight in the mansion on the premises. He had befriended Carson McCullers at Yaddo back in '42; his return visit saw an introduction to Katherine Anne Porter, and they roasted wieners on her nearby farm.

Hughes wrote during the day. He had started a column for the *Chicago Defender* before going to Yaddo, and the fan mail that arrived at Yaddo about the column charmed him. Some evenings—his writing and reading finished—he made his way over to the Saratoga racetrack. He enjoyed hobnobbing with the Negro stable-hands. Evening found him back in his cabin, usually reading more mail. "I'm getting wonderful fan letters thru my column," he wrote to his friend Arna Bontemps. "Three today, one from two house servants in darkest Mississippi; another from the colored sailors on a Pacific battleship."

The United States military had been issuing regular reports for the public about the thousands of troops Louis and Robinson had entertained. It was good public relations to counter the news stories of sporadic racial unrest in parts of the country. So plans were fixed for them to take off for Europe in early 1944.

American confidence about the war was rising rapidly as the new year dawned. "Good news comes in from every battlefront," a White House assistant informed President Roosevelt. But the president himself—who had gone on grueling international forays in late 1943 to augment the final Allied push, traveling to Casablanca to meet with Winston Churchill and Tehran to confer with Russian premier Joseph Stalin—warned against overconfidence in his 1944 State of the Union address. "If ever there was a time to subordinate individual or group selfishness to the national good, that time is now," Roosevelt said to the nation.

In preparation for their overseas assignment—Robinson expressed little relish for the mission—the Louis and Robinson assemblage was sent to Fort Hamilton in Brooklyn, where they'd make final preparations for the trip.

Robinson, however, did not complain about being back in the Manhattan area—if only for a short stay. The fighters were delighted with their new surroundings. Robinson was simply back home. They were far removed now from the rural South and all those odd and menacing stares. Wartime Manhattan may have been nervous and exhausted—but it was also hopping. In Times Square and along Broadway, the movie-house marquees glittered brightly.

Hollywood had stayed busy during the war, offering its movies to the hungry public and to servicemen. Wartime movies were a heady mix of melodrama, comedy, the spies-among-us concoction, and of course the always intoxicating romantic tale. Greer Garson was stalwart—and lovely—in the 1942 *Mrs. Miniver,* a William Wyler–directed film which portrayed an English family's togetherness through wartime bombings, deaths, and separations. Mrs. Miniver read *Alice's Adventures in Wonderland* to her sleeping children in an underground shelter as German bombers flew overhead. (Churchill loved the movie and would say that all the Mrs. Minivers had been crucial to England's success in the war.) A standout in 1943 was the Bette Davis film, *Watch on the Rhine,* adapted from a Lillian Hellman play and set against a Washington backdrop where Nazi spies strolled in the shadows. But perhaps no film merged such an array of different genres—sarcastic comedy, war, romance, patriotism—as *Casablanca* did. Moviegoers were enraptured with Rick, the mélange of characters who populated his café, and the dramas that swirled around them. There were Vichyites and Nazis. There was unforgotten love. There were flashbacks to romantic Paris. And there was the music of Dooley Wilson playing Sam—Lena Horne had been considered for the role of the black piano player before they'd gone with a man—as he serenaded the joint with "As Time Goes By."

As time went by at Fort Hamilton in Brooklyn for Robinson and Louis, who were waiting to travel to Europe, the pugilists couldn't help but consider postwar plans, which meant their return to the ring. Deep in the minds of many, however, the reality had set in that the best years of Louis's career were behind him. His last authentic bout—more than two years before, not counting exhibitions—had been in March 1942 in New York against Abe Simon, whom he knocked out in the sixth round. (Louis donated those winnings to the war effort—causing his fan base to swell even more—and entered the Army soon after.) Robinson had managed to have several fights during the first year of his wartime duties, affairs that carried plenty of Sturm und Drang but were often overshadowed by war news.

Louis and Robinson again hustled over to see promoter Mike Jacobs while based in New York—"[t]o put the touch on him," as Robinson put it, which meant having Jacobs stake them money against future bouts. (The German, Max Schmeling, who had been a paratrooper in the war, was in Berlin telling news correspondents that he'd soon be landing in Mike Jacobs's office himself, via parachute, to discuss a future Louis bout—which never was to be.)

Jacobs—always of the hard grin, the slick glance—fortified Robinson and Louis with cash: "And we were finding ways to spend it," Robinson allowed. Away from the military base in New York, food, wine, and the treats that the fighters bestowed upon women cost much more than in the haunts of Florida, Mississippi, and Alabama.

There were movies to see, drinks to buy. The music remained intoxicating. There were old Harlem friends of the duo's who needed a buck or two. (Edna Mae Holly—the girlfriend Sugar Ray was most serious about—kept reminding him how she couldn't wait for him to come home for good; he wondered about nightclub dancing, what smoothies might be sending her gifts.) There were hard-luck soldiers they had befriended on the Brooklyn base, who also needed a little help with dough. Louis got lost in the part of patriotic messenger for the Army; the role was so full of the respect he was often denied from society at large—save when he had a foreign foe such as Schmeling standing in the ring with him. The war had given him a stature beyond Negro America; he thought he saw freedom on the horizon and equality for all. (Robinson saw duplicity and felt that was an assault upon his own personhood and future.) Louis's eagerness to fight in the ring seemed to be ebbing. There had been telltale signs of his shifting feelings during the war. Before the Louis-Robinson contingent had taken off for Mississippi, Louis spent time with some reporters in New York City. "I'd like to fight again, I guess," he said, without emotion, "but I don't know—it's more than just a personal matter. We have more than that to talk about now." He liked the feeling of being a man with a grand mission, and he held a belief that racial woes could be fixed within the jubilation of a united home front and that Hitler could be defeated because of that unity. It was a mirage—great civil rights battles surely lay ahead—but it bewitched him. He was also going through domestic travails, of which he said little. His wife Marva had divorced him in the midst of the war. Louis was made poorer by alimony and a settlement, but still he refused to sulk about the fight opportunities he had lost because of his wartime service.

But Sugar Ray Robinson was staring at a different clock, and he found it hard to shrug off the passage of time. Days and weeks meant lost fights, lost training. The so-called uncrowned champion lacked a belt, and thoughts about the absence of one consumed him. Now came the prospect of Europe and a further distancing from the goal he so cherished. He had concocted a fanciful—and risky—plan to get out of the Army.

Evenings at the Fort Hamilton barracks often found Louis and Robinson and their sparring mates playing cards along with a few other soldiers. On the night of March 29, 1944, the game was straight poker. It came down to Sugar Ray staring across the table at friend Joe Louis.

"Four jacks," Sugar Ray barked. His happy hands prepared to scoop up the money on the table.

"Four queens," the champion retorted, howling.

The laughter of the other soldiers pushed Sugar Ray up out of his chair. He made his way to the bathroom. And with that laughter echoing in his ears, he just kept walking. As simple as that, Sugar Ray Robinson abandoned the sometimes too-quiet life of a Fort Hamilton–based enlisted man awaiting orders to be shipped to Europe and vanished behind a bewildering movielike screen of shadows, deception, imagination, and make-believe.

Otherwise known as AWOL.

He missed roll call. Then he missed roll call again. All of the Negro troops on the base were rounded up and questioned. No one uttered a word. The faces of Army superiors began to tighten. They had previously cautioned Robinson against complaining about the upcoming European trip, at one point going so far as to cite the Articles of War, particularly the part about punishment in light of desertion. Robinson did not care; he had looked good in his Army uniform but felt uneasy about everything else. Army brass did not wish to press Joe Louis too hard, lest a publicity nightmare explode on the eve of his taking off for Europe, but they did request that he phone Robinson's Harlem home. Joe reported to Army officials he'd had no luck locating Robinson. The Army appointed Lt. Col. Frederick Weston to lead an investigation into Robinson's whereabouts. Weston was told if Robinson was located, he was to be brought back to base immediately. His men were told to use force if they had to.

It wasn't until six days later that the Army recorded Robinson's memory of where he had been: He told them, while lying flat on his back in a hospital, that he didn't know, couldn't remember a thing. He said he must have fallen somewhere in Manhattan. He said it all must have begun inside the barracks, when he tripped over some duffel bags and banged his head. He was actually now in Halloran General Hospital, on Staten Island, wearing a white smock and raising his voice: "Nurse . . . Nurse!" Eyebrows were raised among the staff, but the necessary examinations were administered by well-trained doctors—all of this alarmingly close to the departure date for Europe. Manager George Gainford rushed to his bedside. Robinson kept complaining of headaches. Promoter Mike Jacobs made inquiries, trying to track down high-level hospital personnel. (The medical report said that Robinson had been found in the streets of Manhattan and ferried to a hospital on April first—April Fool's Day. Doctors found no brain injury of any kind. Robinson's own self-diagnosis was amnesia. The medical report goes on to state: "He was unable to give any information about his past life or the events leading up to his hospitalization, and he failed to recognize relatives . . . who visited him.")

Aside from the phone calls he had made at the request of the Army, Louis continued to steer clear of the Sugar Ray imbroglio. Joe Louis had certainly intervened on behalf of other soldiers: He was instrumental, shortly after entering the service himself, in helping the onetime UCLA student Jackie Robinson gain entrée to Officer Candidate School when he had been denied admission because of his race. The soldiers Louis had assisted were soldiers who had clearly been wronged, and he knew that the weight of his fame could sometimes right an injustice. In such situations, the heavyweight champion had no qualms about using his War Department contacts, coupled with his close relationship with Billy Rowe, the *Pittsburgh Courier* reporter. But this—amnesia, a forgetful mind on the eve of overseas departure—was something Louis turned away from. It was silly, laughable, a descent into theatre—albeit with consequences that could be severe. Once again, the word "court-martial" swirled around Sugar Ray.

But Robinson had calculated the fallout while unspooling the entire episode in his nimble mind. Being back in Manhattan had convinced him the world was passing him by. Both Gainford and Edna Mae had reminded him of how worried they were about him.

Robinson needed little reminding: One didn't have to trek to Europe for wartime danger. That plane with Carole Lombard in it had gone down stateside. The prospect of being in an accident in Europe—even if it were a goodwill mission—was very real to Robinson. Bombs were falling from the sky over there. Robinson figured he would salvage his rising career—and blunt the criticism sure to come—by becoming a champion. Some, he knew, would believe the medical diagnosis, but perhaps many would not, branding him cowardly. But how much of a coward could one be stepping into a ring with vicious punchers? He trusted his right-left combination more than he trusted Uncle Sam.

Louis and the other fighters took off for Europe without him. Shortly after arriving in London—the seas had been choppy coming over, and there had been a couple of submarine alarms, but they passed without incident—Joe Louis and his fellow pugilists were spotted in central London. Gawkers surrounded them. Newsreel cameramen were also scurrying to keep up. When asked about Robinson, Louis said he'd fallen sick. He was also asked about a story in *Yank* magazine that speculated he'd be getting married following his divorce, and the new bride would be none other than Lena Horne. Louis grinned and said the story simply wasn't true.

Army officials had to think about what to do with Sugar Ray Robinson. His previous run-ins with authority had been relatively minor—but explosiveness had also lurked just beneath the surface of any incident where race and dignity were concerned, a fact Eleanor Roosevelt herself had noticed. And now this, a bizarre spell of amnesia.

Meeting behind closed doors, Army officials decided to thank Sugar Ray Robinson for his military service. He would be granted an honorable discharge.

On June 3, 1944, Sugar Ray Robinson left the Army. Louis and the others were in war-scarred Europe, rallying the troops for the last big push.

Years later, Dave Anderson, coauthor of Robinson's autobiography, published in 1969, wished to put that bizarre incident to rest and implored Robinson to give the details of what really happened. Robinson, then in retirement, hunched his shoulders, widened his eyes, told Anderson he had nothing to add to what was in the Army report. Anderson chuckled, pressed him further, but Robinson was steadfast, which Anderson found strange. "So I just wrote it the way the Army wrote it," Anderson says. "Of course most of the sportswriters charged him with desertion."

Robinson ignored the sportswriters who pilloried him over his military record, explaining that those same writers had long labeled him arrogant, had carried grudges against him since early in his career when he assailed them for not writing about the fighters (read white fighters) who wouldn't give him a shot at the title because they feared him. Nevertheless, at times the taunts would annoy him so much that he'd carry his honorable discharge papers around in his pocket and produce them at the slightest hint of an attack upon his honor. America won the war; Robinson won the prank.

But it lingered. When Robinson was originally contemplating an autobiography in 1952, he asked W. C. Heinz, a highly respected New York sportswriter (Hemingway admired his work), to consider helping him write it. Heinz was intrigued enough to meet with Robinson in the cocktail lounge of the Park Sheraton in Manhattan to discuss the possibility. But he had told himself he had one all-important question to ask Robinson, and it concerned his military career and the reports of desertion. And when Heinz did ask about the Army and the matter of going AWOL, the conversation grew awkward. Robinson denied desertion; Heinz wanted a fuller explanation, told Robinson he couldn't rest until the "conflicting versions" of his military stint had been resolved. Robinson got a quizzical look upon his face. Heinz made up his mind then and there—he would have no part of Robinson's project.

"I'm sorry, but I just can't do the book," he said.

"That's all right, old buddy," Robinson told him. "I understand."

Years later Heinz would say of Robinson: "He was a guy you'd like to have as a friend. But you couldn't trust him. He was a great con man."

The war-weary nation scented victory when the Allies invaded Normandy that June. The liberation of Paris brought much celebration. The French capital was in ruins, but the wine flowed.

As for Sugar Ray's mind—his memory—it was now wickedly clear: He had been a professional for four years. He had no intention of waiting that long to gain a championship belt.

Harlem was buoyant in the summer of 1944, when Robinson returned home. Many had jobs. A little money had been saved—in banks, under mattresses. The anxiety of war was winding down. The Tuskegee Airmen had proven themselves: They flew 1,578 missions; they would come to be awarded one hundred Distinguished Flying Crosses.

And with Joe Louis still in Europe during those waning weeks, Sugar Ray Robinson had the streets of Harlem to himself. Now the children—who used to run after him and Louis—only had him to scamper toward, and he spun with delight at their smiles when they saw him.

The poet Langston Hughes had written a song for Congressman-elect Adam Clayton Powell Jr. in the summer of 1944. Powell had become the first black man elected to Congress from the Northeast. The poem was titled "Let My People Go—Now." (Hughes also made his debut that autumn on the stage of Madison Square Garden, at a human rights rally.)

Lena Horne got invited to the White House that winter, summoned by First Lady Eleanor Roosevelt. Horne was being thanked for her work on behalf of the war effort. The nightclub star—who had also become a pinup girl against the backdrop of muddy battles in the Pacific and European theatres—took orchids to present to Mrs. Roosevelt.

The young trumpeter from St. Louis, Miles Davis, arrived in Manhattan by train. He was just eighteen years old. He had been accepted to Juilliard, but already he was dreaming beyond formal education. He would recall: "I arrived in New York City in September 1944, not in 1945 like a lot of jive writers who write about me say. It was almost the end of World War II when I got there. A lot of young guys had gone off to fight the Germans and the Japanese and some of them didn't come back. I was lucky; the war was ending. There were a lot of soldiers in their uniforms all around New York."

As for Sugar Ray Robinson, the fighter just released from the war was flexing his muscles inside a Manhattan gymnasium.

They were all coming through the curtain of post–World War II America now. They had struck their first blows for freedom—Robinson and his battles on military bases; Horne in her demand to Hollywood that she only be offered dignified roles; Hughes in his activist and rebellious poetry; young Miles in slipping away from East St. Louis. They were in the vanguard now. There was something political in their artistic pronouncements—and stylish in their individual demeanor. Let my people go now, Hughes and Powell may have cried, but no one had to argue for freedom on this quartet's behalf.

They were already gone, away from the things that might have confined them. Their admirers were left to wonder everything about them—not least the mystery of where they had each acquired their individual taste and style.

Robinson had gone into the military believing it a lark and thinking that his rising celebrity would shield him from the orderliness of military life and responsibility. But for the first time in his life he'd been confronted with social humiliation, something that could carry a deeper hurt than poverty itself. And that humiliation had been heaped on not only him but on his hero Joe Louis as well. It was a bewildering thing to see up close. Sgt. Walker Smith Jr.—honorably discharged—was less a con man and more a nonconformist.

Now out of uniform, he began swaying toward the *Esquire* style sweeping certain parts of Manhattan and the country.

Gentlemen of great means and prestige strolled about the Manhattan metropolis. They were men who had an allegiance to art and style. Many—the Vanderbilts and Astors among them—were known to take their high tea at the Waldorf Astoria. Their magazine of choice, *Esquire,* had come into being in 1933. That had been a year fraught with economic pain. But style, the artistry of it, managed to keep at bay so much that seemed uncertain and unwelcome. The pages of *Esquire* offered a kind of balm. A writerly and visual presentation to prove that the proceedings of life would go on.

Above 125th Street, the periodical was being flipped open by jazz-playing hands, by young writers and dancers, by young pugilists. It advertised features on "Fiction, Sports, Humor, Clothes, Art, Cartoons." By the time that milieu had been mixed and soaked into the brew of uptown, a whole crop of men had emerged, joining the well-heeled and their progeny to let them know that they too believed in the magic of art and style. Only these individuals felt compelled to add their own music. And so it was jazz that colored their *Esquire*-loving signature and came to flood the senses of the young Sugar Ray.

1945–1946

Esquire men

SUGAR RAY ROBINSON was a man of music—you could see it in the way he fought. And it was jazz in particular that moved him, curled his mind into delicate introspection and observation. Those stuttering jazz stanzas were like big canyon-wide flashes of light, with musical sensations flying out and above patrons. All as if the world were being born with melody right before the eyes. Jazz seemed to carry a language all its own, and it was a language that comforted Robinson. The men he admired—Lester Young, Charlie Parker, Billy Eckstine, Miles Davis, Cootie Williams among them—had seemed to bring the same discipline to their craft that he brought to his: It was the discipline of science, coupled with the fleetness and derring-do of improvisation. "He was, like them, an entertainer," says Budd Schulberg, the Hollywood fixture and screenwriter. "And I think that appealed to them. He was hard to resist." Sugar Ray told reporters that he himself fancied playing the drums. He paid attention to how Buddy Rich handled his drumsticks, to how Max Roach held his rhythm.

His youth had been peopled by older men—the men in the gymnasiums nodding to him; the shadowy men in the corners betting on his skills; the promoters who wanted to be around him and bought him dinners of liver and onions at Harlem eateries. The men with skin that had a sheen to it, who held his hand a little too long when they shook, making promises and predictions; the men who caught him eyeing the cut of their suits and the softness of their fedoras, commenting on what they just knew to be a bond of mutual admiration. The trainers and promoters—like George Gainford and Mike Jacobs—were all older men, as were the jazzmen whose freedom he relished. His skills had hastened his maturity. The ladder that he had already climbed so high simply put him out of the reach of childhood friends, and so they vanished away from him. Left in his world were older men.

Born too late for the 1920s Jazz Age, Robinson found himself at the doorway of modern jazz in early 1940s New York, the time period that paralleled his own rise in boxing circles. He only had to walk into the Palm Café, uptown on 125th, to hear the kind of music he loved. "I would say it was one of the most popular clubs in New York, and they catered to a sophisticated bourgeois," remembers Robert Royal, who had first met Robinson while working at another club near the Palm.

The Palm Café was especially noted for its jazz, which was broadcast throughout the city from a radio station based inside. They had a quartet of deejays; each would become a notable figure in his or her own right. One of them, Evelyn Robinson, was gorgeous: She had a café au lait complexion and bright eyes. (Evelyn unabashedly saw currency and instant recognition in utilizing her brother's last name.) Weather permitting, she liked fur draped around her shoulders. Her hair was often pouffed up, in the manner of a Hollywood actress expecting cameras to flash. She was Sugar Ray's sister, and she beamed when he showed up, grinning in her direction, the music crowd nodding at him as he moved slowly toward a table.

The men of Sugar Ray's world—jazzmen—seemed to jump right out into the haunting, ecstatic, worrisome, and finally victorious world of the 1940s. When World War II was over, plenty of musical instruments got unpacked. A lot of hepcats were snapping their fingers, making plans, hunting down nightclub owners in hopes of lining up engagements. And before long, there they were, on the stages of East Coast clubs, beneath glowing bulbs. Club denizens would rush out the next morning to get their vinyl records. But there was something else that brought their music—and style—out into the open.

In that seminal year of 1944—Sugar Ray back home, the war ending, citizens coast to coast full of joy and hatching new plans—a pipe-smoking man by the name of Arnold Gingrich, editor of *Esquire* magazine, began nosing around New York jazz spots. Those uptown journeys set him right in the heart of Harlem. Gingrich, a bon vivant, a man who possessed high literary tastes, a man who knew F. Scott Fitzgerald and Ernest Hemingway and John Dos Passos and many of their lesser contemporaries, was in search of something to complement his literary tastes. And when he found it—jazz, jazzmen—he knew he had found something special. It was a world he wanted to know more about, because in that world there was the kind of music that made him smile. Arnold Gingrich soon realized that what was in front of him, before his own eyes, was a distinct convergence of men, music, and style. This cultural convergence was far from universally appreciated at the time. Mostly, in fact, it was only known in places like Kansas City, New Orleans, San Francisco, New York City. Gingrich became so enthralled by this world of rhythm and nightlife that he began making plans to devote a whole issue of his *Esquire* magazine to the music, the craze—the hot jazz. A certain style—the dress code, the supper club air—would inform everything presented in the magazine. The celebrated issue, called *Esquire's Jazz Book,* hit the stands in 1944. It featured many of Sugar Ray's acquaintances, and for him it merely confirmed the reach he was undertaking with his own personal style and presentation and sensibility. "In Harlem Sugar Ray hung around all the musicians," says jazz critic Albert Murray, who'd been a devoted *Esquire* reader since the magazine's origination. "These were men who liked excellent fabrics and nice shoes. Everybody of my generation went for the things in *Esquire* magazine. You were dressing out of *Esquire*—but you gave it a Harlem touch."

Arnold Gingrich was born in 1903 in Grand Rapids, Michigan. A serious-minded youth, he became an inveterate reader. He combed through the stories in literary magazines—*Collier's, Harper's, The Saturday Evening Post, American Mercury, Holiday*—looking for tales of young love, the gunfire and unpredictability of war, the requisite bravery and gallantry of it. His leisure passions, too, veered toward the adult: He loved fly-fishing even when he was young, and became highly skilled in that demanding sport, which requires reasoning, imagination, and focus. (He would later write extensively about it.) Soon after graduating from the University of Michigan (Phi Beta Kappa), Gingrich began work in Chicago as an advertising copywriter. He liked the city, the pace of it, all those tall buildings that seemed to suggest business at hand, a place for earnest ambition. Chicago was a place where a man might welcome new ideas and ventures and seize upon them with zeal. Gingrich met Dave Smart, who ran a direct-mail advertising company known as the Men's Wear

Service Corporation. Smart—who rode horses for a hobby and was known as a clothes fiend, seeming to change attire as often as Fitzgerald's Jay Gatsby—hired Gingrich in 1929 to sell fashion booklets to haberdasheries. "He had a great flair for style and a canny instinct for what would come off as 'class,' " Gingrich would recall of Smart. Smart's snazzy, handsome publication, *Apparel Arts,* showcased high-class clothes for gentlemen. It was like a store catalogue with some magazine content. Gingrich took the job of filling the editorial pages. (When Gingrich went on the road, Smart simply reached into his pocket and sliced money from his roll—$50 bills as Gingrich would remember—and hand it over to him. Then Gingrich was gone, out the door, introducing fashion and high style up and down the East Coast.) The publication—in hardcover no less—became a hit. Among its eccentricities were French captions, left untranslated.

Smart and Gingrich, along with William H. Weintraub—another Smart business partner—had formed a close enough bond that they began hatching plans for a new magazine. They imagined it as a kind of men's *Vogue.* It was brave to float such a plan during hard economic times, and their mission seemed to carry a kind of stylishness of its own. They alerted writers, cartoonists, artists. Such new ventures caused serious writers to raise their eyebrows, wondering about the pay scale and the possibility of making some dough. (Gingrich tossed out figures ranging from a hundred to two hundred bucks for an article.) The trio named the magazine *Esquire,* and one issue made it onto the stands at the end of 1933 before the magazine went monthly in 1934. That first issue was a potent and stylish salvo that heralded things to come: It featured work by the likes of Ernest Hemingway, John Dos Passos, and Dashiell Hammett; Harry Hershfield contributed humor; there was writing by Ring Lardner Jr. and Erskine Caldwell; and cartoons came from, among others, William Steig and E. Simms Campbell. The advertising was colorful and handsome. One page was destined to become a constant: "That was the Cadillac page," Gingrich would recall. "We had that sold before we even had a magazine to run it in. And, except for the back cover, it became and remained the one advertising page in full color in the first issue of the magazine." (In time New Yorkers would learn to spot Sugar Ray's Cadillac—the color of a pink rose—cruising Broadway to Harlem, or idling in front of the jazz haunts on Fifty-second Street, or parked on the gravel at his Cabin-in-the-Sky training camp. His specially designed Cadillac, its chrome as shiny as a barracuda, would become a vehicle as commented-upon and ogled as the Vanderbilt and Astor autos had once been.)

In those first three years the magazine sold upwards of ten million copies. It was an astounding figure. *Esquire* had arrived. Gingrich knew talent, and one of his earliest hires—at least in person—was so obscure as to be almost invisible.

With plenty of pages to fill in those early days, Gingrich wanted to hire a talented cartoonist. Russell Patterson, an artist Gingrich knew, heard of his plight and recommended a kid in Harlem. Patterson promised the kid was gifted, although unknown, and definitely in need of work. But Patterson also told Gingrich there'd be a problem if he crossed "the color line," because the kid, E. Simms Campbell, was a Negro.

A graduate of the prestigious Art Institute of Chicago, Campbell lived on Edgecombe Avenue in Harlem with relatives. Young, impecunious, eager, he'd often trudge through Manhattan, from one magazine office to the next—dressed neatly, perfect manners—trying to sell his drawings. But he could never get past the receptionist, never even get an interview scheduled. Sometimes he'd be sent away in the politest of tones; other times the matter was handled rather curtly and there he'd be, hustling onto the A train, heading back home, uptown to Harlem: No jobs for Negro cartoonists in those fancy offices. Patterson—as Gingrich would recall—had also said something else about Campbell: "He knew that this kid was from hunger."

Walking up on Edgecombe Avenue, himself quite hungry for good cartoons to fill the pages of the magazine he was putting together, Gingrich made his way to the apartment where Campbell lived. He would remember that there seemed to be children everywhere, on the walks, on the stoops, up and down the hallways. Elmer Simms Campbell was quite delighted to see this urbane figure standing before him. It was a rare and welcome relief for him: The young artist was saved from the embarrassment of going downtown yet again. An editor had come to him. Campbell led the way through the apartment and showed Gingrich his work. He had drawings that were finished and drawings that were still in progress. He seemed a young man who had been working away for years, hoarding his work, quiet about his inability to showcase it. Gingrich couldn't take his eyes off the drawings. The young man standing next to him possessed a gift, and Gingrich instantly knew it: "I wanted to yell Eureka, because I saw at a glance that my troubles were over." Gingrich carried his checkbook around when planning to charm artists and writers for his publication. He pulled it out and offered Campbell a $100 check on the spot, with promises of more payment to come. Back at the office, when Gingrich showed Campbell's work around, other editors expressed equal delight. (Campbell's cartoons would appear in *Esquire* until his death nearly four decades later.)

Before that first issue, Gingrich had ruminated on what the new magazine would mean: "To analyze its name more closely, *Esquire* means . . . that class just below knighthood—the cream of that middle class between the nobility and the peasantry."

When *Esquire* took off—discussed in salons and men's clubs, in barbershops and uptown in Harlem, praised on college campuses for its fashion content and literary contributors—Arnold Gingrich was quite a happy man. To start a magazine during a depression, and to have that magazine find a foothold, was a near miracle, and he realized it: "Conceived during the Bank Holiday, when the national anthem was Brother, Can You Spare a Dime? And born a few weeks before Repeal, when nobody booed as the bands played Happy Days Are Here Again, *Esquire* was Depression's child, married to a sweet young thing called Recovery."

The jazz critic Albert Murray could feel the influence of *Esquire* on Harlemites, on the jazz players, and on Sugar Ray Robinson: "All these guys were influenced by *Esquire* magazine."

Gingrich and Campbell became friends, and the Harlem that Arnold Gingrich began seeing through the eyes of his cartoonist fascinated him. Musicians seemed to be everywhere. And in time, Gingrich befriended potent talents. He began hobnobbing with Coleman Hawkins and Lester Young, with Billie Holiday, Benny Goodman, and Lionel Hampton. Some he'd met at war bond affairs during wartime, others at gigs downtown or uptown. He met Charlie Parker and Roy Eldridge; Duke Ellington of course—and Johnny Hodges too. The jazz swirled around him; the jazzmen smoked their cigarettes and he smoked his pipe and the music hummed and floated, dipped and rose. The transformation surprised even him, because these musicians and their music, as he would put it, had overnight "become my cup of tea."

And around these figures floated sportsmen, men who loved both jazz and sporting events. These were the men who leaned in to murmur words of advice into Sugar Ray Robinson's ear when he was fresh out of the Army. One of those men was Oscar Barnes, a native of the U.S. Virgin Islands who had a stake in the New York Black Yankees, a Negro League franchise. Barnes would take his son Arthur to see Sugar Ray's fights in the 1940s and 1950s. A nod from Oscar Barnes gave you special cachet, and Oscar Barnes—who knew enough about those early sporting years in Harlem that Francis Ford Coppola would later ask him to serve as an adviser on his film *The Cotton Club*—often nodded in Sugar Ray's direction. It all introduced young Arthur to a certain kind of style. "The most important influences were music then," Barnes recalls. "On the jukeboxes we had Lester Young, Ben Webster, Duke Ellington, Count Basie's band. Jimmy Rushing was singing 'Sent for You Yesterday.' "

So the men snapped their fingers around Sugar Ray Robinson. "They were proud and attracted to Sugar Ray because of the nerve he had," says Arthur Barnes. (In the mid-1940s, before Miles Davis befriended Sugar Ray, Sugar had struck up an acquaintance with Dizzy Gillespie, and the two were seen strolling the streets of Manhattan together, Sugar bending Dizzy's ear about the music and the road. Passersby rushed toward Dizzy, not always aware who the string-bean figure next to him was.)

It took time to get fight cards organized. For the first nine months of 1944, Sugar Ray Robinson had no scheduled fights. So he was a man in training, reintroducing himself to Harlem, bopping in and out of the jazz clubs.

If *Collier's* magazine could highlight Walter Camp's All-American football team annually—as they had been doing—then Arnold Gingrich and his team at *Esquire* now saw no reason why they could not take their readers down a different path. They named an All-American Jazz Band in a special edition, the 1944 *Jazz Book*.

And when it arrived—as Joe's and Sugar Ray's and Clark Gable's and Ike's and Jimmy Stewart's war was coming to a close—the publication could hardly be missed on the newsstands. It measured fourteen inches in length and ten in width; it was ninety pages of thick-stock paper; it had gorgeous photographs and illuminating essays; it had artful drawings by a onetime poor kid in Harlem who had proven to be a discovery; and it was all wrapped in an eye-catching scarlet-red cover!

And while the photographic production was handsome and wholesomely representative of Negro and white musicians alike, never before, it seemed, had such a large contingent of Negroes been gathered to showcase their artistic muscle in one publication.

The *Jazz Book* essays were learned and informative; pieces of erudition still impressive decades later.

Paul Eduard Miller's essay—"Hot Jazz: Prophet without Honor"—sought to explain the struggles of jazz "for a justifiable place of recognition in a hostile world." Miller's writing swept across the decades of jazz, remembering how hard a journey it had always been to keep the music alive, how difficult the late twenties and early thirties had been: "By 1932 Joe Marsala had done a stint as a truck driver; Jack Teagarden, Miff Mole, Red Nichols, and a host of others succumbed to the lure of radio money; Rappolo was in the madhouse, Beiderbecke, Teschemacher and Lang were dead." Miller knew that deep within the music lay all kinds of secrets and mysteries; that those accustomed to the status quo, the expected, the routine, would have to alter their senses and open their minds to the appreciation for a new art form. Jazz—from the alley, the stoop, the drug needle, the smoky throat, the St. Louis eyes of Billie Holiday, and the cockiness of the young lad, Miles Davis, on a bus just now arriving in Manhattan (he would tell friends later in life how much *Esquire's Jazz Book* had inspired him)—was climbing up and up.

Paul Eduard Miller's reference to the jazz soloist's search for recognition could equally have applied to a young pugilist, home from war. All kinds of mysteries unto himself, trying to direct his own life now and to give his brand of boxing to the world, the young Sugar Ray was not unlike the young solo jazz musician. Robinson identified so easily with jazzmen because they made valiant efforts to control their own destinies; figures like Dizzy Gillespie and Lionel Hampton had lifted themselves from the confining world of so many in Negro America. The musicians seemed as independent as a Negro could be in 1940s America. And they respected codes of dress and refinement. ("Sugar Ray wasn't the type of guy to wear a fucking leather jacket," remembers the writer Jimmy Breslin.) Robinson also liked the way jazz musicians canvassed the world around them—street corners, sidewalks, nightclubs—when they were not playing. Their eyes seemed to always be roving, calculating—much like Robinson's eyes inside the ring. In *Esquire* Miller would opine: "Over and above the beat surges the soloist. Pitting himself against the limitations—the throb of the rhythm section—he seeks release from the confinements of society. With ecstatic abandon he pursues his unattainable objective. But the percussionists do not allow him forever to wander the heights. They recall him; he subsides, merging once more into the restrictions of the orchestra where, resolving with dignity his fanciful flight, he again affirms life."

Esquire's Jazz Book came with biographical sketches of numerous jazzmen—the known and unknown, the gifted and the extraordinarily gifted—and discographies.

Of course there was Louis Armstrong and William "Count" Basie, Sidney Bechet and Harry "Bing" Crosby; Cabell "Cab" Calloway and others of that rising tribe whose names had appeared on marquees coast to coast. But who knew of Walter Brown? *Esquire* did: "Featured as vocalist with the Jay McShann orchestra, a Negro group from Kansas City which has come into some prominence during the past year." What of Arthur Bernstein, who played string bass, who had chucked his law books because the music got inside him, claimed his heart? "A one-time lawyer, now in the service, he has concentrated most of his activities with free-lance work in the New York area," *Esquire* informed its readers. Arthur had recorded with the likes of Eddie Condon, Benny Goodman, Sharkey Bonano, and Billie Holiday. For all involved it seemed such a privilege, such a coup, to have made the *Esquire* cut. To slip into a barber's chair and open the red-covered publication and spot yourself. Of course Art Tatum made it; so, too, Jack Teagarden and Teddy Wilson. They were men and women who lived, for the most part, like vagabonds, traveling the country, spreading the jazz, toting their instruments, pleasing the crowds.

And there appeared on nearly every page of the periodical a touch of E. Simms Campbell, his drawings in the margins, almost pencil-like etchings with dark shadowings: Someone with a bass guitar, someone holding a trombone, someone leaning back and blowing into their trumpet. A womanly figure with something flowery in her hair, her shoulders thrown back and standing at a microphone: Campbell wanted you to imagine seeing "Lady Day," Billie Holiday, herself. He wanted you to imagine seeing Benny Goodman—the man in silhouette with a clarinet. And Duke Ellington—the figure hunched over the piano keys.

But it was the array of photographs—black and white, soulful and expressive—that genuinely captured the imaginative scope of *Esquire*'s offering. They had been culled principally from three sources—*Jazz* magazine, *DownBeat,* and *Metronome*—and they had the effect of forming a kind of documentary through still photography. Here is the great Sidney Bechet (Sugar Ray talked incessantly about his genius) and two others, Earl Hines and Rex Stewart. The three men, their hair pomaded, are captured in a Chicago studio, recording a tribute to a friend, the late Johnny Dodd. Hines sits at the far right, a jazzman's smile on his face. His paisley tie is tied, tight. Rex Stewart, horn player, stands in the middle; he's staged a quick getaway from Duke's band. Bechet and Stewart have wide waists—too much chicken and gravy on the road, too many spoonfuls of mashed potatoes. Long leather belts are holding up their beautifully pleated slacks. Here is Benny Goodman, a page all alone, the background black, as if Benny is his own lightbulb. He's leaning to the left just a bit, holding his clarinet, dressed in a tux. He has the courtly look of a corner druggist. He's been playing since childhood and he's been famous since 1936, hopping around the country, heading his own band, playing music both sweet and lovely ("Cabin in the Sky," "Honeysuckle Rose," "Sing Me a Swing Song"). Negro musicians are wild about him: he has assailed convention and integrated his bands, gallivanting about the South with a poetic grin on his face.

It is unmistakably Billie, shot from the waist up, the gardenia a giveaway, like the hairstyle and the slitted eyes and the smooth skin. She's standing at a microphone (the E. Simms Campbell etching come to life) and showing a wide smile. For four years, leading up to 1944, she has been singing solo, having broken away from Count Basie's band and Artie Shaw's band. Somehow—maybe it's the magic of the Speed Graphic—it is never the ravages of drugs that comes through in photographs of her, but the musicianship. One wishes that she were photo op and voice only ("That's Life I Guess," she sang).

It's a dandy of a photograph: Duke Ellington on the left, film-maker and boy wonder Orson Welles in the middle, and Cab Calloway on the right. They appear to be seated along the back wall of some nightspot. The caption talks about Welles's onetime plan to film the story of jazz, centering it around Louis Armstrong's life. (The film idea fell apart while the jazz kept humming.)

They are men and women—mostly men—pushing the doors of jazz open wider. They are in suits and ties; they travel at times on the Twentieth Century Limited express train; they travel in the backseats of old Model T Fords and new Cadillacs; they can slip a town if need be and leave everything behind if they must—everything save for the instrument.

Sportsmen adore them, lean into them and their music, buy them drinks. Theirs is a world of melody and newness. It is a world that Sugar Ray Robinson easily gravitates to. These are men who recognize style, who dress as he does—with an attention to detail, a surprising flourish against a backdrop of sedateness. "He was the unofficial ambassador of entertainment in Harlem," Robert Royal says of the young fighter.

Robinson, an inveterate reader of boxing publications, had astutely studied the careers of both Jack Johnson and Joe Louis. Johnson had given up much because of his constant cavorting with white women (whom Robinson avoided) and because he showed no inclination to ingratiate himself into any black community. Louis tried, bouncing between Chicago, Manhattan (Harlem), and Detroit, but failed to become a permanent and visible fixture in any one locale. Robinson would stake his claim to Harlem because of its ready-made backdrop of entertainment venues—where sportsmen gathered—and because he so easily fit into that scene. Then, too, Johnson showed no inclination toward musical entertainment during his boxing career; Louis did, but looked awkward trying to catch a beat. Robinson, because he had made efforts at studying music, fit in gracefully. His appearance at nightclubs in Harlem always raised the profile of those clubs, and the owners began to consider him wonderful publicity. And, finally, there was Edna Mae Holly, the gorgeous woman on his arm.

Edna Mae liked to go swimming. It was at an outdoor pool in

1941 in upper Manhattan that she first met an up-and-coming prizefighter. Sugar Ray would go there after sparring sessions, quite proud of himself and his physique as he lolled around the pool staring at the young ladies. Edna Mae, there with her girlfriends, had emerged from the swimming pool one afternoon looking as lovely as a bronzed mermaid might look. Robinson felt he was gawking at "the prettiest pair of long legs I'd ever seen." They were, in fact, a dancer's legs. "She walked with a little wiggle," Mel Dick, a lifelong friend of Robinson's, would recall of the young Edna Mae.

Born in Florida but raised in New York City, Holly hailed from a family of middle-class achievers. She studied for a time at Hunter College but then confounded the family's conventional expectations by becoming a dancer rather than a teacher or social worker. She was one of the beautiful young women who had danced with Lena Horne on the stage of the Cotton Club. At the time Sugar Ray met her she was employed at the Mimo Club. (Even though Robinson had only been fighting professionally for a year when they first met, his reputation had already spread.) She recognized Sugar Ray when she saw him and some of his friends sitting one evening at a table at the club where she danced. When he approached her, she played coy and uninterested. He wooed her by sending roses. He made a nuisance of himself at the Mimo by dropping by to watch her rehearse. She told him she had other suitors; he twirled his fedora and smiled at her. One of those suitors—the one she paid more attention to than the others—was Willie Bryant. Bryant, often referred to in the press as a Manhattan playboy, was a radio deejay and part-time actor. He was Hollywood-handsome with slicked-back hair, thin mustache, and cool features. Women swooned over him. But Sugar Ray dismissed Bryant and continued to pursue Edna Mae with flowers and gifts— among those gifts, a mink coat. The mink caught her attention. "Ray took Edna Mae from Willie Bryant," says Robert Royal.

And then there she was, ringside at his fights. They married quietly and almost secretly in 1943 on one of his Army furloughs. Now this rising, silky fighting machine in the well-cut and tapered suits, who bloodied men as an occupation, was hers. The season of the *Esquire* men marked their coming-out party. Musicians took them to dinner; there were soirees in their honor. Edna introduced young Robinson to Lena Horne, to Duke Ellington, to all the entertainers she knew. (Celebrities had long already introduced themselves to him, but he played along.)

They talked about clothes and fashion crazes. She proved a complement to the insights he had gleaned about style from his jazzmen friends. They moved into an apartment on St. Nicholas Avenue. "He really admired her," says Billie Allen, a dancer who sometimes socialized with the couple. "He always strove to meet her standards."

"She knew how to handle him," says Evelyn Cunningham, who knew the Robinsons when she was a young writer in Harlem.

Owing to her beauty and those dramatic entrances she had perfected at social gatherings—the stop-on-a-dime halt, then a slow stroll forward—Edna Mae began to appear in the society columns quite frequently. (From a Chicago newspaper columnist: "You cannot steal a party that is given for Lena Horne or Edna Mae Holly . . . Edna Mae, who is the wife of Sugar Ray Robinson, proved that when charming Ann Helm feted her [the] other night. Edna Mae with her grand looks was the whole show just as Lena would have been.")

"Edna Mae and Sugar Ray reminded me of the love story in *Carmen Jones*," says Billie Allen. "I think Sugar Ray exemplified the extraordinary black male—virile and handsome."

When bigger fight purses began to come in, Sugar Ray and Edna Mae moved into a larger home in Riverdale. He introduced her to glittering nights after his victorious fights. The photographers caught them both, arm in arm, dazzling in their stride. They had bewitched Manhattan and its environs. "Edna Mae was quite glamorous," says Billie Allen, "but after a while I think she became concerned about his whereabouts. I got the feeling he was a bit more rough-hewn than her."

Sugar Ray Robinson used to sing songs in the company of his wife, warbling out jazz standards. He particularly liked "The Very Thought of You." It made her smile. But she began to catch him in white lies, then bigger lies, and she realized he had a penchant for being unfaithful. There were heated arguments, separations, then Edna Mae's unannounced visits to training camp. Then long nights of lovemaking after the reconciliation. Their only child, Ray Jr., was born in 1949. He was a handsome and gregarious boy, but his daddy was on the road a lot. "My business was boxing, not babysitting" is how Robinson put it.

The fighter window-shopped on Fifth Avenue. He filed away the names and locations of tailors recommended to him by Duke Ellington and seconded by Edna Mae. He listened intently to music, parsing the different rhythms practiced by jazz combos. Conversations about boxing were fine, but when he sensed they were going on and on, and the information supplied to him was useless, things he already knew, he changed the subject—even if he was talking to George Gainford—with a grin and turn of the head.

He dreamed of himself in the jazzman's world more than in the grubby and wicked and unforgiving world of pugilism. He admired the jazzman's demand for respect, took it to heart. In the autumn of 1942 Robinson was wooed by Boston officials for a fight in that city. He decamped with aides to Boston to look things over. He scoffed at the proposed venue—the grubby and pedestrian Mechanics Hall—and requested the more charming and famed Boston Garden. When showed possible hotels for his accommodation and that of his traveling mates, his face grew pinched: He considered everything the officials showed him below grade. He suggested the Copley Plaza Hotel with its chandeliers and soft carpeting and classy address. (It was sometimes referred to as "the Costly Pleasure," a sobriquet its operators hardly minded.) Movie stars and high rollers stayed at the Copley Plaza, strolling through its lobby as sweet piano music drifted through the air. Boston boxing officials listened to Robinson's requests and eventually told him they could not meet either of them. Whatever clout they had, they didn't wish to use it up getting a twenty-one-year-old Negro boxer and his entourage into the Copley Plaza Hotel. Robinson left town and abruptly backed out of the fight. But the matter did not end there. It ignited a verbal brouhaha in the New York press, principally between Dan Parker of the *New York Daily Mirror* and Dan Burley of the *Amsterdam News.* Parker was livid that Robinson had refused Boston officials: "Ray Robinson has class as a fighter but in no other respect," Parker opined, citing the Boston incident. "He's the direct antithesis of Joe Louis." That charge met with fury from Burley: "The ungracious grumpy Mr. Parker's blasting of Ray's refusal to Uncle Tom in Boston and accept accommodations in a regular dump of a flophouse smells of [U.S. Sen. Herman] Talmadge and Georgia . . ." He goes on: "Ray Robinson is only reflecting the spirit of the new Negro who today refuses to bow and scrape before erstwhile royalty, and who is demanding his full pound of flesh in the distribution of all the [sic] Rights citizenship in these United States affords."

It was, of course, the blood and guts that made the dreams of Sugar Ray Robinson come true.

Not long after *Esquire*'s jazz edition was published, Sugar Ray got in contact with Vertner Tandy Sr., a celebrated Manhattan architect. For more than a year Robinson had been contemplating a foray into the business world. He discussed his idea with Edna Mae, her dancer friends, and his own musician friends. Robinson and Tandy took a stroll down Seventh Avenue, idling on the block of 124th. Sugar Ray looked around, up and down the block, into the traffic. And then he began to imagine seeing his name in lights, just as he had as a kid when he looked up at the names of the big Broadway stars.

He found himself with time on his hands. Home from the war, it did not take him long to become disenchanted with the quest for a shot at a title fight. Prizefighters were avoiding him and his deadly left hook, denying him the opportunity to be named champion. Champions rightfully demanded larger purses. Even his handlers were dubious about whether the time was right. "Robinson is impossible now," Mike Jacobs, the promoter, had confided to a publicity hack in the world of boxing shortly after Robinson's return from the military. "Imagine dealing with him as a champion."

Jacobs—playing both ends—tried to assuage Robinson's frustration by mentioning that he'd make plenty of money by fighting non-title fights. "I didn't need money," as Robinson would put it, "I needed glory."

And Sugar Ray, for once in his life, really didn't need money. He had savings now. While awaiting his title shot, he leaned into music dreams. He wanted a place where jazzmen and jazz lovers could come, where someone writing protest poems might wish to come and think. A place where he could pour champagne himself, and slip the mink wraps off the shoulders of lovely women.

He had started out as little more than an urchin, a hustling little child in Detroit, then New York City. But now Sugar Ray Robinson had propelled his own dreams into reality. Ideas of his future continued to excite him. He convinced himself he could travel further into mainstream America than either Jack Johnson or Joe Louis had done. The shortsighted among his fans and critics might wish to link all Negro prizefighters together, but it was his intention to carve a new model.

There was something intoxicating about the Manhattan of 1945. It wasn't just that the civilized world was still standing upright, that the forces of evil had been beaten back. It was all of that tripled by celebration and opportunity—and music. War had famished everyone; now it was over, everyone seemed ravenous. Charlie "Yardbird" Parker and Dizzy Gillespie were kicking up a hurricane on Fifty-second Street. Billie Holiday was wailing; Louis Armstrong was in and out of town with his band. Musicians were back home from Paris. You couldn't fling a scarlet-covered jazz publication ten feet without it flapping by the doors of some jazz nightclub. They were large and small; they stretched from Broadway to Harlem. Headline makers like Joe Louis and Henry Armstrong now had nightclubs. The competition hardly seemed to faze Robinson.

Armstrong, the onetime triple crown boxing champion, had an establishment—the Henry Armstrong Melody Room—located on St. Nicholas Avenue. The Doles Dickens quartet held forth as the establishment opened in the winter of 1946. But Armstrong didn't really seem to go with the backdrop: He was too quiet a man. With his boxing heyday over, his club seemed an idea hatched by others and his passions seemed elsewhere. Joe Louis's place was at 11 West 125th. It seemed, more than anything, a place that wished to make its reputation on the heaping portions of food served. "And the prices, considering [the] high price of food these days, are not out of line either," one account noted. Louis, never an animated conversationalist and hardly a bon vivant, grinned at his guests and shook their hands. The operation of any type of business establishment—looking over account books, weekly grosses—seemed to tax him in ways he did not wish to be taxed. He was happy to bolt back to Detroit at every opportunity.

But as with all great and romantic men, Sugar Ray Robinson's own dreams outpaced the desires others had for him with a blinding speed. He had an almost messianic drive, and wherever others saw limitation, he saw opportunity. Where others saw the confinement of the athlete, he saw the athlete in transcendence, using his drive and skill for other creations, especially those of an artistic nature. He had proven to newspaper reporters that he would go around them—appealing directly to the New York State Athletic Commission—when they would not back his quest for fair treatment in getting a title shot. (He had begun hoarding legal books and documents to prove his case.) He had told church elders who thought he might be behaving too aggressively—given his youth—that he was sure of his goal. He was simply bending Harlem to his will. A nightclub, then, seemed merely an extension of the man he happened to be. Jazz was the music just beyond his left jab and his right uppercut. The brighter the lights of his imagination, the better his mood. He considered himself more in tune with music and its trappings than either Armstrong or Louis, whose movements about Harlem he had watched intently. Armstrong had made his reputation in the featherweight and lightweight divisions; they were not marquee divisions. He walked Harlem hardly recognizable, a near relic. Louis was an anthem indeed, the glory and rhythm of American patriotism, his fists having bloodied the Nazi regime along with Schmeling himself. But Louis now seemed a figure frozen in time, his slow delivery in any conversation too much the echo of his rural upbringing, and hardly the kind of personality a nightclub might spin out of. Sugar—"Suguh Ray" as they yelled at him when he was seen around the great metropolis—was different. He was a New Yorker. He was improvisation; he was independence. His vibe was new: He was the soloist—jazz in the background—at work in a hostile world.

He forked over $100,000 to buy the property where his club would be, on 124th and Seventh Avenue. (Commercial banks were loath to loan blacks large sums of money, so Robinson set up his own realty company and used his earnings to acquire three other properties on the same block. He had a barbershop—which quickly evolved into a kind of hepcat hair salon for men—an office for George Gainford and himself, and a lingerie shop for his wife Edna Mae. Robinson and Gainford positioned themselves as businessmen who appreciated style and decorum, imagining a mini-empire that would sprout from these beginnings by virtue of Sugar Ray's fists and Gainford's devotion.)

Robinson told Tandy, his architect, to make the club beautiful— as beautiful as he could imagine.

Vertner Tandy had the right credentials for what Robinson envisioned. Tandy was a denizen of Strivers' Row, that stretch of Harlem that served as home to the highest achievers of the community. He had become the first licensed black architect in New York. He had attended, first, Tuskegee Institute, then Cornell, graduating from its architecture school. He wore lovely suits (he became another *Esquire* reader) and had an office on Broadway. He achieved acclaim in 1917 when he designed Villa Lewaro, the much-ballyhooed mansion of the Negro hair magnate, Madam C. J. Walker. Both blacks and whites were astonished at the majesty of the structure—located in Irvington-on-Hudson—and the accomplishments of the once impoverished little girl who grew up to become a business titan. Just before the mansion was finally completed, a *New York Times* reporter came out to visit. "The structure is a three-story and basement affair with roof of red tile, in the Italian Renaissance style of architecture, and was designed by V. W. Tandy, a negro [sic] architect," the *Times* noted. "It is 113 feet long and 30 feet wide and stands in the centre of a four-and-a-half-acre plot. It is fireproof, of structural tile, with an outer covering of cream-colored stucco, and has 34 rooms. In the basement are a gymnasium, bath and shower, kitchen and pantry, servants' dining room, power room for an organ, and storage vaults for valuables." The account went on: "Plans for finishing the house call for a degree of elegance and extravagance that a princess might envy. There are to be bronze and silver statuary, sparkling cut-glass candelabra, paintings, rich tapestries, and countless other things which will make the place a wonder house."

Sugar Ray's establishment would be considerably smaller, of course, but Tandy realized he had been summoned to the task because of his architectural stylishness and inventiveness.

As the weeks rolled into months in 1946, Sugar Ray took on an impressive number of foes. His constant pressure against the New York State Athletic Commission had opened doors—though he and Gainford still seesawed between optimism and pessimism about his shot at a title. He averaged more than a fight a month, and by the time the cold winds began whipping around Manhattan in November, Robinson had already fought fifteen times. Sammy Angott (a former lightweight titleholder) and Izzy Jannazzo had taken him to ten rounds, as had Norman Rubio, Ossie Harris, and the dangerous puncher Artie Levine. He told boxing authorities he'd take on welterweights or lightweights. Then the stalling came again. His suspicions about fight promoters and boxing managers only deepened. He complained yet again to the New York State Athletic Commission about the shenanigans he saw all around him: titleholder Red Cochrane seemed to be avoiding him, even agreeing to fight Marty Servo, who, it just so happened, Robinson had already beaten—

twice! The New York State Athletic Commission, feeling heat from Robinson and his camp, agreed to the Cochrane-Servo bout, but with a caveat: The winner had to meet Robinson in his next bout. Servo knocked out Cochrane and was awarded the belt. But as his destiny with Robinson approached, Servo's camp announced the new titleholder had "nose trouble." It was yet another twist in the dodging of Sugar Ray. So many fallen foes, and yet he was still without a crown. The logic of the athletic commission made no sense to him: Robinson was told the title was vacant for so long because of the war; that the sport was just getting back to its prewar momentum; that his time would come. The postponements and excuses left Robinson, as *Newsweek* magazine noted that year, "just where he has been for the last four years—holding the highly unofficial title of Uncrowned Champion."

Robinson or Gainford may not have given it any currency, but being without a crown did add to his mystique: The sportswriters and sportsmen had already anointed him. They talked of him in tones of reverence, the way those who had yet to see Charlie Parker in the flesh were talking. They were both—Robinson and Parker—figures cloaked in the whisper of the sensational; in the marvel of heightened expectation.

Robinson had fought so many bruising and scintillating bouts that viewers of the sport, writer and fan alike, had to wonder if the inevitable bout where he would grab his crown—thus ensuring larger purses, of course—would measure up against his already celebrated victories. Arthur Daley of *The New York Times* imagined why Robinson's march to a title shot—he had seventy-five pro bouts behind him—had been so long in coming: "He plays too rough. The welterweights have been disinterestedly looking in the other direction whenever he appeared on the scene."

Then, at long last, following behind-the-scenes negotiations between both camps and boxing officials—and with the welterweight crown the prize—a bout had been announced for December 20 between Robinson and Tommy Bell. It would take place in Manhattan, against the backdrop of Christmas cheer. Bell, the Youngstown, Ohio, fighter whom Robinson had beaten in ten rounds back in January 1945, was not to be underestimated: He was quick, his right was harsh, and he had more than enough arrogance to give Robinson and Gainford worries. "Nobody wanted to fight

Bell," remembers trainer Angelo Dundee, whose brother Chris Dundee managed Bell. "He was a very tough fighter."

Robinson turned his attention from nightclub concerns and left for his Greenwood Lake training camp. The wind there sliced across the hills and through the naked tree branches. As camp went on, Robinson seemed a bit unfocused. His attention was divided between Gainford and Tandy, his nightclub architect. Robinson would disrupt camp by bolting into Manhattan to look at the progress of the club and confer with his architect and decorators. Given that a championship bout was looming, it was a strange pattern of behavior. At such times, Gainford's lack of control over Robinson was all too apparent. "I was taking Tommy Bell lightly," Robinson himself would later confess. Many conceded Robinson was the favorite going into the contest, but there were those who had concerns and critical observations, the sportswriter Joe Bostic among them.

Bostic wondered why Robinson's hands were always plunged into a bucket of ice following bouts. He imagined them vulnerable, prone to injury and more than the average amount of swelling. "Will they stand up?" he asked. "That's the big question mark. He'll need 'em both—and in good shape—if he's to lick a stiff punching capable adversary. Which is what Tommy of Youngstown definitely is."

Promoter Mike Jacobs had cast a wary eye upon Negro-Negro matchups. Jacobs—his mind whirring back over Joe Louis–Max Schmeling, Joe Louis–Jim Braddock, Joe Louis–Max Baer, then further back to Jack Johnson and any one of his white opponents—had peered deep into the American economic psyche. Interracial matchups, he knew, carried potential for higher earnings. Bell, a Negro, squaring off against Robinson, meant a contest absent the social and psychological underpinnings that sometimes drew the crowds. But with white fighters dodging Robinson—and Bell eager as Robinson himself for a title shot—the athletic commission felt they were at least fielding an estimable confrontation, and one they could certainly market.

Sugar Ray Robinson fretted when a title shot was coming up. He would read about his prey in boxing publications and glean tidbits from Gainford, prying loose any news he might have picked up from boxing camps and other managers around the New York City gyms. When solid information was hard to come by, he cursed, stalking his prey in his mind like some silent jaguar with moonlit eyes scanning a landscape. He had speculated to sportswriters that perhaps he'd end up in a nursing home before winning a title. He complained and wondered how much was being denied him because he was unwilling to conform to deals brokered by the likes of Frankie Carbo, also known as Paul John Carbo, also referred to by his threatening moniker—Mr. Fury.

Frankie Carbo was a menace and a thug, roving around professional boxing like a dancing bear, his paws touching nearly everything.

In the aftermath of World War II, it was Frankie Carbo who supplied much of the criminality that infected a sport already known for its shaky allegiance to honor and ethics. Carbo—so conscious of his short stature that he wore elevator shoes—was a gangster and former convict. (Many in law enforcement would come to believe Carbo was the triggerman in the slaying of the wild dreamer and casino builder Bugsy Siegel in Los Angeles in 1947.) Carbo had wheedled an alliance with James Norris, who was heir to a family fortune and who also happened to head the International Boxing Club. Like more than a few men who had come by wealth honestly or by inheritance, Norris seemed bizarrely stimulated by the prospect of having a crook like Carbo by his side in the hunt for even more money. Using violence and threats, Carbo bullied Norris into acquiescence as he sidled up to fight managers, taking behind-the-scenes control of fighters, their purse strings, and their futures. George Gainford tried to limit the damage done to himself or his fighter through the association, but the more he dodged, the more difficult it appeared for Robinson to find challengers.

Robinson hated the business of the fight game, and as he watched Carbo and IBC officials, his distrust grew. He sniffed graft and imagined conspiracies. He saw sportswriters gallivanting with Carbo and his men; he saw promoters being handed gifts. Low-pitched conversations and overheard whispers fueled more skepticism. Often he'd look upon his Cabin-in-the-Sky (Lena's influence) training camp—the wind and the trees, the hills and the floating clouds—as a cleansing escape from it all. There was one more reason for caution that had lodged in the mind of Sugar Ray, and it was the ballad of Charley Burley.

Burley, a Negro who made his home in Pittsburgh, had turned professional in 1936. He quickly established himself as a dazzling and dangerous fighter in the ring. He was also quite proficient at dodging blows. The more his victories mounted, the more difficulty he seemed to have getting a title shot. Burley began to fight across weight divisions—welterweight, middleweight, heavyweight—believing it would increase his marketability. He sometimes fought men who outweighed him by more than forty pounds. With no title shot offered, he concluded it was because of his race and nothing more. Burley believed that the sinister shadow that hung over boxing—and the melodramatic villains who stalked in and out of the sport—would not limit him; that his accomplishments would thwart them because the public demanded it. But he was naïve. His own managers often made deals behind his back and kept Burley from the fights he wanted most. It was the breath of Frankie Carbo at work. Burley would also tell writers and fight camps that he would not be involved in any type of shenanigan where a fight was expected to be thrown. (Late in his career Burley unspooled a story about having once been approached about a three-fight matchup with Robinson—provided he take a dive in the first encounter. Burley never fought Robinson, and Robinson never commented on Burley's tale.) Robinson avoided the fate of Burley because he took an obsessive interest in his own career from the outset, hammering George Gainford with questions and inquiries. Burley was also prone to switch managers, never forming an impenetrable allegiance. Gainford did not busy himself with other fighters, concentrating on Robinson. If Negro fight managers were stymied by the psychological—and real—weight of the racism that permeated the sports world, George Gainford unleashed another sensibility: He was a black man born in the South whose family had West Indian roots; he brought an aggressiveness to his dealings with those who pulled the purse strings of fights. "Gainford was brilliant. He knew how to deal with white folks," says Robert Royal.

The Bell fight fell into place for Robinson, but only after he had beaten everyone in his path and dismissed the overtures of the Carbo gang. It was his romantic vision of the world—that through sheer willpower he could right things, that there existed writers who respected, privately if not always in print, his honorable devotion to the craft. He sensed a generational shift from the fans of Joe Louis to his own: His were coming around to his artistry; his expected a combination of vengeance, grace, and beauty. Sugar Ray knew the world was cold, but it was not in his interests to succumb to that coldness.

The double-dealing and wickedness—the corruption and racial dynamics that had long haunted his sport—were things he believed he could overcome. And unlike his hero Joe Louis, he felt he would step beyond them. Every move he made was wrapped around his belief in the athlete as necessary Renaissance man.

Christmas week of 1946 found poet-lyricist-dramatist Langston Hughes in Philadelphia, part of a troika of writers working on *Street Scene,* Elmer Rice's celebrated play about life jammed inside the tenements of New York. Rice, Kurt Weill, and Hughes were working feverishly to prune the play, now being adapted into an opera, for a Broadway opening. (The 1931 film version, directed by King Vidor, had featured Sylvia Sidney and Estelle Taylor; it received fine reviews.) Hughes had long admired both the play and Vidor's film treatment. He was especially moved that Rice had recruited him, a Negro, to aid in the writing of a play about whites. Hughes, by 1946, may have been a cosmopolitan figure (Gingrich's *Esquire* magazine had already published some of his poems, which had been illustrated by none other than E. Simms Campbell), but he knew the hardness of street life. "That I, an American Negro, should be chosen to write the lyrics of *Street Scene* did not seem odd or strange to Kurt Weill and Elmer Rice," Hughes would muse years later. "They wanted someone who understood the problems of the common people . . . I did not need to ask them why they thought of me for the task. I knew."

Lena Horne had emerged from World War II as a full-fledged black sex symbol. The sheer reality of it bewitched Hollywood, which had hardly any roles for her. The war had given blacks a pronounced civil rights posture: Sugar Ray and Joe scuffling with white soldiers; protests in munitions plants over equality on the job; the rise into the public consciousness of New York congressman Adam Clayton Powell Jr. and activist A. Phillip Randolph. Horne did appear in *Ziegfeld Follies* in 1946. She had also fallen in love with Lennie Hayton, a highly respected Hollywood movie director whom she had met while filming *Stormy Weather.* (Hayton happened to be white, which is why the affair was kept hush-hush.) But she was really excited about appearing in the 1946 Radio City Music Hall Christmas show. Her presence in the extravaganza—it also featured, among others, Frank Sinatra, Judy Garland, Angela Lansbury, and

June Allyson—sent prideful sparks through Harlem and black America. She was the only black featured in the show, which was titled *Till the Clouds Roll By.*

By now the young musician was residing in Los Angeles, blowing his trumpet up and down fabled Central Avenue, playing with Lucky Thompson's band. "They were some country motherfuckers," he would conclude about the blacks who caught the band's Los Angeles performances, "but they used to like the music we played because they could dance to it." Miles Davis thought Los Angeles was too slow; he missed the frenetic pace of Manhattan. He had Bird to keep him company. Bird was shooting heroin and gulping huge quantities of whiskey, in between the brilliant playing. When Davis began making his way back East, he was floored by some sweet news: "*Esquire* magazine had voted me its New Star award for trumpet, I think because of my playing with Bird and B's [Billy Eckstine's] band."

The starlet, the poet, and the trumpeter were forcing cracks in the world around them—just like the club-owning pugilist.

There were more than a few boxing writers who referred to Tommy Bell as "one of the great welterweights" of the early 1940s. In 1943 he had registered ten knockouts in the ring; a year later eight opponents suffered the same fate. It is—with rare exceptions—the poor man who fights and the well-to-do man who watches from ringside. Tommy Bell's background was a symphony of hard labor, more Woody Guthrie than jumpy-sweet Charlie Parker. In his youth Bell wound up in one of those FDR-inspired Civilian Conservation Corps camps in Georgia. Working in the outdoors, sleeping in barracks. He sometimes ran the barracks card games, which could turn into emotionally charged and rowdy affairs. There were fights over winnings. One night he saw a fellow camper jumped by other campers while he was sleeping. With his winnings one night—figuring he'd be jumped too—Bell snuck off toward the woods to sleep. Then he left the camp altogether. He returned to the North, where he worked at Republic Steel, shoveling ore. He worked inside a foundry, putting clamps on molds. He turned to boxing, picking up matches where he could. Once a fight manager stole his winnings and left him stranded.

The day before his bout with Robinson, Tommy Bell was spotted in New York's Central Park, getting in some light work. Passersby stared and gawked; wisps of frost floated from his mouth.

Tommy Bell always looked forward to that moment before the start of any fight when the lights were turned off and "The Star-Spangled Banner" played. He'd move his head just a little, left to right, and he'd stand there, thinking, becoming emotional. He was alone, but he wasn't sleeping in the woods anymore. He actually felt himself to be a lucky man, who made his living in a dangerous avocation.

One of the Manhattan cartoonists weighed in on the looming fight: "Tommy Bell's Right Threatens Ray's Title Dreams!!"

More than fifteen thousand fight fans hustled into Madison Square Garden on the evening of December 20, 1946. The weather outside was awful, soggy snow turning to rain, and yet they kept coming. Sportsmen in long wool coats and fedoras; women fussing with their hands to clear snowflakes from their collars. Promoter Mike Jacobs—now ill, having suffered a brain hemorrhage—shouldn't have worried: The gate receipts would exceed a healthy $82,000. Robinson was the sentimental favorite. A good many in the crowd had followed him since his local Golden Gloves days. There was also another reason for the excitement he elicited: The mighty flame of Joe Louis was flickering. He had fought just two times that year. His followers were reduced to figures not unlike subjects worrying after their king. But now another flame was flickering, and they decided to cross the valley where the flame of Robinson had begun to shoot upward, claiming their attention.

As the musical strains of the national anthem faded, photographers jostled for position, reporters flipped open notebooks, radio announcers checked their microphones. Among the throng in attendance—turning to the music of their names being yelled and the popping camera flashes, squinting and scanning the Garden, which on so many nights had been their Garden—were Jack Dempsey, Gene Tunney, and Joe Louis.

George Gainford told his fighter to beware of Bell's right. In his corner, Bell was being reminded of Robinson's speed.

The vicious punch—described as "a sizzling left" delivered "like a cobra striking"—arrived in the second round, not from Robinson but from Tommy Bell, and the gasps heard throughout the arena seemed to portend an unexpected struggle for Robinson. He tumbled to the canvas with referee Eddie Joseph circling—and the muscled Bell sneering. "My face was on the floor before my ass was," Robinson would remember. James Dawson, the *New York Times* writer, sensed danger for Robinson: "The Harlemite was hurt by the blow," he knew. The champs—Louis, Tunney, and Dempsey—all made animated movements in their seats as Robinson struggled on the canvas. He willed himself up from a seven-count knockdown. Bell hardly let up, constantly pummeling Robinson in his midsection and the jaw. Toward the last seconds of the fifth round, Bell landed another vicious right to Robinson's jaw, which, the *Times* man noted, "staggered Robinson." Bell—who appeared to be in better shape than his opponent—meant to tire Robinson quickly. Leading up to the fight, Tommy Bell had had no distractions; there had been no nightclub opening to worry about; no worries about selecting a particular type of wood for a bar; no pondering over the size of a mirror to stretch along the wall behind it. Gainford's cries from the corner seemed to meld with all the other cascading voices near ringside. And then it happened—a Robinson left, followed by a Robinson right; a wobbly Bell suddenly wide-eyed; the Robinson followers twisting in their seats, sensing something; Gainford leaning over the ropes. If there had been a feeling, beyond the sixth round, that Robinson was in an uphill battle, by the ninth, he had clearly turned it around. In the tenth, Bell went down for an eight count. And in the eleventh came the feared right-left Robinson combination, an exchange that clearly hurt Bell and seemed to starkly alter the momentum. Robinson was relentless in rounds thirteen through fifteen, and when the bell finally rang—the crowd hissing and rocking in anticipation of the final decision—Robinson leaned into Gainford, his own voice filled with emotion, and told him he had won; he just knew he had won; the crown was his. Seconds later, when the official announcement poured from the center of the ring, Robinson was declared the victor on points. But there was some booing from those who believed the Ohioan Bell deserved better. "For Bell made a fight of it all the way," as Dawson of the *Times* would write. But the pandemonium began to rain down, as the decision confirmed what so many had for so long predicted: Walker Smith Jr., Sugar Ray Robinson, was a champion fighter; his moment of glory had long been inevitable; now it was upon them, having arrived on a cold December night in 1946, and it sent the reporters fleeing for the phone booths and back to their offices, just as they had done on those history-making nights of Louis, Tunney, and Dempsey.

Gainford turned on his heel, looked out over the crowd, and figured it best to get his newly crowned champion away from the throngs of people.

"Clear that aisle," he snapped, leading Sugar Ray through the outstretched hands and the thunderous noise and the flashing camera bulbs—a New York policeman parting the way for them—to the dressing room. Strangers pushed close enough to catch the whites of Robinson's eyes, but Gainford kept moving forward with the authority of a Roman general, as the vanquished Tommy Bell receded into the shadows. It was a telling scene, however, and it had a little of the character of a drama acted in pantomime. Robinson and Gainford's cool disposition gave the moment a look of inevitability, suggesting that the slow start and the fierce battling in the late rounds were simply Robinson's assertion that a champion must find ways to come back; that champions are defined by artistry—and guts. It was as if Robinson had merely dropped by the Garden to pick up something that had been rightfully his for years now; something he was forced to wait to claim because of the racial dramas and politics of his sport. The next day the newly crowned champ was game enough to pose sitting down and holding aloft a copy of the New York *Daily News* with the resounding headline: ROBINSON OUTPOINTS BELL. He was dressed in silk, his face looked baby-smooth despite a noticeable cut above the left eye, and his hair gleamed in waves.

The respected New York sportswriter Dan Burley was quick to recall that his own earlier predictions had come true on the wintry night before: "From the beginning, way back in the days when nobody actually knew the kid was a potential all-time great, this column was plugging for Ray Robinson," he wrote. He went on to say of Robinson: "He'll reign the welterweight king as long as he wants to, or until he can get a middleweight title match with Tony Zale, which he asked for back in 1941 when Cochrane started running out on him."

Yes, the entire night had merely been a delivery on all those long-ago expectations, held by so many, that he'd be champ someday. They had gotten accustomed to his lightning punches—the hook that seemed to arrive so powerfully that it was like something crashing through a locked door. They had gotten used to the way he would strut away from his opponent after a bout-shifting left-right combination that delivered his opponent to the mat. It was a matador's strut—his back arched with ramrod discipline, hands at his side—as he shifted his gaze to the fans, and then back to his prostrate opponent and finally into the glittering light of the Speed Graphic flashbulbs. The men who wrote about the sport in respected publications had imagined this moment. It was back in June 1942 that Nat Fleischer had put Robinson on the cover of *Ring* magazine. The issue boasted a headline—"Ray Robinson—Colored Welterweight Champion of the World"—that was more a benediction than reality, given that Robinson's crowning was four years away. In 1942 Robinson had not quite been two years removed from amateur status. But Fleischer was such a known authority on the sport that his opinion carried a powerful cachet. Fleischer did, however, express one concern about Robinson, and it came to him after witnessing Robinson's March 20, 1942, bout against Norman Rubio: "The stringy colored sensation showed in his fight with Rubio, a tough, two-fisted clouter, that he possesses everything, even an abundance of cockiness that some day is likely to bring deep regret to him and his followers."

Fleischer's sentiment was articulated well enough, but it was given in an old-fashioned key that was not in Robinson's register. His cockiness was merely another manifestation of artistry. Charlie Parker skipped notes and found his own rhythm in compositions, bending the jazz to his tone. ("We heard him and knew the music had to go his way," Dizzy Gillespie said of Parker, adding, "He was the other half of my heartbeat.") The Charlie Parker fans out there, in the cities—in the gallery—relished something new: that cockiness, that break from tradition. Style—Sugar Ray Robinson in his one-button-roll suit, waving his felt fedora, smiling beautifully and softly following another ring victory—spun cockiness in a different direction. By the time he had evolved that signature style of the *Esquire* man with a touch of Harlem, his followers and admirers simply allowed themselves to be awed. He had given them echoes of jazz from within the twenty-four-foot-square ring, which comprised enough space for a tight big band—or a soloist. He spoiled them to the point where they expected nothing less from him.

The timing of Sugar Ray Robinson's coronation dovetailed so perfectly with his nightclub dream that it smacked of a Hollywood movie—the crown, then the champ's name in neon lights on 124th and Seventh.

Less than a week after his championship bout, the first ads heralding Robinson's club began to appear. He had ventured outside with his club's work crew one evening, and they treated him to a moment that made him giddy when they flicked the lights on outside. The red cursive lettering above the awning, cast against the darkness, gave it a theatrical glow: *Sugar Ray's.*

They came on opening night, and they seemed to be spellbound. It was the décor, and the music, and the champ himself, smiling and smiling (LaMotta or Jackie Wilson or Sammy Angott—no one could diminish the wattage of that smile), and the twinkling of champagne glasses, and the long mirror behind the long bar. Vertner Tandy had built the interior of the club to resemble the first-class quarters of the Twentieth Century Limited express train. Shortly after its opening, a Harlem publication expressed ecstasy over the club: "Nothing like it in town, in fact, not in the country . . ." Robinson meant to be a presence on the premises, and loved slipping in—those words champ champ champ floating around him like feathers—then gliding behind the bar, reaching for a bottle, taking an order. One reviewer talked about "Sugar Ray Robinson's cleverly designed bar . . . doing about the best business in town." It went on: "Maybe because Sugar himself gets behind the bar and mixes the drinks with his own famous hands." There were other nearby nightclubs to compete against—the Shangri-La, Small's Paradise, Frank's, Joe Louis's and Henry Armstrong's places among them—but Robinson's establishment had something the other establishments didn't have: "They didn't have Sugar Ray," says Charlie Rangel.

Because of his presence, Sugar Ray's club would become, through the years, a touchstone, a place for downtown sophisticates and European tourists alike; a spot for Harlem sportsmen and gorgeous women and jazz musicians. (Robinson was often seen in the company of Billy Eckstine and his wife, June, another dazzling beauty.)

If jazzmen were, through their extraordinary music, confounding their listeners—and Sugar Ray was giving his admirers the type of boxing they'd never seen before—it is little wonder the landscape of the fighter and the jazz players intersected. "He was a wonderful person for them to know," Robert Royal says of the jazzmen who roamed in and out of Sugar Ray's club. "He was a gentleman."

Robinson had handpicked his nightclub staff. Mike Hedley took the position of day manager. Hedley possessed some charming qualities in Sugar Ray's mind: He was a bandleader, and also a singer with a lovely falsetto. Gus Levine was Robinson's host—the gentleman who'd meet you at the door, who'd tell you if the owner himself was on the premises if you hadn't spotted him and you just needed to know. Gus also happened to be one of Sugar Ray's sparring partners.

It didn't take Robinson's club long to acquire a certain lure in Manhattan circles—not unlike Jock's, Toots Shor's, El Morocco, or the Stork Club. His was certainly a club for the nobility, not for the peasantry. On his fight nights in succeeding months and years, his admirers would celebrate his victories by hustling over to his club, where Mike Hedley and Gus Levine were waiting to grin them right through the doorway. During out-of-town bouts, Robinson, of course, couldn't be there, but they didn't seem to mind. They converged on the club anyway. The revelers were the anonymous souls of Harlem: transplanted Southerners, unknown musicians, Pullman porters as far away from the train whistle as they'd like to be; hospital workers, subway workers, factory workers. Now and then a crowd of them would gather outside the club to pose, men in fedoras and long wool coats with happy smiles on their faces, the cacophony of worship in the air. "You'd ask yourself after a fight, 'Where was Sugar Ray?'" remembers Arthur Barnes. "And you'd know he was going to his bar. And you'd take your girl." And he adds: "Sugar Ray's place didn't get the intellectuals. Sugar got the 'players.' They would go there looking for the good times."

The truth of the matter was that every big city where blacks had settled after the Great Migration of the 1920s would come to have one: a Negro nightclub on the Negro side of town. In Cleveland it was Gleason's; in Atlantic City it was the Harlem Club; in Columbus, Ohio, it was the Trocadero. They dotted the country from coast to coast, modest in size but often host to outsized plots, political ruminations, dramas, and dreams. They were like little Negro-populated movie sets, dark and glittery and full of perfumed women and men flashing bills; others whispering in corners beneath the spilling low-wattage lightbulbs; a half dozen or more souls seated at the bar and alternately nodding to the music and peering over their shoulder to catch the passing image in the mirror; saucy barmaids and gin-and-tonics coming right up; that bell ringing only the cash register at the end of the bar; that stack of flyers by the door just the latest advertisement and plea for participation in the next antidiscrimination rally; and the knot of whites from the brave hipster set across town, always catered to with overdone kindness so they'd be sure to come back, to spread the word about the tasty chicken and lima beans and peach cobbler. For a few hours each day, the Negro nightclub was a place free from the turmoil of the outside world; its denizens breathed of freedom and the lush life. And on those Gillette Blue Blade fight nights, the clubs jumped with a special kick.

To own a club like that, a club that hummed, with an allure that spread beyond the local zip code, was like magic.

As Joe Louis had stood in the glow of admiration, now stood Sugar Ray.

Sugar Ray Robinson had rushed with unstoppable force—even if in fits and starts—toward his own glory. He never doubted it would come. His talents and gifts were now undeniable. His stylized sense of self and business acumen—for now at least—mocked both Jack Johnson and Joe Louis. White sportswriters looked upon him with a squint on their face: They had never seen anything like him. Jack Johnson had toyed with sportswriters; Joe Louis could never find the right words for them. Robinson displayed a cocky flourish with artistry in the ring, but outside of it, he offered a hypnotic humility. He had chosen economic justice—which he construed as financial independence—over the cry for social justice. Civil rights organizations pleaded with him to join their cause in public. Instead, he donated money and welcomed them into his nightclub, where they might lull their heartache over food and drink.

The turn of events—unable to get championship fights for so long, but now the undisputed champion, now the fighter with a swanky nightclub—left Robinson exultant: "And now the lights were flashing on Seventh Avenue, my name in lights."

He moved through Manhattan like a man of destiny. The Negro baseball players, the actors and actresses in the barely respected but pride-swelling Negro cinema, the poets and writers—they all recognized him and waved in his direction.

Sometimes, though, he looked at his life as if through a split screen. On one half the life he currently led, and on the other, a life that entranced him—the life of a dancer-musician. He began taking dance and music lessons from Jarharal Hall, who operated a popular Manhattan music studio. (Hall, who had the copper features of someone of Indian descent, moonlighted as an entertainer; there were many who admired his silky singing voice.) Beyond the applause he garnered from the boxing ring, Robinson would always be dazzled by the way a gifted entertainer commanded attention: It was the alchemy of Duke Ellington's band, of Billie Holiday's voice, of Charlie Parker's blowing, that caused him to constantly marvel.

Along with Billy Eckstine, *Esquire* magazine's E. Simms Campbell, Duke Ellington, and crooner Billy Daniels, among others, Robinson was named to a list of "Outstanding Male Dressers" in Manhattan in 1946. They were all men who looked as if they weren't trying, and yet they appeared joyfully splendid in their dress. It gave them the look of being effortlessly elegant. (Langston Hughes received an honorable mention on the list.)

In welcoming them all into his world—his nightclub, and also his newly opened barbershop, which sat next door—Robinson beamed. You could spot Lena Horne sitting at the bar, or Langston Hughes. Or hear the bark of newspaperman Walter Winchell. Robinson's nightspot benefited mightily from being within walking distance of the popular Hotel Theresa. The hotel was home for many traveling jazz musicians as well as the leggy showgirls who danced at the Apollo Theatre. Many of the female entertainers who stayed at the Apollo had a special request for young Charlie Rangel, who was a hotel desk clerk before his political career took hold. They wanted to get over to Sugar Ray's, but it was dark outside, and they didn't want to walk unescorted; and he'd tell them he didn't even know if Robinson was over at the bar, telling them Sugar Ray might be on the road for a fight, or he might be in training. But they didn't care; they were in dressy attire and the night was young and they demanded he escort them. "Bar hopping was so important at that time," recalls Rangel. "When I was a desk clerk at the Hotel Theresa, I stayed sharp, and when the lady dancers and entertainers needed an escort to go bar hopping, they'd ask me. We went to the

The Harlem poet Langston Hughes was an habitué of Sugar Ray's nightclub. He also dreamed of roles Robinson might play in one of his theatrical productions.

Baby Grand, Sugar Ray's, Jock's, the Red Rooster. You'd go to Sugar Ray's with these ladies, and I'd tell them they probably weren't going to see him, but they wanted to go anyway."

Robinson's barbershop stocked the finest hair tonics; Negro men of a certain class—Robinson, the poet Langston Hughes, jazzmen Louis Armstrong and Roy Eldridge, men in urban locales all over the country—were partial to having their hair "marcelled," which meant a greasy concoction was applied overnight to give it both a sheen and a wavy appearance. It was a time of suits and silk ties, of hair that shined like molasses, of Yardbird's horn and Duke's baton; of jazzmen strolling through the lobby of the Hotel Theresa in their Nunn Bush shoes; of Gus Levine over at Sugar Ray's nightclub signaling, with the dip of the sun, that it was time for the lights over the awning to be turned on.

Sugar Ray Robinson's barbershop seemed to draw as many names as his nightclub. "Duke Ellington used to come into the barbershop and say hello to everybody," recalls Edward Allen, the New York dentist and jazz aficionado. One afternoon in the barbershop, Allen turned to look through the window and saw a commotion going on outside. Men and women had gathered in a semicircle. Cars were slowing. "Outside on the sidewalk," he remembers—still a thrill in his voice all these decades later—"Sammy Davis Jr. was trying to outdance John Buck of Buck & Bubbles!"

It was a time when you could be stopped dead in your strolling by that one-of-a-kind Cadillac coming your way. In the late 1940s there were an estimated two million cars crisscrossing Manhattan intersections every day. But there was only one flamingo-colored Cadillac, because there was only one of its kind in existence, and it had been special-ordered by Sugar Ray. It was a convertible, and it had whitewall tires, and the hubcaps were as silvery as new coins, and he'd wave, and if he were stopped at a light, he'd shake a hand, then caution the soul to please get out of the street, and they would, turning this way and that way, following him with stunned eyes as he cruised out of view. "Sugar had gone down to Miami and fell in love with the color pink," says Frankie Manning, the Savoy dancer who often spotted Robinson at the nightclub.

He patrolled the city in his Caddy, rolling from Sutton Place to Gramercy Park, from the Bowery to Chinatown, from Greenwich Village back up Sixth Avenue—above the rumble-rumble of subway trains beneath him—onward through the golden glow of the trees in Central Park, past Grant's Tomb, along 125th Street and over the Triborough Bridge. His violent hands rested softly on the steering wheel. "That car was the Hope Diamond of Harlem," its owner mused. "Everybody had to see it or touch it or both to make sure it was real. And to most of them it literally was the Hope Diamond because if skinny little Walker Smith could come off the streets to own a car like that, maybe they could too."

Not many months before the war-scarred and jazz-soaked 1940s would come to a close, an eloquent writer by the name of E. B. White, chronicling New York City, wrote: "A poem compresses much in a small space and adds music, thus heightening its meaning. The city is like poetry: it compresses all life, all races and breeds, into a small island and adds music and the accompaniment of internal engines. The island of Manhattan is without any doubt the greatest human concentrate on earth, the poem whose magic is comprehensible to millions of permanent residents but whose full meaning will always remain elusive." He went on: "At the feet of the tallest and plushiest offices lie the crummiest slums. The genteel mysteries housed in the Riverside Church are only a few blocks from the voodoo charms of Harlem."

In the spring of 1949, *Holiday* magazine, in an impressive issue devoted to New York City and its culture, food, politics, and fashion, dispatched young writer Ann Petry to essay Harlem. Petry's versatility astonished: She'd been a pharmacist and an actress; she had also studied at the Harlem Art Center—all that before turning to writing. In 1945 she received a Houghton Mifflin Literary Fellowship Award. She used the $2,500 prize money to finish her novel, *The Street,* which was published in 1946 to raves. (Its heroine lived and struggled in Harlem.) But it wasn't Petry's prose—fine enough—that distinguished the *Holiday* spread. Nor was it the accompanying poetry of Langston Hughes with its requisite lyricism—"Golden girl/in a golden gown/in a melody night/in Harlem town . . ." Instead, it was the rapturous photography of George Leavens that stunned the eyes. His camera, on the opening page, landed right outside Sugar Ray's nightclub and it seemed to linger as the neon jumped from the page. The red lettering of the famous fighter's name shone atop the awning, which stretched from doorway to near the curbside.

In those magic years it is clear that Sugar Ray Robinson has transcended his sport. With his image in national magazines evoking style and grace—and the reflections in the mirror of his nightclub tossing about the images of Lena Horne, Duke Ellington, Jimmie Lunceford, Jackie Gleason, Billy Eckstine, Charlie Parker, and others of their pedigree—he has ushered in a new way to think of the fighter and his prowess. He unashamedly confers as much with George Gainford, his fight manager, as he does with Jarharal Hall, his dance and voice teacher.

There are nights when he roams about. He runs into acquaintances from his youth, boys who are now grown men but whom he once sparred with over at Salem Crescent, the gym of his youth. Only they didn't make it, because the sport did not allow for the untalented to prosper. Some went into athletic work, some into church affairs, still others into manual labor. And there are those clearly suffering, looking him up and down, commenting on his attire and prosperity, telling him about the sound of his fights on the radio one moment, then the next about their hard-luck stories. He will slip a little money over, promise free drinks, a haircut, a meal. "He was generous to a fault," remembers Robert Royal.

Sometimes, as quietly as he can, he checks on the competition. It amuses him that there are three nightclub establishments owned by boxing champs—or former champs—operating in Harlem: Joe Louis's and Henry Armstrong's and his own. But it is Armstrong who, after their handshake and pleasantries exchanged in the moonlight, stays on Sugar Ray's mind.

Years earlier, he'd hung around Madison Square Garden—poor as pennies, yet dreaming and dreaming—watching Henry Armstrong in the ring, bobbing his own head against Armstrong's punches; then following Armstrong and his silky robe through the throngs and stopping, just staring when he couldn't get any closer; then bouncing back down into the Salem Crescent gym the next morning, swearing to himself he was going to be just like Henry Armstrong, and pleading with George Gainford to explain to him what made Henry Armstrong so great; what, exactly, made him Henry Armstrong, a three-time world champion. You might even say—as Dizzy had said of Charlie Parker—that Henry Armstrong was "the other half" of young Walker Smith's heartbeat.

At first his life was full of the American song of pain and heartache—groveling to put food in his belly—and then came that dizzying whoosh that brings unexpected glory. It's a wonder, though, that fever or flood didn't erase him from the landscape, spilling him into the masses of the forgotten.

He was born in Mississippi in 1912, the first year of the great floods that would haunt and drown that landscape for months. Negroes suffered the worst—there were cries they were used as human sandbags—but the misery seemed bottomless for both races. With the fear of floods, the lurking web of slavery, and pangs of hunger, his family fled Mississippi in his youth.

In St. Louis, the young and impish Henry Armstrong played children's games along the riverbank. Sensing some kind of lyricism in life, he wrote poems in his quiet moments. Another Missourian, Samuel Clemens—aka Mark Twain—might have loved him, the way he lit out for the territory, across America and through Mexico, battling and finding his way as a professional fighter. During the menacing shadow of the 1930s Depression, young fighters like Walker Smith—aka Sugar Ray Robinson—and many, many others all about the country uttered his name with a reverence that became almost mystical.

a lovely setup for the old man

BETWEEN JUMPING ROPE, pummeling the punching bag, and sparring, the young fighters inside New York City's Salem Crescent Athletic Club were forever discussing recent professional bouts—the knockouts and the fifteen-round slugfests that had taken place downtown at Madison Square Garden. They heard the day-after commentaries from shoeshine men, from subway riders and men on stoops, from grocery store clerks and aging city dwellers. For there was nothing like the day after a memorable battle at the Garden—the reactions became a type of city music all its own, unsolicited soliloquies that hummed all day long from borough to borough around the great metropolis. And inside Salem Crescent, it gave the young pugilists even more inspiration to pay close attention to trainer George Gainford and to Roy Morse, the founder of the club and himself a product of the city's streets. They'd run farther, skip rope longer, do additional sit-ups—anything to keep them imagining that one day they'd become part of the citywide verbal jousting that followed evening radio broadcasts and fight headlines. Sometimes Gainford and Morse would cadge tickets for their young charges to get into the big fights down at the Garden. The boys were impressionable young fighters, and they all had heroes. Young Walker Smith described the great Henry Armstrong as "my boyhood idol."

In 1937, the year before the unmatched success that brought him triple title ownership, Henry Armstrong fought twenty-seven times. He fought three times each during March, July, August, and September of that year—a backbreaking feat for any mortal. Not only were there twenty-seven bouts, but there were twenty-seven victories; all but one of them won by knockout. Millions marveled at his feats. In black-and-white newspaper photos, he seems a little tyro in billowing black trunks—he stood a mere five feet five—but his gaze was steely. Henry Armstrong never complained about the relentless schedule set up for him by Eddie Mead, his manager at the time. He simply packed his bags and pushed himself through the months and seasons, believing that given the distance he had come in life, it would have been ungrateful to complain about anything as he stood awash in boxing glory.

He was born in 1912 in Columbus, Mississippi, the eleventh of Henry and America Armstrong's children. (The kids hardly knew what to make of the raised eyebrows when strangers heard their mother's first name.) The Armstrongs were sharecroppers. Which meant they picked cotton, lived practically hand to mouth, lit kerosene lamps at night, obeyed the rules of segregation, and prayed as if Jesus Christ lived right alongside them in their log cabin. Their most consistent visitors were traveling evangelists. Desperate as their circumstances were, Henry's mother never turned an evangelist away from the dinner table. Little Henry resented the Scripture-quoting men scooping up corn bread and tomatoes and chicken, knowing he'd be hungry later in the night and much of the food would be gone. Because of his small size, family members called him Rat. The little boy went for long walks in the woods; he was prone to having visions and dreaming. One night he dreamed that he was "being led across a river of water by an angel—and such an angel!" Armstrong would recall. Young Henry's father moved to St. Louis with his older sons in 1915, and months later sent for his wife and the younger children, who had stayed in Mississippi. They gathered at the train station, embarking on their journey to Missouri, surrounded by friends and relatives there to bid them goodbye. Gospel songs began to flow from the throats of those gathered—"Lead, Kindly, Light," and "On My Way to the Kingdom Land," among them.

Henry Sr., who had found work in a packing plant, settled the family into a brick house on the South Side of St. Louis. In grade school, little Henry was astonished at all the schoolyard fights he witnessed. Fighting and scrapes seemed to be a natural and beguiling pastime in his new surroundings. Gangs of youths stalked, neighborhood to neighborhood. Henry—short but stout—wrestled with young enemies. Then, as he grew, he switched to hitting with his fists. He purchased a pair of boxing gloves and offered to take on all comers, the pair of gloves thrown over his shoulders as much a dare as a gunslinger's holsters. The death of his mother was a blow that changed everything. There were mouths to feed and he wanted to help his father. He worked in a bowling alley, he scrubbed cement stoops for small change. He graduated high school with a proud honor: He'd been named poet laureate of the graduating class.

The poet laureate found work quick enough, driving stakes for the Missouri Pacific Railroad. He wasted little time in telling railroad workers about his dream to box. Aging men who worked for the railroad—and who had once boxed themselves—regaled him with stories of their own ring ventures. He didn't know which tales to believe, but the utterances excited him. Henry bought a sandbag and trained while circling it in his basement. Laid off from railroad work, he washed dishes. Laid off from washing dishes, he found work in a hat store. A trainer noticed Henry working out at the colored YMCA in St. Louis. Spotting potential, the trainer entered him in local AAU contests. (He started out fighting under the name Melody Jackson—thus the name, in later years, of Armstrong's Melody Room nightclub in Sugar Ray's Harlem.) In Missouri he became an AAU champion. Henry moved to Pittsburgh with another fighter and manager hoping to better his prospects, and in 1931 he won his first two pro bouts. But the earnings were meager, and he found himself back in Missouri. He was soon invited out to the West Coast, and he began dreaming of what California might have to offer: "Oranges falling like manna from heaven . . . luscious nights under the star-studded dark blue dome of heaven . . . $5,000 purses . . . classy clothes and a diamond ring . . ."

Utilizing his experience of railroads and railyards, Henry Armstrong—without sufficient funds to catch a train or plane—tramped his way to California. It was not an easy trek. Brakemen had been specially trained to watch out for hoboes: "They weren't friendly to hoboes, and they were downright dirty in their handling of Negro hoboes, striking at those who were slow in getting off the train at their command," Armstrong would remember. Armstrong and his traveling mates hopped from train to train, survived mostly on bologna and crackers, and finally made it into that big, open, and bountiful land of California. They slept at missions as Henry sought out fight gyms during the day. Impressing trainers at the local Main Street gym, Armstrong was soon back in the ring. A roundhouse right had become his specialty. "It was neither jab nor hook, nor swing," Armstrong would explain. "It had less preliminary, but more consequences, than any of them. And the glove traveled only a few inches in its round trip." Between 1932 and 1934, Armstrong—fighting all his bouts in California save for three in Mexico City—amassed thirty-two victories against four losses and five draws. (In Mexico City he fought in outdoor bullfighting rings; the locals, furiously attached to their own homegrown fighters, pelted him with orange peelings.) He was soon known as a West Coast sensation from Mississippi—never mind his lengthy wanderings and his arrival by freight train. Nat Fleischer's *Ring* magazine took note of Armstrong, placing him sixth in its 1934 rankings.

By 1936 Armstrong had a new manager in Eddie Mead. Mead had been managing fighters since the 1920s. He was a tough character, once accused of having placed an iron bar inside one of his fighter's gloves. (Mead was a close consort of actor George Raft, who was in turn known for his ties to gangsters. Mead knew of Armstrong's star-filled eyes and made an introduction.) On August 4, 1936, Armstrong defeated Mexican-born Baby Arizmendi in Los Angeles. He was named California-Mexican featherweight world champion. The honor meant little east of the Mississippi, but what Armstrong did in the following year—those twenty-seven bouts and twenty-seven victories, winning his first world championship—meant everything. It meant his name was suddenly on the lips of Walker Smith Jr. and the other young souls inside Manhattan's Salem Crescent Athletic Club.

The sportswriters began referring to Armstrong as "Homicide Hank." His windmill blows were crushing. He had solidified a reputation that stretched coast to coast. "I lived in Los Angeles when Armstrong was starting out," says Budd Schulberg. "He was a nonstop fighter. He would go three minutes without stopping—and he was so fast. It was more than a punch a second. He was really remarkable."

Joe Louis worshippers might have considered 1938 Joe's year, inasmuch as he avenged his previous loss to Max Schmeling by knocking him out before those seventy-five thousand screamers at

Yankee Stadium. But, in reality, it was Henry Armstrong's year. First came the announcement of a matchup with the revered Barney Ross. (Joe Louis invited Henry to train at his training camp. Armstrong was a jumpy and excitable youngster still astounded at his own success—nodding, grinning, hanging on the words uttered by Joe's trainers. Louis liked his disposition.) On the day of the much-publicized bout, thirty thousand showed—Joe Louis among them— at the Madison Square Bowl out on Long Island to watch Armstrong attempt to take Barney Ross's welterweight crown. Ross was in trouble from the outset. Round after round, Armstrong threw powerful left jabs at Ross's jaw, connecting time and time again. Ross's right eye swelled; blood poured from his lips. "Armstrong hooked two lefts to the body and then shot a left and right to the head," the *New York Times* account of the fourth round would record. "Ross jabbed a left to the face but Armstrong moved in and pounded the body with both hands. Armstrong shot a left hook to the jaw." It never eased for Ross. The referee looked toward Ross's corner at the top of the eleventh, wondering if the champion's team might want to call it quits, but they did not and Ross battled on. "Like a human tornado," James Dawson of the *Times* would write, "Armstrong cut Ross down." The fight opportunist, Mike Jacobs, was in the crowd, suddenly salivating at the chance to represent Armstrong himself. (He'd make his way toward Armstrong's camp like a barracuda— albeit a smiling one—in the aftermath.) Dawson added: "In a word, Ross had not a chance, because he was unsuited to the style of the young Negro who hammered him out of his title and because he had not the stamina, the resistance, the reserve, the strength to come on against youth."

Henry Armstrong ended the phenomenal career of the Chicagoan Barney Ross that night. Reporters who chased Armstrong to his dressing room were stunned to see he was without a single mark; that he seemed, in fact, not at all exhausted after a bout that went fifteen rounds. They needed quotes. He tried mixing humility with insight: "It was the easiest fight I ever had against a really good fighter," Armstrong said.

Ross was the stalwart fallen hero. "This was my last fight," he promised on the night of his defeat. "I've been around a long time, and I've been on top most of that time, and I guess I'll have to step down." It was rare for a fighter to stay true to such a proclamation, but Barney Ross did. His next fight was against enemy forces during World War II on Guadalcanal as a Marine. He received a medal for his bravery, and sympathy when it was revealed he had become addicted to the morphine that was used to kill the pain of his injuries.

They toasted Henry after his huge victory at Small's Paradise nightclub in Harlem. The Ross bout had happened in May. Immediately after, Armstrong turned his sights elsewhere. Already holder of the featherweight title—and having beaten Ross for the welterweight crown—Henry Armstrong squared off against Lou Ambers in New York on August 17 for the lightweight crown. Ambers fought fearlessly, cutting Armstrong above the eye and causing blood to flow in his mouth. Armstrong—the onetime hobo, the child who had had dreams and visions in the Mississippi woods—dispensed with his mouthpiece and swallowed the blood so the fight wouldn't be stopped. Ambers pounded away, just like Armstrong; fans screamed loudly. In the end the onetime hobo won a split decision, becoming a triple titleholder, and tumbling into boxing history.

He spent his earnings lavishly. He was an easy touch for a handout. The sight of beggars moved him, and he dug into the pockets of his pleated slacks. (Out of the ring he wore suits and white shirts; the open jacket often revealed suspenders. He dressed like a banker.)

In future matches, however, the titles began to get away from him.

October 4, 1940, was Sugar Ray's first professional bout in New York. He scored a technical knockout against Joe Echevarria in the second round, marking what would be the start of a three-year period of uninterrupted victories. But Robinson would remember that day for another sentimental reason as well: He was on the early part of the same card that featured Fritzie Zivic and Henry Armstrong. There were many who felt Zivic was nothing but a dirty brawler. (Photos of him angling his gloved fist below the midsection of his opponents hardly dispelled that belief.) So there was young Robinson finishing off his opponent Echevarria, his arm being raised, his first thrilling pro victory, compliments of his volley of rocketlike punches—then hurrying to his dressing room, getting dressed, and getting back out to the arena, moving fast through the crowd of well-wishers and breathing with excitement because he was so eager to get a seat where he could see his idol, Henry Armstrong, defend the welterweight championship. He had to sit there and watch, round after round, squirming, as Zivic went for Henry's eyes, and gasps filled the arena because Henry's welterweight belt was at stake. Henry complained about Zivic's low blows to the referee, but it didn't matter, and at the end, the arms of Fritzie Zivic were raised. Young Robinson's victorious night had ended with the defeat of Henry Armstrong. He cried to Gainford that Henry had been the victim of a badly called fight. He added to the around-town soliloquies the next day, repeating his belief about the wrong done to his hero. He vowed he wouldn't forget what he had seen the night before. (One year and three weeks later, Robinson avenged the hurt by delivering a punishing whipping to Zivic in a ten-rounder in New York.)

The next few years saw Henry Armstrong—who had already relinquished his featherweight title—based back in California. During the war, actor George Raft formed a stateside outfit called George Raft's Caravan. They provided entertainment for the troops; Raft asked Armstrong to join up, and he did, staging exhibition bouts just as Robinson and Louis were doing. By then Henry had announced his retirement, and his name all but faded from the headlines.

It turned out to be money woes—of course—that pulled him back in the summer of 1943. He was pounding the pavement one day in Manhattan, on his way to ask promoter Mike Jacobs for a loan. And it just so happened that on that day, Joe Louis and Sugar Ray Robinson were also visiting Jacobs on one of their Army furloughs. But, in a bit of vaudevillian hide-and-seek, Robinson and Louis never came face to face with Armstrong. Jacobs commandeered Robinson and Louis, leading them into his inner office from a small outer office. There were jokes and greetings. Then: "*Shhh,*" Jacobs said, "be quiet." Louis asked Jacobs why. Jacobs explained that Henry Armstrong was on his way up. "He's trying to put a touch on me for five hundred" dollars, he said.

When Henry knocked, Jacobs refused to answer the door. He eventually went away.

It was the curse of boxing, and Robinson knew it and understood it in a far sharper way than Louis: Money made a rising, gifted fighter and his cornermen smile; championship belts made the same fighter unreservedly trust his managers. The losses that caught up to the fighter as he aged would eventually send him reaching for money that was gone, that had vanished. Sam Langford—who had once fought Jack Johnson and to whom Johnson denied a rematch after winning the heavyweight title because Langford had skills that frightened even Jack Johnson—was sometimes seen on the streets of New York in the early 1940s. Among those who saw him was Sugar Ray Robinson. Langford was old and blind by then, and he was kept afloat only by the concern of a group of sportswriters who banded together to start a charitable fund for him.

"Did you see what Mike Jacobs did to Henry Armstrong?" Robinson had said to Louis once they left Jacobs's office. "Did you see how he treated him?"

It was hardly lost on Sugar Ray Robinson that the career of a prizefighter was always sliding toward its end. In Armstrong and Louis, he could see grace and beauty up close, but also the savage timeclock of the sport. To survive as long as he could, he hewed to two particular principles: the need to keep his body well conditioned, and the importance of never underestimating an opponent.

The cupboard was bare during the war as far as boxing was concerned, because so many pugilists were enlisted. Mike Jacobs loathed the fact he had fewer and fewer big fights to promote.

In 1942—he had been away from the ring since January of 1941—Henry Armstrong announced he wanted to fight again so he could pocket at least $100,000 in savings before quitting for good. He had a wife and children and assorted relatives he was caring for. The plan was to barnstorm the country—just as, in his youth, he had rumbled around his St. Louis neighborhoods with gloves flung over his shoulders—looking for contests. It was the silly dream of an aging fighter, the dream heightened even more as Armstrong began falling under the spell of alcohol. But he hit the road, fighting in Colorado, Utah, Nevada; he had to have a personal driver at night because his eyes were going bad from all the damage. He fought unknown fighters, sometimes a mere fourteen days apart. He turned his gaze toward the sound of train horns out there in the hinterland, which reminded him of his youth; he thought of poetry but couldn't get the poems out of his head onto paper. He ate bad food and drank beer and racked up victories against nobodies—save for Fritzie Zivic, whom he fought again, beating him on October 26 in San

Francisco. No one seemed to care, though; Zivic wasn't champion anymore either.

Just before Christmas 1942, a report floated in the press—obviously planted by members of Armstrong's camp—that Henry Armstrong was ready to take on none other than Sugar Ray Robinson himself. The ruse upset Gainford. Robinson dismissed it: "I'll never fight Armstrong." Gainford's thinking was businesslike and directed toward the future: His fighter was only two years into his professional career. Though few would have bet on Armstrong beating Robinson, Gainford knew Armstrong was cagey and experienced, and the last thing he needed was for his own fighter to be surprised by a snarling has-been entering the ring on past-glory emotions. There was no upside. Gainford issued a quick dismissal of the Armstrong challenge, insisting that the "rumors" of a matchup stop. "Ray Robinson definitely does not want to box Henry Armstrong," Gainford said.

But with his out-of-town victories stacking up and drawing media coverage, it seemed that Armstrong's trajectory would inevitably cross with Robinson's anyway. Reporters sniffed the air and sensed something. Dan Burley, writing in the *Amsterdam News,* felt if Armstrong were to keep winning bouts in his comeback bid that "promoters would be blowing their hot, sweaty breath on Ray's neck with offers for him to meet the former triple title holder." Expressing great admiration for both fighters, Burley—obviously building interest in just such a bout—said he believed that fight fans would not wish to see the two clash: "That's something few real fans want to see. Armstrong has been an idol of Ray and Ray has been dear all along to Armstrong."

Nine months after Burley's words appeared, Robinson agreed to the fight, despite more protests from Gainford. Mike Jacobs said he could bill it at the Garden. He told Robinson the fight would get Armstrong closer to his goal of accumulating a sufficient retirement fund. Jacobs also told Robinson that he was the only fighter with marquee value who could guarantee a handsome amount in gate receipts. Jacobs knew such a contest—former triple titleholder against rising welterweight, hero-worshipper against none other than his hero—would garner publicity.

Thus the setup of the old man—Henry Armstrong—was arranged.

It was the inverse, however, of the dive, of criminal skullduggery, of money changing hands. Instead this was mere old-fashioned melodrama, which sometimes hacked its way into the fight game minus menace. Events like these originated in sentimentality, which was the peephole through which Robinson was staring out and over the career of Henry Armstrong.

Reporters visited both fighters during workout sessions. When Sugar Ray was asked by Hype Igoe of the *New York Journal-American* if he would be able to hurt Armstrong, who was someone he so obviously admired, Gainford interrupted, his tone sharp. "You remember his first Golden Gloves final, Hype? You remember how he knocked down that Spider Valentine boy? They were pals for years. Shot marbles together. Did everything together. But that didn't stop Robinson from knocking him down. No room in this business for friendship, Hype." Robinson hit the bags, imagining himself wily enough to become a great actor—to win but not destroy.

And yet, Henry Armstrong believed, really believed, he could beat Sugar Ray Robinson. He trained with determination; there was talk of his steely resolve and of the messianic mission he was on before quitting. Reporters took note of his twenty-six bouts in this comeback, and the fact he was victorious twenty-three times.

He was broke and in need of money. He was dreaming; he was Rat again.

A *Chicago Defender* reporter, however, weighed in with an opinion of a Robinson-Armstrong matchup: "God Forbid."

In a column in the *St. Louis Post-Dispatch,* Armstrong's hometown newspaper, there was a gentle warning offered to Robinson: "[N]ever before has he met a man of the experience, strength and indomitable will-to-win of Armstrong," John Wray wrote. Still, Wray conceded that Armstrong was facing a "much younger, faster and more virile" opponent in Robinson.

On the eve of the fight, Sugar Ray Robinson paid a visit to Armstrong's Manhattan workout headquarters. Robinson was dressed in his military uniform, and he was smiling that movie-star-in-the-war smile: the armor of glamour. He seemed loose as a jazz drummer. Armstrong himself was in workout attire. He was lacing up his shoes; he still had work to do; he aimed to beat Sugar Ray Robinson; he looked resolute and dead serious. He had no time for smiling or guffawing.

Mike Jacobs had hustled hard promoting the bout and was able to announce to *The New York Times* he expected a "near capacity" crowd of around sixteen thousand for the Garden event.

Jay Gould—a snappy Negro and a syndicated columnist writing from San Francisco—usually covered the horse-racing scene. But he often weighed in on upcoming boxing bouts. The Negro gamblers and bookies around the country knew him, and he tapped them for insights and scuttlebutt about pending fights. "Rooster Hammond of Detroit, biggest sepia bettor around the country on fights," he wrote, "made Sugar [Ray] Robinson a 1 to 4 favorite in New York to beat Armstrong."

They shook hands during the weigh-in as the cameras clicked. Henry was shorter but more muscled, even though Robinson was five pounds heavier. Garden observers wondered if military life had softened Robinson ("never a champion," the *New York Herald Tribune* reminded readers), depriving him of the strict regimen of workouts he was able to have in civilian life. Armstrong, as the former featherweight-lightweight-welterweight champion, had his admirers in the Garden crowd, who remembered his great battles—and that hyper trot he'd take around the ring after his victories, sometimes patting his opponent on the cheek with his gloved fist, as if to apologize, then continuing the trot, his arms raised so happily and joyfully.

The tone was set right after the fight began, with a staccato series of Robinson punches that were followed by a reprieve. It was like a bear begging a cub to stay inside the cave because danger lurked.

Every time Armstrong approached, a lightning-quick Robinson jab pelted him. He seemed a lost fighter in the ring, a slow-motion tyro up against Robinson's dancing speed. Robinson stayed back now and then, as if Armstrong might be worn down by exhaustion and fade, but the battler would crouch and charge and then Robinson fired as a form of defense. From high in the stands, Armstrong seemed a blur of caramel against the darkly hued Robinson. The *New York Times* account allowed as to how Robinson "merely pecked away at his 31-year-old opponent, riddling him with a ceaseless spray of long lefts to the head." End of the fourth round, over in his corner, Armstrong was rocking his head, that gladiator look in his eyes an echo of the past and certainly not the current proceedings. Armstrong knew only one way to fight—the windmill motion, the hard charge—but his punches aimed at Robinson landed in the wind. There were those in the stands aghast at Robinson's domination—the quick movements; striking only when he wanted; all of it like a pro conducting a clinic. By the sixth round, it all struck the *Times* man as rather repetitious: "Armstrong would snort in leaving his corner, shuffle toward his foe, his head weaving from left to right, then suddenly find his head bobbing back and forth under the force of Ray's long and sharp left hands." There were some catcalls from the stands, voices demanding a knockout—that smell of blood, the gaggle of photographers on their elbows at ringside— but Robinson was fighting with sentimentality and caution. He merely wished to keep Armstrong at bay and not hurt him. From the perspective of Jesse Abramson, covering for the *New York Herald Tribune,* Armstrong was utterly lost. "The man who rose to fistic fame and glory with three championships through the piston-like fury of his two-handed attack could not lay a glove on Robinson," Abramson observed. "He tried to spear him with a leaping left and always missed. When he got in close, Robinson tossed him around like an empty barrel."

At bout's end, Armstrong retreated to his corner with his usual prideful gait. But Robinson, to no one's surprise, was named victor in a fight that Joseph Nichols of the *Times* called a "spectacle" as "tame as a gymnasium workout between father and son."

Henry Armstrong had never seen anything like this; never seen someone so fast. His muscles and terrifying reputation meant nothing, absolutely nothing at all, to Robinson. It was as if the boxing gods had been keeping some kind of secret away from Henry and all of a sudden the velvet curtain had been torn back, revealing this specimen before him: feral, blessed with blazing footwork, not so much stalking the ring as dancing around inside it. After every round Henry Armstrong told his corner he'd adapt to Robinson's style, and then the round would be over and he'd be breathing hard—even the actorly blows from Robinson had a stinging effect.

The young fighter had overtaken his idol. The *New York Herald Tribune* headline—ROBINSON OUTPOINTS ARMSTRONG IN GARDEN BOUT BEFORE 15,371—was far kinder than the *Amsterdam News* headline: OLD MASTER TAKES BEATIN' LIKE MASTER.

In his dressing room, Henry Armstrong, surrounded by admirers and furiously scribbling reporters, announced—yet again—his retirement. "I'm through," he said, all the blood wiped from his swollen lips. He said he might try managing fighters himself. He said it all forlornly. He tried, in fits and starts, to explain what had happened this night, to utter words about Robinson's speed, hardly a ring secret. "I know it looked bad," he said. "It's my style of fighting. If Robinson had come in, instead of staying away, it would have been different." No one believed him, though no one challenged him on such a melancholy evening.

In their dressing room, Sugar Ray Robinson and George Gainford took the position of paying nothing but full respect to Armstrong. Robinson said the pugilist was "the greatest I ever fought." He added, not quite convincingly: "I never could get him in trouble." Both fighter and manager were cautious in what they said, lest they tip someone off, such as the New York State Athletic Commission, as to what Robinson's intentions had been all along. "At times Ray, failing to take advantage of openings that were obvious to the spectators in the second shelf, appeared particularly careful of Henry's welfare," said the AP report, which landed in the *St. Louis Post-Dispatch*—giving Armstrong's family and friends a chance to read about what had happened.

With a day behind them to reflect on what they had witnessed, the New York sports columnists began to weigh in, analyzing the event from a different perspective than the beat reporters. And what they produced while bent over their manual typewriters was pointed—and cutting. "The New York press was pretty bitter about the Ray Robinson–Henry Armstrong fight," the esteemed Stanley Woodward of the *Herald Tribune* offered after taking the measure of his colleagues. According to Joe Williams, of the *New York World-Telegram:* "It was highway robbery at $16.50." In something of a backhanded compliment that might have come from an old showman himself, Woodward was more charitable toward Robinson and the fight: "The boxing clients for years have spent their money on baloney . . . They are experienced in the market. They do not need protection."

Robinson ignored the words hurled by the columnists. Sugar Ray Robinson never courted reporters—not in the way Jack Johnson or Jack Dempsey had courted them, not inviting them into his home or sharing intimate details. Reporters and columnists made him wary. He questioned the company (Frankie Carbo) they were sometimes seen around. Either they didn't take him seriously enough, dismissing all of his complaints about having to wait and wait for a championship bout, or they took him too seriously: For what was the harm in going easy on an aging champion like Henry Armstrong in the ring! (Robinson's relationship with the press was so testy that he would later hire PR agents to serve as intermediaries between him and reporters, ostensibly to foster better relations. But he used the third parties to widen his distance from the Fourth Estate, leaving them to label him, forevermore, eccentric and uncooperative.)

"I couldn't hurt an old man," Sugar Ray would reflect years later about the bout, "but I couldn't go through the motions either. I'd hit him enough to get him in a little trouble, but whenever I felt him sagging, I'd clinch and hold him up. I didn't want him to be embarrassed by a knockdown."

It took the old fighter five months to break his retirement vow. He was back in January—the George Raft exhibition gig had ended—fighting out West again, in Portland, Oregon. Sometimes he averaged two fights per month. His opponents were unknowns. He was also, in a manner, fighting for his country: Now there were personal tax bills; he owed Uncle Sam thousands. So he fought all across the country through 1944, taking care of his debts. The last bout of his great and wondrous career took place on Valentine's Day, 1945, against someone name Chester Slider. The bell rang in a ring in Oakland, California. After a full ten rounds, Slider had a victory notch over a former triple-crown champion. "The old speed was gone," Armstrong had finally, at long last, come to realize.

He made pipe-dream investments—motion pictures and restaurants. He never saw a dime's worth of profit from any of his ventures. His Manhattan nightspot didn't last long; many simply preferred Sugar Ray's and the other livelier places.

He tried managing, but too often there were loud arguments with the fathers of young fighters. They wondered if he knew what he was doing. He soon abandoned the manager's dream and headed back to California.

His thirst for beer turned to whiskey, which he drank and drank. In January 1949 he was tossed into the drunk tank in Los Angeles. He had been hanging out on Central Avenue, that hepcat stretch of the city, roaming in and out of the bars. He climbed behind the wheel of his yellow convertible and proceeded to crash it into a lamppost. He yelled to authorities that he was Henry Armstrong; reeking of alcohol, he reminded them of his fame and glory. They slapped on the cuffs and drove him off to jail. The story began making the rounds that Henry Armstrong was locked up. "You're letting a million boys down," the judge told him, her voice full of shame for Henry. He got out and walked the city, stared at like a bum, a Negro bum. He didn't drown in the Mississippi River, but Rat was drowning on the streets of Los Angeles.

He started reading the Bible, poring over its pages, reciting certain passages out loud. Unlike when he'd been a hungry youth at the dinner table back in Mississippi, evangelism now appealed to him. Former drinking buddies eyed him suspiciously; he didn't care, and when a minister invited him to say a few words in his pulpit, his new career began to unfold. He spoke to men on the street, his Bible in the fold of his muscular arm. He spoke to hoboes, telling them, with a glint in his eye, of his own railroad journeys.

He started a youth foundation in California. He got Sugar Ray Robinson, Barney Ross, and other notables to serve on its advisory board. (Robinson would long remember the joy it gave Henry to work with kids.) Henry Armstrong seemed happier than ever. The years moved on, but by the 1970s he had relocated back to St. Louis. He worked with pride at the Herbert Hoover Boys Club (Hoover being one of the heroes of the long-ago Mississippi floods) for more than fifteen years. "He had films of his fights," an executive director of the Boys Club would remember of Armstrong's work. "He'd get a bunch of kids up in one of the conference rooms and he'd give them a commentary on his fight films. The kids just loved it. He shared his moments. He shared his life." He ate at the same Burger Chef every day for lunch. He didn't at all mind playing checkers with the kids. He carried a briefcase around town. And he much enjoyed being known as a minister. As he walked home, men would see him and point him out to their sons, telling them about the great fighter, Henry Armstrong, and his ring accomplishments. Inner-city St. Louis was tough at the time, and Armstrong's eyes were hardly what they once were. Two punks mugged him in 1978, leveling him with vicious blows. "To think that two guys would do this to me," he said. "In my prime, I would have whipped both of them."

His third wife convinced him in 1982 to leave St. Louis and

return to Los Angeles. It happened abruptly, and family members were distraught, but Henry loved his wife. "He had a lot of fantastic friends here," his daughter Edna would lament about her father's hometown. Months would go by and family members would not hear from him. They blamed his wife. The great fighter Archie Moore—like Armstrong, born in Mississippi but calling St. Louis home—was asked by the family to look in on Henry. Moore reported back to Henry's family that Armstrong looked wan and seemed unhappy.

Every now and then he ventured out in Los Angeles, wearing a suit and straw hat and leaning on a cane. He'd take in some of the pro fights. Mike Tyson pulled up a chair and took a photo with him while on a visit to LA. He was in and out of hospitals in the last months of his life. He suffered from malnutrition and anemia; his mind was slipping, along with his sight. He died October 22, 1988, in Los Angeles. October was always one of those California months when the winds hummed down off the Santa Ana Mountains, passing over the masses of Los Angeles County residents—the well-heeled, the scuffling hoboes—and right out into the ocean. It was always a fine month for dreaming.

Jim Murray, a *Los Angeles Times* columnist, was one of the few writers still around who had seen Armstrong in the ring: It was back in 1944 and he had caught Henry at the end in two Los Angeles bouts only ten days apart. "He'd charge a rhinoceros," Murray would write a day after his death. "He made his fight like a guy running for a bus. He walked through people like turnstiles." It was a lovely column, full of boxing knowledge and tenderness. "He got the position in history no man should get," added Murray, "the part of the bill where they put bird calls—between the eras of Joe Louis and Sugar Ray Robinson."

In those wondrous days when he first drove his shining Cadillac around 1940s Manhattan, you'd often see Sugar Ray pull over and stop upon spotting Henry Armstrong, climbing out of his car to chat. There they stood, two proud pugilists, idling, catching up on old times, which were still new times for Sugar Ray.

It was there, hovering, like something unfathomable. Hardly anyone wished to talk about it; the possibility was kept out of sight like an old yellowing newspaper clipping, one that proved it had happened before. Sure as water rushing over Niagara Falls, some night in yet another arena it would happen again, and there would be those redundant gasps of horror and worry. There were always photos in the aftermath, showing the fighter in earlier times looking so lively and prepared. Tousle-haired Jimmy Doyle, grinning to beat the world. Hell if he'd turn down an eighteen-grand payday. No sir, not in hurting 1947 America. In 1947—never mind Sugar Ray's reputation: the canonlike kick to his punch, already two victories against fearsome Jake LaMotta—that's enough dough to buy a home, which is just what the grinning fighter aimed to do. Later, some of the ones who were there will rewind their minds: If only he'd ducked that punch, or that whistling bolo; yes, the bolo, because that thing looked as if it landed right on the skull. But that was wishful thinking: You never see the fateful punch coming.

Forever after, the two—the killer and the killed—are intertwined and linked. Not unlike the great couplings from the world of entertainment: Astaire and Rogers. Burns and Allen.

Robinson and Doyle.

1947

killer

WHEN SUGAR RAY ROBINSON'S TRAVELING ASSEMBLAGE arrived in Cleveland, ten days before the scheduled title bout, it was hot and sunny. He was a little miffed because not all of his luggage had arrived on time. He and his willowy wife Edna Mae—she still had her dancer's body—and his manager, George Gainford, took time out to visit some of their familiar haunts in the downtown area. They had friends on the East Side of the city, where so many of the black citizens resided. Fighters led nomadic lives; cities blurred, save for the faces of old friends.

The punch that Jimmy Doyle never saw coming. The punch that would never be forgotten.

Robinson had long conducted himself with the aura of a champion—making suggestions to those around him; challenging himself with his workout regimen; appearing unfazed by the flash-bulbs going off around him. Not so George Gainford. Just months earlier George Gainford had been that anonymous Negro seen at the corner drugstore; looked at—and straight through, as if he were not even visible—inside yet another hotel lobby; passed by on the street without comment or nod. Now he was a fight manager who managed a world champion. Now newspapermen were sidling up to him for quotes and scraps of information about his fighter, Robinson. They'd ask him about the welterweight division, about the special gifts of other fighters. Now George Gainford had currency and armor. And when looking into the eyes of fight promoters, he was suddenly more determined. He could see a mighty bright future ahead. All these years rubbing down the shoulders and arms and back and fists of his fighter, Sugar Ray, and whispering instructions in his ears, over and over. He was the giant Negro in a white T-shirt in the dressing room with ointment on his fingertips.

As soon as they arrived in Cleveland, Sugar Ray and Gainford scheduled a private meeting with fight promoter Larry Atkins. They wanted to talk to him about proceeds from the nationwide radio broadcast of the fight. Sugar Ray and Gainford both liked the feel of cash and knew of too many fighters not quick enough of mind to reap full revenue benefits from their fights.

Whatever it is that fight promoters do in their spare time—scout new venues, slide their palms across the tops of new automobiles as they glisten on lots, sweat about money lost in recent contests, hum along to old jazz standards—they most assuredly dream. Larry Atkins was a dreamer. And for years he had dreamed of holding a title bout in his native Cleveland. By the time the news began racing around Cleveland, up and down Euclid Avenue, past the fight arena itself, out to Shaker Heights where the swells lived, then back to the East Side and past the barbecue joints and dilapidated homes and exhausted day workers, and over the phone wires, and into the shoeshine parlors and onto the lips of the shoeshine men themselves—before the moon began rolling across the darkened Cuyahoga River and the barstools were being claimed in the downtown drinking establishments—he was awash in pure joy.

His dream had come true.

The fight game in twentieth-century America required a huge stage, which is why so many championship fights took place in Manhattan, at Madison Square Garden. The Garden—like the Roman Colosseum–inspired Yankee Stadium, which lay far across the trees and rooftops of the city—was a perfect venue. It certainly helped—indeed it meant everything—that Manhattan had the kind of cast to augment the proceedings: high rollers, jaunty newspapermen, powerful fight promoters, entertainers, gangsters, showgirls. In Manhattan, even the not-so-old lions, Jack Dempsey and Gene Tunney, could still be seen grinning in restaurants. And up in Harlem, around 135th Street, you could sometimes get a peek at the Brown Bomber himself, Joe Louis, in the flesh. As a fighter, he was in decline in 1947. But the legend, the cocoa-colored warmth and hugeness of it, was still something to behold.

So when a championship fight found a home in another city, locals had a cause for celebration. It mostly happened because of the back-slapping and hustle and grit and wizardry on the part of that host city's best-known promoter, whoever it happened to be. In some cases, though, it was due to the eagerness and gullibility of the town itself: On July 4, 1923, Dempsey fought a championship bout in obscure Shelby, Montana, against Tommy Gibbons. Dempsey's manager, Jack "Doc" Kearns, sweet-talked the Shelby elite (cattlemen, bankers) into forking over a $300,000 advance to Dempsey. Dempsey won, but the crowd was smaller than expected and the town nearly went broke, angering many. Dempsey and company had to escape Shelby in a hurry by train.

It was first announced in May 1947 that Sugar Ray Robinson would defend his recently won welterweight title, and do so in Cleveland. That in itself was news: There hadn't been a championship bout in Cleveland in sixteen years, since 1931 when the German Max Schmeling knocked out Young Stribling, a handsome Georgia country boy who was as beloved by rural fight fans as he was by the Ku Klux Klan. This, then—the return of a title bout to Cleveland—was a wondrous moment for Larry Atkins.

Atkins was a hometown promoter. Born in 1902, he had grown into a man with a huge lived-in face and deep-socketed eyes. He bore a resemblance to the comedian Jack Benny. Law school had bored Atkins, but not the fight game, nor the slapstick quality of wrestling, which he had promoted during the Depression after venturing to St. Louis.

Atkins had begun hitching himself to boxing promoters in the early 1920s. Mostly, he did publicity work, elbowing his way into radio offices and newsrooms, reminiscing and jawboning into the wee hours with anybody willing to listen to him hold forth about his fighter. After a stint in Chicago—a rollicking and fight-crazy city— he got his dream job: doing publicity for his hero, Jack Dempsey. Atkins was in Chicago, at Soldier Field, on September 22, 1927, when champion Dempsey squared off against Gene Tunney, a cerebral fighter who had been reading Somerset Maugham's novel, *Of Human Bondage,* on the eve of that fight. It was their second battle; Tunney had won the first a year earlier in Philadelphia. More than 145,000 were at Soldier Field; upwards of fifty privately piloted planes arrived, having flown barons, heiresses, and Rockefellers into town. Local denizen Al Capone had been skulking about, inquiring about fixes. The long count of that fight—Tunney knocked down by Dempsey and getting a reprieve due to a count mix-up, Dempsey lurking vulturelike and not retreating to his corner quickly enough—would be discussed for decades, spun so dizzily the loss would come to seem a kind of victory in the minds of Dempsey partisans. Late in life, Atkins would recall that 1927 bout: "I was Jack's press agent for that fight. He was my idol and always will be."

His bona fide credentials in hand, Atkins returned to Cleveland in 1940. He meant to shake up the fight business in town. He befriended fighters, fight managers, newspapermen, boxing commissioners. Still, it would take seven years before he got the kind of glittery announcement he so often witnessed in Dempsey's world— the title bout—and that he had dreamed someday, somehow, would be his very own event to orchestrate. He'd show the New York promoters that his heels clicked just as hard as theirs. Robinson's challenger would be Jimmy Doyle, a young Los Angeles–based fighter, only twenty-two years old and a rising and fearless welterweight. Flush with the deal, Atkins found no problem getting anyone on the phone at the *Cleveland News* or Cleveland *Plain Dealer* to write up the announcement: He'd previously been employed in the sports departments of both publications.

Hard times lay over Cleveland in 1947. The city still shivered from its post-Depression blues, which seemed to spill into post–World War II blues. There were industry jobs, just not enough. The shanties in and around the Cleveland Flats were still horrific; the impoverished sought handouts. For years it had been a city more crooked than straight. A hardworking crime fighter, Eliot Ness, had made a name for himself working in the city's Prohibition Bureau. He got corrupt cops thrown from the force; he staged raids on clubs with his convoy of trench-coated and fedora-wearing men. Crime took a truly bizarre turn in the city beginning in 1935. Bodies, some beheaded, began showing up on roadsides, in parks, and along alleyways. Fear was everywhere. Doors were bolted; mothers gripped the hands of their children, tight. The killing spree went on for at least three years. Suspects were arrested and then released for lack of evidence. Ness never found the killer, whom the press referred to as the Cleveland Torso Murderer. During World War II Eliot Ness left Cleveland to work for the Federal Security Agency. But 1947 found him back in Cleveland, launching a run—many deemed it quixotic; it was on the Independent ticket—for mayor against Thomas A. Burke.

As Ness went after voters, Larry Atkins went after fight fans. (A good many he simply bumped into at the downtown bar he ran.)

The New York Times reported in its April 5, 1947, edition that the Robinson-Doyle fight would take place in Cleveland on May 30. That report came two days after Robinson beat Fred Wilson in Akron in a three-round knockout and three days before he dispatched Eddie Finazzo in Kansas City, Missouri. But Robinson's route to Cleveland had one more scheduled stop, which was back in Manhattan, where he took on George Abrams on May 16. Abrams took Robinson ten rounds before Robinson was declared the victor in a split decision. The cuts above Robinson's eyes from the Abrams fight made George Gainford a bit nervous; the manager contacted Atkins and asked for a delay in the fight so Robinson's cuts would have time to heal. June 10 was mentioned, then abandoned. The final date settled upon was June 24.

The Cleveland Arena, site of the fight, was a twelve-thousand-seat in-the-round arena with the seats stretching for more than sixty rows. Located downtown on Euclid Avenue, it was made of cinder block and was the architectural creation of Al Sutphin. Sutphin owned the Braden-Sutphin Ink Company in town. He loved sports and built an arena that, in time, came to play host to professional basketball and hockey teams, as well as the rodeo, the circus, and bike races. But it was amateur and professional boxing that held a special lure for the local populace.

The big marquee fronting Euclid Avenue lit up on fight nights.

The cheap tickets for bouts at the Arena—the "A" was capitalized atop the roof of the place and you could see it at a great distance— went for six dollars; all others were ten and fifteen. But there were some bars out around Euclid Beach where you could get under-the-table tickets for as cheap as a buck. Inside the Arena, you could sit on the floor in chairs, then scoot the chairs up closer, provided there was room and you had the gumption. Sometimes there'd be five ten-round fights in one night. There were a couple of local kids, Carl and Louis Stokes, who heard about the Robinson-Doyle fight and would have loved to get tickets, but they couldn't afford it. Carl was a young fighter himself and reveled in the attention the city got from the upcoming match. He circled the clubs where he knew both fighters would be sparring and gawked, along with his brother Louis. (The Stokes boys would grow up to make their marks in another arena, that of politics. Carl would become the city's first black mayor; Louis a U.S. congressman.)

Ten days before the bout, a report came out of the Greenwood Lake training camp that Robinson was having difficulty getting down to the 147-pound weight limit. Gainford laughed the worry off. Robinson would come in under the limit, proclaimed Gainford, "now that Ray is training seriously."

Robinson—"New York's crack Negro boxer from Harlem," is how the *Times* described him—was indeed seven pounds overweight. His challenger, Doyle, who had arrived in Cleveland on Sunday, June 15, a day after Robinson, met the weight limit and looked to be in excellent shape. Robinson's extra weight seemed to worry everybody except him. In fact, a few days after arriving in town, Sugar Ray Robinson went golfing, ferried out to Highland Park, a local golf course, with all the insouciance of a country gentleman on holiday. He cut a fine figure on the golf course too, the ball flying from the end of his club, up, up, and away. He even sank a twenty-foot putt, which he bragged about to his cornermen and some of the local citizenry. It all felt so good, so wonderful. He returned a day later, under sunny skies: more golfing; more fun times.

Still, Gainford had respect for Doyle. Locally, Robinson set up workouts at the Fox Hole gymnasium. When fans and admirers could get in to watch the welterweight champ, they'd elbow for better views, rising on tiptoes. At one session there were upwards of three hundred onlookers. The attention finally caused Gainford to threaten—albeit good-naturedly—to conduct his fighter's remaining workouts in private.

Three days before the fight—with Larry Atkins whirling about, hoping and praying that Robinson would meet the weight limit test—Robinson stepped up on the scales in his dressing room following a workout. Sweat poured from his brow. All around eyes widened as the dial on the scale came to a stop. Then came the grunts and exclamations of approval from his camp: Gone were the seven extra pounds he had arrived carrying. He weighed exactly 147. He smiled. (One of Gainford's secret admonitions had been for the champion to take a constant round of steam baths.) "Don't know what all the fuss is about," Robinson said coolly. "I knew I could make it all the time. Don't think Mr. Gainford would let me take two days off this week to play golf if he was worried too."

Robinson and Gainford were rebuffed by Atkins, however, in their efforts to reap some of the expected proceeds from the radio broadcast. Far as Atkins was concerned, Robinson and Gainford were arrivistes. And he was not about to grapple with a radio conglomerate over putting more money into their pockets.

Over at his training headquarters—the old Johnny Papke Gym—Jimmy Doyle was beating the bags like a man on fire. His manager Paul Doyle (no relation) was giving him advice, and sometimes the manager couldn't tell if the kid heard him because he'd just nod and keep on punching. When the welterweight challenger heard that Robinson had made his weight limit, he simply shrugged. "Not that I ever suspected for a second that he wouldn't make that welterweight limit," Doyle offered from his base. "He'd make it if he had to cut a leg off, I hear—or get a haircut, anyway."

During photo sessions for the Cleveland media, Robinson and Doyle faced each other with gentle grins on their faces, extending their arms, softly tapping each other about the shoulders as the flashbulbs went off. Robinson's grin seemed light and easy and wide; he was sporting a lovely tweed jacket at one session. Jimmy Doyle's grin had a little peculiarity to it. One couldn't tell if he was grinning because he was half in awe of Robinson—or because he was secretly feeling insulted about the way the newshounds had been dismissing him. Or even perhaps because of those tales of Sugar Ray out at Highland Park, golfing and horsing around. There were fighters that Jimmy Doyle had put on their backs with his gloved fists. He'd fought beneath the lights at fabled Madison Square Garden, same as Sugar Ray. He boasted a record of forty-six wins against five losses. Jimmy Doyle did not come to Cleveland to be disrespected. Yet it had been that way all his life—fighting for respect, fighting to be taken seriously. No one ever called Jimmy Doyle pretty. He had a fighter's face, as lined as Dempsey's. But there were folk around Cleveland who knew not to dismiss him. "Doyle could fight," remembers Jimmy Bivens, a Cleveland heavyweight who watched Doyle work out at the time. "These guys would think they could get in the ring with him and beat him up while sparring. And Doyle would end up beating them up!" Decades later, Bivens could still cackle at the memory. "He wasn't afraid of nothing."

Jimmy Doyle didn't come to Cleveland to play golf. He had no time or inclination to play golf. In fact, if Jimmy Doyle had been asked to putt a golf ball into a hole—even just several feet away— he'd likely pick the thing up and ram it right down the hole with his bare hands.

The city of Los Angeles was not known for producing boxers. The sport simply had too much to contend with, not least Hollywood and the allure of acting and entertainment and the magic of movies. But there were fighters who emerged from the palmy sunshine of that city. In the beginning, if they were good enough, they got on fight cards at the Olympic Auditorium. They had to make a name for themselves before they got that prized invite: a ticket to the East Coast, the epicenter of the fight game.

Jimmy Doyle was born James Delaney but took the name Doyle in homage to a onetime welterweight star. Jimmy Doyle had all the hard luck of the Irish in America: He was poor, he dreamed, and those dreams often got smashed. But he kept dreaming. As an amateur, Doyle impressed his trainers Duke Holloway and George Tolson. Eventually he landed with Tony Palazola. Palazola liked the fierceness of the kid and pointed him out to fighters and boxing legends alike who found themselves passing through Los Angeles. When boxer Jack Johnson, the former heavyweight champion, was rumbling around Los Angeles in the 1940s and took an interest in Doyle, it was an unimaginable boost to the young fighter's confidence. Johnson's interest was matched by that of Jim Jeffries, another heavyweight. But not just any heavyweight. Jim Jeffries was the white heavyweight who came out of retirement in 1910 to take the championship belt from Jack Johnson. The fight was staged in Reno, Nevada. It had the dramatic weight of racism circling it: Jack London, the writer, had been pleading with Jeffries to come take the title from Johnson. The outcome brought tears to the eyes of white men and women alike. "Once again," Jack London was forced to write from Nevada, "has Johnson sent down to defeat the chosen representative of the white race and this time the greatest of them. And as of old, it was play for Johnson." Now these two champs, race-laden and history-soaked, were watching the young Doyle and seeing much to admire.

Jimmy Doyle—curly-haired, his nose flattened from so many bouts already—turned pro at the end of 1941. He was single and he still lived at home. He was determined to make money to support his mother.

He acquired a reputation of ferocity and impressive technical skills. Patrons were aghast when one of his fights turned into a brawl with another fighter, and both men tumbled out of the ring—because Jimmy wouldn't let go. He simply kept fighting, kept swinging. It was as if he were seized by something otherworldly.

On July 7, 1944, Doyle beat Nick Moran in Los Angeles. Then he and his manager got the invitation they'd been waiting for: Jimmy Doyle got booked for a series of fights on the East Coast. And he dazzled.

On November 30 he beat Sammy Daniels in a ten-round fight in Baltimore. For his first fight at Madison Square Garden on January 12—by now some were calling him Irish Jimmy, by now he had amassed six East Coast victories and many followers—Doyle was matched against Frankie Terry. More than twelve thousand fans packed into the Garden that night, among them former mayor

Jimmy Walker. Walker—so beautifully turned out in suit and jewelry that he fairly glowed—was beloved by fight fans for restoring legalized boxing to the city. He waved around to his fellow New Yorkers, then enjoyed the bout. In the next day's *New York Times,* James Dawson, the *Times's* estimable boxing writer, gave Doyle plenty of credit for a fight that resembled a kind of clinic, with Terry, Doyle's opponent, on the losing end. "A right to the body in the fourth round staggered Terry," Dawson wrote, "and in the fifth a left hook opened a cut over Terry's right eye and he fought the rest of the battle blinded somewhat." Terry outweighed Doyle by eight pounds. Dawson added: "Doyle was too good a boxer, too smart a ring general, for Terry to make even the faintest impression."

A little less than three weeks later Doyle tossed off his robe inside the Broadway Arena in Brooklyn and beat Pittsburgh native Johnny Jones. *The New York Times* described Jones as "rugged." It mattered little to Doyle. "Jimmy Doyle last night chalked up his eighth straight victory since he came to this section of the country five months ago," the morning-after *Times* account noted.

In December, in a much-publicized fight, Doyle found himself in Cleveland in a scheduled ten-rounder against Lew Jenkins, a former lightweight champion. Jenkins's career had been bewildering: He was a gifted fighter—whose first wife, Katie, often took a stool inside the ring between rounds, dispensing advice to him while in frilly attire and pretty hat—but he could never pull himself away from the bottle. He was known to step into the ring inebriated. He joined the Navy during World War II, and, once out, convinced himself he could regain his boxing title.

One of the few writers enamored of the Los Angeles fight game was Budd Schulberg. Schulberg's father, B. P. Schulberg, was a much-admired Paramount studio executive. His son, Budd, educated at Dartmouth, liked to write poems and short stories and hang out in fight gyms. (Budd's novel *What Makes Sammy Run?* created a sensation with its portrait of Hollywood insiders and won acclaim in the literary season of 1941.) The young novelist, who would go on to write gritty screenplays, saw Jimmy Doyle in Los Angeles early in the fighter's career. "He was a good little fighter," remembers Schulberg. "A big gamer. He took a punch. He usually won on points. He wasn't going to knock you out. He was not easy to beat."

It was two years earlier when Robinson and Doyle first began appearing in the same newspaper stories. In 1945, the Boxing Writers Association released their yearly rankings. Freddie "Red" Cochrane was the reigning welterweight champion. The number-one contender in that class was voted to be Sugar Ray Robinson, followed by Marty Servo. There was a tie for the number-three contender: Tippy Larkin, and Jimmy Doyle.

On the eve of their Cleveland fight, both Robinson and Doyle were quiet. "We hope to put Doyle away inside of six rounds," pronounced Gainford. "That, we think, would be much the smartest thing to do."

Tommy Dorsey and his brother Jimmy were in downtown Cleveland that week with their big band, playing their sweet syncopated music. Their "Marie" and "Boogie Woogie" were big hits. It was summertime indeed in Cleveland: Over at B. B. Baker, one of the finer stores in the city—located right down the street from the Arena—snappy Panama hats were going for $10. The swells who lived out in Shaker Heights were already plotting weekend getaways to their nearby summer cottages.

When Clevelanders awoke on the morning of June 21, they awoke to front-page headline news about the California murder of gangster Bugsy Siegel. Siegel had been sitting at home, reading the newspaper, when the bullets slammed into his skull. (A photographer wielding a Speed Graphic got a gruesome photo: Bugsy, in a light-colored suit, slumped back on the sofa, his face covered in blood, his right eye still open, as if he were looking at something across the room. The glass ashtray on the end table was sparkly clean.) Authorities quickly concluded it was a professional hit: Bugsy was said to have angered mob insiders because of cost overruns in the Flamingo hotel, whose construction he had overseen in the Nevada desert.

Meanwhile, Larry Atkins was predicting a full Arena—and it would prove to be so. Just prior to the fight, he let it be known that should young Jimmy Doyle win, there was already a contract drawn up for a rematch to take place in—where else?—Cleveland, on July 22. Fight promoters thought it was quite a savvy move on the part of Atkins.

Those who were backing Irish Jimmy Doyle had already imagined in their minds how he could win: "They insist the Californian will be the champion if he survives eight rounds," wrote Dawson of *The New York Times.*

The local writers, however, were a little more wary, a little more circumspect.

A ghost hovered at the door of the the Robinson-Doyle matchup, a ghost by the name of Artie Levine.

Levine, a Brooklynite and former Marine, was a vicious puncher who had fought Robinson here in Cleveland on November 6, 1946—six weeks before Robinson won the welterweight crown by defeating Tommy Bell. Levine landed a punch in the fourth round of that bout—bringing Larry Atkins, who had promoted the fight, and so many others, up out of their seats—that floored Robinson. The confused Robinson struggled up off the mat from a nine-count knockdown, eventually pulled himself together, and went on to knock out Levine at the end of the tenth round. He'd never forget Levine, though, and would often comment upon the impact of his punches. Earlier that year—March 1946—Levine had been here in Cleveland matched against Jimmy Doyle. At 160 pounds, Levine approached the middleweight limit, but the welterweight Doyle was indeed a gamer, unbothered by the weight disadvantage. Doyle fought that night without his trainer Tony Palazola in his corner; Palazola was gravely ill in a hospital back in New York. Doyle was matching the hard-hitting Levine punch for punch, thrilling the Cleveland fans. Judges had Doyle leading on points well into the fight, but then Levine "rallied from way behind"—as one sportswriter put it—to land a flurry of dangerous punches to Doyle's head, knocking him unconscious. Doyle suffered a concussion in the bout and had to be carried from the ring on a stretcher. There were examinations and consultations. Doyle was young and doctors saw no need to risk further injury. The doctors suggested he quit fighting, owing to the indeterminate severity of the concussion.

After that fight, and all the post-fight sentiments expressed, a sullen Jimmy Doyle retreated to his Los Angeles home. He didn't fight for nine months. He grew itchy, couldn't stand the idleness, told family members he missed the ring. So he started a comeback— though Los Angeles boxing commissioners were too nervous to allow him to fight there. He hit the road, amassing several victories before his arrival in Cleveland to face Robinson. Franklin Lewis, the respected boxing writer for *The Cleveland Press,* spoke to Doyle a week before the bout. "You see, Levine had hit me all through the fight. Look at this face now. It's been hit." Young Doyle possessed wit—and also a seeming need to prove himself again: "I fought against the fear I might be punch-shy," he said of the bouts that preceded the Robinson match.

It was as if Cleveland—and Artie Levine—was Doyle's Waterloo, as it had nearly been Robinson's.

Word seeped from his camp that Doyle would be showing a keen interest in the area around Robinson's eyes, which the Robinson foe Abrams had injured in their last fight. A fighter with warped vision is a fighter in trouble and one who enters the ring with a telltale weakness. "All's we gotta say is that it's the big shot—the shot Jimmy has been aiming at so long, and we're gonna give it everything we've got," offered Doyle's manager, Paul Doyle, on the eve of the fight. "And we've got a right to think that'll be just about enough to do the trick."

So, with the ghost of Levine by the door then, the lights twinkled on inside the Cleveland Arena.

Promoter Larry Atkins was clearly overjoyed with the cachet of hosting a championship bout. Along with more than eleven thousand other paying customers—Teddy Horne, Lena's father, among them—he made his way to his front-row seat. A great many others, including the Stokes brothers, Carl and Louis, would listen on the radio. There was a sentimental factor mixed in with the excitement: Robinson was the reigning world champ and thus the beneficiary of instant respect, but both fighters had fought in and around Cleveland several times before and they both received generous and enthusiastic applause as they were introduced. Jack Davis would be the evening's referee.

Then came the ringing of the bell that set Sugar Ray Robinson and Jimmy Doyle in motion, toward each other.

It was astonishing—there were gasps from the crowd—to see the quickness and sharpness of the punches Robinson threw. It took just a nanosecond of an opening and he was inside Jimmy Doyle's arms, delivering punch after punch. He'd step back, like a man admiring the cut of another man's suit, then step forward, right back into Doyle. Doyle had always been adept at knocking away punches, but these punches were coming too fast. Some of the Cleveland writers—leaning, scribbling—wondered when the Robinson knockout punch would come. Doyle had other thoughts, namely to survive round to round. He threw a litany of punches in the third round, and some of the onlookers howled that he had won the round. "A solid right cross to the head brought some respect from Ray in the third round," noted a *Cleveland Call & Post* writer. Doyle had gotten off nice punches in that round, but they were not without consequences for him: A wicked Robinson punch in the fourth closed Doyle's left eye.

Then, in the fifth round, Robinson landed seven unanswered punches. Doyle suddenly began to show signs of exhaustion. His legs were heavy, far less springy than at the fight's beginning. The reporters and the promoters and the fans wanted a fight, a long fight, something for their money. Robinson's manager, Gainford, wanted his fighter to put the scrappy Irishman away. But Robinson couldn't. He would later express wonder at the punches Doyle withstood. Jimmy could take a punch. He always could. He took punches from fighters who laughed at him in the early rounds of fights, only to find himself staring them down with his arms raised in victory. Some of the pre-fight reporting talked about how Jimmy Doyle was a slow starter, how he always required rounds to get himself angling toward peak performance. To get the adrenaline really going it seemed as if Jimmy Doyle had to be convinced he was truly in a big-time fight. In the sixth round, it came—a rock-solid Doyle punch, landing right where he wished it to land, above Sugar Ray's eye. It stunned the fighter for a moment. The blow drew blood. But as quick as Doyle tried to follow through, Robinson tied him up, with referee Davis leaning into both. Nevertheless, Doyle had fought a cagey round, which Davis would later contend he had won. The men in Doyle's corner were on their feet. Their thinking was, the longer Doyle remained in the fight, the better his chances of pulling it out. And there he was, in the seventh round, standing toe to toe with the world champion, taking hit after hit, and drawing more blood from Robinson's cut. "Man," Robinson would later sigh, "I threw everything at him but my brassie [a golf club] and he still wouldn't go down." It was as if Jimmy Doyle meant to prove to the crack Negro boxer from Harlem that he wasn't anybody's quitter.

In the middle of the seventh, however, Robinson let loose with a barrage of fierce punches.

When the bout was already under way, a telegram arrived at the main ticket window. It was for the Doyle camp. It came from a group of Doyle's California friends: GOOD LUCK, JIMMY.

Jimmy Doyle, who had tasted the sweat and spittle of Jim Jeffries, and of Jack Johnson, those two giants who had seen enough in him to tutor him, to inspire, had confided in relatives before coming back East that he wished to continue fighting long enough to help his family—he mentioned his mother specifically and purchasing her a house—and then maybe he'd find something else to do. He was a reader of books; he knew there lay a world outside of boxing. And yet, he was a dreamer. Some days he'd wake up and all he wanted to do was box, to be a world champ.

Some black fighters out in LA sang his name inside those gyms in sort of a singsong, hipster manner: Jimmaay; Jimmaay Doyle. He loved it, the way it sounded, the way it cut the air, sailing on the respect he had earned.

It was in the eighth round that Robinson saw his opening. Doyle had left his chin unprotected. The punch came before it came; it was just that quick. It landed in the dead center of Doyle's chin. A bite of a sandwich, a long gulp of a drink, and you might well have missed it. "The left hook that lifted Doyle off his feet, crossed his eyes and turned his face gray," wrote Bill Corum in the *Los Angeles Herald Express,* "must have been as clean and perfect a knockout blow as was ever landed. The writer can only say [what] must have been, for, truthfully, he didn't see it. The round was drawing to an end and I had turned my head to pick up a piece of paper on which were scribbled some notes when that ripping left cut Jimmy down." There was no need for a follow-up punch—Jimmy Doyle was already falling. His left leg remained straight, but there was a bend in his right leg. He instinctively reached his right hand out to catch himself on the ropes. A tuft of air rose inside his dark trunks as he was going down and it gave him the appearance of a man floating backward. Cameras flashed; lights blinked across faces at ringside;

bifocals caught the illumination of light and flash. And as Jimmy Doyle was falling backward, into unconsciousness, Sugar Ray's eyes were locked on his, with the kind of intensity someone has as they watch the hapless traveler tipping over the side of the ocean liner, into oblivion.

He thumped onto the canvas, his head taking a hard bounce. His manager, the aging Paul Doyle, looked, swiveled around, lowered himself as he peered into the ring. He moved about in a small space like a hyperactive gnome, yelling for his fighter to rise. But he couldn't. There were wheezing movements from Doyle as the count began. Referee Jack Davis—sensing something amiss—motioned for Doyle's manager to come into the ring and get his fighter; Gainford leapt to his feet and protested, demanding the call for a knockout. Finally Davis went and held Robinson's hand aloft. Doyle's cornermen were now in the ring, because their fighter was not moving. They lifted him up but he was puppetlike; it was like trying to lift a sleeping person from a bed. Robinson's cornermen, now sensing something wrong as well, quickly entered the ring to see if they could help. There was angst in the seats, rising up and into the farthest back rows, where the humming volume of the tense worry began to stretch. It must have reminded many of the Doyle and Artie Levine fight, the one in which Doyle had been knocked unconscious. It all seemed a spooky bit of déjà vu. In the ring a dozen men—two doctors among them—now stood over Doyle. More kept coming through the ropes. Boxing commissioners rose from their seats and made their way to ringside. Photographers checked the film in their Speed Graphics. They moved about to get better angles inside the ring. Five minutes turned to ten, which turned to fifteen, and Doyle remained quiet and unmoving.

The cursory examination in the ring told the doctors that Doyle needed medical attention. An ambulance was racing out to the Arena from St. Vincent Charity Hospital. When the ambulance arrived, the attendants rushed the stretcher right into the ring—onlookers stepping aside, hands cupped over mouths—and lifted Doyle gently onto it. They lifted the stretcher up slowly. His right arm—his punching arm—dangled to the side until someone raised it.

Manny Berardinelli, who would later serve as cornerman for his brother, Joey Maxim—a gifted Cleveland fighter destined in time to have his own classic confrontation with Robinson—was in the crowd that night. "I never seen anybody leave on a stretcher except for that night," he would recall.

Gainford and Robinson watched Doyle being taken away through the darkened arena. Then Gainford got his fighter to his dressing room. Robinson needed a bit of medical attention himself. Doyle had opened that nasty cut over his eye. In his dressing room, Robinson asked after his challenger; Gainford told him he'd find out as soon as he could. Cornermen rushed back out into the arena, trying to glean any news. "I didn't think I hit him so hard with that left hook," Robinson said, while being bandaged. "I threw a lot harder punches, and ones he didn't catch with his gloves."

Jimmy Doyle lay silent in the back of the ambulance. Its siren blaring, it had to cut across the city, past Chester and Prospect and Carnegie avenues. Upon reaching the hospital at Twenty-second Street—they arrived in under seven minutes—doors swung open. It was against the glow of moonlight and with low-pitched voices that staffers rushed Jimmy Doyle inside.

Doctors must work quickly when there is a serious head injury. It took Dr. William Miller, the chief of surgery at Charity Hospital, no time at all to order brain specialist Spencer Braden—revered as one of the best in the country, let alone Ohio—summoned from nearby Chagrin Falls to look at Doyle. Doyle had a blood clot on his brain. There would have to be surgery right away to release the pressure caused by the clot.

It didn't take long for word to spread from the hospital about the severity of Doyle's injury. His manager was on the phone to California with Doyle's family, trying to reassure them. Robinson and Gainford left the Arena and made their way to the hospital. Larry Atkins was already there. Public officials were demanding updates on the fighter's condition; there were those already asking Atkins if Doyle—given his concussion from the Levine fight—should even have been allowed to fight. The questions and insinuation pained Atkins. He said he wouldn't talk, not now, glancing around the hospital. But he did say that he certainly didn't suspect "anything serious" wrong with Doyle leading up to the fight.

The surgical procedure began at three a.m. Doctors made incisions on both sides of Doyle's skull. Peering inside, Dr. Braden did not like what he saw; there was "extensive damage" to the fighter's brain. Braden conferred with other medical experts on the premises; X-rays were pored over. Things looked grim. Time—measured in minutes—would tell the tale. At one point Doyle's breathing stopped; then it was revived. But as minutes passed into half-hour increments, there seemed to be no overall improvement in his condition. The prognosis looked to be worsening. Medical staff, conferring with the Doyle camp, began thinking of summoning the hospital chaplain to his room.

Doyle's family phoned from California again, seeking another update.

"I'm sure sorry," Robinson murmured as the night deepened. "I didn't have any idea he was seriously hurt when I left the ring."

Doctors and nurses kept a vigil around Doyle, moving him in and out of an oxygen tent to aid his breathing.

Johnny Katcich, a Doyle friend who had come all the way from Los Angeles to watch the fight, was crestfallen: "He told me after the Levine fight that 'If I don't go back to Cleveland and fight in the same ring again I'm not a man' and he meant it."

The morning after the fight, Jimmy Doyle was on the front pages of American newspapers—right up there with accounts of the mysterious murder of Bugsy Siegel on the other side of the country, in Jimmy Doyle's hometown.

By noon of the following day, his breathing grew weaker, then quite faint. Rev. James W. Nagel, the chaplain, arrived to read the fighter his last rites. A few hours later, Jimmy Doyle was pronounced dead. He had lived seventeen hours after being taken from the ring.

Law enforcement authorities told Robinson and Gainford they could not leave the city. They informed Gainford that his fighter would likely be charged with involuntary manslaughter. It was a formality, they intoned. But the news rattled both Robinson and Gainford: In most cases the charge of involuntary manslaughter carries a penalty of between three and ten years in prison.

Within hours, County Coroner Samuel Gerber was vowing a wide investigation. And with things now spinning at a rapid clip—both wire service reporters and local reporters were demanding answers to their questions about Doyle's medical history—Gerber went on to make dark hints aimed directly at the city's criminal and civic nexus. There had been "unholy pressure" upon him, he said, to forgo an investigation. (Apparently these individuals did their angling while Doyle lay dying.) He would not name the perpetrators, but the pronouncement cast sudden suspicion upon practically everyone connected to the fight. Gerber said he had told the individuals who had come to him that "no power whatsoever will prevent me going through with it."

Meanwhile, a moratorium was declared on all upcoming bouts in Cleveland until the completion of Gerber's probe. That unnerved town fathers—and Larry Atkins—because fighting in Cleveland was big business.

Doyle's death marked the first time in modern boxing history that a fighter had died in a world championship bout. It was also the first professional ring death of 1947—although three nonprofessional fighters had died as a result of ring injuries.

Robinson and Gainford made a trip to the morgue to view Doyle. Hours earlier he had been bouncing on his feet, swinging punches. Now this—his curly-haired head against a white sheet. They left the morgue in silence.

Just before beginning his inquest, Gerber gave the public a more detailed description of the "unholy pressure" he had cryptically referred to. "Why not consider this an accidental death?" he said someone had whispered to him. "Why have an investigation? Why not just try to live down this unhappy incident as quickly as possible?" Rather than lower the volume on an already-brewing controversy, Gerber, according to *The Cleveland Press,* ratcheted up the suspense. It only made reporters hungrier, and they turned on Gerber and demanded to know the name of the person who had made the request. "I will not identify him," Gerber shot back, "but I will tell you this much: It was nobody connected with Ray Robinson."

Gerber, a severe-looking but dapper man who wore his hair neatly parted on the right, then got his probe under way by summoning witnesses to his office inside the county morgue. His secretary adjusted the office furniture so that witnesses would be seated directly across from Gerber as they began to unspool their memories about the events that took place on the night of June 24. Each witness had to take a sworn oath that they were telling the truth.

One of Gerber's first witnesses was Edward Delaney, Jimmy

Doyle's brother, who had arrived in town a day after the fight. Gerber wanted to know about Jimmy's condition in Los Angeles in the weeks following his fight with Artie Levine, when he had been hurt. Delaney—thin, rubbing his eyes—said his brother seemed changed following the fight with Levine fifteen months earlier. He seemed sullen; he was no longer shadowboxing and "sparring around" the family house, Delaney said, breaking into tears. Instead, he said his brother sat reading, staring off into space. He didn't even like to go dancing anymore, one of his favorite pastimes. The implication was that Jimmy had suffered an injury that had not healed and that had obviously altered his personality. Paul Doyle, Jimmy's manager— old and gray-haired, and now looking even more so—seemed somewhat confused by the proceedings. He recited Jimmy's prior fights leading up to the Robinson engagement and said Doyle had acquitted himself nicely in those fights, all of them victories. Paul Doyle could only vow that his fighter was in "tip-top" shape when he had entered the ring against Robinson.

For public consumption—and certainly with an eye toward future promotions—Larry Atkins issued a statement to the Cleveland media. In it he said Doyle seemed physically fit and ready to fight upon completion of the medical examinations that he had to take once he arrived in Cleveland. Atkins's statement—issued on behalf of himself and fellow promoter Bob Brickman—included the revelation that New York officials had already deemed Doyle fit to fight there in anticipation of future engagements in that city.

If Sugar Ray Robinson and George Gainford had waltzed into Cleveland with the scent of boxing royalty about them—the champ and his manager taking up the first title defense of their crown— within minutes of Gerber's grilling they looked otherwise. With their slack and unsmiling faces, and Gerber's relentless questioning, and a stenographer nearby recording their every word, they looked like two Negroes caught on the wrong side of the law in a sometimes lawless metropolis. Edna Mae had tried her best the night before to console Robinson, but she also had the unmistakable look of worry as she reminded her husband that the fight game was a dangerous business. (Gerber, as if in a concession to the distraught Robinson, excused him from having to testify under oath; not so Gainford.)

Gerber minced no words, however, with either man, and he expected succinct answers.

"Did you personally rank Doyle as a worthy opponent?" Gerber asked Robinson.

Robinson, dressed in light-colored pants, dark shirt, and a pair of sandals, alternately rubbed his forehead and chin. He looked exhausted during the round of nighttime questioning.

"Well," Robinson offered, "Doyle had a very impressive record up until the time he lost the fight with Artie Levine. He had not been beaten for about two years."

Gerber continued: "Isn't it a fact that you considered yourself personally a much better fighter and strictly outclassed Doyle in the last nine months?"

"It is a fact that the champion in each class is supposed to be the best," Robinson answered, fidgeting.

"Did you notice during the fight that Doyle's right eye kept dropping?" asked Gerber.

Robinson: "I was too busy fighting to notice."

Gerber soon switched to Gainford. He asked Gainford if he had noticed anything strange or disconcerting about Doyle's appearance before the fight.

"I'm not a physician, sir," Gainford answered. "I have no connection with Doyle, only Ray Robinson."

The social mores of the period did not augur well for sharp-tongued replies on the part of two out-of-town Negroes, no matter what their sports pedigree. Gerber proved as much when he announced that both Robinson and Gainford were being "smart" and even "evasive" with him. The manner in which he was steering the inquest forced some to conclude Gerber was being unfair and accusatory toward both Robinson and Gainford. The press weighed in. An editorial titled "Manslaughter in the Ring" appeared in the *Chicago Daily Tribune.* In it, Robinson found an ally. "If there are any manslaughter charges lodged they should be made against the men who permitted Doyle to go into the ring and not the man who struck the fatal blow," the editorial opined. "Robinson did what he was supposed to do, which was to knock out his opponent."

The Cleveland Press also targeted authorities in an editorial titled "Did the Doctors Know?" "The rugged business of fisticuffs is a little out of this page's province. But it is of general editorial concern that prizefights are supervised and regulated in the public interest. Medical examiners and boxing commissions are supposed to protect the ring participants against both mayhem and suicide. In these protective chores for the Robinson-Doyle match, it looks as though the Cleveland authorities failed somewhere."

On the final day of hearings—after Gerber had summoned promoter Larry Atkins, referee Jack Davis, Arthur P. Hagedorn, the boxing commission's physician, and Andrew G. Putka, who chaired the city's ring board—several boxing officials let it be known they felt Gerber had cast aspersions upon them and their professionalism.

Gerber said he would issue his findings as soon as possible.

Mayor Burke, who was fighting an election battle against Eliot Ness (Burke would handily win), urged that the report be released promptly.

Gerber worked fast, issuing his findings on June 30. Local and national publications eagerly reported on them. Of crucial interest was the fate of Robinson. The coroner cleared the fighter of all possible charges resulting from the death, calling Robinson "absolutely blameless" and stating that he "was unfortunate in being the opposing contestant at the time of Doyle's fatal injuries." Gerber also went on to absolve all Cleveland parties connected to the contest; he stated that the city's boxing commission "should not be considered negligent in having allowed Doyle to fight."

The results of the Gerber probe ushered in some changes within the Cleveland boxing scene. From now on any fighter, like Doyle, who had suffered a serious head injury in a previous fight would not be allowed to fight in Cleveland. A fighter's medical records would now be more strenuously examined. (Taking a cue, many other states would adopt these guidelines as well.)

Robinson wished to do something for the family of Jimmy Doyle. He quickly announced he would hold benefit fights in the very near future, with most of the proceeds going to Doyle's family.

If Jimmy Doyle, unmarried, had a girlfriend, no one knew, no girl came forward. If there was someone he might have written love letters to while on the road, glorying in his pain and talking about the beauty of being a fighter who was keenly respected and nationally ranked, no one knew.

Those who had fought against Jimmy Doyle, and the managers and promoters who knew him, began replaying his career in the newsreels of their minds. He had seemed to bring something into the ring with him. It was more than skill, or a hard punch. He charged and charged at his opponents. It would have taken more than golf clubs—as Robinson knew—to beat him back. Some of Doyle's childhood friends who had traveled cross-country, sadly to watch him die in Cleveland, kept mentioning how much moxie he possessed. There was that, but there was also something else: Jimmy Doyle had a sweet rage about him.

When the press referred to him as Irish Jimmy Doyle, it must have pleased him, for he was quite proud of his heritage. There is a line from the poem, "The Balloon of the Mind," written by the Irish poet Yeats: "Hands, do what you're bid."

Bigger and better fighters had long snickered at Doyle. But he had surprisingly found a way to whip them. He looked, too, like he had been in fights, in lots of fights. He was as unhandsome as Sugar Ray was handsome. Except when he was raising his hand in the ring, sweat dripping, nothing but his bag of books and magazines waiting for him back in the hotel room. Then Jimmy Doyle was quite beautiful.

His body was taken back to California, where he was buried, in the soft soil.

Fight managers spend countless hours trying to decipher a fighter's psyche. The practice can be as fruitful as reading the cosmos. "I don't know how it will affect Ray's fighting in the future," Gainford said before departing Cleveland. "He's just like anyone else and is bound to have some reaction. How it will manifest itself . . . Time will tell."

Sugar Ray Robinson was six months into his world championship now. The welterweight division was such an unpredictable one before his ascendancy; there had been long stretches where the title had been vacant. Sometimes gifted contenders came out of nowhere. He had beaten Tommy Bell for the crown—but Jimmy Doyle had also beaten Bell in a non-title match. It was not that the fighters were interchangeable, just that the division was yet to be solidly claimed by anyone. Which is what Robinson wished to do. He wanted to own the division, to stake his claim to it, just the way his onetime Army buddy Joe Louis had controlled the heavyweight division.

Of those two much-talked-about killings in the country that week—Bugsy Siegel and Doyle—both had been nighttime appointments. One was done in the serene moments of a man's plain domestic life—reading the evening newspaper. There were bullets and shattering glass and the whispering flaps of the newspaper falling to the ground. No one saw a thing. The other killing had taken time—the way unforgettable cinema takes time—melting into the senses, as smoke does into cloth. It had been done in front of thousands. The victim lay dying against the silent end credits and the hushing sound that swept through the Cleveland Arena. Cinema vérité. And standing over the fallen man, a feral and ferocious figure. In Cleveland, doing his job.

Robinson had never been a boisterous fighter. If only he could have helped Jimmy Doyle up, the way he used to help those Golden Gloves boys up off the canvas in Chicago and New York City after he had battered them.

He was at the dawn of his full potential now, imagining ways to invent a whole new kind of prizefighter. He would jump weight divisions. It was scary—for it would take the will of a Houdini to jump weight divisions and still win. He knew he would have to be as methodical as a scientist.

Gerber, the coroner, had asked him: "Well, did you notice that Doyle was in trouble at any time?"

And he had answered: "Getting him in trouble is my business as a boxer and a champion."

He came through on his promise to Doyle's family, staging several bouts in the weeks ahead on behalf of Jimmy, and giving part of the gate receipts to Doyle's mother. Gainford was unhinged by it all, believing his fighter might be needlessly hurt—fighting out of guilt and sentiment—by someone trying to make a name for themselves. Gainford needn't have worried. Sammy Secreet and Flashy Sebastian were both knocked out in the first round. Enough money was raised through the bouts to set up a trust fund for Doyle's mother. The last fund-raising fight was staged right in Los Angeles, inside the Olympic Auditorium, the place where young Jimmy had first gotten noticed, had first heard the roar of people shouting his name.

Sugar Ray Robinson had long seen death and dying—it had been a constant in his Harlem. There were gangland slayings, and wife-husband domestic horrors. There was the killing of numbers runners, their bodies laid out on the pavement for all to see. The downtown publications—*The New York Times* and the *New York Herald Tribune*—might not have covered those killings all the time, but the two Harlem papers, the *Amsterdam News* and the *New York Age,* certainly did. They wrote the stories up with tabloid fanfare. There were killings by poison, killings by butcher knife. At times it seemed like the Harlem metropolis where Sugar Ray Robinson had spent some of his formative years was a breeding ground for death. In the years to come, Jimmy Doyle's death would be looked upon as a witchy footnote, and even though Robinson would remark now and then that he had dreamed of it in the months prior to the bout in 1947, it sounded too pat, too made-up. None of the articles written leading up to the fight mentioned a bad dream. They did mention the eye injury from sparring at Greenwood Lake. Sugar Ray was smart enough to realize that dreams could not be qualified or verified. His actions in the aftermath had been noble. Jimmy Doyle's mom would always have food on the table. Gainford indeed continued to worry now and then, as any manager would under the circumstances. There were tales of fighters and ring deaths before Robinson, and, sadly, there would be more afterward. Four years later another fighter, Roger Donoghue, was responsible for the blows that killed George Flores in a bout that took place at Madison Square Garden. The death haunted Donoghue. He soon quit boxing, was seen shadowboxing inside Manhattan bars, mumbling to himself, joking, a man in pain. "You killed a man," a kid once piped up to him. "I'm going to tell everybody." And Donoghue had replied: "You don't have to tell everybody. They already know." Donoghue would find work, though: He'd befriended writer Budd Schulberg, who wrote the screenplay for Elia Kazan's 1954 movie *On the Waterfront* and got Donoghue work training Marlon Brando for his role as failed boxer and union hero Terry Malloy. No one ever taunted Sugar Ray. And soon, George Gainford's worries fell away.

Some sportswriters, Bill Corum among them, had started to fret in Cleveland that perhaps Robinson had peaked. That maybe they had seen the best he could do. Before coming to Cleveland, Robinson had become engaged in a war with Jake LaMotta, having already fought him five times, losing once. But they would glance back over their shoulders in the months and years ahead and realize that great and wondrous battles lay beyond Cleveland. Everything was mere prelude in the world of Sugar Ray.

By the time Sugar Ray Robinson left Cleveland, his poise had begun to return. Edna Mae had wrapped her lovely arms around him. George Gainford was calling him champ, champ, champ. The summer wind was in his face.

Up, up, and away then, over the Highland Park golf course where he'd swiped at balls; over the Cleveland Arena where he had fought a foe who had come into the ring with a fire given to him by those legendary heavyweights Jim Jeffries and Jack Johnson; away from the shadow of death; into the future where he believed he had beautiful worlds—boxing, fashion, dancing, boxing again, worlds that were often at odds with one another—to conquer.

In the years beyond his ring life, when the fame had mostly fallen away, when Sugar Ray had settled into his sixth decade on earth, living in sunny Los Angeles with Millie, his wife, the love of his life (who had replaced Edna Mae); in those seasons and years when his hands had gone slack, he was given to shoving his fight films into an old Super 8 and showing them to houseguests. He'd sit in a chair, neatly dressed of course, and his shoulders would roll a little as the figures clashed on the screen. The smile was serene and his eyes would widen as he pointed out little things—the fighters, the difficulties they presented, the arenas and cities—to his guests. The names of the opponents—Carmen Basilio, Jake LaMotta, Randy Turpin, Kid Gavilan, Bobo Olson, Gene Fullmer—would come off his lips in that whispery and hoarse voice of his. (All those fighters, just like him, cursing the air some mornings, trying to dodge ailments that seemed to search for them and haunt them long into the night, complaining about mattresses being either too soft or too hard. So many fighters with so little to do now. The memorabilia craze, which would have corralled them to moneymaking signings, had not yet taken off.) But Sugar Ray refused to have a copy of the Doyle fight in the house. Why would anyone wish to have a film of a death they had been so close to causing? Why would anyone wish to have a ghost flitting around their house? In all those days and weeks in the aftermath of the fight, he had told Gainford that he was fine, that the death was not bothering him, that George should just keep his mind on the future bouts, on securing the next paycheck.

But there he sat, all those years later, dodging Jimmy Doyle, who had grown up just miles from the house in LA where the TV now flickered in front of champ Sugar's face. Dodging Jimmy Doyle—as if such a war of the conscience could be won.

It was one of Sugar Ray's realities that he was in perhaps the most savage of all sports and that sometimes it repelled him. Not long after the Doyle fight he would begin saying to acquaintances that he could walk away from the sport anytime; that sometimes it bored him; that he controlled it and wouldn't let it control him; that he realized the claws of time were upon his back. But the fight business provided income and glory, which he welcomed. So he was forced to unleash his savagery—as if it were beyond his control, like an eagle ascending through air after prey—and when awful damage had been done, he would attempt to salve his conscience with dignified actions: walking across the ring to lift the shoulders of his fallen Golden Gloves opponents; helping Doyle's family realize Jimmy's dream of purchasing a house for his mom. Fight fans would watch him in the aftermath of Doyle, and on those occasions when he held a punch, when he motioned to the referee to intervene during a clutch—on behalf of the opponent he was whipping badly—they would be obliged to wonder: Was Sugar Ray pulling back? Would caution be displayed—Gainford's deepest fear—when it should not be? Those who watched him had no way of knowing. But he did suddenly become a philanthropist—not huge sums, but in the 1940s and 1950s small sums could help a family stave off disaster. He started to visit poor schoolchildren and orphanages, dispensing gifts. He would battle with one hand and give with the other. It was the manner in which he forced himself to understand the brutality that he unleashed in life.

Their episodic war stretched nine years. They fought across World War II and into the Korean War—and through three presidential administrations. Their sagas shared newspaper space with Roosevelt's steeliness, Truman's resolve, and Eisenhower's steadfastness. A mélange of life's characters came together around their battles—gangsters, bookies, whores, hotel doormen, pimps, Pullman porters, gents from the Old Country (Italy), restaurant workers, newspapermen, prison inmates, old pugilists, gents from uptown (Harlem). "I fought like I didn't deserve to live," Jake LaMotta once said, as if ascribing demons to his very existence. Sugar Ray Robinson professed to have no demons, although his paranoia rested in a dark place. Without the song of patriotism floating over either—as in Joe Louis against Max Schmeling—people were left to crawl toward their baser instincts: "On the streets, it was the 'nigger' versus the Italian," remembers Robert Royal, a Sugar Ray acquaintance. A feverish ethnic pride broiled inside many. LaMotta knew there were those who called him a wop, though never to his face.

Years before, in Italy, men like LaMotta's father, who had nothing, were marked as being from the proletariat class. From high above, Robinson vs. LaMotta seemed a collision of cultures—the artist and the proletarian; the proletarian fighting like someone pushing mightily to the other side. But the artist had convinced himself he was fighting for the ages. The archetypal enmities of each gave their half dozen clashes a grave and haunting timelessness.

1942–1951

an opera in six brutal acts

BEFORE ALL THOSE BEAUTIFUL PEOPLE started to gather around Sugar Ray and before his name was etched in neon up in Harlem, before he'd killed a foe, before he even held that precious first title, the biggest and hardest war of his professional life had begun.

It was a ring rivalry that held the nation in rapt attention, the kind that could not have been designed or plotted in hotel suites or the back rooms of boxing clubs. There had been

The Robinson-LaMotta feud lasted more than a decade, becoming one of the greatest rivalries of all time. In the wake of the savage opera lay scandal, beautiful women, heartbreak, and plenty of blood.

other rivalries of similar weight and fascination. Before he fought Joe Louis, Max Schmeling had German history behind him: the leader of the Third Reich sending him to America to conquer the boxing world. History between fighters could also ignite passionate interest. Rocky Graziano and Tony Zale, two hearty and rather robotic pugilists, first clashed in 1946. Zale won in a sixth-round knockout. The following year, in Chicago, Zale was at it again, punishing Graziano so badly into the third round that Graziano partisans feared the bout would be called. Blood was gushing. But Graziano thundered back, lifting fans from their seats, and by the sixth it was over. Graziano emerged the surprising victor. Immediately, there were cries for a rematch. A rivalry had taken root. It was the kind of moment that kept the bookies cheerful. The third bout was announced, but it wasn't to be. A story broke in the press that Graziano had served prison time, and had even been given an additional prison sentence while in the military for striking an officer. This led to more probing, which revealed that he'd failed to report an attempted ring bribe in a timely manner. Officials held closed-door meetings, and Graziano lost his license to fight in New York City. But much of the public, especially the working man in the shadows—coal miner, factory worker, construction worker, ditchdigger—sympathized with Rocky. The sentiment echoed around a feeling that Rocky was a stand-up guy; that he had gotten a terrible rap; that he was a tough sort because one had to be tough to survive in the world. And soon enough he was being talked about in glowing terms—a onetime dead-end kid who had created his own damn luck in a crazy world; a guy who maybe didn't have class, in the traditional sense of the word, but who had guts, and his guts had gotten him to where he could look anyone on Park Avenue in the eye and stand tall on his own pride. A poor man bent out of his pride could understand such a thing. He lost the third fight against Zale, but his legion of fans grew. A deeper kind of glory awaited him outside the ring. Ordinary men rushed up to him, simply wishing to touch him. He'd become a workingman's good luck charm, a hero. He called his autobiography *Somebody Up There Likes Me.*

It was on February 5, 1943, that the Sugar Ray Robinson–Jake LaMotta rivalry genuinely took hold. Their first bout, four months earlier in New York, had been won by Robinson. It showcased dueling portraits and starkly different styles, hinting at an allure, teasing the public's appetite. But it was in Detroit that those portraits exploded, that tough automotive and steel city that truly told of things to come—of the blood and the fury.

In New York circles, Jake LaMotta was known as "the Bronx Bull." "A fight," the Bull expressed, "is all of a piece, you get moving in a certain rhythm, you can't stop, it's all got to go along. It's true that you have to stop at the end of every round, but once you've started you have to keep going, you don't stop till you get to the end." He thought every fight might be the end. If not for him, then, he hoped, for his opponent.

He was the child of immigrants. They came on big hulking liners across the Atlantic, getting seasick, dreaming, becoming hungry, praying. Between 1900 and 1910, 2,045,000 Italian immigrants entered the United States. That was triple the number of the previous decade. Even before they shuffled down the gangplanks of those ships—staring wide-eyed amidst the clatter and chatter of Ellis Island—there already existed the foundation of the social and political turmoil that would test their resolve. It took little time for the accusations to emerge, and they came from many corners. Never mind the intelligentsia, the scholars and tradesmen and seamstresses among them. It was another social element that took hold. An 1884 letter to the editor in *The New York Times* read, in part: "The Italians who come to this country with a hereditary respect for brigandage, and find that the men who are most talked of here are the Jesse Jameses of the West and the Jay Goulds of the East, naturally think that there is a fine field in America for genuine Italian brigandage. The wonder is that they have ever thought of engaging in any other industry." There were countless other letters printed of similar opinion.

In 1890, a lynching took place in New Orleans that cut crushingly deep into the Italian immigrant sense of insecurity in a foreign land. David C. Hennessy, the New Orleans police chief, was murdered right in front of his home. Hennessy had been conducting an investigation of crime wars in the city that pointed to members of the Mafia. As he lay dying, Hennessy is reported to have uttered the identity of his killers: "the dagoes." Arrests were swift. One arrested man was shot as he peered through the jailhouse doors. The others—

all men of Italian lineage—were pulled outside by a screeching and cursing lynch mob. Their bodies swung in the open and charged air. There was outrage among Italians across America. A group holding a rally in Troy, New York, to protest the lynchings was pelted with rocks; gunshots were fired at the gathering, but miraculously no one was hit.

Italy's fascism kept the immigrant tide flowing toward America's shores. Not surprisingly, in 1901 the Society for the Protection of Italian Immigrants was formed.

Then came the convulsive drama that would echo for years to come.

In 1920, Bartolomeo Vanzetti and Nicola Sacco, a fish peddler and shoemaker—in addition to being anarchists who had drawn the attention of federal agents—had been arrested and accused of being involved in the holdup and murder of a payroll guard and paymaster in South Braintree, Massachusetts. The men were, without a doubt, of a criminal mind; the FBI had accumulated files on them and some of their acquaintances. But what sent spasms of outrage through the immigrant community as the murder trial got under way was that the evidence was so circumstantial. The judge, Webster Thayer, appeared blatantly biased in favor of the prosecution, verbally taunting both defendants within earshot of court observers. Both men proclaimed their innocence. There were rallies on their behalf. Each received the death sentence.

It was the law then—and it continued to raise ire—that the same judge who sentenced the men could also hear their appeals. Judge Thayer seemed to relish the opportunity, and his second ruling only rubber-stamped his first. There were letters written to high-placed politicians as the drama of their innocence or guilt spilled across newspaper pages for years. The poet Edna St. Vincent Millay wrote an impassioned letter to Gov. Alvan T. Fuller on the eve of their scheduled date to die: "I cry to you with a million voices: answer our doubt. Exert the clemency which your high office affords. There is need in Massachusetts of a great man tonight. It is not yet too late for you to be that man." The governor felt otherwise.

Sacco and Vanzetti were each led into the death chamber just before midnight on August 23, 1927. Their deaths ignited protests throughout Italy, but also in London, Paris, Geneva, and Johannesburg. Millay wrote a poem about them called "Justice Denied in Massachusetts." Woody Guthrie sang a ballad.

It was hardly as weighty as the discrimination meted out against blacks, but the Italian immigrant was caught in a prism of political and social upheaval that unfairly multiplied their sins and belittled their contributions.

In New York City, a great many of the Italian immigrants settled on the Lower East Side, as Joe LaMotta did when he arrived. He hailed from Messina, a region in southern Italy. Northern Italians looked upon their part of the country as cultured and were condescending toward their brothers to the south. LaMotta and his wife and children, struggling in Manhattan, moved to Philadelphia not long after World War I. He sold fruits and vegetables from a horse-drawn cart. He became bitter and took his anger out on his wife by hitting her across the face. One of his children, Jake, was constantly bullied at school. He cried to his father, upon which he received two things: a vicious slap—and an ice pick to defend himself. He wielded it with abandon: "It was the first time I can remember really having someone afraid of me," he would recall. "I can still remember that feeling of power flood through me. An icepick in my hand—and I was boss!" His enemies, in time, would scatter.

Back in Manhattan, Jake's father entered him in back-room fist-fights when he was eight years old: two kids going at it in an open space for the amusement of gathered men. Money was thrown at the feet of the winner. Joe LaMotta pocketed most of his son's earnings, and the son hated him for it. In time, Jake began stealing—small things, candy, radios. He quit school. He raised the stakes of his stealing when he assaulted men in alleys—sometimes with a lead pipe to the skull—and fled with the money he'd found on them. He ran unrepentant through the naked city like a little demon. He saw his father hit his mother, time and time again, rattling the furniture, frightening the children. Young Jake LaMotta's whole childhood seemed stitched together by violence.

When the authorities caught up to the teenager he was sent to the State Reform School at Coxsackie. The sentence was one to three years. His father uttered unkind things about him, while his mother fretted with worry.

At Coxsackie, his rough Bronx-boy demeanor only hardened. Jake sassed guards. He kept to himself, a moody and distant figure, as stony as the brick around him. He ran into Rocky Graziano, an old neighborhood acquaintance also doing time. Graziano told LaMotta to walk a straight line so his time would pass quicker; LaMotta said he had no intention of doing that, and Graziano dismissed him as "nuts." Jake walked up to colored inmates—the races banded together for security—and told them flat out they should steer clear of him. They did. His escape plot was stolen from a Grade-B movie: He was caught trying to flee in the back of a truck. The truck never made it beyond the reformatory walls. The warden—who thought him a "goddam [*sic*] moron"—sent him straight to the hole, which was below ground, a blanket of darkness. On sleepless nights he balled his thick fists and hurled foul words at the walls.

The prison chaplain interceded and got him out of the hole in two weeks, then suggested he get into the prison boxing program, which he did.

For the most part, he trained himself, a grueling exercise of sparring and jumping rope, lasting until he nearly collapsed. His ring style was aggressive and relentless, crouched low and stepping forward.

No one understood why LaMotta wanted to take on the prison champ, a huge and feared fighter within those walls, but he insisted on the chance. He trained for months, while guards snickered that he'd take a merciless beating. On fight night the gym was crowded: the warden and the guards with their sallow complexions, and even the prison chaplain. LaMotta refused the glove-touching ritual, his enmity against the champ—who had laughed watching him in the ring months earlier—heightening by the second. They gasped when the champ took a barrage of blows to the head and guts, finally crumpling at LaMotta's feet. The air grew hot and heady; those in their seats began to stir like penguins as they tried to replay and chatter about the vicious knockout they had just seen. LaMotta stalked around the ring, looking out over those gathered. He had no friends, save for the chaplain, and he didn't care.

He gathered up his meager belongings on the day of his release. He had little to say to anyone. He saw the chaplain, and of course the warden, who gave him a quick lecture about going straight.

Then Jake LaMotta—sprung from the stone walls where the Bull had been born—walked out the front door to his freedom.

Back home in the Bronx, LaMotta, determined to become a professional boxer, got himself entered in some unsanctioned bouts that were held in warehouses—down-and-dirty affairs with beer and loudmouthed men. (Some of the warehouses fronted as porn movie theatres when they weren't hosting these ad hoc boxing events.) The scene of desperately poor people and their sporting fetish—"home relief and boxing," as LaMotta put it—depressed him. He finally got himself over to the Teasdale Athletic Club. There he was surrounded by trainers and other fighters hoping to enter the pro ranks—an environment that offered a hint of organization and success.

His straight-ahead style attracted some attention and encouragement. He entered the Diamond Belt fights, local charity events that featured up-and-coming fighters, and got some press attention because people got dressed up—women in diamonds!—in evening attire to attend. The headlines—LA MOTTA WINS FOURTH STRAIGHT; LA MOTTA WINS IN SIZZLING FIGHT WITH ZEKE BROWN; LA MOTTA WINS DIAMOND BELT LIGHT-HEAVYWEIGHT TITLE IN FINALS—left LaMotta reeling with joy.

His Bronx pals told him he was ready to turn pro—and then pointed in the direction of the Mob, which held a powerful sway over boxing and could speed the prospects of a promising fighter. LaMotta didn't want anything to do with the Mob; he didn't trust them. So he went his own way.

On March 3, 1941, Jake LaMotta fought his first professional bout, a four-round victory held in New York. (It took place five months after Sugar Ray Robinson had fought his first pro bout in the city, so they were breathing the same air, carrying the same dreams.) LaMotta had grinned on his way to the dressing room following that initial victory—though in the ring there had been something akin to an animal's fury in his eyes. He fought often in Detroit and Cleveland in those early years, the better to escape the clutches of the New York Mob. He eyed Negro fighters with great and fevered curiosity: "Many of those colored six-round fighters would have chased some high-priced top notchers right out of the ring. A lot of them would have to fight with handcuffs on just to get a pay night here and there." He held no pity, however, regarding the uneven social and political dynamic faced by any colored pugilist: "You would just about have to kill them before they'd give up. Well, I had something going for me, too, on that score—I was just as hungry as they were. In those days there wasn't anybody I wouldn't get in the ring with. Not only did I fight the colored bombers, but I took on guys in any weight class."

In time, fight followers became convinced LaMotta was another version of Harry Greb, the native Pittsburgher who fought from 1913 to 1926. Greb—known as "the Pittsburgh Windmill"—had a fearless and cocky straight-ahead style. Greatness was predicted for him early in his career. It was amazing how often he fought: In a thirteen-year career Greb battled 299 times. It was quite a feat— and quite maddening. He appeared to be a man only at peace between the ropes. Greb's battles against Gene Tunney—one loss, one win, two no-decisions—were legendary and blood-spattering affairs that left both fighters looking like reddened zombies. Between those Tunney battles, Greb had dropped down to mid-dleweight, and he took that crown in 1923. The most remarkable evidence of Greb's toughness, however, is that he fought for years half-blind: His retina became detached in a 1921 bout against Kid Norfolk. Like a man on a wartime battlefield, all he needed to keep going was consciousness. Four weeks after the eye accident he was fighting again. In 1926 Greb was in an automobile accident. Sur-geons aimed to repair some of his facial injuries from the years of boxing while attending to his injuries from the accident. But Greb never came out of surgery. Even if he was past his prime, his death stunned many. He was thirty-two years old.

In 1942 Sugar Ray Robinson was becoming agitated regarding future championship possibilities. He was like the welcoming wel-terweight host, only no one of stature wished to come to his party. The belt's titleholder was avoiding him. The delicacies he offered— sudden headlines if he should be defeated, a bigger purse in an expected rematch—were not enough for potential challengers and their camps. Back in the summer of 1941, in Philadelphia, he had fought the lightweight champion, Sammy Angott and beaten him. But that was a non-title fight. So in 1942, he stood across from weak foes in the ring. Who was Maxie Berger? Or Harvey Dubs? Who were Dick Banner and Reuben Shank? Mere victims of his in merci-less engagements he took while pining for better foes.

He began trolling for challengers out of his weight division.

Sugar Ray Robinson, who had spent part of his youth around the Bronx and knew the environs well, had heard of the hard-puncher from up there and—always with an eye toward the marquee matchup—he began pondering a LaMotta match. The upside thrilled him: It would mean being ushered into the middleweight ranks against one of that division's most talked-about fighters. The downside—a loss that might darken his unblemished record—was something he simply chalked up as the inevitable danger of any fighter without a loss. When he instructed George Gainford to approach the LaMotta camp, Gainford's nerves went haywire. La-Motta outweighed Robinson by nearly fifteen pounds. The number of those pounds could fluctuate now and then, but that hardly lessened Gainford's concerns. LaMotta could flat-out hit and hit hard. Gainford lived on Robinson's fists, and he knew well that many a fighter had been prematurely pushed into another weight division, a march that sometimes led them right to their breaking point. Robinson—whose self-confidence was a thing of unbending resolve, even beauty—also declared that he had no intention of bulking up. Gainford heaved a sigh, then began making inquiries on behalf of his impatient fighter.

Aside from Gainford, there were more than a few who looked upon a potential Robinson-LaMotta matchup with worry. According to Dan Burley of the *Amsterdam News,* there had been "a lot of shaking of the head going on" regarding the potential clash. Burley wondered if the lighter Robinson would be able to avoid the muscle of LaMotta, and noted, "Robinson has an alarming tendency to get in close with rough, tough, bear-like individuals when there is no need to do so, mainly because Sugar likes to prove to himself and to the fans that it makes no difference to him whether he's punching at a distance or mauling in the close-ups." Burley sensed trouble for Robinson if he allowed himself "to be sucked in" by LaMotta, which would leave him at the mercy of LaMotta's "blind swings."

Both Sugar Ray Robinson and Jake LaMotta were fighters who directed the course of their careers over and beyond the will of their managers. "Sugar Ray was the boss," LaMotta would say decades later. "Whatever Sugar Ray said, went. Just like me. We fought anybody. No one could tell us who to fight and who not to fight. It was really like Sugar Ray didn't have a manager. He was his own manager."

"Sugar Ray took on LaMotta because there was no one else in the welterweight division," the trainer Angelo Dundee said.

The fight was announced for October 2 in Manhattan.

And immediately, from barstool to tenement stoop, from sandwich shop to radio station, from political-club back rooms to fight gyms everywhere, the clack of chatter began. About LaMotta's strength, and Robinson's guile. Prognosticators rehearsed and debated memories of each fighter's previous fights: old Italian men on the city's East Side and down in Greenwich Village, conjuring a LaMotta victory into their passionate minds; smooth uptown figures in long coats—fall had arrived, the air was crisp enough for tweed or wool—believing in Sugar the same way they had believed in Louis. The fighter's styles, obvious to many, were a fire-and-rain contrast. "A fighter who performs in the windmill style of Harry Greb or Jackie Kid Berg, LaMotta keeps charging forward at all times and throws punches incessantly," one New York publication noted, with an obvious tinge of worry. "It is a style that Robinson doesn't relish, and that has always given Sugar Ray his most uncomfortable evenings in the ring." The *Chicago Defender* made mention of Robinson's thirty-five-bout winning streak: "A surprisingly large number of boxing experts expect it to end at that figure."

Two New York boys from distinctly different worlds setting off on their odyssey, preparing to taunt the social, political, and cultural realities that jumped in the air around them. The Harlem Dandy and the Bronx Bull.

On that lower frequency where some minions of the boxing universe lingered, there was another way of expressing it: the nigger and the wop.

Unlike Robinson, LaMotta wasn't a student of boxing history; but he knew enough to familiarize himself with a welterweight's mind-set. He actually harbored a suspicion about welterweights. "The welterweights, you know, are tricky and fast, so you learn to duck and weave so that when you get into your own weight class you're not a sitting duck." The newspapers printed thousands of words about the upcoming bout. Hype Igoe of the *New York Journal-American* believed LaMotta would pull out a victory. *The New York Times* conceded that Robinson was "favored" but allowed that LaMotta could pose problems because he was a "hard puncher."

More than twelve thousand showed at Madison Square Garden for the ten-round bout. Leaves blew through the streets of Manhattan as George Gainford taped his fighter's delicate hands. There was much chatter among the throng indoors about the thirteen-pound weight advantage LaMotta had over Robinson. Joey LaMotta—a sometime fighter himself—tended to his brother Jake in their dressing room along with manager, Mike Capriano.

Robinson's loose gait and relaxed appearance were a contrast to LaMotta, who seemed coiled.

Robinson surprised LaMotta in the first round by engaging in close battle with him, trading short stinging jabs, immediately communicating that he would give no ground regarding his foe's strength. LaMotta's corner would catch moments when a blow from their fighter—if delivered now!—would inflict damage, only to see that Robinson's head—peekaboo—had vanished to one side just as quickly. In rounds two and three, Robinson had stepped back effectively, peppering LaMotta with jabs that seemed like tentacles reaching out for blood. The Bronxites in attendance urged their fighter to inch in closer to Robinson, but Robinson always slipped away. Gainford instructed his fighter to forget about a knockout, worrying that the kind of hitting it would require might damage Robinson's hands, which were prone to swelling. It was in the fourth that Robinson—as if on a fast carousel—connected with a torrent of blows: "a flood of nerve-jarring right and left hooks, jabs and bolo wallops to the head and kidneys, wild, roundhouse swings to the head," in the words of an *Amsterdam News* man. The onslaught cut a gash above LaMotta's left eye. The *Times* writer Joseph Nichols sensed Robinson's evolving strategy of quick hits: "The Harlem fighter worked along these same long-range lines through the seventh and often staggered his heavier rival with well-placed rights to the jaw."

This was a different type of "colored" fighter than LaMotta had ever faced. The judges agreed, giving Robinson the victory in a unanimous decision, extending his undefeated streak. Clusters of blacks erupted with joy over Robinson's win, a reaction that had the effect of taunting every soul from the Bronx. The *Times* referred to LaMotta as yet another "victim" of the wily Robinson. To Dan Burley's mind, Robinson had slid around LaMotta "with the grace and artistry of a ballet dancer," confounding the Bronx challenger all night long.

There were grins inside Robinson's dressing room amid the flicker of camera bulbs. Gainford took the spotlight. "There's a lot of things Ray can do that the experts don't know about," he said, sounding as if his fighter possessed the trickiness of Houdini, as if the best was yet to come. Sugar Ray rested his hands in ice water and listened, still such a surprising portrait of welterweight wispiness despite the evening's just-completed battle with a heavier foe.

"Beating middleweights is among them," Gainford went on, explaining Robinson. "Look at him: There's not a scratch on him. He's been like that right along. That's why he can fight every week or every other night if he wants to." The reporters were scribbling it all down. "He knows how to keep out of the way and at the same time, mess up the other fellow," Gainford said.

Robinson, however, admitted that LaMotta's blows had been delivered with menacing power. "He hit me one left hook a little high on my head and I saw stars," he said. "He hurt me a couple of times. I have never met a fighter strong as he is."

LaMotta cursed long into his Bronx night, telling his brother and cornermen he could have beat Robinson; that Robinson was just quicker than he had imagined.

But what promoters listened to and heard was the amount of fascination with the fight, the aftermath in which there was a pouring forth of raves about the tussle. Robinson won, but the punches flew and flew and neither man hit the canvas. And for a wartime audience known to spend conservatively on leisure activities, the $29,434 gate receipt was nothing to snicker at.

When approached, both fighters quickly agreed to a rematch. Robinson's motive was easy to understand: Now that he had climbed into the company of middleweights, he wished to remain there. It was the financial end that appealed to LaMotta. He had been fighting and scuffling for bigger paydays. Robinson's name on a boxing marquee ensured big crowds; big crowds meant larger purses and more money for him. LaMotta had received more publicity surrounding the Robinson fight than ever before, even if some of it rankled him. There were reporters who had written profiles of him, and inside those profiles—scanning the words and sentences— he felt they were trying to make him out to be "a poor ignorant Italian." (He hated that many of the stories mentioned that he ate a lot of macaroni, intimating his was a poor man's diet.)

It was the simmering anger of the proletariat.

There was a natural belief the rematch would be held in New York. Then Boston promoters made a grab for it. But Nick Londes, a hard-hustling Detroit matchmaker, also made appealing offers to both camps to come to the Motor City. He offered the Olympia, which was a fine and celebrated venue; he promised a large crowd. Robinson, having won the first fight, had the upper hand when it came to picking out the location. He agreed to Detroit, and some of the reasons were certainly sentimental: It was his hometown; old friends who had seen the childlike hunger in his eyes when he was a little boy still resided there. LaMotta had no reservations about Detroit. It was a lunch-pail town, an underdog metropolis. In fact, the colored population of Detroit had become well acquainted with Jake LaMotta. He had already whipped two tough fighters there—Jimmy Edgar and Charley Hayes—leaving those who had witnessed his victories awestruck.

Sugar Ray Robinson arrived in Detroit a week before the fight. A deeper maturity—he was all of twenty-one years old—had seemed forced upon him in recent months, and there had been changes in his life. Bolstered by his enterprising belief in himself he had formed Ray Robinson Incorporated, and the move had quickly swelled his payroll: Now, in addition to Gainford, he was traveling with Bill Miller, an adviser; Clyde Brewer, an additional trainer; and Al Linton, a secretary. Evelyn, his stunningly beautiful sister, was along as well: "I'm his good luck charm and travel to all his fights," she offered shortly after his arrival in the city. His stature in boxing circles had also risen. For his achievements throughout 1942, Robinson—just weeks before arriving in Detroit—was named "fighter of the year" by *Ring* magazine. (His victory over middleweight LaMotta had been an obvious exclamation point.) The praise from *Ring* magazine was not an honor that could be downplayed, since Robinson had dethroned Detroit's own Joe Louis, winner of the designation for the preceding four years. There was warmth and an assuredness in Robinson's smile now. He seemed joyful that his sister was at his side to bask in his glory and, at times, tend to his slights—both real and imagined.

The Olympia stadium was already selling standing-room-only tickets, owing to the interest in the bout and its two combatants. Worrying about news of heavy betting on the fight, boxing commissioners announced that they would not name the boxing officials until the night of the fight.

Seen around the city in the days before the bout, Robinson and his group had the loose and jovial comportment of a jazz ensemble. Their long winter coats flapped in the breeze. Pedestrians eyed them with curiosity and gave them space. The surroundings elicited memories, and Robinson talked about his childhood with his companions, pointing out street corners and girls he had wooed and lost, stores where he had bought candy bars, porches where he had jitterbugged with a child's unharnessed energy. "Not much space for . . . worthwhile roadwork between school and home was there?" he remarked to his entourage as they all looked around, standing in front of the Balch Elementary School, which he attended, and his home, which was right across the street. Among them all, there was sweet, comfortable laughter in honor of that child then—and the man now. "There's where you learned tap dancing, eh Ray," one of his walking companions said, pointing to the school. Moving around town, he talked about the fancy stores his family never could afford to shop inside, about the bright theatre marquees he ogled; he pointed out play areas and alleyways. He bear-hugged old acquaintances, then quickly pointed to his sister Evelyn—her fashionable attire drew many admiring comments—as if to prove that the Robinson family beauty had not only held up but improved with time. (Few could deny that both siblings had a magazine-pictorial attractiveness.) He saw shoeshine men and janitors, scavengers and hoboes, city sweepers and garbage workers—the very type of occupations that might have claimed him had he not gotten away, fighting before he was a fighter to make all his dreams come true. His memory was lit yet again while standing on Ferry Street: "Oh, oh, I wonder how that gal of mine is getting along. Let's see . . . Mmmm . . . Mmmm . . . She was pretty too. That's it, Lorraine." He scanned nearby faces awaiting smart-alecky retorts. "I was only ten then," he said. Delighted to be back in Detroit, he found himself in a comfort zone. He made time to go bowling, young ladies squealing at the sight of him as he shone beneath the bowling alley's fluorescent lighting. He was able to hear some fine music in the city. There were hours when he vanished completely from Gainford's sight; his New York aides who had accompanied him to the city imagined he was availing himself of opportunities for quick romantic adventures.

On one of his outings—an inevitable trek—Robinson and his group went over to the Brewster Recreation Center. It was bound to touch his senses, for it was a showcase of Negro pride and accomplishment in the city. And it was where, as a youth, he had spent so much time, where he first met Joe Louis, where he had stared at other fighters with awe, where he first slipped on a pair of boxing gloves. There was much laughter and joy at his appearance, voices rising and hands reaching out to touch him. His gray fedora sat back on his head as he and Leon Wheeler, the center's director, caught up and talked about old times. He brightened at the sight of Delmar Williams, one of his earliest mentors who was still working there. The familiarity of everything overwhelmed the young Sugar Ray. He couldn't resist a light ring workout for the gathering. He threw some easy punches and offered a peek at his fast footwork. Delmar Williams nodded and told those near enough to hear that he had first spotted this wondrous talent back in 1932. Ray broke a sweat in the ring; his sister's eyes stayed glued to him, ready to caution against too much exertion. "I used to carry Joe Louis's gloves and bags into this room here," Robinson said, pointing. While heads swiveled, he stepped from the ring. Williams, the old mentor, had seen enough of his former pupil: "Yep," he said jazzily, "there's gonna be a jam session at Olympia Friday—and that LaMotta boy is in the jam."

Jake LaMotta and his traveling crew set up sparring sessions at the Motor City Gym. The Italians in the city were overjoyed at his presence. He shook hands with the locals and swapped a few Bronx stories. To relax he played pool with some pros passing through town. He had a habit of keeping his laughter to a minimum, a persona he had created but one that fit naturally with his rather severe disposition.

There was talk on the street and throughout the city about advantages and disadvantages each fighter would bring into the ring. Robinson's height and rangy reach over LaMotta were believed to be hugely in the fighter's favor—as was apparent during the first meeting. But LaMotta scoffed at such theories. "People pay too much attention to the physical advantages of prize fighters," he said. "They seem to think that if a fellow has longer arms than an opponent he will beat that opponent. That's the bunk. If the men who bet on fights used those things as a basis for their calculations regarding the winner of a fight they would all be broke." Nevertheless, LaMotta's manager had employed the Youngstown fighter

Tommy Bell, tall and long-limbed like Robinson, to spar with La-Motta and, in effect, to mimic the dangerous and elusive Robinson himself. (At this time Bell was three years away from his own destined date with Robinson.) It was LaMotta's belief that surprise in the ring must be accounted for: "Often one good punch will decide a fight and knock all calculations into the water bucket."

Street-corner chatter and theories ricocheted around the Robinson camp as well, one being that LaMotta had trimmed his weight for the first fight and it had sucked some of his power away. It was a mistake, the naysayers believed, that he wouldn't make again. Gainford snickered, and when he addressed the issue, it was with an easy bravado. "When Ray defeated Jake in New York the people said he did so only because he made LaMotta come in at 157 pounds. They contended that Jake was weak at that weight. Well, Jake claims to be a legitimate middleweight. So we are taking him at the middleweight limit here. When we beat him he will not have any excuses," he proclaimed. One afternoon Gainford spotted a member of LaMotta's camp at one of Robinson's workouts—spying!—and after demanding the intruder leave, he complained to promoter Nick Londes, who promised it would not happen again. Denizens of fight camps were hardly above trying for an edge by angling for nuggets of information from the opposition.

At the weigh-in LaMotta was sixteen pounds heavier than Robinson. "It's His Big Night," the *Detroit Free Press* said in a caption beneath a photo of LaMotta on fight's eve. In the picture LaMotta, in silk boxing shorts, is crouched and looks quite brooding against the 1940s film-noir shadow of newsprint.

In the hours leading up to the fight, Canadians crossed the border into the United States and Michigan; Ohioans crossed the state line. When the sun dropped and the skies darkened over the Olympia, all reserved tickets had been sold. A couple of hours before the ten p.m. starting time, however, promoters announced that tickets for "the gallery gods" would go on sale. The gallery gods were the stragglers, the poorer souls, the ones who'd brave standing around in the cold. The gallery gods had scrounged up coins that very day, itching for their moment to scoot over to the Olympia.

Up high, the gallery gods were in heaven, seated among the more than 18,930 in attendance—the largest crowd ever for a Michigan

bout—and clutching their $1.20 lowest-priced ticket as a keepsake.

Both fighters received loud applause during the introductions, but Robinson's was thunderous: The hometown boy, his sister, and the Brewster Recreation Center gang up close—every moment of it unleashed such emotion and revelry.

The vicious LaMotta right sends Robinson tumbling through the ropes in front of his hometown crowd in Detroit in 1943. The victory convinced LaMotta he was the better fighter. Robinson believed otherwise. And thus the stage was set for all future battles.

From the outset LaMotta rushed Robinson—"Jake stomped me with his first left hook," Robinson would recall—leaning on him with his weight and firing punches. "The crowd let out a roar of expectancy as the men came out of their corners fighting in the first round," noted the *Detroit Free Press,* "and it roared from then until the finish." Robinson matched LaMotta with punches, but it was obvious that LaMotta's were having the more desired effect. By the third round LaMotta's strategy was clear: He was going to go after Robinson's body, not his head. He was going to wear him down. He was going to use his extra weight to full advantage. The punches kept plowing into Robinson's stomach and kidney area. Now and then LaMotta would take aim at Robinson's head—but he'd hear that whistle as if it were the only sound landing in his ears—and he'd immediately aim his punches low again, into the stomach and kidneys. Robinson grimaced. LaMotta banged at Robinson's head again, and again there came a piercing whistle from ringside, which no one paid attention to—not with the photographers and radio announcers and everyone else elbowing and jostling. LaMotta had trained to hear that whistling shriek because it came from a member of his corner who whistled hard every time LaMotta began focusing too much on Robinson's head. It was the cue to get back to pounding the body, which LaMotta did. And the more the Bull pounded Robinson's body, the more he became convinced he could win. Gainford pressed his hands into the rope at ringside, urging his fighter to stay away from LaMotta; but LaMotta kept barreling into him. Then, in the eighth round, a LaMotta strike landed so viciously, so hard, it sent Robinson backward, bent over, reaching for his groin, and flying through the ropes all in one motion; LaMotta's body language hinted he just might charge out of the ring after his opponent. Robinson's sister Evelyn gasped. It was as if he had been lifted and thrown by the force of a hurricane. Photographers angled their cameras and the flashes popped. There was Sugar Ray: frozen for that millisecond, bent like candy-store licorice. LaMotta wanted more of Robinson. But Robinson rose slowly, into the referee's count. Before the eyes of men and women whose front porches he had tossed newspapers onto as a kid; before women who were once girls he whistled at. There were church folk and funeral-home workers in the audience whom he knew by name. He had posed in the days leading up to the bout with old acquaintances, grinning like a handsome star of Negro cinema. And now this: their Detroit-born fighter on his butt, his face contorted and eyes honey-glazed like those of a suffering animal. The Bull had stormed into Sugar Ray's china shop with a vengeance. They screamed for him to get up; the old gadflies from the Brewster Recreation Center, old friends of Joe Louis's, all pointed and extended their arms, raising the sweaty cry for Robinson to rise. The gallery gods up high screamed, they screamed because this was what was so exciting about boxing; anything could happen and through their squinting eyes they were seeing it all, the telltale moment that would put them right in the middle of the soliloquies to come about what had transpired down there; that made them even with the rich man who was sitting down front, because they were there this night as well.

LaMotta kept heaving during the count. And then that little shift began, the shift where the borderline sentimentalists become converts, angling with emotion toward the better fighter. And Jake LaMotta, having already whipped one Joe Louis protégé in Jimmy Edgar, seemed to be angling for another one now. In the racially haunted universe of boxing, LaMotta knew that many white fighters were wary of the Negro boxers, fearing that two losses in a row to a Negro would doom them and imagining that their manager might get interested in the Negro and forget about them. LaMotta had pondered such thinking and kicked it to the ground: He looked for Negro fighters, went after them like some Great White Hunter stalking about the Midwest and the Eastern seaboard. Now here was Robinson, a 3-to-1 favorite, flying through the ring. Who was the poor ignorant Italian now? LaMotta stood there, breathing hard above Sugar Ray, his thick neck and thick shoulders turning to the crowd. This was their Sugar Ray, their boy, whom he had knocked from the ring, shamed in the glare of the Speed Graphic bulbs. LaMotta simply hated Robinson's silkiness, that way he floated about the city—be it Manhattan or Detroit—as if the air had been scented for him to walk through; as if he owned things not yet his—such as a championship belt! Robinson got up in time, got to his corner, only to be scolded and hissed at by Gainford, who took him to task about his gallivanting around Detroit before the bout. Robinson appeared bewildered, still taking in the sting of LaMotta's fists. Two rounds later it was all over. His winning streak—amateur and pro included—of 130 rounds had come to an end. In his hometown. Stunned faces stared into the ring; noise swooped backward all the way up to the gallery gods.

The newspapers over the next two days—reporters and columnists from Detroit to New York and elsewhere—would point to LaMotta's weight advantage as having been crucial. "When Jacob LaMotta brought the Sugar Man down with a body punch in the eighth round after bombarding his midsection at every opportunity in each of the seven preceding rounds," said Charlie Ward of the *Detroit Free Press,* "the ears of the fight wise went up like the ears of so many startled rabbits in a midnight pasture." It was no mystery to LaMotta why he'd won: "When I met Ray in the Garden last fall

I had to scale down to 157 pounds. That took something out of me and I didn't have enough steam at the finish."

Heavier now, he grabbed at his moment of glory. The *Detroit Free Press* headlined proclaimed: JAKE IS CITY'S CINDERELLA. Before the teletype machines had finished clacking off the reporters' wired-in dispatches that night; before the photographers had developed their final fight pictures (they knew the editors would want that one showing Robinson flying from the ring!); before the Canadians had ventured back across the border, and the Ohioans slipped back into Ohio; before the gallery gods had made it back to their apartments and rooming houses and dropped off to sleep from exhaustion and excitement, there had been whispers of a rematch, snaking in and out of the fighters' dressing rooms, Gainford nodding, vowing revenge. Robinson was Robinson—his pride foretold of a destined rematch.

"I still think I can defeat LaMotta and I hope I get another chance at him," Robinson said, his voice heavier than usual.

A rivalry's prerequisite—the nation's attention—was now a certainty. The *New York Times* headline pointedly said: END OF ROBINSON STRING SHOCKS RING WORLD.

Two weeks later the promoter Londes raced off to Greenwood Lake, Robinson's training camp. The phone calls had come to an end; now it was time for the formality of signing the contracts for the third bout. It was cold and stark when Londes reached Greenwood Lake. Robinson felt he needed the disciplining climate following the debacle in Detroit and was now pushing himself very hard in training. Contracts signed, Londes took off.

But LaMotta, as the victor, now had the pick of location. The city of Detroit had grown on him. He liked the hard and cold feel of the place, and Detroiters had taken to him too. Dale Stafford, the *Detroit Free Press* columnist, agreed that LaMotta "had given Detroit a brand of fighting which has appealed to the public and resulted in this great revival of professional boxing." Stafford added: "Of course the city has been good to him, too, and it is doubtful that he could have gotten either the money or opportunity elsewhere that he has been accorded here."

While Robinson had received 35 percent of the gate receipts, LaMotta got 25 percent in Detroit. For LaMotta, that figure came to $39,399. "That's the biggest check Jake ever got," his manager said, beaming.

LaMotta wanted—and got—a return to Detroit.

Promoter Londes had left Robinson in the cold of Greenwood Lake. The fight date would be February 26, only twenty-one days after their earlier bout. The emotionally wounded young fighter ran and climbed the hills; he ran through the bright light and he ran into the spreading sunset. His welterweight-to-middleweight dream suddenly lay in doubt. He brooded about the defeat he had suffered in front of so many friends and family. And now, with the contracts signed, pushing himself along the pathways—Act One and Two over, Act Three looming—it was impossible for him to ignore how high the stakes were. This fighter, this Bull, had knocked him from the ring. No one—auto magnate, factory worker, shoeshine man, or gallery god—would forget it.

After LaMotta beat him, Robinson defeated Jackie Wilson at Madison Square Garden. LaMotta was at ringside during the match—snorting, blinking, turning as fans patted him on his broad shoulders, his Bronx allies sitting close by, glorying in his growing stature.

LaMotta arrived in Detroit three days before the fight. He took workouts—unsmiling—again at the Motor City Gym. Robinson, who had refused to stipulate any weight limits on LaMotta, lest anyone think he needed an advantage, arrived the next day. Gainford kept a tighter rein on his young fighter's movements; coming into the city just forty-eight hours before would lessen opportunity for carousing. Because of the war there had been air-siren practice runs in the city—as well as in many cities across the nation—and the metropolis could seem somber one day (air raid!) and dizzy with excitement the next if a big-time fight was looming. Robinson obliged his fan base and invited them to a brief workout at the Brewster Recreation Center once again. His partisans—gathered, on their feet, staring up at him in the ring with the concentration of bird-watchers—commented among themselves that he seemed in wonderful shape. But there was concern that had trailed him from Manhattan, and it seeped into the minds of local boxing officials. It was believed that Robinson had injured his delicate hands in the Jackie Wilson fight. N. H. Schiafer, a physician who worked for the State Athletic Board of Control, would have to examine the fighter's hands before giving the final go-ahead on the bout. Schiafer put

Robinson's hands through several exercises. Robinson grinned as onlookers stared with worry. "This boxer is in unusually good condition," Schiafer finally said. Robinson's blood pressure after a workout had been 110 over 70. "That is very good," the doctor said, as if to reassure anyone who imagined their own blood pressure had risen during the proceedings. (In the next day's edition of the *Detroit Free Press,* there appeared a photograph of Robinson's fists—no face or body, just the elegant fists—balled and resting on a table. Darkly hued hands; the thumbnails looked freshly manicured. The photo caption said: "Sugar Ray's Dynamite Knobs As They Appeared Wednesday After Getting Examination Okay." The caption continued: "Now he can turn 'em loose against Jake in return bout at the Olympia Friday night."

Only once before—in 1930 for a welterweight title bout—had the Olympia fight promoters raised tickets all the way to $10. There was grumbling on the street, but the tickets sold at a feverish clip. (The gallery gods need not worry; their $1.20-priced ticket went unchanged.) For this bout each fighter would receive 30 percent of net receipts, a figure that told of LaMotta's new equality against Robinson.

Strategies evolved. "Ray is a boxer of the old English school," Gainford ventured to explain. "Just plain speed and clean cut boxing—that's his specialty. Naturally he wants a lot of room for his style and the ropes hamper him. Yep, we gotta stay away from the corner and ropes." Robinson's sentiments echoed his manager's: "He'll have a tough time flagging me out there in the open," he said of LaMotta.

Maybe it was the air raid sirens, or the rationings that were in evidence, but Jake LaMotta—who sprang from a childhood that left him believing all manner of enemies conspired against him—paid particular attention to the military alertness of Detroit. The wartime reports on the radio, the sirens, the photographs of Detroit boys who were away at war in the local newspaper—all of it toyed with his mind. LaMotta didn't serve in World War II because of an ear problem, but in Detroit, on the eve of his third match with Robinson, it began to rankle that Robinson was getting such good, patriotic-themed press. He wondered to himself if the Army-inducted Robinson might garner sympathy from the judges on fight night. The more his camp told him he was imagining things, the more convinced he became he was right. The Bull believed what the Bull believed.

LaMotta couldn't escape the rags-to-riches story line that trailed him now. Two years earlier he had been treated to nearly worthless fight-night paychecks. His manager, Mike Capriano, reminisced with local reporters about his fighter's financial odyssey: "For a long time," he said, "Jake was a $25 fighter. That's what he got for his first pro start and that's what he got when he fought Johnny Morris, Stanley Goicz, [Lorne] McCarthy and others at White Plains, N.Y.; when he fought Monroe Crewe, a heavyweight, at Ridgewood Grove; when he met Johnny Cihlar at the Broadway Arena and Morris in a rematch at the New York Coliseum. We thought we'd struck it rich one night in the Queensboro A.C. when we pulled down 85 bucks for a fight with Joe Baynes. We never made as much as 100 bucks until we came West for the first time."

LaMotta sat beside Capriano during his recitation, looking bored. The here and now was the here and now.

ACT THREE "I didn't lose it, he got the decision."

From the opening bell Robinson hewed closely to instructions given him by his corner and Gainford: Steer clear of the ropes and sting LaMotta with punches when close enough. LaMotta's strategy was to attack, and he kept coming, making it difficult for Robinson to escape. But Robinson surprised LaMotta by holding on to him. It was as if a big disoriented penguin—one side black, the other white, which was actually close to what the gallery gods themselves were seeing—was tussling with itself. The clutching kept LaMotta from forcing Robinson to the ropes. "The crowd didn't like that but it was sound and effective practice," *The Detroit News* would say of the Robinson strategy. Going into the third round Gainford urged Robinson to ignore LaMotta's lower body and go for the head. It took another round before he was able to do so with effect: A flurry of rights to the head—"and two jarring uppercuts"—staggered LaMotta and drew blood from a cut above his left eye. A sudden and guttural symphony of crowd noise washed over the Olympia. Robinson kept swinging, "trying for a knockout," sending LaMotta twisting along the ropes. It was sheer will that enabled LaMotta to stay on his feet, shaking the blows—as a pedestrian does snowflakes—at conclusion of the round. When the Bull reached his corner, his face red, having survived the round, he found himself greeted with applause: This was his Detroit as well. And he was benefiting from the emotion of those who had been neutral; those who wished merely to see a good fight. Robinson's corner was quite confident. Their fighter was meeting LaMotta's strength with caginess. In the seventh round, LaMotta had inched Robinson toward Robinson's own corner—near where the souls from the Brewster Recreation Center sat and where his beautiful sister sat—and he unleashed a pounding left punch to Robinson's head. Robinson collapsed; Gainford's fleshy hands gripped the ropes; the referee stepped in and commenced with the nine count. LaMotta's manager had seen his fighter wallop other fighters in such a fashion; he imagined it was over. The Brewster crowd watched, then erupted as Robinson rose, beating the count. LaMotta's failure to finish Robinson off would prove costly. In the remaining rounds Robinson fought as if starting the fight anew; his flinty punches rocked LaMotta in the last three rounds as the Bull showed signs of tiring. As both fighters retreated to their corners at the final bell, each believed he had won. But it was Robinson's hand that was raised at center ring. The raining of boos surprised him. In those seconds of pure and raw emotion, his hometown connection held no magic. The boos kept coming. "So deafening and so prolonged were the howls of protest," noted *The Detroit News,* "that [announcer George] Wise had to give up the idea of introducing the principals for the next bout."

Though composed, LaMotta felt robbed of a victory. Some in the crowd—it was a record-breaking $60,000 gate—shook their heads as they made their way toward the exits. In the hours afterward, LaMotta himself would begin replaying the details of the event, focusing on those minutes before the fight's beginning when the fighter Jackie Wilson, at ringside, was introduced to the crowd—and introduced as "Sgt." Jackie Wilson. It was that military-patriotic inclusion that he now wondered about, pondering what role it might have played in Robinson's win; wondering if Robinson's own military record might have kept the judges—even subconsciously—from making a harder and, in LaMotta's mind, fairer decision. "If they say I lost," LaMotta said, "I'm willing to take their word for it." But that comment was suffused with disenchantment; he sulked and remained bewildered. Among the other notables at ringside were Larry Atkins, the Cleveland fight promoter, eyeing Robinson, four years away from bringing him to Cleveland to face Jimmy Doyle.

Robinson's dressing room was a joyful cacophony of the cheers and congratulations of elbowing well-wishers. He strained to see over their shoulders, trying to spot familiar faces as they inched toward him. A Falstaffian lightness had returned to huge George Gainford's appearance; he was smiling. Robinson needed ice for his hurting hands. "He really hurt me with a left in the seventh round," Sugar Ray said. "I was a little dazed and decided to stay on the deck for the count of eight. That was the only time I was in trouble and my plan of staying away worked the rest of the time."

But a cloud lingered over Robinson's win. Many felt he had been beaten. And even before the fighters had left the city, the demands for a rematch were already buzzing. Both camps, within days, agreed in principle to a fourth bout. "I didn't lose it, he got the decision," LaMotta would say of that third bout years later.

The loss bore into LaMotta, like darkness in the inmate hole at Coxsackie. The world, he felt, belittled him, shoved him around; believed him to be little more than "a wop." He had flattened Robinson in the seventh round, put him on the canvas. And he hadn't failed to take in the shock and boos from many in the audience when Robinson was announced the victor. "That's when I began to think about Robinson as a nemesis."

So now they were conjoined. They were linked—and cursed—like sibling brothers, each of whom ferociously wanted what the other possessed. LaMotta also wanted revenge. The Bull was angry at Jackie Wilson and at Sugar Ray: He hadn't forgotten all those patriotic hosannas thrown Robinson's way in Detroit. He knew he wouldn't be able to sleep peacefully until he had righted this perceived wrong. The boxing gods had conspired against him—he'd never get to face Joe Louis because of those weight divisions. But he had no intention of letting Robinson get away.

As for Robinson, however, he had bigger goals in his sights—the reigning middleweight champion, not to mention the welterweight belt. He wanted a fair chance to claim glory even if he had to trek across weight divisions to get it. And yet, economics mattered: Robinson-LaMotta had broken gate receipts in their joint appearances—STANDING ROOM ONLY, the Detroit placards said—at the Olympia. They confused bettors and bookies, igniting constant curiosity within both groups.

They were big box office, and the shadow of each—pulling writers, fans, jazzmen, the young and old—loomed over the other. They were pure athleticism. "Watching those guys was like watching two fighters in a brawl down on Pier 6," recalls David Dinkins, a young fight fan in those days and later mayor of New York City.

They were opposites who attracted. Having fought three times, they now knew each other's styles well enough that one's ring knowledge seemed to cancel out the other's ring knowledge. The clacking of the fight bell started each saga anew. That old racial animus hovered—but it never burst into full fury as it did with Joe Louis and Max Schmeling; instead it just sent off a few sparks and splinters—little-boy ruffians who sided with Robinson or LaMotta, who were broiled in ethnic rivalries tossing epithets as they strolled home through the tough streets of New York City, the sinister words dying before they had a chance to incite anything.

Detroit lay behind them—and blood between them. One felt conspired against; the other had been anointed by virtue of gifts and hunger. Such were the requisites of a rivalry and the planting of its deep seed, one that would sprout in the hurt face of the Italian and the swooning pride of the distressed Negro.

Within twenty-four months there would be crowds clamoring and jostling for tickets to see them again, this time in Manhattan, the jazzy metropolis Robinson considered far more his backyard than Detroit had ever been.

The months—with war and victory and big-themed speeches and Billy Eckstine crooning and a certain draftee, Sugar Ray Robinson, home from war (the amnesia gone!), and all the kissing and hugging and lovemaking—passed by as if in a blur.

INTERLUDE **Sugar, Meet Sugar**

An "uncrowned" champion, as Sugar Ray Robinson was being called, couldn't escape the spotlight. To certain overactive minds, such a fighter became a mark for other fighters who were trying to forge a reputation. This was true, at least, for the brave fighter whose camp thought he could upset the uncrowned champion and snatch the spotlight for himself. George Costner was such a fighter.

Costner, a welterweight and native of Cincinnati, Ohio, had turned pro in 1939, a year before Robinson's ascension. He was rangy, had reach, could hit—"and moves about the ring like a tiger," noted one publication. Promoters were eager to book him. Many began thinking he possessed Robinson-like skills. Costner would not argue otherwise; he even adopted the nickname Sugar, and reporters started writing him up as George "Sugar" Costner. Robinson did not appreciate the thieving of his moniker.

On January 19, 1945, Costner knocked out Richard "Sheik" Rangel just a minute and twenty-two seconds into the first round of their Chicago Stadium engagement. The knockout brought fans out of their seats. As he strolled around the ring, Costner heard them calling his name: Sugar, Sugar, Sugar. The Rangel knockout got Costner a date with the other Sugar. (Costner's camp knew that Robinson had once knocked out Rangel—but it had taken that Sugar a full two rounds to do so.)

The interest in the bout, orchestrated by Chicago promoters Irving Schoenwald and Jack Begun and scheduled for February 14, 1945, was immediate and fevered. "This bout is a natural," Begun declared. "This boy, Costner, is a honey and it wouldn't surprise the followers of this Cincinnati scrapper if he upsets the dope cart and wins." There was a feeling in some boxing camps that LaMotta had exposed Robinson's vulnerabilities, that now he was ripe for the taking. "We never had such an advance sale since Tony Zale defended his middleweight title against Al Hostak in the Stadium four years ago when 15,087 paid $48,475 to see Zale . . . knock out Al in the second round," Begun said.

Costner expressed confidence in a win, and he had his followers: "If he does [win]," the *Chicago Defender* offered, "it will not only be a big upset but will back thousands who are of the opinion that Costner is about the best welterweight in the country today."

In early February, the original Sugar asked for a one-week

delay in the bout. He was suffering from a sore throat. It was rescheduled for February 14. Supporters of Sugar II wondered if Sugar was worried.

The seats inside Chicago Stadium filled early on the evening of the bout. "Not since Joe Louis fought James J. Braddock in Comiskey Park in June 1937 has Chicago been host to so many out-of-town sepia sport and boxing fans," proclaimed *Chicago Defender* columnist Fay Young. The attendance was put at 20,193; the gate a muscular $94,000. In George "Sugar" Costner's previous twenty-three bouts, he had recorded twenty-three wins; twenty-two of his victims suffered knockouts.

Each fighter's quickness was evident at the bout's beginning. Sugar Ray saw a waling right coming for his head toward the end of that opening round, at the two minute and fifty-five second mark. His duck was quick, fluid, and natural, and with that he stepped in close and feinted with his own right. Sugar II prepared to go under the feint, but the feint was just a feint and Sugar Ray let loose with a powerful left hook. The hook connected and Sugar II went down—never having seen it coming—taking the effects of the follow-up right blast with him. Those in their seats who didn't see it—blinded by the ref or at an odd angle in the stadium—let out a grating gasp because the accompanying sounds told them they had just missed something spectacular. Sugar II was on the canvas. Sugar Ray stood glowering at him. Sugar II heard the counts—one, then four, five, then eight, then nine—and couldn't rise. He took the full count on one knee. The much-hyped bout was over. A knockout in the first round. What had gone wrong? Costner had never fought before a crowd this large. Some imagined jitters, noting that in previous bouts he had always seemed jumpy and coltish in the moments before a fight. But on this night he had seemed strangely quiet and still in his corner—like a child approaching a high dive for the first time.

The men in their shined shoes and the women in their fur hardly planned to let the evening pass so quickly. Many headed over to the Negro side of Chicago, known as "Bronzeville." And Bronzeville, according to the *Chicago Defender*, "jumped" in the hours after the bout: " . . . [A]ll you had to do was to drop in your favorite bar and you'd find a friend from out-of-town who had come to see the two gladiators battle at the Chicago Stadium." Robinson sped through the wintry night with an assemblage of Chicago and New York friends until they reached the cozy warmth of the Grand Hotel bar, where he relaxed. Admirers came to him, men and women. Sugar Ray grinned as he signed photographs of himself and shared harmless gossip about his friend Joe Louis and life in Manhattan and Harlem. (Someone in his camp always carried press photographs of the fighter.) Not long into the night, there was a bit of noise, a gentle commotion; nothing to worry about, but someone else was approaching and the appearance was causing a stir. Heads craned back and forth: It was George Costner. There was an embrace—two foes, but no ill feelings on Sugar Ray's part, which is why he had insisted Costner drop by. Sugar Ray introduced Costner to his beguiling wife Edna Mae. More photographs were handed out. There was music; the tinkling of ice in glasses as drinks were poured. The warmth of the bar suited Sugar Ray nicely, the glint of jewelry shining from necks and wrists, the wide smiles cast in his direction. Sugar's defeated foe stared about with a mixture of amazement and amusement. And as George Costner readied to leave that night, looking about, witnessing the constant waves of adulation that radiated toward his opponent—the lovely victorious moments ticking by, that old mixture of boxing laughter and nighttime style playing like its own symphony—he knew exactly what the others gathered about knew: There was only one Sugar.

ACTS FOUR, FIVE, AND SIX It's on TV! Blood on the TV Screen

The fourth Robinson-LaMotta bout was announced for February 23, 1945. In the 727 days that would pass before the event—it would come just two days shy of the two-year anniversary of their last encounter—the country existed in that haze of wartime worry. Still, political and cultural events churned on.

In 1943 a stringbean singer from Hoboken, New Jersey, made his first appearance on *Your Hit Parade*. Many—and not just bobby-soxers and Italians—were enraptured by the voice of Frank Sinatra. That same year a new subway system was unveiled in Chicago. The New York Yankees won the '43 World Series. On the college grid-iron, Notre Dame took the football crown that year. There was plenty of music on the radio. A big hit was "Don't Get Around Much Any-more," by the Ink Spots; "Let's Get Lost" by Vaughn Monroe also moved listeners. The following year, 1944, saw Roosevelt elected to his fourth term, and the Missouri senator Harry S. Truman assumed the vice presidency. (Truman, who had been a haberdasher back in Missouri, dressed in a style right out of *Esquire* magazine.) That year also saw the cancellation—a by-product of war—of both the U.S. Open golf tournament and the Indianapolis 500. One of the more curious events in the sports world in 1944 involved the Cincinnati Reds. They used a fifteen-year-old left-handed pitcher—youngest major-league player in the game's recorded history—by the name of Joe Nuxhall for part of an inning against St. Louis because their ranks were so depleted. The St. Louis players, however, paid little mind to the novelty and went on to whip their opponents 18–0. Little boys and girls rushed for the comic strips with the premiere in 1944 of the *Batman and Robin* serial.

Among the flamboyant personalities that flourished during the tumultuous 1940s was a new kind of tough character: the outsized newspaperman. Figures like Damon Runyon, Hype Igoe, Stanley Woodward, and Jimmy Cannon—all sportswriters, and all quick to quote literary giants if only to prove the depth of their knowledge beyond the sports pages—were as well known as the sporting fig-ures they covered. In New York City especially, home to more than half a dozen major newspapers, the competition for scoops and sala-cious information was fierce. In the days leading up to the fourth Robinson-LaMotta bout, one of the most tantalizing and gossip-fueled stories revolved around Sugar Ray Robinson's military record, which had taken on a boomeranglike life of its own. And the talk made him seethe.

Robinson's quick knockout of George Costner in Chicago—along with the other fights he had fought and won since his military release—had been brought to the attention of the Army discharge board, which had granted his release based on medical reasons. If

Robinson could have recovered so quickly, the board now wondered, might they have been duped? The board contacted Robinson, demanding that he show up for a reexamination immediately following the upcoming fourth LaMotta fight. Military impropriety was a serious issue, especially as seen against the emotional backdrop of wartime patriotism. A fighter risked losing fan approval if found to have shirked military responsibility in any way. It was Dan Parker of the *New York Daily Mirror* who had written of Robinson's bewildering exit from the Army. (Parker was a tireless crusader against the corruption that had infected professional boxing, and thus any impropriety on the part of a fighter and Uncle Sam's Army would certainly have piqued his curiosity.) Now, on the eve of a big fight, questions were being raised in the press about Robinson's character and military record. George Gainford was incensed about the story, particularly its timing, feeling it might have an adverse effect on his fighter's concentration. Robinson, whose paranoia took off on flights of fancy with little or no encouragement under normal circumstances, blamed Parker's writing for the imbroglio and also privately wondered if the LaMotta camp had anything to do with it. (Other publications around the country had picked up the story.) It was Jesse Abramson of the *New York Herald Tribune* who came to Robinson's defense. "All the rumors and suspicions involving the military career and current status of Ray Robinson . . . are being aired again this week," huffed Abramson on the eve of the fight. Abramson felt that the airing of these "lurid details" of Robinson's military discharge was unfounded, and reminded readers that boxing boards—which had access to military records—had approved Robinson for fights in Illinois as well as New York after his military discharge. Abramson also possessed shrewd boxing insight into how two of the nation's most well-known fighters were currently perceived: "Every one likes Joe Louis, not every one likes Ray Robinson." Despite his anger, Robinson stayed mum about it all, not wanting to give the public or the promoters ammunition that might affect contract negotiations and radio rights, or even result in last-minute withdrawals from bouts. (Robinson would indeed undergo a new military examination, but nothing would come of it. His military career was officially over, even though the issue of his service would be revived again a decade later during congressional hearings about favoritism shown athletes and entertainers regarding military service.)

Many of the familiar faces—entertainers, bookies, sportsmen, newspapermen—were eagerly looking forward to the fourth matchup. There was a feeling that the bad blood between the two fighters was truly roiling. "They were out to kill each other," says Arthur Mercante, the onetime Golden Gloves referee. There would be one figure, however, missing from the proceedings, and both Robinson and LaMotta would lament his absence.

No one knew how old Hype Igoe—the longtime boxing writer for the *New York Journal-American*—really was when he died twelve days before the Robinson-LaMotta match. He had covered Louis-Schmeling, Braddock-Louis, Louis-Baer, and hundreds of other memorable encounters across America and into Puerto Rico. Igoe was one of the first writers to sense nuance and cultural sensibilities in the Robinson-LaMotta pairing, scavenging for new angles as he wrote about each fighter. Over the years there had been more than one "sixty-fifth" birthday party for Hype. His coterie of admirers came anyway, laughing into the wee hours. He was overweight, obviously vain about his age, enjoyed the remoteness of woodsy boxing camps, practiced magic tricks in idle moments, was an admired cartoonist, wore a signature fedora, and could often be found atop a Manhattan barstool. There were plenty of odd and eccentric occurrences in the life of Hype Igoe. He once hitched a ride out to the Indianopolis 500 with the great flying ace Eddie Rickenbacker piloting the plane. A voluble sort, Hype moved easily amongst the Hoosier crowd. In a field, whiling away some time, he began displaying his magic coin tricks, turning nickels into pennies, dimes into quarters. Both children and adults gathered. But there was confusion about the speed at which money was changing hands. Law officers came closer and weren't amused by the trickery. They quickly suspected Hype of being a con artist from back East and whisked him into custody. Colleagues helped convince authorities Hype meant no harm. He seemed to like everything about the heartbreaking fight game—the way heroes (Joe Louis) could come out of nowhere; the sheer will of the comeback champion (Braddock); the business acumen practiced as if it were all part of a carnival act by so many fight promoters (Mike Jacobs); the falling-apart heroes (Joe Louis again) who he thought had some kind of majesty in their efforts to hang on. He was a sightseeing passenger with a notebook on a vessel that moved between Madison Square Garden, Chicago Stadium, Yankee Stadium, and smaller joints in between. The old newspaperman of indeterminate age had a Runyonesque guys-and-dolls sensibility. (Runyon was at the funeral out on Long Island.) Caswell Adams, writing in the *New York Daily Mirror,* would refer to Herbert "Hype" Igoe as "a definite legend in the curious business of writing sports."

The LaMotta camp announced on fight's eve that their contender would weigh in at 159 pounds for the engagement. In fighting against the likes of Robinson and others in his class, LaMotta had unwittingly cursed himself: He had started his career as a light heavyweight; now, he was backtracking, forced to keep a careful eye on the weight scales as he prepared for fights in the welterweight division. The tactic created more drama than it should have and outright frustration on LaMotta's part when he stepped into the ring with a lightning-quick fighter—fast of feet and fist—like Robinson. Robinson had loosened his demands for the previous two fights, allowing LaMotta to fight heavier, at 165 pounds. But for this bout, a 160-pound contract was in effect, and LaMotta needed to come in below that earlier figure. "There are only three or four pounds involved, but they are mighty important pounds for LaMotta," the *New York Herald Tribune* noted.

There were times, given his haphazard training regimen, when LaMotta's weight was known to have ballooned to 170 pounds or more. With a scheduled bout at hand, the weight would come off, but the Bull hated the toll the regimen exacted.

Both fighters felt supremely at home in Manhattan and naturally gravitated to their respective watering holes (jazz clubs for Sugar Ray; Italian social clubs for LaMotta), where patrons wished them well. Robinson was favored—3 to 1 by some oddsmakers; only 2 to 1 by others—but LaMotta partisans held on to the fact that LaMotta was the only fighter who had beaten the previously undefeated Robinson. They were also quick to point out that LaMotta had never been knocked to the canvas by *anyone.*

Robinson did his pre-fight workouts at Fred Irvin's uptown gym while LaMotta sparred at Bobby Gleason's gym in the Bronx. The fight would mark Robinson's first return to Madison Square Garden since that gentle defeat of his idol Henry Armstrong a year and a half earlier.

Fight promoters were strangely caught off guard by the public's eagerness to see the two fighters again: The lowest-priced seats—accommodations for the gallery gods—had sold out midafternoon on the day of the bout. And two hours before the ringing of the bell, there were only standing-room tickets left. Promoter Mike Jacobs predicted fifteen thousand for the bout. Instead, more than eighteen thousand would arrive at the Garden—couples; loners over from the Bowery; denizens of Broadway; photographers and newspapermen, all shuffling to their seats. The photographers were toting their Speed Graphics, their press credentials hung from their neck or tucked in the brim of their fedora.

Just seconds into the first round, it became clear that Robinson's early ring strategy had shifted to one of outright aggression. Robinson quickly fired several rights and lefts at LaMotta, all of them connecting. LaMotta was stunned and showed a deep cut on his forehead in that round, as Gainford yelled at his fighter to keep hitting. In the third round LaMotta—with his one-dimensional though powerful fighting style—decided to charge Robinson, "pawing away at the body," as Jim Jennings of the *New York Daily Mirror* put it. It was an unwise move; Robinson let loose with a left that snapped LaMotta's head back and bloodied his upper lip. There were frenzied whoops from the crowd. Jennings saw LaMotta as a "slow-thinking" mauler in this ring and concluded that he was up against a meaner and more determined Sugar Ray. In round four, a Robinson strike—"a murderous left hook," as *Herald Tribune* writer Jesse Abramson described it—hurled LaMotta into the ropes. The Bull stopped himself from hitting the canvas; it would have been a first in his career. LaMotta, showing pure rage, had to be pulled away from Robinson: Jake continued swinging at the sound of the bell. It might have taken LaMotta this many fights to realize it, but Robinson had a tough, hard jaw. And there was something else: Robinson had begun keeping an eye on the clock—a move, those who knew him would say, adopted from his former foe Fritzie Zivic—in an effort to time the intervals of his punches to draw more points from the sitting judges. "His left was a classic" throughout, noted the *Herald Tribune.*

By the fifth round, LaMotta looked woozy and certainly dazed. But it was a scheduled ten-round bout, and Jake always believed a fight could turn on just one devastating punch. It was in the sixth—the Bull having cornered Robinson—that the temper of the noise shifted and suddenly rose to a deafening level: a resurgent LaMotta began pummeling Robinson's face and midsection; the photographers clicked as LaMotta bore into Sugar Ray, who had bizarrely dropped his hands and took the punishing blows standing near the ropes. More than ten seconds passed. Gainford waved his fighter away from LaMotta. The reporters tried to decipher the words spewing from Gainford's mouth. Some sensed a knockout, believing LaMotta had revived himself and this was his moment to turn the bout in his favor. But just as quickly—like a deer at rest in the woods before an unseen noise shocks it into movement—Robinson, his dark trunks shimmering against the lights, danced away, back to the center of the ring. And once there, glove to glove with LaMotta, he unleashed a versatile array of blows—"right crosses, upper cuts, bolos, left hooks, left jabs"—that left LaMotta reeling and toyed with the unsettled loyalties of the agitated crowd. The astute observer could now see that standing as still as a mummy and taking LaMotta's punches was a ruse on Robinson's part, an effort to tire his challenger and lure him to the center of the ring—only to unleash his own sustained fury. (It was a strategy the old magician Hype Igoe might have loved witnessing.) The Robinson maneuver was "one of the slickest bits of gallery playing on record," noted Dan Burley of the *Amsterdam News.* LaMotta looked bewildered at what was happening. He had gone into the fight with a ten-pound weight advantage over Robinson, but it mattered little as Robinson's strategies—attacking early, the whirling mind games—seemed to vanquish LaMotta's heft.

LaMotta had anchored his prowess as a fighter to raw power. At times he seemed to be encased in cement, his feet moving only when necessary. He was indeed vintage—a throwback to an 1890s or 1920s boxer, when a fighter met power with power. But Robinson was something new, unseen by the likes of LaMotta or anyone: He moved like someone on a great movie musical soundstage. He brewed power with artistic flourishes. His feet moved with the quickness of grasshoppers. The deeper LaMotta believed in his method—moving by inches in its tight dark shadow—the more unwittingly he exposed himself to the myriad gifts of Robinson. Robinson checkmated LaMotta's power and brutishness with speed and round-by-round mental adjustments. Whereas LaMotta hewed to only one musical note, Robinson jumped to a jazzy vibe, thus turning the boxing canvas to the musical stage syncopations that best suited him.

Suspense circled the Garden at bout's end, evidence of contentment at a memorable battle having been fought. But Robinson had carried the evening: Referee Eddie Joseph scored it six rounds for Robinson and four for LaMotta. The two other judges differed starkly in their assessments: Bill Healy gave six rounds to Robinson, three to LaMotta, and called one even. Jack Gordon gave seven rounds to Robinson, calling two even, with the other round going to the Bull.

"Class," said James Dawson of *The New York Times*—using a word more often associated with artistic or stylistic interpretations and not fistic matters—"told against bull-like strength" in the ten-round matchup. Many saw heroics in LaMotta's mere survival: "How LaMotta stood up under all that fire is a major mystery," said the *Amsterdam News*.

Purists would come to note that changes had taken place in the fighting style of Sugar Ray Robinson during the LaMotta battles. Because LaMotta simply would not go down, Robinson had learned patience in the ring, taking punishing body blows and all the while adjusting his mental resolve. There would be bruising; there would be blood. He adjusted the artistic bent of his fighting game—he had a habit of humming jazz tunes to himself between rounds—to withstand power from the other direction. It was a determined reaction to LaMotta's style, but it would also supply him with the confidence to extend his career when others cautioned against it. Inside that strategy, of course, lay a downside: blows to the head can result in long-term damage.

As the fighters made their way to their dressing rooms, and as the bettors collected themselves up in the stands; as the loners descended the steps angling toward the night air, and the reporters rushed to meet their deadlines, a sentiment hovered that the two fighters were hardly finished with each other. "You don't keep fighting unless the fights are close," LaMotta would say years afterward, believing that each of his losses, up to this point, had been so close that he could have won with more charitable judging.

Gainford hovered over his fighter down in the dressing room, applying ointments and massaging his muscles. Robinson's lips were bruised purple from the blows he had taken. Though comforted by the victorious outcome, he lay on a table with a look of exhaustion. Many of those gathered wanted to know about those climactic moments in the sixth round, when it seemed as if LaMotta might send him through the ropes again, as he had done in Detroit. "I was getting a little tired, so I figured I could rest while I made him miss," Robinson said, aiming for levity. "My eye wasn't so good," he went on. "I rolled with some punches and I rolled into others." While cornered, he sensed something in LaMotta's eyes—raw fury—and admitted that he had to make a quick adjustment, which had him dancing back to the center of the ring.

In the much more somber environment of LaMotta's dressing room, the defeated fighter offered that he thought Robinson had been toying with him in that sixth round.

Both fighters now believed that each encounter had put them closer to supremacy over the other. Robinson's logic was plausible, as it showed in the cross-country headlines and the decrees of the fight judges; LaMotta's was emotional, anchored to his belief that since each fight was—in his mind—scintillatingly close, there wasn't much that separated the two. He put forth theories about newspapermen who wrote about him and Robinson, believing they had maligned him: "There was a time when there wasn't more than two or three of them I was on speaking terms with, and why? Because they said all I knew how to do was get in there and slug, I didn't have any style or what they call finesse, not that any of these writers were ever in a ring themselves."

Jake LaMotta was that odd figure, in whom losses only fortified will and confidence. Hadn't he knocked Robinson from the ring? And had Robinson ever put him on his rear end? He had not.

With four thrilling fights now behind them, which were seen by tens of thousands in person and listened to by many millions more on radio, they had created their own cinema. They were magnetically linked. Both had now possessed the American imagination. They were connected not only by klieg lights but by the blood they were willing to spill to outlast each other.

One might have imagined, in the aftermath of the fourth battle, that the two required distance from each other. But distance would only serve to frustrate, as if they were antsy gladiators stomping upon sand in the middle of the stadium. "I knew what I wanted, and he knew what he wanted," LaMotta would say years later. "We were two of the best fighters in the world."

The calls for another fight erupted immediately. By fall, the plans were in place: Expectations were that the fifth bout would be in early September 1945, in Chicago—a place where the autumnal winds blew hard and fierce.

President Roosevelt, the man whose voice had trilled over the radio wires into the lives of so many—Joe Louis on the march against Schmeling, Henry Armstrong hoboing across the country, Sugar Ray in his crisp Army uniform, the LaMotta family in the hard tenements of New York; millions of other citizens—died in Warm Springs, Georgia, on April 12, 1945, seven weeks after the most recent Robinson-LaMotta bout. His body was carried North on railroad tracks, and thousands who had gathered along the tracks, ragamuffin and well-heeled alike, stretched their palms outward as if they might somehow make that huge man visible one last time. Harry S. Truman assumed the presidency. The deaths caused by the dropping of the atomic bombs which Truman had ordered ushered in the end of war. Many Americans were able to start lives anew. Rationing, which had spread to shoe purchases and canned goods among so many other items, was slowly lifted. It was now okay to begin filming fight footage again—film stock had been a precious commodity during the war—to use in newsreels advertising upcoming fights in movie houses across the country. The velvet curtains would pull back in the darkened movie theatres, and there they were again, fighters in grainy black-and-white footage, claiming our darkest dreams—to inflict pain upon one's enemy.

Sugar Ray Robinson did not always find it easy adjusting to domestic life. Edna Mae had no intention of sitting home and simply becoming Mrs. Sugar Ray Robinson. She had friends from the world of entertainment and nightclubs before she met him, and she did not wish to lose them. Robinson depended on his sisters and mother to keep Edna Mae company when he was off on extended golf outings or training for fights, but Edna Mae did not always relish their company. She came from an educated class of Negroes; the Robinsons did not. But for Robinson there was a trade-off in contending with the cumbersome details of the relationship—Edna Mae's large family, the marital expectations of both—and it was the star quality of Edna Mae herself. She was beautiful. As a couple they looked dazzling on the streets of Manhattan together, fur wrapped around her, his evening suit fitting him just so. Jazz figures desired their company. They socialized frequently with Billy Eckstine and his beautiful wife, June. "She complemented Sugar Ray," Arthur Barnes recalls of Edna Mae. They went house hunting during those seven months in 1945 between the fourth and fifth LaMotta bouts, eventually purchasing that lovely home in the Riverdale section of the Bronx. It had a large lawn, and on summer evenings friends would come by and Edna Mae would light candles. Everyone listened to Duke Ellington and Charlie Parker beneath moonlight. It was the kind of living Robinson had long ago dreamed of and Edna Mae simply expected.

During that seven-month interval leading up to the outdoor September fight in Chicago, Sugar Ray adopted a far more conservative schedule than usual—obviously concerned about wear and tear as he prepared for LaMotta—and fought just three times. He took on Jose Basora in Philadelphia. That fight was more difficult than Robinson had envisioned; he had to settle for a ten-round decision. Prognosticators imagined a spirited challenge as well from Jimmy McDaniels, a tough Los Angeles fighter who had never suffered a knockout in his career. Sugar Ray introduced him to the experience: It came one minute and twenty-three seconds into the second round. And Jimmy Mandell suffered a fifth-round TKO in Buffalo.

LaMotta, on the other hand—as if to remind the world of his fearlessness and addiction to the ring—fought seven times. He fought twice in both March and April. He won all of his bouts, though not without sweaty effort: Jose Basora—the fighter Robinson had required all ten rounds to beat—took him to nine rounds. Those keeping track of the fighters, their opponents, and their respective records noted that George Costner—the imposter who had been beaten in one round by Sugar Ray—hung on with LaMotta for six before losing.

Chicagoans had long reveled in their city being a prime fight town. Their Comiskey Park, where Robinson-LaMotta would unfold, was a cherished venue. The Windy City crowd had become enamored of Robinson's fight style when he was appearing in the city years earlier on behalf of the New York City Golden Gloves team. But even as a pro, Robinson had a Chicago streak going: He had knocked out all three opponents—Tony Motisi, Lou Woods, and Costner—whom he had faced in the city. "What makes Robinson doubly anxious to keep his local knockout record clean," offered the *Chicago Defender,* "is the fact that LaMotta has been able to withstand Ray's murderous punches for 40 rounds so far."

The fight was being promoted by Jack Kearns, onetime manager of Jack Dempsey. Kearns—who had tried for his first riches by running off to join the Alaskan Yukon gold rush in his youth—was eager to stage the engagement. Weeks before the bout, he ushered a gaggle of newspapermen, radio announcers, and members of the Chicago Boxing Commission to a meeting at the Morrison Hotel. He slapped backs and grinned, though the grinning faded when reporters started talking about the fact that Robinson wanted his opponent at 160 pounds or under—a demand that had yet to be guaranteed by LaMotta. It was obvious Kearns still had work to do to appease both camps. In mid-September, Robinson sought a delay because of back pain, and the final date settled on was the twenty-sixth. When Kearns staged his second press gathering, it was to announce that both fighters would arrive in Chicago two weeks before the bout to continue their training.

Two things about their fight would be different this time around. First, it would be staged as a twelve-rounder, two rounds longer than each of their previous encounters. The additional two rounds were seen as favoring LaMotta, since endurance was one of his major assets. And, second, Robinson himself aimed to fight heavier, at 150 pounds, because he believed he would need the extra weight to counter LaMotta's strength. Kearns, the promoter, was predicting the gate would crack $100,000. Wilfrid Smith, the *Chicago Daily Tribune* writer, was not the only one to remark that the Robinson-

LaMotta matches had caught the nation off guard. They were two fighters fighting out of their divisions, and yet, as Smith knew, in the past three years they were simply "the best money match of the war period."

Both fighters' arrivals in Chicago caused instant excitement. History was now swaying upon the shoulders of each. Negroes had begun reaching out to Robinson with growing affection and curiosity, as they had once done with Joe Louis. Sugar Ray was viewed as an inevitable champion, thus drawing the interests of politicians, real estate magnates, lawyers, physicians, and gimlet-eyed hustlers. The musicians that he knew from town to town had turned into an adopted choir now, jawboning and preaching asides about the wicked-punching prizefighter they knew from Harlem. "We'll wager the best fists to be tossed at Savoy [a nightclub] during Sugar Ray Robinson's training period will come from the battler himself . . . ," the *Chicago Defender* announced.

As for LaMotta, he couldn't set foot in Chicago without his own internal musings: Chicago was where Tony Zale—the onetime middleweight champion—had fought so many times, and where he had been adopted as a fighter. Zale belonged to Chicagoans. In 1934 Zale fought twenty-one times, and all but three of those matches were in Chicago. As much as LaMotta wanted a crack at Zale— LaMotta's "ultimate goal is a fight with Chicago's Tony Zale," the *Tribune* reminded readers—he couldn't have it because Zale was off in the war, unavailable to fight between 1943 and 1945. So Zale was the invisible figure that hovered over LaMotta's middleweight title hopes. No matter how much he fought or who he whipped, LaMotta had a realization that gnawed at him: "I still was no nearer a crack at the title." Still, with its large Italian population, Chicago showed affection toward him: The Italian social clubs sent emissaries to greet him, inviting LaMotta out for dinners, pleading with him to visit recreation centers and CYO clubs where Italian youth congregated and became bright-eyed at the prospect of meeting him. (LaMotta's exploits had recently begun drawing the interests of the Italian press overseas as well.) But everywhere LaMotta looked— especially in the big hard fight cities of Detroit, New York, Cleveland, and now Chicago—he saw the influence of the Mob at work;

and they were the men he loathed, who he believed were keeping him from getting his chance at a title shot.

The two combatants did their training at local CYO gymnasiums, the Chicago reporters scribbling notes about the look of each fighter: LaMotta looked bulky as ever, but Robinson had also added a few pounds. There were those who wondered right away if the extra weight would slow him in the ring, stifling his stamina if the bout should last the full twelve rounds.

When scheduling outdoor fights, promoters are always at the mercy of the weather. For several days preceding the bout, there had been rainfall. But the rain held off on the day of the event; the temperature of fifty-six degrees on the evening of the fight suggested proper attire: Topcoats, scarves, tweed jackets, and lamb's wool were all draped over the attendees. (Some thought Kearns might delay for a day, but he couldn't: The Chicago Cubs were in the World Series and scheduled for a game at Comiskey the next day.)

As the throng made its way to stadium seats, the whole scene— like so many outdoor fights—managed to offer a kind of spectral beauty: A mass of souls snaking along the aisles; klieg lights draping Comiskey; stars in the sky with the deepening of evening; two fighters seen bending beneath the ropes and into applause, nodding and rolling their shoulders and their necks, getting looser, going to their respective corners—everything set against the sounds of nature and unfolding beneath raw sky.

Among the fourteen thousand plus in the crowd was a figure rarely seen on such occasions: Leila Smith, Sugar Ray's mother. She sat with Marie and Evelyn, her two daughters. And, as was her habit, she prayed for her son's well-being.

The two fighters stood against the moonlight. They touched gloves, retreated to their corners, then emerged eyeing each other without mercy.

LaMotta aimed to be the aggressor and it showed in the very first round. Fighting at a weight that made him more relaxed, he charged early and often in the first three rounds. Robinson countered with fast left jabs, but LaMotta bore in, punching at Robinson's stomach and sides. It wasn't until the fifth round that Robinson's lightning-quick punches began to show dividends: He stung LaMotta several times. In the sixth, Robinson did more clutching than usual, buying time for rest. LaMotta's moves were staccato during the round, quick steps toward Robinson. Sugar Ray began fighting backward, a strategy that mixed offense with defense: As he moved away from LaMotta, he also fired punches. He was one of the few fighters who could attempt such a feat and make it work, as it demanded a super-human effort at balance and body adjustment. The strategy so angered LaMotta that at one point he urged Robinson to charge him, motioning with his hands palm up in the manner of a school-yard bully. Robinson refused to oblige. But then, a round later—the seconds ticking toward the end of the seventh—Robinson approached LaMotta and let loose with a battery of right-left, left-right punches. LaMotta took the blows. The scene lifted the crowd; Robinson's sisters screamed. People thought a knockout might be imminent. But stamina had always been one of LaMotta's prized assets. And by round nine, sure enough, LaMotta had reversed the momentum: He had begun fighting, noted Wilfrid Smith of the *Chicago Daily Tribune,* with an "inspiring" edge that seemed to carry him through into both rounds ten and eleven. LaMotta's punches proved relentless; Robinson was "visibly tired" at the end of the eleventh. If the fight had ended then, the judges might have had a difficult time determining the winner. Robinson's backing-away strategy had actually drawn some boos from the crowd. In the first minute of the final round, both fighters traded perfunctory blows. Then, with a minute to go, it happened. Robinson struck in a fero-cious manner: His left slammed into LaMotta's jaw; the Bull spun. Robinson then unleashed another left, but it didn't fully connect, so he brought a right "out from nowhere" which clearly shook La-Motta. And then the bell sounded across the klieg-lit darkness of Comiskey Park, and it was all over.

The fighters stood waiting on the decision as the judges huddled and flashbulbs popped. The twelve-rounder had indeed favored LaMotta. But Robinson's late rallies in the middle rounds and dur-ing the final round had been powerful.

Sugar Ray Robinson—standing beneath the moody and churning sky, his opponent fervently believing he had won or at least fought to a draw, both corners nearly breathless as they strained to listen for the decision—was declared the victor. There erupted more than a smattering of boos. The referee, along with one of the judges, scored it 61–59 for Robinson. But the third official tallied 63–57 for La-Motta. It was the kind of disagreement the two fighters had become accustomed to, and it showed what made their boxing wars so unforgettable. The next day the *Chicago Daily Tribune* referred to the bout as a "close victory" for Robinson. But two days later, the publication was referring to the judges' vote as an "unpopular decision." The *Amsterdam News* allowed as to how Robinson's "last ditch stand" in the final round had played a large role in his win. A United Press dispatch referenced a years-long pastime of Robinson's while summing up all their encounters: "And as in the others, it was Robinson's superior boxing skill, his speed, his in-and-out punching, that won for the former tap dancer."

Robinson was full of praise for his opponent afterward. "LaMotta is the toughest man I have ever fought," he said. Gainford and his corner had noticed a swelling lump behind Robinson's right ear from a LaMotta wallop and were treating it. "I have fought him five times and hit him with everything I know how to throw but he still stands up."

The Bull was obviously distraught. He hightailed it back to New York City, but before leaving he confessed: "I thought I won all the way."

Sugar Ray Robinson decided to stay on in Chicago. Why, there were such good restaurants in the city, so many wonderful spots to hear jazz in and around Bronzeville. Most important, though, he wanted to see the Cubs play in the World Series. Chicagoans spotted him on the streets in the days after the LaMotta battle and called his name; this was hardly unusual for him. He'd been fighting—athletic club, Golden Gloves, professional—nearly a decade now. And he was still only twenty-four years old. For a long time he had recognized his power and personal appeal. His public image may have been practiced, but the magnetism couldn't be manufactured. He turned to those who called out to him with a tender generosity—like a tap dancer at performance's end who knows compliments are about to float his way.

There was something else in 1945—in addition to their five bouts—that linked Sugar Ray Robinson and Jake LaMotta so closely. Neither, at that point, had been given a shot at fighting for a title. They had yet to figure how to navigate the turbulence one had to go through in dealing with promoters, mobsters, publicists, and rival fight camps. They both stood suspended in their title dreams— pummeling each other in the meanwhile. The perceived unfairness bore into them. "The only thing I really wanted was that title," LaMotta would say of his middleweight hopes. In boxing, the title-holder is king, but you could never become king without a shot at the title and the attendant coronation. Both fighters were impatient, and both saw sinister forces conspiring against them. Robinson would get his shot a year later, though not with Red Cochrane, as he should have, but with Tommy Bell.

The Bull would decide to take a darker—and far more unfor-giving—route to his title shot.

INTERLUDE **Dreaming Sugar**

The little boys of Coney Island had plenty to keep them busy in the late 1940s. They flipped through their comic books, constructed cardboard airplanes while spitting buzzing noises from their mouths, did their arithmetic, drew maps for geogra-phy class. The hum of sports, of course, hung heavily in the air. Baseball was beloved, and many of the little boys on Mel Dick's Coney Island block chirped on and on about the great Joe DiMaggio, their hero. In the local park where they played baseball, they'd swing their bat while howling DiMaggio's name. But not little Mel. He had another hero, and his name was Sugar Ray Robinson. "I studied everything about him." There sat twelve-year-old Mel, in 1946, in his bedroom, thumbing through the New York papers, racing to the sports section, reading top to bottom every article about Robinson. He'd neatly fold the articles, stash them away for safekeeping, then retrieve them and read them all over again. A weeks-old article thrilled him anew upon reading it for the fourth and fifth time. It turned into a sweet obsession. The other boys had their baseball phenoms; he had Sugar Ray. He daydreamed, alone, about his hero. "My parents thought I was nuts."

He was the son of Russian and Austrian immigrants— William, a portrait photographer, and Sonya, a housewife, both of Jewish ancestry. Little Mel was blessed with the gift of gab and a willful personal determination. He had to meet Robinson. Nothing could stop him. From reading the newspapers, he had learned that Robinson often trained at Grupp's Gym in Harlem. It was quite a trek from Coney Island into Harlem, but he plotted it all out. There was no way he could tell his parents. On the decided day, playing hooky from school, he marched out the front door as if someone, far away, was calling his name. He took a trolley car to the subway station, then the uptown Seventh Avenue train to Harlem, and found Grupp's Gym. He had a couple bucks; it cost twenty-five cents to watch Robinson train. He paid his quarter and walked up into the gym. He spotted Robinson in the ring, sparring. He stared wide-eyed and found a seat. "Hey, young fella," said a man who seemed ancient to him. It was Harry Wiley, he'd later discover, one of Robinson's trainers. He came back the next day, and a third day. By then he'd become noticeable. And on that day, when Robinson finished sparring, he jumped from the ring and angled his way over to the punching bag. He began pummeling it. Mel had no idea what the nods and grunts and gentle smiles coming from all the men gathered about—the boxing gym chorus—meant: the champ looked good, is all. The champ caught the kid—the only white kid who had showed up for three straight days—out of the corner of his eye as he finished with the punching bag and walked right over to him. "Hey, who are you?" Robinson asked. Mel told him his name.

"Where do you live—and do your parents know you're here?" Robinson wanted to know.

Mel confided that his parents were at home; he said he had come to Harlem to meet him—Sugar Ray Robinson. Robinson chuckled; Harry Wiley chuckled.

"Why?" Robinson asked.

"You're my hero," he said. Then little Mel blurted: "And I love you."

Robinson ran his hands through the kid's mop of hair. The fighter seemed both moved and tickled.

Sugar Ray turned on his heel and told Mel to follow him. He simply couldn't believe it. Walking alongside his hero! Robinson plopped himself on a table in the dressing room for his rubdown and asked this just-made friend about home, about school. He asked Mel if there were other boxers he admired. There really weren't. "He said to me, 'You ever meet Joe Louis?'" Mel would remember decades later. "I told him no. Then he said, 'Go over there, will you, and pull that curtain back on the shower.' So I walk over and pull the curtain back and there is Joe Louis standing in the shower! They all start laughing. I walked right into the shower and shook Joe Louis's hand!"

It was the beginning of unimaginable events and moments in the life of Mel Dick. Robinson would send gifts out to his Coney Island home: boxing gloves, fight programs, photographs. Mel himself would troop alone into Harlem; he had an open invitation to watch Robinson train. He'd run by his nightclub during the daytime and peer in at the windows. "What I felt," he says, "was an admiration and love for black people. Because they were so nice to me. That was a special feeling—how they welcomed me. I never worried about anything." He would dash into his home in Coney Island, pick up the telephone, and call Robinson's office. "His secretary—I called her Mrs. Phyllis, would answer. She'd say, 'Hello Mel. How are you?' And I'd say, 'Fine.' I'd say, 'How's Ray doing today?' 'How much does he weigh?' 'Is he ready for the next fight?' I was trying to impress my friends!"

In high school, when he had begun driving, he'd bring dates by Sugar Ray's nightclub. He'd stop when he saw the pink Caddy. He'd hop out, run inside, and beg Sugar Ray to come out and meet his date—for the girls never seemed to believe during the ride into Harlem that he really knew the fighter. "And he'd come out to the car and introduce himself to my date! And always just before I'd drive off he'd lean into the car and say, 'Mel, you be good.'"

He told his famous friend about the local boys' Coney Island baseball team. They had talent, he swore, but never decent enough uniforms. Sugar Ray bought them new ones. They named themselves the *Sugar Rays*. The team was all white, save for one tall Negro: Lou Gossett Jr., future Academy Award–winning actor. In his late teens, Mel was a constant guest at Greenwood Lake, the training camp. It was rustic, but to him it was paradise. On his first visit, walking up to the house, he was startled when he heard piano music. Inside, at the piano, sat Sugar Ray himself. "He was pretty good too. He'd play tunes like 'Sweet Georgia Brown,' 'Boogie Woogie.' He loved playing." He goes on about the training camp: "You'd be walking down a road and you'd see Frank Sinatra. On another day Duke Ellington and Miles Davis."

When Mel proposed to Bobbi, in 1957, he knew there was only one friend he wanted as best man. First Bobbi said yes, then Sugar Ray accepted best man honors. (Sugar Ray declined an invitation to appear on *The Ed Sullivan Show* because the taping would interfere with the wedding.) "And when he arrived—dressed so beautifully!—he said to me, 'You see my cufflinks, with the Star of David?' And then he pointed to his tie clip. And it also had a little Star of David. Then he went to the reception and all these ladies were saying to him: 'You're Melvin's friend—the fighter!' And he would say, 'Yes I am. And you are?' It was something else. He knew how to wow people."

It would all last—dinner, good seats at the fights, nightclubs, training camps, the birth of children, the mutual family heartaches, the love—until death claimed the great prizefighter.

Who cared that there was a sepia world spinning out there? That there were those—far from the lynch rope, far from the Northern or Southern jail cell or chain gang—who lived and clapped hands and spun records and took high tea and wrote verse, altering their own universe?

The late 1940s were Lena Horne's European years. She went in search of beauty. "We actually left home because of race and politics," her daughter would confide.

Lena Horne sailed for London in the fall of 1947 with Lennie Hayton, her beau. (She aimed to marry Hayton in Europe, far away from the contentious eyes of Americans.) In postwar London, she sipped tea, looked gorgeous against the chill, and stood agog at the rebuilding efforts. War veterans talked to her about her music—those Artie Shaw sessions! She wowed audiences at the London Casino, a theatrical venue. Among her admirers were English actor

It is little wonder the beautiful Lena Horne fell prey to the lure of big-time prizefighting. Negro America's biggest celebrities came from its ranks. She dated Joe Louis and befriended Sugar Ray.

James Mason and the poet Dylan Thomas: her beauty seemed to transfix both. But where to marry? Tabloid reporters seemed to be everywhere in London. Paris beckoned. She played the Club des Champs-Elysées there. Her audiences were spirited. French entertainers sought her out—Yves Montand and Edith Piaf among them. A district mayor in Paris married Lennie and Lena; Lena wore Balenciaga. She phoned daughter Gail in America and told her to keep the marriage secret. When she herself was back on native shores, Lena Horne was invited to sing at Truman's Inaugural Ball. She enjoyed the moment, but, in time, McCarthyism began to engulf the country. She had befriended activist Paul Robeson; she knew where it was all going. So she sailed again for Paris, "dripping ermine" aboard ship. Paris was a springboard for other European destinations— Monte Carlo, Glasgow, Edinburgh. She sang in swank clubs; she dressed beautifully, much of her attire purchased from couture designers. Her circle of friends grew: Noël Coward, photographer

Robert Capa, Marlene Dietrich. She piqued their curiosity; she could see it in their eyes. Paris enchanted her, and she enchanted Paris. Some nights she could be heard singing at Club Galerie, backed by a small ensemble of French musicians. "It was a special club," Herbert Gordon, one of the Galerie's cofounders, would explain. "Artists were invited there to express themselves and to meet other artists, mostly Americans, but also Danes, French, Swedes, who would come there to discuss art and music, and to exchange ideas . . . You had to be hip and sensitive." *Life* magazine caught up with Horne and her husband in Paris, and they appeared in its July 10, 1950, edition. They were photographed outside a Paris café. In gazing at the picture, it remains nearly impossible to avert one's eyes from Horne, dressed as she was in her "quadruple pearl choker, Jacques Fath suit, and seriously frivolous French hat." Even on a distant shore, she remained the queen of sepia America.

In sessions that spread over 1948 and 1949, the young man with the trumpet picked some musicians—Gerry Mulligan, Max Roach, Kenny Clarke among them—and made some recordings for Capitol Records. They were lovely and tender. "I wanted the instruments to sound like human voices, and they did," Miles Davis would remember. Among the tunes were "Hallucinations," "Godchild," "Move," and "Darn That Dream." Those were the beginnings of the landmark *Birth of the Blues* album. Now when he was nodded at by other musicians, there was reverence in those nods. Like Lena, Miles Davis also headed for Paris: He landed there in early 1949, his first foray abroad. He and some fellow musicians played the Paris Jazz Festival and drew applause. And he met notables—Pablo Picasso, Jean-Paul Sartre. He fell in love with Juliette Gréco, a bohemian and well-known singer. He might as well have been in a fevered dream: "Even the band and the music we played sounded better over there. Even the smells were different. I got used to the smell of cologne in Paris and the smell of Paris to me was a kind of coffee smell." But every Paris dream seems to end and he was back on American soil before the decade closed.

He would claim that a bone-deep loneliness for his Paris lover pushed him toward heroin. Seen on New York street corners—shaking, snot dripping from his nose—Miles Davis seemed to be sabotaging his splendid gifts. He could die, drifting away on somebody's stained sofa. But he had a need to see Sugar Ray Robinson up close, and when he saw him in the ring, he believed his salvation lay in what Robinson had shown: discipline, fearlessness. He liked the beauty of movement merged with the fearlessness. So he began to hang out with the great prizefighter, who was himself a softie for musicians, whether struggling with demons or not. Robinson tutored him, introduced him to sparring partners, welcomed him to his nightclub. Miles began to fill his dope-hungering spells with sober hours at the gym, watching fighters, watching Sugar Ray. As Sugar Ray danced in the ring, Miles stared quietly, convincing himself he was seeing beauty and music and jazz—just in another dimension. An acquaintance would recall accompanying Miles on visits to the gyms: "Miles didn't go there to be seen. He went there to watch—watch the boxing and to see that courage and loneliness . . ."

In that sweet-smoky world of sepia America—off the beaten path, but all the more buoyant for being so—Langston Hughes reveled in his renown. On April 24, 1947, he attended the opening of the Gershwin Memorial Room on the campus of Fisk University in Nashville. He stayed around to do some lecturing, reciting his own poetry in a mellifluous voice. The students were quite delighted to see, up close, any published Negro author. He couldn't touch down in a Southern city without well-heeled Negroes and liberal whites offering to host a tea party on his behalf—and there he would be, alighting from an auto, climbing steps into strangers' homes, regaling them with stories of Manhattan and the Apollo Theatre as books were pushed under his nose to autograph. His honey-colored skin shone; his hair was swept back in that marcelled fashion, just like Billy Eckstine's, just like Sugar Ray's. Like Horne, he wasn't immune to political currents: In the coming months, Red baiters would hound him out of several speaking engagements because of his affiliation with and sentiments toward radical organizations. Backed into one corner, he came out swinging from another and proceeded to write more operas, ballets, and librettos to keep his bills paid. He was delighted when Gwendolyn Brooks—he had helped get her first poem published in *Negro Quarterly*—received the Pulitzer Prize in

1950 for her book, *Annie Allen.* "Practically everybody is going to Rome or Paris these days but us," Hughes sighed to a friend in 1950. But there was much to keep him smiling: In 1950 he was interviewed for the first time on national TV to talk about his book *Simple Speaks His Mind,* a collection of his newspaper columns. (It would eventually sell an impressive thirty thousand copies.)

Hughes's 1950 television introduction came the same year Sugar Ray Robinson made his own debut on national TV. Robinson's was on November 8 in Chicago in a bout sponsored by Pabst Blue Ribbon. He was matched against San Antonio native Bobby Dykes, eight years his junior. Dykes had made his reputation with a feared right hook. He entered the ring first; Robinson kept the crowd waiting. Down in the dressing room, his cornerman Pee Wee Beale was doing what he did best—tending to Robinson's hair. And when Robinson pushed back the hood of his robe after finally entering the ring, his hair indeed looked as if he had just come from a salon. Robinson outweighed Dykes by ten pounds, but that was hardly the only advantage: He was also quicker and more elusive. By the second round Dykes was bleeding from the nose. By the eighth he looked genuinely bewildered. Robinson's punches seemed to come out of nowhere; several times he leaned forward on his left leg while his right leg was crooked in the air—like Astaire in mid-pirouette—and delivered left hooks. Other times he yanked his head left to right as Dykes's blows landed in open air. He was toying; perhaps mocking. It was both theatrical and professional; in this bloodiest of sports, he seemed to be enjoying himself. He did not appear to want to leave the stage. The announcer deemed it "the mark of a true professional" that Robinson would not inflict unnecessary damage; the longer the fight went, the more it seemed merely a showcase for Robinson's wide arsenal. It had been a sensational way to introduce himself to the TV audience. And there would be more engagements to follow.

Langston Hughes was right: It did seem as if everyone, save himself, was leaving for Paris that year. Following his bout against Dykes, Sugar Ray immediately embarked for Europe, sailing from Manhattan on the good ship *Liberté*. He was traveling with nine others, including his valet, his barber, and his lovely sister Evelyn. They were all stalwart members of his nightclub set, prideful Negroes elevated—as if by helium—in the wake of his footsteps. Their bustling caused a stir on deck. As Robinson knew, "It wasn't usual for nine Negroes to be sailing on the *Liberté,* and sailing together." They nodded at the curious stares from fellow passengers. A steward glided past and Robinson overheard him say to another: "The boxer, Sugar Ray Robinson, and his entourage." The boxer rolled the word around in his mouth and delighted in it. "Entourage": an old French word meaning a group of attendants. Robinson cackled and proclaimed to his sister and the others that he no longer had assistants— but an entourage!

He would have one bout each in Geneva, Brussels, and Frankfurt. There would be two matches in Paris. All the bouts were fairly uneventful: five fights, five wins. With his music and entertainment leanings, he couldn't help but be charmed by the City of Light. Paris had long welcomed black American artists—Josephine Baker, Sidney Bechet, and Lena Horne most recently—into its cultural bosom. Parisians by the thousands clamored to greet the American fighter, whose sense of style and decorum were so attractive to them. He ate at elegant restaurants, always in suit and beautiful tie. Other patrons ogled as he dined with the great French fighter Georges Carpentier, who had been light heavyweight champ from 1920 to 1922. Carpentier had fought against Jack Dempsey in 1921 before eighty thousand in Jersey City. Dempsey would claim a fourth-round knockout, but Americans were impressed with Carpentier, and he would always have friends across the Atlantic. Robinson strolled the Champs Elysées, shopped, befriended local musicians, saw the naked dancing girls at the Lido, and practiced his French. A new snack was suddenly on the menus at some of the cafés of Montmarte: They were made of sweetened rice and called Sugar cakes, in honor of the visiting American fight champion. The *Chicago Tribune* reported that Robinson had "captured Paris more completely than Hitler." He might well have lingered longer on the continent—Paris seemed to melt right into him—but there were pressing opportunities back in America.

Sugar Ray Robinson had begun considering the inevitable— jumping to another weight class. It was a prospect that made him think of a far loftier goal than previously imagined: a Joe Louis–like parting of the curtains and the kind of attention mostly reserved for heavyweights.

While Sugar Ray Robinson was in Europe, Jake LaMotta was grappling with the darker forces of his own nature. The ebbing away of marital love can be a lethal blow to any man. LaMotta wrestled with that, but also something else: mobsters who fixed fights. The combination plunged him into the same darkness he had experienced early in life and that had put him behind bars.

Fighters want what they can't have; fighters in the serious hunt for a championship belt often get prizes they would otherwise miss.

She was Bronx-born, beautiful, tall, blonde, and when lounging on the beach in her two-piece swimsuit (it wasn't for swimming), her legs were as devastating as torpedoes. Her real name was Beverly Rosalyn Thailer, but she changed it to Vikki; her friends didn't believe "Beverly" had the right seductive timbre. Her father, a small-time gambler, would go into rages and beat her: it was her beauty, it was her staying out late; she couldn't understand the abuse nor the silence of her mother. She got a job working in a nightclub where the men dressed like women. The cross-dressing bewildered her, but she needed the money. Sometimes she herself danced onstage. One night a gangster promised her and another girlfriend a good time—dinner, some drinks. Instead he raped her, took her virginity, and she was too frightened to go to the police. Life darkened: "Yet here I was, fifteen years old. I'd been beaten by my father and found no one to protect me. I'd been raped and hadn't told a soul what happened."

The woman-child, gorgeous though quite bruised, let it be known she wanted to meet the local Bronx fighter everyone was always talking about. As soon as she was introduced to the Bull, he was mesmerized. "She looked like a beauty-contest winner, like the blonde who plays the lead in one of those movies about the queen of the campus," the non-collegiate LaMotta would remember of their first meeting. He reminded her of John Garfield, the tough-guy actor. They married in 1946—within three months of their initial meeting—and it was largely because she had become pregnant. She was sixteen years old.

His hovering seemed, at first, warm and protective, but then it turned into outright control, his paranoia stoked by her every move. "He was jealous of other men—I couldn't talk with the butcher or grocer—but he didn't want me talking with other women either." The beatings would be followed by makeup sessions, and now Vikki LaMotta—in furs and jewelry paid for by her husband's fists—was living in torment again. After one assault, she told him she'd rather be dead than live any longer with him. They made up. Fears of abandonment lashed at the cursed Coxsackie child: "I remember one of the Robinson fights, Robinson had me but I just wouldn't give the son of a bitch the satisfaction of knocking me down, so I told the referee I'd murder him if he tried to stop the fight. I got my arm wedged around one of the ring ropes and stayed there defying Robinson to knock me down. He couldn't, but I got about as bad a beating as I've ever had. So help me God, I'd rather take a beating like that than listen to my wife tell me she'd rather be dead than living with me."

The more Jake LaMotta scanned the boxing world, the angrier he became. He could glance across the calendar of 1946 and notice that Robinson had gotten his crack at fighting for a championship belt— but Jake LaMotta had not. He had ignored the entreaties from mobsters, and where did that get him? He felt punished. He slept in the arms of a woman who had the beauty and mystique of a mermaid, and yet he was still full of anguish. His paranoia convinced him he didn't have her true love at all.

His brother Joey—long hovering like some kind of spectral tempter at his brother's shoulder—took Jake to meet some people.

On March 14 of 1947, LaMotta defeated Tommy Bell in New York in ten rounds. In June he bested Tony Janiro in New York, also in a ten-rounder. But on September 3 he suffered a defeat at the hands of Cecil Hudson in Chicago. The Hudson setback wobbled his confidence at getting a title shot.

It was soon announced that LaMotta would fight Billy Fox of Philadelphia on November 14 in New York. Fox's record was stunning: He was 49–1. He was only twenty-four—two years younger than LaMotta—and there were many in boxing circles who admired him. But the consensus was that LaMotta would beat the young fighter. James Dawson, the *Times* writer, predicted that LaMotta would "be trying his rushing, crashing, close-range fighting style, against a combination boxer-fighter, who also boasts a paralyzing punch."

On the night of the fight, a strange aura circled the ring beginning in the second round. While LaMotta fought in his usual hard-charging style against Fox in the first round, it was different from then on. In rounds two and three he seemed to vanish, taking unreturned blows from Fox. "Then he backed across the ring under a right to the head and acted as if his knees were buckling," Dawson wrote. Many in the audience thought LaMotta—as he was sometimes wont to do—was simply playing possum; that the fury would be unleashed in due time; that the Bull was about to make the youngster pay. There were more than eighteen thousand on hand; the box receipts exceeded $100,000—the most money taken in for a fight in the Garden all year. In the early part of the fourth, Fox snapped LaMotta with a sharp right. It drove LaMotta into the ropes, where he surprisingly cowered. Upon bouncing back to the center, LaMotta was met again by Fox, who proceeded to pummel him with "numerous lefts and rights." Then, in the same round— cries of "Stop the fight!" being howled now, an unfamiliar sound in the ears of the Bull—LaMotta, standing at center ring, took another volley of blows from Fox. The referee had seen enough and stepped in and stopped it. Jake LaMotta had been beaten, upset in the fourth round. FOX KNOCKS OUT LAMOTTA IN FOURTH ROUND BEFORE 18,340 AT GARDEN, the six-column *Times* headline screamed.

It was an amazing victory for young Fox. Both fighters quickly made their way to their dressing rooms, and New York state athletic officials quickly followed. They peppered LaMotta with questions about having fought such a lackluster bout. LaMotta pointed to Fox's record, said the kid was the better fighter on this night. Officials seemed to accept the explanation, but decided to withhold both purses until further investigation. LaMotta soon offered another explanation: that he had a hurt spleen and had kept quiet about it. The fighters received their money, but LaMotta was suspended from fighting for seven months for concealing his injury. (A more sinister truth lay in the shadows: The people his brother Joey had taken him to meet were mobsters. LaMotta admitted to a U.S. Senate subcommittee in 1960 that he had thrown the Fox fight—on orders from Frankie Carbo, the mobster—for a chance at a title shot. Fox had long been a Mob-linked fighter.) But in 1947 the public was led to believe LaMotta had been suspended because he had been untruthful about his injury—the New York athletic investigators were none the wiser themselves.

LaMotta stewed during his suspension, a cheater, a faker, a man hoarding a secret because he believed it would get him to the ultimate goal: that championship bout. His brother Joey delivered news of the okay from Carbo and his gang: Jake would now have his chance at the belt. However, he had to fight—and keep winning— before it could happen, in order to remind the public that he deserved the opportunity.

LaMotta fought and won five times in 1948. He started out 1949 with a ten-round loss, however, to Laurent Dauthuille—a vicious-punching French Canadian—in Montreal. His next three fights, though, were impressive victories. Then it was announced: On June 16, LaMotta would go up against world champion Marcel Cerdan ("the Moroccan Bomber") at the outdoor Briggs Stadium in Detroit. (Before he faced off against Cerdan, though, the Mob demanded $20,000 as matchmaker's fee: Vikki had to pawn her engagement ring to help raise the dough.)

Cerdan, the French champ, was dashing and elegant, a figure whom the French loved because he loved their Edith Piaf. They were a smashing couple—Piaf sang to him from the stage whether he was in the audience or not—and each constantly buoyed the spirits of the other. (Cerdan was married. Piaf ignored this inconvenient fact and the French, being the French, didn't seem to mind.)

A half dozen French writers trailed Cerdan from Europe to Detroit to witness the first defense of the crown he held. The excitement surrounding the bout was not only due to an American challenging a foreigner but because the locale was Detroit—a city that had long embraced LaMotta. "The popularity of LaMotta here is explained by the fact he has engaged in fifteen local bouts," wrote the *New York Times* man James Dawson, "all of them exciting, including a victory he scored over the world welterweight champion, Ray Robinson."

On June 15, the day of the bout, rain muddied the Briggs Stadium field, and organizers—among them Joe Louis, in temporary retirement mode and employed by the recently formed International Boxing Club as their boxing activities director—had to huddle to debate a day's postponement. All parties agreed to reschedule, but when the Cerdan camp learned that in keeping with LaMotta's wishes there would be no new weigh-ins the next day, they exploded in anger. Lew Burston, who was Cerdan's American representative, believed the move favored LaMotta, whose weight monitoring was always a last-minute worry. "I want an authentic world middleweight championship bout," Burston fumed. "I do not want Cerdan to defend the title against a light-heavyweight, and LaMotta will be a legitimate light-heavyweight unless he is compelled to weigh again tomorrow." At ten-thirty the next morning, the two men stepped again onto the scales, and shouts of delight were heard as both fighters made weight. That evening, the rain held off.

There were more than twenty-two thousand on hand at Briggs Stadium. Vikki had never seen her husband fight in person: Afraid to see his face bloodied, she preferred listening on the radio back at a hotel. But Jake pleaded with her to sit ringside on the night of the Cerdan fight, and she did. Before the fight, LaMotta—so fond of Detroit, the city where he had defeated all those Negro boxers, where he had shamed Sugar Ray Robinson—promised his wife Vikki that he'd win.

Paranoia, shame, anger, confusion, and a tawdry kind of gleefulness followed him into the ring that night. He knew he had critics—sportswriters and fans of the fight game alike—and he cared not at all about them.

Not long into the first round the two fighters became entangled; LaMotta wouldn't let go. He had emerged from his corner in the first round in a state of agitation. Still entangled, he finally shoved Cerdan off; the Frenchman slipped and grimaced as he landed on his right shoulder. LaMotta was quickly waved away by the referee. Cerdan got to his feet again, but for the rest of the fight he seemed at a disadvantage. The Frenchman fought gamely in the second round, though, connecting with a flurry of left punches. It was also in that round that LaMotta broke a knuckle on his left hand. Still, utilizing his demonic grit in rounds four, five, and six, LaMotta punched with strength and savvy; his cornerman Al Silvani was screaming at the top of his lungs for him to keep it up. Vikki LaMotta was beside herself; this was her husband, in the flesh, at the top of his game: a fearless and remarkable punching machine, outboxing a world champion right before her eyes: "And it was a thing of beauty to watch," she would remember of the night. The crowd began to sense a shift. By the end of the seventh as he made his way to his corner, Cerdan—five years older than LaMotta—looked both exhausted and unsteady. His cornermen suggested he give up in the eighth round; Cerdan adamantly refused. But he had nothing left.

When the Frenchman couldn't answer the bell for the tenth, the noise started rising; the police contingent started moving closer around the ropes, and Vikki LaMotta's eyes lit up. And then there he was, the Bull, at center ring with his arms raised. The world middleweight champion; up high, the gallery gods were twisting and turning. There were some boos, but LaMotta ignored them, offering only his hard dockworker's grin. Then he paraded around the ring, side to side, so everyone could see him, so the photographers could get their pictures, so that all those who had counted him out all his life—just another wop, a dago, a fool—could see this: Jake LaMotta, champ. Cerdan had come up short, as one reporter put it, "against a huskier, stronger, more savage" foe. And there now was Vikki in the ring, too, looking, with her porcelain beauty, like something that had descended from the bright ring lights. And then there appeared inside the ring Sugar Ray's old Army buddy Joe Louis. Joe's soft face gleamed against the light. He was holding the specially designed belt—of gold, sapphires, and rubies, at a cost of $5,000—in both hands, the way someone might hold a fur coat walking across a dirty puddle. When he handed the belt to Jake, deep emotions caught the Bull. His eyes watered.

Later that night—after all the noise and handshakes and bear hugs and tears—Vikki and Jake retreated to their spacious hotel suite. At long last, a night they would remember forever. Vikki slipped into the bathroom. When she emerged, she was wearing "white silk stockings, a white string bikini, and the championship belt." The Bull might as well have been in heaven: His wife knew that "That was Jake's moment. "He was at the summit with the woman and the title of his dreams."

Few would deny that Cerdan deserved another chance at LaMotta. Many boxing observers believed that were it not for that first-round shoulder injury, the results might well have been different. LaMotta had no choice but to grant Cerdan a rematch, since just such a clause had been written into the original contract. The bout was announced for December 2, 1949, to take place at Madison Square Garden.

The great Frenchman—a bigger-than-life hero in both France and Morocco—arrived at Orly airport in Paris on October 27 for his Manhattan-bound flight, leaving himself plenty of time to set up training headquarters. Photographers had trailed him and began clicking away. For days leading up to his departure, he had been the topic of excited conversation in Paris cafés. Many recalled the 1948 fight against Tony Zale in Jersey City when he had captured the championship crown. At Orly, Cerdan was accompanied by his manager and cornermen. He was in a jubilant mood. "With all my strength I want to get back that title that I so stupidly lost," he told a group of well-wishers. "For those who say I'm washed up I can say that, despite my thirty-three years and 110 fights, I feel myself at my peak." And shortly thereafter, the Air France jetliner was cleared for takeoff and zoomed skyward.

About 1,500 miles out, the pilot sent a simple message: "Having accomplished first part of trip normally, ready to land at 2:55 on Santa Maria Airdrome, Azores, weather being clear." But the plane suddenly hit a stretch of terrible weather, rain and fog; villagers below heard the boom against the mountainside. All forty-eight on board were killed. It took rescuers the better part of a day to reach the wreckage. The grief was wide and deep, especially in Morocco and France. The sudden loss "had plunged the nation into mourning," the great French boxer Georges Carpentier said. Edith Piaf, who had long felt thwarted by the promises of love—that is, until she met Cerdan—collapsed when word of the crash reached her. She kept singing her songs ("La Vie en Rose," "La Marseillaise") but told her friends she'd never be the same again.

Absent Cerdan, Jake LaMotta fought five fights in 1950; two were title fights. He defeated both Tiberio Mitri and, in their rematch, Laurent Dauthille. The Bull now strutted like a peacock around Manhattan, a champion who wanted everyone who didn't already know to hear about the accomplishments of Jake LaMotta. He laughed too loudly and ignored social graces. Walking along one evening, he and Vikki ran into the comic Fat Jack Leonard on a Manhattan street corner. Fat Jack blurted out a joke to everyone he met. Jake listened, then, bizarrely, belted Fat Jack in the stomach. The comic cringed in pain. "What did you expect?" LaMotta said, his voice edgy. "You make your living telling jokes. I'm the champ. That's how I make mine."

After mid-September of 1950, LaMotta didn't fight for the rest of the year. In 1951, the public began clamoring for him to get back in the ring. It was time for him to defend his crown. And, if not a champion, they at least wanted him to fight a contender.

On August 9, 1950, Sugar Ray Robinson fought Charley Fusari in Jersey City. The fight went the full fifteen rounds, with Robinson retaining his welterweight crown. But it had become mighty difficult for him to keep making the welterweight limit, and he decided after the Fusari fight to move up to the middleweight division. As soon as he started calling himself a middleweight, the public saw what was coming.

It all began as conjecture, then shifted to heady and fast-moving gossip. Finally, promoters realized the marquee attraction of such a matchup. In time, emissaries for the Robinson and LaMotta camps huddled and began negotiations.

What LaMotta had—the middleweight belt—Robinson now wanted; what Robinson had—a smooth and elegant image outside the ring—LaMotta craved.

The fight was scheduled for Valentine's Day in Chicago. The public swooned.

A tenseness gripped the country at the time; President Truman had committed forces to the Korean conflict. Old generals from World War II and battle-tested American soldiers—along with U.N. forces—were pushing through the mud of Chipyong in Korea in an effort to defeat Communism. Gen. Douglas MacArthur remained wary of integrating military units. President Truman, however, got rid of him in favor of the more amenable Gen. Matthew Ridgway. And pride swelled in Negro establishments—Sugar Ray's nightclub, Joe Louis's restaurant—that, at long last, military units were now integrated.

Early in 1951, Sugar Ray Robinson was being honored at a Boxing Writers Dinner at the Waldorf Astoria in Manhattan. They were annual black-tie affairs. The heavyweights always looked as if they were about to burst from their tuxedos. Not Sugar Ray: Robinson was wonderfully proportioned—as if he had been put together by a men's fashion designer conscious of perfect measurements—and seemed born into his attire, formal or otherwise. Dignitaries were sprinkled about the evening audience, along with women in gleaming jewels, catching the wattage of Sugar Ray's smile. Not everyone who had been invited could make it, and an assortment of telegrams were read from the podium, addressed to honoree Robinson. SEE YOU FEBRUARY 14 IN CHICAGO, one said. MAKE SURE YOU'RE THERE. JAKE. Beneath the glittering chandeliered light—elbows at rest upon white linen tablecloths—everyone, including Robinson, chuckled.

It was as if the rivalry had been in stop-time since 1945, and now it was suddenly being resumed. There would be one marked difference, however, this time: It would be televised across the nation. The whole country would be able to see for themselves what the Robinson-LaMotta wars had been about—and why they still had such powerful currency.

In 1948 there was a significant rise in the number of broadcast television stations across the country. The medium was still precious enough to be considered a novelty. In the 1948 television season, coaxial cables began linking the East and Midwest. Suddenly, television was a national phenomenon; shows could be circuited right to the West Coast. The first huge TV stars—Arthur Godfrey, Ed Sullivan, and Milton Berle—had also come onto the TV scene between 1948 and 1949.

Retail stores often experienced a bump in the sales of TV sets prior to the broadcasting of big nationally televised events and fights. Ad salesmen realized this, and the newspapers were full of endorsements of which sets to purchase. There were, as well, trade-in opportunities—smaller sets for larger ones! DuMont was a huge manufacturer of TVs, and a mainstay of its product was the DuMont Lifetone Picture guarantee: "This exclusive DuMont picture circuit gives the finest range of 'whites' and 'blacks' in the most lifelike telepicture possible today." One New York outlet, Davega, crowed about trade-in opportunities: "Davega Will Take Any Size TV Set— Any Make—and Offer a TRADE-IN ALLOWANCE Towards a New 17″ or 19″ EMERSON!"

Fight promoters often had to work hard to secure their fight venues, fitting their bouts in around other events already scheduled inside big city arenas and stadiums. February 14 was the date that promoters found available for what would be the sixth and final act of the Robinson-LaMotta drama, a date that struck many as ironic inasmuch as their fights had always been full of bone-jarring and wounding fisticuffs. Now its next installment would take place on a day reserved for roses and sonnets.

At a Chicago fight luncheon days before the bout, Robinson—with LaMotta sitting nearby—instructed a waiter to bring him a cup of red juice from a raw steak. When the beef blood arrived, Robinson offered a sip to LaMotta. "Keep it," a puzzled LaMotta snapped. Robinson then proceeded to drink the blood. The Bull, aghast, shook his head: Robinson—supposedly the smooth and silky persona—was fucking with him and he knew it.

On fight night, the national TV cameras panned across the audience inside the Chicago Stadium, and the edgy and excited murmurings of thousands could be overheard. But beyond the stadium—in all those homes—an estimated thirty million would tune in. That was one-fifth of the American population. The fighters' wives were in attendance; both Edna Mae and Vikki looked gorgeous. They sat on opposite sides of the ring.

Robinson's hands were being taped tight; Gainford and trainer Harry Wiley feared the bruising his knuckles might take as they rammed into LaMotta's skull. Robinson's demeanor worried Wiley. "You look too cool," Wiley told him.

LaMotta, in his dressing room, made a strange request to his brother: He wanted a shot of brandy—and got it.

The familiar voice of Ted Husing, even and sonorous, would be announcing for Pabst Blue Ribbon. "This broadcast tonight is making history," he proclaimed. "Never before has any event been heard and seen by so many people. Not only here in America but right around the globe. It is being shortwaved to Australia and New Zealand, ten thousand miles away . . ." The Voice of America would pipe the fight to military camps in Korea; Pan Am flights would begin carrying it at the sound of the bell on their aircraft flying around the world. Press representatives were in attendance from Canada and France. Italian dignitaries were in the audience, representatives of LaMotta's native land. "The bout the world's been waiting for," Husing said.

For the first time, Sugar Ray Robinson and Jake LaMotta—a crown merely a dream for both when they originally met back in 1942—were meeting as individual champions. Also, a championship belt was at stake. Not since the days of Henry Armstrong had a champion from one division stepped into a ring to face a champion from a separate division. A nation, its DuMont and Emerson TV sets at the ready, was primed.

LaMotta entered the ring in an eye-catching leopard-spotted robe. Robinson's robe was rather simple: black silk.

Soon as the bell sounded, LaMotta rushed in at Robinson, unfolding a strategy similar to the other confrontations—charge and charge and charge—the two becoming entangled until the referee stepped in to separate them. Robinson was still backpedaling from LaMotta in round two, but LaMotta kept charging, going after "Ray's lean ribs," as the *Chicago Tribune* noted. Robinson's counterpunches began to connect in the third, and a streak of blood could be seen dropping from LaMotta's nose. "A right obviously hurt LaMotta," announcer Husing explained. But just as quickly LaMotta landed a right to Robinson's face and his nose was also bleeding. LaMotta's aggressiveness had clearly put him ahead going into the fourth.

Just into the fourth, Robinson unleashed a bolo punch—drawing *ahhs* from many of the estimated 14,800 on hand—and it stilled LaMotta for a moment. Seconds later, however, LaMotta landed a solid right as the light from the Speed Graphic flashbulbs at ringside erupted. Robinson's trainers, Gainford and Wiley, were quite pleased at the taping of Robinson's hands: he stood taller than LaMotta, and his fists—the taping held off swelling—continually fell upon LaMotta's head. In the sixth round, the fighters fought evenly; LaMotta's right eye was puffed, as were Robinson's lips. "I just couldn't level away with him with my right hand," Robinson would say of the sixth. LaMotta's endurance surprised him: " . . . the more I kept punching the more determined he seemed to stay on his feet."

And then in the ninth, it happened: Sugar Ray began unloading unanswered punches with a vengeance. He would later admit this had been his and Gainford's strategy all along. LaMotta, as he imagined, would be exhausted by now. The punches seemed to come like big scattering stones; his energy bedeviled LaMotta. It was as if LaMotta's head was a nail and Robinson's fist a hammer, and he was hammering the nail. The punches rained down and down. LaMotta began wincing from the blows. Robinson hardly let up in the tenth, managing to brush off a wicked LaMotta right hook and then quickly opening a gash over LaMotta's right eye with a stinging blow. LaMotta showed distress as he made his way to his corner to end the round. He came out in the eleventh and offered a quick fusillade, but, as *The Washington Post* would put it, it was just "a dying swan gesture." Robinson stood in a corner and took those blows: "Then he pulled the switch," the *Post* noted. He fired punch after punch into LaMotta, staggering him to within inches, it seemed, of going to the canvas. "No man can endure this pummeling," announcer Husing cried. It was sheer personal pride that kept LaMotta on his feet in the twelfth, taking the blows like a puppet in a ferocious wind. His wife Vikki had already buried her drained face in her hands, where it would remain for the final two rounds. At the beginning of the thirteenth, Jake LaMotta looked truly spent, and a final Robinson volley brought referee Frank Sikora in between the two; he had seen enough and ended it all, two minutes and four seconds into the round that had seen LaMotta take an astonishing fifty-six blows.

The sounds rose slowly, then began cascading in operatic fashion. The world had a new middleweight champion. Gainford and Wiley saluted their champion. Leila Smith, mother of the new champ, pressed against her two daughters with unalloyed joy.

LaMotta, descending from the ring, pushed aside the hands that reached toward him to help him through the ropes. The organist piped up "For He's a Jolly Good Fellow" as a salute—strange as it might seem—to LaMotta's having withstood such punishment. Reporters scampered toward the respective dressing rooms. LaMotta fell onto a table and was immediately given oxygen. His wife Vikki, her high heels clacking swiftly into the room, was shocked at the sight of her husband connected to the tank, his face horribly swollen. She had grave thoughts her husband might expire then and there, but a physician managed to calm her. "I'm here with you as always," she said soothingly to the Bull. It was hours before he was in a condition to leave the stadium.

The worldwide sporting event played out on the front pages of newspapers, right alongside news of the Korean war conflict. A six-column headline—CHINESE REDS LOSE 10,225 IN DAY—was spread across the top of the next morning's edition of *The Washington Post,* and the front-page photo beneath it showed Robinson lashing a right into LaMotta's jaw: ROBINSON TKO'S LAMOTTA IN 13TH TO WIN TITLE. Gainford was telling anyone with a pencil or pen that his fighter now would be aiming for the light heavyweight crown.

The televising of the fight—and Robinson's "spectacular" showing, as *The New York Times* put it—introduced Sugar Ray Robinson to more fans than ever before. He was a lethal, fist-flying presence, suddenly as near as the television set. But not everyone was enamored of such living-room intimacy. In a front-page editorial, the *Indianapolis News* attacked the proceedings: "At least a million Hoosiers last night saw a world championship prizefight over television. For most of them it was their first. They saw two athletes swing at each other's jaws and stomachs like savages in a jungle; they saw blood drip from battered noses; they heard 15,000 fellow Americans roar a sickening tribute to brutality." It went on: "When Jake LaMotta was permitted to go into the thirteenth round unsound of mind, unsound of body, wobbling and with a mentality that didn't know whether it was 10 o'clock or the Fourth of July, the 'sport' showed its true colors. It is a throwback to the Cromagnon man . . ."

Sportswriters—and the fight-watching public as well—quickly found a summing-up title for the final Robinson-LaMotta encounter: "The St. Valentine's Day Massacre."

Neither Sugar Ray Robinson nor Jake LaMotta, of course, had invented the sport. They simply played by its rules, unfair as they often were. It was war, up close and in the trenches. It was as dark and grave as a cemetery at midnight. LaMotta knew that innocence had nothing to do with the fight game. Darkness, in fact—and a need to escape a life of criminality—had led him into the ring in the first place. Robinson, a Negro, had found glorious movement across the landscape as a fighter. The lyrics of "Sweet Georgia Brown" played in his heart as his hands showed a killer instinct. His fists gave him freedom, allowing him to believe he owed the sport everything he could give it.

Three days after the bout, Robinson and his wife Edna Mae boarded a train for New York City. Well-wishers and Chicago acquaintances crowded the platform to see them off. They waved and smiled as the train pulled away, receding into the distance, finally vanishing.

The saga of Jake LaMotta wasn't over. A year and a half after the last Robinson bout, he moved his family to Miami Beach.

Vikki thought it might save the marriage. Things only grew worse. The money began floating away. There were bad investments, a hilarious attempt at playing the trumpet in hopes of joining a band. He tried affecting the manners of a man of leisure. He was seen rushing in and out of bars, his gut heaving, loud Hawaiian shirts on his back. He whispered into the ears of game young ladies. There were run-ins with Miami police: LaMotta punched a shoeshine man who had asked him to leave his stand. The assault charge was dropped, but he had to make a financial settlement to the poor soul. His last bout—he would fight only ten more times after the final Robinson meeting—was against Billy Kilgore, a nobody, in Miami Beach on April 14, 1954. He lost.

In 1955 he opened Jake LaMotta's, a bar on Collins Avenue. He held court, brought in celebrities to entertain (Buddy Hackett, Milton Berle), told horrible jokes, and ordered up drinks for young Lolitas: underage girls in lipstick sitting in the smoky shadows. But, in time, bar attendance dropped, the clientele went from upper-crust to low-life. There had been complaints about Jake's boorish behavior. Vikki hated the riffraff he brought home from the bar. The following year she left him, eventually filing for divorce.

In January 1957 Jake LaMotta was arrested on several charges, among them promoting prostitution, conspiracy, and contributing to the delinquency of a minor. A fourteen-year-old girl who had been arrested on a prostitution charge told police she plied her trade at LaMotta's bar. LaMotta professed ignorance of the girl's age. The scandalous news went national. He was eventually convicted on two counts of promoting prostitution. He served six months, sitting, at night, in the darkness, just like at Coxsackie all those years ago. Some days, chained, he trudged to the back of a big pickup along with other cons, and was deposited on the side of a highway to do roadwork. A shotgun-wielding prison guard watched over everyone. Inside jail the rednecks hated him and he hated them, daring any of them to lay a hand on him. They kept clear.

Upon his release, he was finished as a businessman and seen as a joke. There was additional shame, in time, when he went public in 1960 about having taken that dive in the Billy Fox bout.

Sometimes reporters and sports junkies would come around and want to talk to Vikki LaMotta about her onetime husband. He was the father of her children; she preferred talking, for the most part, about when things were good; when the Bull was smiling and happy and fighting and loving her and looking beautiful in the ring against Marcel Cerdan. She did believe, though, that the fighter who had chased and captured her Jake time and time again over a nine-year period had come to forever haunt the Bull: "Physically and psychologically, Sugar Ray Robinson destroyed him," she felt. "Jake was never the same in or out of the ring again."

Sugar Ray, on the other hand, only continued to soar. On that cold 1951 Valentine's Day evening in Chicago, millions upon millions could suddenly witness the mastery of Sugar Ray Robinson. He became a figure removed from the radio box and all those grapevine soliloquies. What had been mentioned in various corners of the nation about him—his prowess, his frightening speed, his power—proved utterly true. He was photogenic, coldly unemotional in the ring—and a star.

Sugar Ray now stood a decade into his professional fight career. By now the emotional wars that had shaped him had also given him his independence. Walker Smith Jr. had escaped childhood only to be born again as a fighter. The military, he had felt, had been against him and his dream to become a champion, so he outfoxed them too. He was the rare Negro who had rebuked the mob and won. Victory in the LaMotta wars served as a crowning achievement. It was little surprise that admirers seemed to be everywhere. Yes, bad things sometimes happened in and around the environs of entertainment venues in Harlem. But the parishioners at his church, Salem Methodist, forgave him his nightclub ownership. They were convinced he was doing good in his own way. They, too, had been seduced by the champion: If told that Sugar Ray and Edna Mae were coming to church on a certain Sunday morning, the minister in the pulpit was careful not to begin until the couple arrived. Many strained to see the cut of their attire. (Robinson had a habit of stopping cold just inside the church doorway before beginning his stride to his seat.) His church tithing was always generous. He took comfort while away on the road knowing that church members were praying for

him. Growing up in the North—unlike Armstrong, Joe Louis, and Jack Johnson— he had also escaped personal racial trauma. His mother had protected him in the beginning, then the church came to the rescue— deacons and ministers shielding the Salem flock from the lash of racial hurt as much as

The Robinson-LaMotta battles finally came to an end on the night of February 14, 1951, in cold Chicago. Fans kept an extraordinary interest in the long-running and brutal fistic opera.

possible. But a Parisian chanteuse, herself the survivor of a desperate childhood, was about to shake the conscience of Sugar Ray.

INTERLUDE **The Boxer, Madame Baker, and "W.W."**

Just minutes after Sugar Ray Robinson had defeated Jake La-Motta for the last time in that Chicago ring, he made his way over to Ted Husing, the announcer. Leaning against the ropes, he answered a few perfunctory questions. Then—with the national audience watching and millions of others still listening to the radio in homes, restaurants, pool halls, nightclubs—Robinson leaned into the microphone and delivered a message to a friend down in Miami: "W.W., I did the best I could," he said, perspiration still dripping from his brow. Every radio listener, and many in the TV audience as well, knew who "W.W." was: He was Walter Winchell, the powerful and feared Broadway columnist. (Winchell spent several months a year in Miami Beach, doing his ABC radio broadcast, writing his syndicated column, clowning with the locals, and bedding young women who adored his fame and didn't mind his mop of gray hair.) Robinson, from the ring, went on to say to Winchell that he had raised tens of thousands of dollars for the Damon Runyon Cancer Fund while in Chicago—just as he had done during his recent European tour. The fund was a personal crusade for Winchell, and Robinson was committed to it too. Robinson had become involved with the Runyon fund as a way to pay tribute to Spider Valentine, his onetime Salem Crescent boxing mate who had died of cancer. But the face of the fund was the eccentric—there were less kind words used to describe him too—Walter Winchell. The columnist, now back in Manhattan, was about to be drawn into an imbroglio that would involve celebrated expatriate and chanteuse Josephine Baker, Sherman Billingsley, the proprietor of Manhattan's chic Stork Club, and the middleweight champion of the world, Sugar Ray Robinson. The national brouhaha would, for the first time, test Robinson's political savvy.

Robinson had begun courting Winchell back in 1946, during the exciting early days of his nightclub, *Sugar Ray's.* Like a little boy, Walter Winchell was enamored of sports figures, especially the ones who had nosed their way into the culture of entertainment. He would yak about Robinson's nightspot on the radio, sending celebrities and nighttime revelers through its doors. An endorsement from Winchell carried significant weight. There were huge posters on the sides of Hearst newspaper trucks zipping through Manhattan: "Read WALTER WINCHELL—AMERICAS NO. 1 REPORTER—*New York Daily Mirror.*" Winchell and Robinson would be seen together bopping in and out of other Manhattan nightspots—Club Samoa, the Clique Club down on Broadway, the Three Deuces—eyes following them as they moved from table to table. They'd shake hands with patrons, Robinson telling acquaintances to call his office for free fight tickets, Winchell grinning like a vaudeville theatre owner days into a sold-out run. Their joint appearances emitted powerful wattage. (From the age of ten to twenty-three, Winchell had actually been a vaudeville performer. He abandoned the greasepaint to write vaudeville news. Of many sobriquets used to describe him, Walter "Merciless Truths" Winchell seemed to stand out.)

Winchell, like any other New York City newspaperman, had been reading Runyon in the *New York Journal-American* for years. Runyon had become a huge celebrity for his boxing and baseball columns with a literary touch. Hollywood had already discovered his quirky short stories: One such tale, about gambling and bookies and a chirpy-looking little girl with blond curls, became the 1934 film, *Little Miss Marker,* featuring child star Shirley Temple. That same year, another one, *The Lemon Drop Kid,* starred William Frawley and was all about racetrack shenanigans. Winchell and Runyon formed a deep friendship in 1944 following Runyon's surgery for throat cancer. The removal of Runyon's larynx left him unable to speak. He began communicating by scribbling on a notepad. Winchell felt sympathy and insisted that Runyon accompany him on his nightly escapades around Manhattan. Winchell listened to a police radio in his car, and, upon hearing something that excited him, raced off to the scene. Runyon became his sidekick. "He had always scoffed good-naturedly at my habit of prowling New York late at night in my car, listening to police calls on my special radio and chasing excitement where it was happening," Winchell would write of Runyon and those times. "Now, sensing his loneliness, I persuaded him to come along with me. We would meet every night at the Stork Club, where we would sit in the Cub Room with old friends." Teenagers would sometimes spot the two aging men crawling through the night and mistake them for police detectives: Winchell's license plate on his big blue Cadillac said "NYP1"—it stood for New York press—and enabled Winchell to park anywhere he pleased. Little did the gazing teenagers realize that the two men—aging scribes from another era—were much like them, out hunting for action, for fun.

"When I die, if I had one man remember me so faithful despite the many passing years," Runyon had written on his pad to Winchell, "then I'd be happy." Winchell vowed to Runyon— who died December 10, 1946—that he would not be forgotten.

Shortly after the famed columnist's death, Winchell announced a drive to raise money in Runyon's name for cancer research. The cash started coming in immediately. They were readers of Runyon's column, boxing and baseball and football fans, and also readers of Walter Winchell. When Winchell was out screeching through the night, bopping into nightclubs, he was surprised when anonymous souls came up to him, shoving money into his hands and pockets for the Runyon fund. He smiled and his eyes took on a tender glow. Early in the evening he'd sometimes regale everyone with Damon Runyon stories. He enlisted celebrities from Hollywood and Broadway—and Sugar Ray Robinson, who was another type of celebrity. "Winchell really wanted Sugar Ray for the fund," remembers Jess Rand, a young publicist at the time, who knew both Winchell and Runyon.

For many, the two might well have seemed mismatched: Winchell so loud and ego-driven, Robinson quiet and smooth. But they got along, and Sugar Ray's name and nightclub appeared regularly in Winchell's column.

Walter Winchell—whose facial features were sharp as a shark's, who brushed his hair straight back, in the style of film-noir movie stars—considered himself a liberal. Often, he would champion the underdog in his columns. He was sensitive about slights and put-downs. One afternoon while in Miami Beach, along with Robinson, he pleaded with the prizefighter to hit the clubs with him. Robinson, like every other Negro, knew that Miami Beach barred Negroes from its streets after dark.

"You're with me, you know," Winchell said to Robinson.

"Yeah, but you're Jewish," Sugar Ray said.

"I'm Winchell," Winchell reminded him.

Robinson had no intention of letting Winchell down in the fund-raising efforts. The fighter would arrive in a city days before his bout, spend time raising money for the fund, whip his opponent more often than not, and then, before leaving town, present a local hospital with a check for cancer research. Four months after Runyon's death, Winchell himself gave the American Cancer Society a $250,000 check. In time, a board was formed on behalf of the fund; Winchell became its treasurer.

Walter Winchell's Manhattan lair was the Stork Club, specifically an inner sanctum of the Stork Club known as the Cub Room. One had to be a swimmer in that sea of blondes, rich men, tycoons, brunettes, showgirls, and entertainers to gain admittance to the Stork Club; and, once inside, one had to know the proprietor Sherman Billingsley himself to gain entrée to the Cub Room. (The Cub Room was quieter than the main room, where a rumba dance band vibrated.) Billingsley was a onetime bootlegger who had fashioned his nightspot into an elitist's playpen. Kings and queens dined at the Stork Club; Clark Gable and Ed Sullivan and Lucille Ball partook of its wine selection; Jackie Gleason and Bob Hope ate the delicacies sent out from the kitchen, dabbing their fingers on the lovely white cloth napkins. Men wore evening suits; women gowns with silk gloves reaching the elbow. But Negroes did not drink or dine on anything at the Stork Club. Not that the club ever overtly said Negroes were not welcome; it was just an unwritten understanding.

In early October of 1951, Josephine Baker was in Manhattan playing the Roxy. The ads trumpeted: "Extraordinary Limited Engagement! Ned Schuyler Presents The Exotic Rage of Paris . . . in her only New York theatre appearance this season." Baker was the perfect embodiment of a scandalous heroine. In Paris she had danced nude, attended debauched parties. Hemingway swooned over her. Born in St. Louis, Baker had been abused as a child. She got herself to New York City and joined a vaudeville troupe. She found the city rude; store owners wouldn't allow her to try on clothing because she was black. She happily sailed for Paris to appear in a show called *La Revue Nègre*. On stage in the City of Light, she danced and became a sensation. A French theatre director would recall one of her earliest performances: "It was like the revelation of a new world. Eroticism finding a style. Josephine was laughing, she was crying, and the audience stood and gave her such an ovation that she trembled and could not leave the stage. We had to bring the curtain down." Reporters scrambled to sit with her for interviews. She was once asked, in those early days, what had been her biggest joy thus far. "Well," she said, her eyes welling up with tears, "last night after the show was over, the theater was turned into a big restaurant . . . And for the first time in my life, I was invited to sit at a table and eat with white people." During the war she worked with the French Underground; in Paris she was awarded the Medal of Resistance. She counted both male and female among her many lovers. (Physically, there were women far more beautiful than she; her métier was seduction.)

In Manhattan in 1951, during her Roxy engagement, the international star was fussed over; there were dinner invitations aplenty. In previous years Walter Winchell had praised her in his columns. Like Sugar Ray Robinson, Baker had also helped raise money for the Runyon fund. On the evening of October 16, Baker accepted one of those many dinner invitations. Roger Rico—whom the chanteuse had known from Paris and who was appearing in a Broadway show—convinced Baker to accompany him, his wife, Solange, and former Cotton Club dancer Bessie Buchanan, to the Stork. Baker chose a blue satin Dior gown and glided with her party—which also included husband Jo Bouillon—into the cool night. It was a little after eleven p.m. when they arrived at the Stork. They were led to a table in the exclusive Cub Room. Perfume scented the air. Glasses were clinking; silverware shone. Baker ordered a bottle of wine: French. Then a crab salad and a steak. Winchell was seated not far away, absorbed in conversation. Shortly after their arrival, Billingsley, the owner, walked by the Cub Room. He looked around and spotted Baker. "Who the fuck let her in?" he snapped in a low voice to a waiter. Everyone at the Baker table received their meal—except Baker. The diners were aggrieved and complaints were made. A waiter finally told her they were out of crab salad—and steaks. This did not sit well with the party. Baker rose, her sweeping Dior drawing stares, and strode off to use the telephone. She phoned Walter White, the NAACP leader. She told him what had happened.

Within days, the non-dinner event at the Stork took on epic proportions: Baker's party accused the club of being racist; the NAACP complained to Manhattan politicos about the club and demanded an investigation; Baker said Winchell could have intervened the night of the incident but did nothing; civil rights spokesmen demanded Winchell assail Billingsley, the club owner. Winchell refused and quickly became incensed that anyone dared question his progressive credentials. Appeals were being made to Sugar Ray Robinson, who was now a member of the Runyon Cancer Fund board along with the likes of Joe DiMaggio, Milton Berle, and Marlene Dietrich, to give up his seat. (Robinson happened to be out of town.) Henry Lee Moon, who handled publicity for the NAACP, summoned reporters to Baker's dressing room at the Roxy. He said there was to be a major announcement. This contretemps was a big bone and Moon meant to gnaw on it. Heads swiveled and necks craned as the gathering came to order. Madame Baker— a heroine in yet one more scandal—looked regal, surrounded by telegrams, pictures, and flowers, the accumulation of her celebrity. Moon dramatically announced that Sugar Ray Robinson was quitting the board of the Runyon fund. The reporters raced away. Moon, however, had bizarrely not confirmed this with Robinson.

In Manhattan, where scandal, race, politics, and nightclubs all intersected, it proved more electric than the switching on of a hundred klieg lights at a movie premiere. Soon there were pickets outside the Stork. (FAMOUS NITE SPOT JUST A WHITE SPOT, one sign held aloft said.) NAACP leaders told Winchell they expected him to come down hard on Billingsley. Winchell scoffed. The more Winchell was attacked, the more he struck back. He went on a rampage, accusing Baker of anti-Semitism, racism (against lower-class blacks), and even linking her to fascism. Friends told Winchell to calm down, but he could not; he felt he was spreading merciless truths—his stock in trade. Furthermore, he believed the whole affair had been set up, to shame the Stork. And Walter Winchell loved the Stork Club: He drank for free; he got tidbits for his column there; it was his office and dining hangout. As he had told Sugar Ray: I'm Winchell.

W.W. also knew quite well the political temperature of the Stork. That very year, Sugar Ray had breezily suggested to Winchell they meet at the Stork for dinner and talk. Winchell felt squeezed. "I wish you wouldn't, champ," the savvy newspaperman demurred. "Sherman Billingsley doesn't like Negroes and he doesn't want them in the place and if he came down there and he insulted you, I'd have to break with him although I've known him for 23 years." That night Sugar Ray avoided the Stork—but now he couldn't.

When the incident erupted, Robinson was in Boston, where he happened to be raising money for the Runyon fund. Once back in Manhattan, though, he couldn't escape the affair. Reporters were dialing his nightclub, his business office. He said nothing until the evening of the Pal Razor Sports Award ceremony. Stepping through the doors, he looked suave. He had a practiced tendency to move slowly in public situations away from the ring. But there was concern in his eyes that evening. He allowed as to how he felt disappointment that Winchell had not tried to intervene and come to Baker's aid. "I can't tell you how it makes you feel that you're fighting cancer . . . and you have a cancer right there in your own committee." He said he couldn't hold his feelings back any longer and would continue to make them apparent, even in the event that he had to "resign from the Cancer Fund."

Anyone in the middle of the imbroglio was made to feel like a referee trying to get two middleweights to retreat to their respective corners. Baker announced she was going to sue Winchell and the Hearst newspapers, which she did. Robinson—in the middle—began to wonder if Baker had become the victim of her own ego. He slid behind the wheel of his pink Caddy and drove to the Roxy to see her. He was escorted to her dressing room.

"Why are you here?" Madame Baker wanted to know.

"Because I love you," Sugar Ray told her, "and I don't want you to make trouble. Walter is too powerful, he can kill your career."

Robinson had long fought in integrated surroundings as a boxer—the fight game being one arena where white America joyfully came together to watch white battling against black. The fight game had removed the edge he might have held as a social crusader. Other professional sporting affairs, such as baseball, were confined to the Negro Leagues. Baker didn't believe his warning about Winchell. But just in case Robinson was right, she began summoning friends, far and wide, to come to Manhattan to defend her honor and reputation. (She had tried to reach President Truman to express her outrage; White House operators told her the busy man was unavailable.) New York City Hall was more amenable: "I will not go to the Stork Club or any other club that practices discrimination," Mayor Vincent Impellitteri huffed.

Barry Gray was a popular and fearless New York City radio host. He excitedly announced he was going to have guests on his show to go over the entire Baker-Billingsley affair—"a radio trial, if you will," as he put it. Baker arrived at the studio flanked by Walter White, of the NAACP, and Jacques Abtey, one of those individuals who had come from far away to be by her side: Abtey had been her commandant during those dangerous and thrilling days when she worked for the French Underground. (He had also been one of her many lovers.) Abtey said he had crossed the seas "to defend the honor of a war heroine." Baker herself attacked Winchell in breathless tones in two appearances; White read telegrams rebuking Winchell's claim that the Department of Justice and other governmental organizations were in the process of deporting Baker. Gray loved every minute of it. The ratings were high and he kept the discourse up. The attention didn't come, however, without consequences: On two occasions, Gray was attacked. He was forced to get a bodyguard. His attackers got away. Earl Wilson, the Broadway columnist, quipped: "The suspect list has narrowed to 1,000." Gray brought Ed Sullivan on, a onetime popular radio host who was now a popular TV host. Sullivan's face seemed carved from granite. "But of all things that are un-American," said Sullivan—who loathed Winchell from their catty arguments on the vaudeville circuit in their youth—"to me the gravest affront is character assassination. So I despise Walter Winchell for what he has done to Josephine Baker." For good measure, Sullivan added of Winchell: "I say that he's a megalomaniac and a dangerous one."

Then Sugar Ray Robinson came on the show. Despite his earlier comments, he defended W.W., proclaiming him "an ally of black people."

Winchell refused to appear.

The flap continued: There was a ridiculously long newspaper series on Winchell—twenty-four installments—full of critique and gossip, which appeared in the *New York Post* following the Stork Club incident. Among other caustic remarks, it referred to Billingsley as "Winchell's valet." It also said, in part, that Winchell had a thin skin and suffered from paranoia. Winchell complained bitterly not only to allies about the series, but also to the NAACP, claiming the organization was ruining him. He said if he waltzed back into Harlem that his "blood would flow in the streets." Robinson sought to rein in Winchell's paranoia, but it didn't help. As for Josephine Baker, her nightclub engagements across America began to dry up. So she packed her Dior dresses and gallivanted about the world: Argentina, Cuba, back to Europe. She burned her American bridges by denouncing the country of her birth. She began adopting homeless children. The music still wafted from within the Stork Club, but Billingsley was soon besieged by pickets protesting working conditions. Reporters, gossip columnists, and radio broadcasters found other stories to cover—namely the upcoming presidential election.

His support of W.W. had been a rare political move on Sugar Ray Robinson's part. He was an apolitical celebrity. While he considered himself a Democrat, he saw no need to advertise it. He felt for Baker and her plight—if only she had simply come uptown to Sugar Ray's!—but Winchell had been a longtime friend. For the most part, Sugar Ray believed justice was best served from the center of the boxing ring: The hooligans who had jumped Barry Gray knew better than to come near him. When Winchell had cautioned against a visit to the Stork, Robinson heeded the warning: He would not have his pride wounded. He had, of course, his own haven. He was a far more egalitarian proprietor than Sherman Billingsley— hipster whites, French, Greek, Ethiopians, all came through the front door of *Sugar Ray's*. In the aftermath of the Baker incident, Billingsley tried to alter his image even as he was enduring public humiliation and getting several bomb threats. He invited Eartha Kitt to the Stork. She refused; she was spotted on occasion, however, having a high good time at *Sugar Ray's*. So he had his own kind of Stork Club, where the likes of E. Simms Campbell, the estimable *Esquire* artist, could come and relax without fear that his pride would be insulted; where Adam Clayton Powell and his piano-playing wife, Hazel Scott, could spread their glamorous smiles among a kind of sepia royalty; where Billy Eckstine and Duke Ellington could come and just be themselves, sharing all those intimate details about the doings of Negro America—details that never reached the Stork. It was the entertainers who intoxicated Sugar Ray as they came through the doors of his club. He seemed transfixed listening to their tales of performing on the road; it sounded like fun, moments of pure joy. Musicians on a stage; dancers sashaying. Boxing was not joyful; he made it look joyful, but it was a painful exercise. The dark reality was that he took an awful lot of hits. It was the chink in the armor of being a great fighter: Sugar Ray Robinson, the champion, simply took too many punches. He escaped a great many because of his quickness; but a great many he did not. He was already wondering about his future.

He saw time in the mirror, especially on nights like September 27, 1950, inside Yankee Stadium.

Joe Louis had come out of retirement to face Ezzard Charles, the reigning heavyweight champion. Louis, who hadn't fought since June 1948, was fighting because he owed back taxes. Charles pummeled Louis relentlessly; Louis lumbered about the ring like a giant trapped in a haze of fog. Before the fight, Louis's training regimen had been lackluster. In the ring now, he was clearly overweight; boos rang out from the stands. At the end of the fourteenth, he nearly collapsed, stung by Charles's blows. His cornermen helped Louis from his stool to begin the final round. Charles seemed to be holding back from finishing off the iconic figure. In 1948—not quite two years after Jimmy Doyle's fate at the hands of Sugar Ray Robinson—Sam Baroudi died from injuries suffered in a bout with Charles in Chicago. Many felt Charles had lost his killer instinct, leveling off in late rounds when he could have knocked out opponents. So too it seemed with Louis. At the defeat, Louis's eyes welled up. Sugar Ray shadowed his old Army buddy down in the dressing room, helping him put his clothes on. Anguished moans erupted from Louis: He couldn't find his damn shoes. Robinson finally found them and helped the old champion put them on. Sugar Ray—wiping the still-seeping blood from Louis's face—felt "it was like trying to console an old blind man."

The reporters finally came in. They started firing their questions. Then it got quiet, as if they were all suddenly out of breath. Louis scanned the room. His own tears had dried, but now he saw the tears of others—namely Sugar Ray's. It seemed to touch him. "What's the use of crying?" he said softly. "The better man won. That's all." Robinson couldn't shake the night: "I didn't want to make the same mistake Joe Louis had." Tony Cordaro, a reporter for *The Des Moines Register,* would write of the Louis-Charles bout: "It seemed a terrible punishment to take for the income tax." Louis had not left boxing, boxing had left him. Thirteen months later, Louis fought the dangerous Rocky Marciano in New York City. Rocky knocked him out in the eighth round. Afterward, Sugar Ray was again by the former heavyweight champion's side, whispering in his ear, trying to shield him from the klieg lights. It was the unspectacular coda to the great ring career of Joe Louis Barrow.

There were times when George Gainford, Harry Wiley, and others would stand back and watch Sugar Ray Robinson: descending the plank of an ocean liner; shaking the hands of everyone from little children to royalty; chatting with Duke Ellington and Lena Horne; smiling from behind the bar of his very own club; slipping into view behind the wheel of his Cadillac, his name flying from the mouths of pedestrians—Sugarray! Sugarray! Sugarray!—and imagine he was among the happiest men on earth. They chuckled during those times when he casually mentioned retirement, musing about entertainers and dancers—the Nicholas Brothers, Buck and Bubbles, Dinah Washington, Cootie Williams—and the lives they led. How could anyone walk away from being boxing royalty? Gainford and Wiley wondered. They chalked Robinson's threat of retirement up to idle chatter, fallout from all those lovely chorus girls and dapper jazzmen constantly coming into his nightclub, feeding his beyond-boxing dreams.

When he posed for photographers in those halcyon days of the early 1950s, he looked not like an athlete but a man of leisure. Sugar Ray Robinson was now one of the kings of sepia America, rolling in a rich man's mist: dinners at the Waldorf; up-close tickets to big sporting events; swaying on dance floors at those charity balls. Sometimes he'd be spotted standing on a Manhattan street corner, in repose, chatting with some anonymous soul. He'd be holding his fedora by his fingertips, as if he just might flip it into thin air, daring it not to circle back to him. The Negro magazines, especially the ones who fancied themselves arbiters of style and fashion (*Ebony, Our World*), were eager to write him up. But so were the editors of *Life* and *Holiday* and *Time. Time* magazine would feature him on its cover in a 1951 edition, a moment of undeniable proof that he had crossed over into a new light with a bewitching combination of brute strength and silkiness. He convinced himself—not unlike Lena, Langston, and Miles—that the fifties would conform to him and not the other way around. There were hints he wanted to try Hollywood. He had been quietly conferring with entertainment agents. But then Paris called. Cocky brawlers an ocean away wanted a chance at him. So he set sail for the Old World—and a new decade.

THE NEW NEWS QUIZ

TWENTY CENTS   JUNE 25, 1951

TIME

THE WEEKLY NEWSMAGAZINE

SUGAR RAY ROBINSON
Rhythm in his feet and pleasure in his work.

$5.00 A YEAR   VOL. LVII

1951

around (a part of) the world in fifty days

IN APRIL OF 1951, Sugar Ray Robinson was thinking of Paris. The long boulevards and chic cafés; those swank nightclubs and wonderful men's clothing shops. Before he could set sail there were a couple of detours: There was an April 5 engagement with middleweight Holly Mims in Miami. Sugar Ray settled for a decision in the tenth. Four days later, he found himself in Oklahoma City to face Don Ellis. It would be the only fight in that state during his entire career. Robinson didn't linger in Oklahoma City either: Ellis was the victim of a first-round knockout.

The great prizefighter was gallivanting about Paris when this *Time* magazine hit the stands back home. In Manhattan the issue sold out within hours.

It was the European promoter Charlie Michaelis who persuaded Robinson to come to Paris. Michaelis promised a string of bouts that would keep Robinson busy through the summer—while allowing time for plenty of enjoyment and relaxation. Robinson couldn't resist. He informed Michaelis, however, there would have to be first-class accommodations for his entourage, which seemed to balloon by the month. Michaelis agreed to Robinson's demands, and made a request of his own: He thought it would be wonderful if Robinson would arrive with his pink Cadillac. The request perplexed the fighter. He wondered how he would get it there. Michaelis suggested it could come on the same ocean liner that would be bringing Robinson over. "I will pay the shipping charge," he declared, chuckling.

Michaelis went about securing bouts for Robinson. Within a short period of time, he had most of the fights lined up; the lone exception was a possible bout in London. Neither Robinson nor Gainford expressed any worry about the opponents—even if each one happened to be quite well known on the European continent.

The bonhomie and conviviality of traveling jazz bands had entranced Sugar Ray Robinson so much he sought to duplicate it with his own entourage. The disparate personalities in his group were akin to an ad hoc road family. He had been the only boy in a family of sisters and had spent hours and hours alone in his youth. Now he relished company, the mingling of laughter and the sight of familiar faces. Some members of his entourage, however, had jobs, duties to carry out that kept Robinson's stylish image at peak form. So there was a barber, a golf pro, a trainer, a dietician, a secretary. Now and then casual acquaintances—a nightclub owner from another city, a fellow middleweight—would be invited to join, leaving them absolutely thrilled. Don Ellis may have been a first-round knockout victim in Oklahoma City, but he smiled when Robinson invited him on his European excursion. The Robinson entourage, at any given time, could number upwards of a dozen. No one had to be instructed to dress appropriately; they took their cues from the elegant Robinson himself. The men were seen in fine tweed suits and two-toned shoes; the women in silk dresses, heels, and eye-catching hats.

In the days leading up to his late April excursion, Robinson made the ritual stops by his Manhattan businesses. He was a hands-off businessman, taking joy in the hum inside his barbershop, lingerie shop, and nightclub. The movement of so many bodies, the jangling noise from the cash register, convinced him business was good.

A caravan of automobiles made its way to the Manhattan dock for departure. Fight managers had been spooked by the airplane death of Marcel Cerdan, and many began insisting their fighters travel by ship going abroad. (Robinson's pink Caddy eventually disappeared into the ocean liner's storage area. Gainford's black Cadillac was also part of the cargo.) Before boarding, he shook hands and smiled all around. There were plenty of well-wishers—old church members, newsmen, fight fans—to send Robinson and his group off. Ship stewards were astonished at the mountain of luggage. Robinson had packed an assortment of suits. Also, two tuxedos. One was a traditional cut; the other a black tux with tails.

In one sense, this was a different Paris than the one Robinson had visited six months earlier. Parisians had grieved mightily at the loss of Cerdan in that plane crash, and the playing of any Edith Piaf recording continued to summon painful feelings. Robinson, of course, had defeated LaMotta, whom the French loathed because he had not only defeated their Cerdan, but he was the fighter whom Cerdan had been en route to fight again when his plane went down. In the minds of the French, Robinson had avenged Cerdan's nation-shattering death. Unbeknownst to Sugar Ray Robinson, as he sailed toward France, he had become a national hero.

A Negro photographer, who had used all his gifts and photographic talents to get hired by *Life* magazine, got himself a plum assignment in the magazine's Paris bureau. He covered fashion but convinced his editors that Robinson's arrival in Paris would be quite a worthwhile story.

Gordon Parks's life was so rough and incandescent he may as well have popped from an old Western daguerreotype. He was born in 1912 in the dusty town of Fort Scott, Kansas. His father was a dirt farmer. When his mother died in his youth, he was dispatched to St. Paul to live with relatives. There, he found work playing piano—he had a natural ear—in a whorehouse. Thin and dark, he wore his hair slicked back, à la Rudy Valentino. He was a hepcat with ambition, only lacking a direction in which to take it. He hit the road, landing in Sugar Ray's Harlem in the late 1930s.

He eventually left Robinson's Harlem and found work as a waiter on the North Coast Limited train. At stops on the line, he scooped up magazines left by passengers. In one, he couldn't lift his eyes from the pages and pages of photographs: "They were of migrant workers. Dispossessed, beaten by storms, dusts and floods, they roamed the highways in caravans of battered jalopies and wagons between Oklahoma and California, scrounging for work. Some were so poor that they traveled on foot, pushing their young in baby buggies and carts." The pictures had been taken by Farm Security Administration photographers—Dorothea Lange, Arthur Rothstein, Walker Evans among them. Those photographers had gotten their jobs because of the benevolence of the Roosevelt administration and the genius of Roy Stryker, a onetime economics professor who was given a mandate to document rural America. And when Stryker's photographers hit their stride, they found themselves making landmark documentary pictures of white and Negro life in small towns and out-of-the-way places all across the country: Negro workers on a Louisiana plantation; shoeless white schoolchildren in Breathitt County, Kentucky; Negroes snapping their fingers in a juke joint in Clarksdale, Mississippi; white migrant workers in Belle Glade, Florida. It was America—desperate and hungry and drifting and surviving. The images had a huge impact upon Parks. Inside a Minneapolis pawnshop, he forked over $7.50 and walked out with a Voigtlander Brilliant camera. In 1938 a local camera store displayed some of his fashion photographs in their window. Marva Louis—wife of Joe Louis—spotted those pictures and encouraged him to come to Chicago.

In Chicago, Parks got enough work to draw the attention of the Julius Rosenwald Fund. The Rosenwald group gave cultural fellowships to enterprising writers and artists. Parks, to his astonishment, received one in 1940. The fellowship took Parks to Washington, D.C., in 1941 and a prized position as a photographer with the Farm Security Administration. But Parks quickly began to loathe Washington and its racist rituals: store clerks who refused to serve him, restaurants directing him to the back door, theatre ushers telling him yet another show was sold out when he knew differently. Stryker, the FSA head, told him to turn his camera against inequality. "You have to get at the source of their bigotry," Stryker said.

In the very office where Stryker and his team were headquartered,

Parks noticed a black cleaning lady one evening, swish-swishing her mop down the hall. The lady had gray hair, wore a plain dotted dress and severe eyeglasses. Her name was Ella Watson and she was poor as nickels. Parks struck up a conversation. He spotted a big American flag hanging from a wall. He asked Watson if he could take her picture. She was holding a mop in one hand and a broom in the other when the flash went off, her gaunt face staring outward almost as if she had forced herself out of the fabric of the flag itself. The photograph, called "American Gothic," was a sensation, and Parks's reputation began to rise.

Parks spent several years freelancing for *Vogue* and *Glamour* magazines, among others, while living in Manhattan. He befriended novelist Richard Wright and E. Simms Campbell, the *Esquire* illustrator. He shouted into the ring at Madison Square Garden while watching Sugar Ray's bouts and eventually introduced himself to the fighter. In 1948 he became the first Negro photographer at *Life* magazine. Within a year and a half, he had gotten himself that Paris assignment. And when Sugar Ray Robinson and his entourage arrived at Le Havre on his way to Paris on May 2, Parks was there with his camera—along with a beaming crowd of French fans. They wanted to see the fighter who had whipped LaMotta, thus assuaging some of the pain about their Marcel Cerdan. As soon as Robinson came into view, he recognized the four-feet-four-inch figure dashing toward him wearing a wraparound coat and broad smile: It was Jimmy Karoubi, a midget whom Robinson had met on his earlier visit to the country and who had served as Robinson's translator and all-around man Friday. (Members of Robinson's entourage often wondered about his fascination with midgets. But Robinson had arrived in Harlem as the last embers of vaudeville were still visible. Midgets were creatures of vaudeville and carnivals. Sugar Ray's sometime Harlem chauffer, Chico, was also a midget: Chico sat on two phone books in the driver's seat when he was driving Robinson around. He also carried a pearl-handled pistol. "Chico was a badass dude," says Drew Brown, whose father would come to work with Robinson in later years. "He just happened to be a midget.") Now, with Robinson's arm flung down and around his shoulder, the diminutive Jimmy couldn't help but add an extra dash to the exuberant sway of Robinson's band of merry travelers. Ship attendants began unloading the heaps of luggage that belonged to the Robinson party. Finally, after the pink Cadillac was unloaded, the group decamped to the upscale Claridge Hotel.

Hitting the Paris streets the following day, Robinson was caught off guard by the reception. Fans stopped his pink Caddy in the middle of the street, pleading for autographs. Crowds would gather, stopping traffic. It took the intervention of police officers for Robinson to proceed. Shop owners poured out of their businesses at the sight of his traveling entourage; schoolchildren scampered down the streets, with the midget Jimmy cackling and staring at them all from behind the automobile's window. "The return of Napoleon Bonaparte on his white steed," remembered Gordon Parks, "couldn't have charged Paris with much more excitement than did the coming of Sugar Ray" and his camp. Like so many before him, Robinson fell under the sway of the historic and charmed city: "I loved to drive around Paris, with the top down and the radio on loud, and me wearing a beret." Little Jimmy squealed with delight, pointing his knobby fingers out the windows, waving and cackling. Robinson and his entourage seemed tight as a gospel choir. Gordon Parks himself had never seen anything like it. "On the Champs-Elysées in Paris," he would recall, "all it took for movie queues to break rank was for Sugar Ray's fushcia Cadillac to appear. Parisian bicyclists immediately pedaled into high gear to follow, like gulls after a yacht." (Robinson eventually hired a French chauffeur.) Dozens of invitations to parties and soirees were delivered to his hotel; his traveling secretary had to parcel them. In restaurants women tried to be discreet, but when Robinson glided off to the men's room, they followed him through the doors—ostensibly for an autograph. He signed menus, napkins, scraps of paper. He had members of his entourage hand out those handsome black-and-white photos of himself.

French officials were quite prepared for Robinson's visit. He came bearing gifts—in the form of Damon Runyon Cancer Fund checks, which he would dispense throughout Europe—and his generosity demanded the appearance of politicians to express their gratitude. At one charity event, a benefit for aging French comedians held at the Palais de Chaillot, Robinson, dressed in white tie and a cutaway, three-quarter-length tux, surprised onlookers by joining the band and playing the drums. Then he broke into a tap number on the stage, kicking his patent-leather heels to shrieks of wonderment and delight. After the impromptu performance, French starlets surrounded him with heart-stricken looks in their eyes. Monsieur Robinson had become

their dreamboat. Parks realized such a scene could not have played out in America with its racial customs, and he relished all the jubilant mingling. At one event, Madame Auriol, France's first lady, showed up to thank Robinson personally for his cancer fund donation. He kissed the charming lady on both cheeks. Robinson had a scheduled fight on May 21— his first during the visit—against Kid Marcel in Paris; Gainford began worrying about Robinson's socializing and public events. Robinson assured Gainford he'd be fine.

In 1951 Sugar Ray Robinson landed in Europe. Parisians fell in love with him. It was his style, his sense of fashion. (Edith Piaf clamored for an introduction.) Here the great French titleholder, Georges Carpentier, seated at table, far right, hosts a dinner for Robinson. In London, streets would have to be blocked off as thousands angled to get a glimpse of the fighter.

Robinson attended an event to honor the memory of Marcel Cerdan. Edith Piaf couldn't take her eyes off the American fighter. An American-based magazine gushingly referred to Robinson as "Paris' No. 1 celebrity in residence."

While at the fashionable Lido nightclub one evening along with Robinson and his assemblage, Gordon Parks noticed a familiar face: French actress Martine Carol. A voluptuous presence—and France's reigning sex symbol—she was in a sleeveless dress with a fur stole draped around her arms. Her blonde hair flowed; she looked dazzling. Carol—who would celebrate her twenty-ninth birthday on May 16, while Robinson was in the city—had been acting in French cinema since 1943, drawing praise for both her beauty and acting talent. In 1951 she had filmed *Caroline Chérie,* and the reviews were admirable. At the Lido, Parks—always angling for an interesting photo—asked Sugar Ray if he would dance with Carol. Robinson put aside his Coca-Cola: "Sure, if she wants to." He made Parks walk over and ask the screen siren. The actress smilingly agreed. And then there they were, on the dance floor, Robinson's black right hand on her bare white back, both smiling, the music wafting. Parks snapped away, he and Robinson stealing glances at each other, two Negroes quite aware that what was taking place would have been almost impossible on the other side of the Atlantic. Pictures of the dancing couple wound up in the French press, sparking rumors of a Robinson-Carol romance—fragile rumors, it turned out, as Robinson's wife Edna Mae had accompanied him to Paris.

Robinson had grown fond of doing his impromptu nightclub-like performances. (Could he have been rehearsing for bigger things he had in mind?) There were also rounds of golf—he had brought his monogrammed golf bag from America—and dinner engagements and all-night card parties. He would regale a group of American businessmen in Paris with stories about his life—"about Detroit and Georgia and Harlem." Gainford kept reminding his fighter he had come to Europe to fight.

Under the eyes of the first lady, Madame Auriol, along with his entourage and with six thousand others looking on, Robinson entered the ring at the Palace of Sports on May 21 for his bout with Kid Marcel, the reigning French middleweight champion. In the fifth, a Robinson fusillade widened the eyes of Marcel's cornermen; they feared for their fighter's well-being. Shortly after that the ref determined the Kid had been punished enough and called the bout. Robinson donated his earnings to the French Cancer Fund. Other foreign fighters might have been booed after besting a native fighter on his home turf, but not Robinson. It doubtless had something to with the fact he so charmed the French—they were "at his feet," as Parks would remember—in the days leading up to the Kid Marcel match.

On May 26, Robinson was in Zurich for a bout with Jean Wanes, a Frenchman. Wanes had announced before the contest he might well suffer a defeat, but he aimed to go the distance in the ten-rounder. The Frenchman hardly inspired confidence as he tumbled to the canvas in the third round from a Robinson blow. It happened again two rounds later, but he gamely popped up. In the seventh round Wanes hit the canvas yet again—this time it was a vicious Robinson right—sending shivers of additional concern through his cornermen. But there appeared flashes of an odd little smile upon the Frenchman's face, giving his countenance a rather sweet fearlessness. Wanes lay on the canvas in the ninth, taking a nine count. "But even this blow could not damage the Frenchman's ardor," as the AP would put it. Robinson was awarded a tenth-round decision and could only offer Wanes—still grinning—his compliments. Two weeks later, in Antwerp, Belgium, Robinson was pitted against Jan de Bruin. It seemed to be a scrappy battle, though anyone could see de Bruin was taking the majority of the blows. In the eighth round, de Bruin, obviously desperate to bring a stop to those Robinson blows, did something that had a touch of slapstick to it: He grabbed Robinson's arm and lifted it over the champion's head, signaling the winner before the ref could. Robinson had a perplexed look on his face; members of his entourage swiveled their necks like owls looking at one another. "You are too good for me," de Bruin simply told Robinson. No one disagreed.

On June 24 Robinson found himself in West Berlin, at the outdoor Waldbühne Stadium to battle Gerhard Hecht. Hecht was the country's highest-ranked light heavyweight. There were an estimated thirty thousand in attendance and the air was warm as the watching Germans munched on pretzels and drank beer. Gainford and Robinson both noticed the large contingent of American soldiers in the audience—just the type of scene that made Robinson reflect momentarily upon his own military service, strange as it happened to have been. The German crowd was excited; it had been more than two decades since a world champion had appeared in a West Berlin ring. Toward the end of the first round, Hecht crumpled to the canvas after taking "a combination of smashing blows" to his head. A cascade of boos erupted: Hecht's corner complained to the ref that Robinson had hit their fighter with a kidney punch—which was illegal under German rules. Hecht needed extra seconds between the first and second rounds to be attended to. Gainford and Robinson couldn't understand the booing and the finger-pointing from Hecht's corner. The bell rang for the second round. Robinson needed only ten seconds to put Hecht down again. This time Hecht's cornermen leaped into the ring. "Foul! Foul! Foul!" they cried out, charging Robinson with another kidney punch. Anger now seeped from the grounds into the ring, Germans yelling in protest. "Just like Schmeling!" they howled, recalling Schmeling's claim that he took some illegal punches in his second matchup with Joe Louis. Robinson stood at center ring, listening as the noise took on an ominous tone. Then came the nasty clamor of beer bottles flying through the air and shattering inside the ropes. Fans popped up from their seats, flinging their seat cushions toward the ring. Those seated at ringside were forced to scamper beneath their seats. Robinson realized this was cause for concern; Gainford and his corner motioned to him, Gainford flinging a protective arm around Robinson, and they all began to move from the ring. But on all sides, fans were angling toward them. Members of Robinson's entourage were attacked; his wife Edna Mae suffered a nasty bruise on her leg. They knew they couldn't navigate through the throng and dipped beneath the ring, which was elevated. They continued to hear the cacophony of the angry crowd, hissing in their German tongue. Without help, they couldn't move. It finally arrived, after nearly five minutes and a spike in George Gainford's blood pressure. Nearly two dozen police officers pulled the Robinson contingent toward safety. They were soon joined by a group of American soldiers, bolting into action from deep within the crowd. When Robinson and Gainford and the others had reached safety, it was quickly determined best to leave West Berlin as soon as possible. An hour after the melee, Robinson and his entourage were hustled aboard a U.S. military train and happily bid the city goodbye.

Robinson now longed for a return to those gentle evenings in Paris. Instead, there was an engagement in Turin, Italy. Robinson and his traveling companions found the Turin surroundings—with the Italian Alps in the distance—quite lovely. They were also impressed with service at the Principi di Piemonte Hotel, with its high ceilings and richly textured interiors. Gainford browbeat the hotel staff with questions about food and lodging and who would get the final bill. He was assured the fight promoter, Signor Agnelli, would handle expenses. (Gainford could never shake the worries he'd had when traveling with the Salem Crescent boxing team, counting dollar bills and fretting about expenses.) But Agnelli—the gentleman promoting the Turin bout—happened to own the luxurious hotel where Robinson's entourage was staying. This brought a smile to Gainford's face.

Nearly twenty-five thousand showed for the Robinson bout. They had a short stay: Cyrille Delannoit, Robinson's opponent, held on for just three rounds before succumbing to a TKO.

When Robinson returned to Paris, Gainford told him that negotiations for a final bout on the Continent were under way. Robinson relaxed in his light-filled hotel suite. When Gainford had completed the contract, it was announced Robinson would be going to London to take on Randy Turpin. Turpin was a brawler whom Robinson knew little about. The fight was announced for July 10. Robinson and his entourage packed up and headed across the Channel. Again, the pink Caddy was part of the luggage.

He wasn't in America that summer, yet in America Sugar Ray was everywhere: On June 25, 1951, he appeared on the cover of Henry Luce's *Time* magazine. It was a potent tribute to his acclaim. The headline—"Sugar Ray Robinson: Rhythm in his feet and pleasure in his work"—seemed to acknowledge both his deftness as a hoofer and his skills in the ring. But more significantly, it cemented his presence in the cultural brew of America. The narrative on the pages is rather bloodless, too plain and stark for the figure described. Still, Sugar Ray had become only the third Negro—after Louis Armstrong and Joe Louis—to appear on *Time*'s cover. With his wavy hair, dark complexion, and thin mustache—offset by a red shirt buttoned to the neck, plaid suit jacket, and gentle smile—he has the insouciance of a jazzy bandleader. Behind his head on the cover sits a circular globe, and on it are a set of boxing gloves hanging from a piece of string. Each glove has two spindly legs attached—artwork signaling Robinson's march across Europe and his fistic victories. In Sugar Ray's Manhattan, young fighters made beelines to corner newsstands to purchase copies.

He was mobbed in London. Fans flooded the entryway to the Savoy Hotel, where Robinson and his party had checked in. Right away

Gainford began to worry about what the noise and throngs of people would do to Robinson's concentration. Within hours of his arrival, there were overeager fans galloping up and down the hallways, trying to find his suite. Savoy staffers became alarmed. With a nudge from hotel management, which was in a tizzy over the pandemonium. Gainford announced he and Robinson would find someplace else.

Gainford, a savvy negotiator when pressed for time, found a massive fifteenth-century stone building miles from the center of the city and, flashing cash, commandeered it. The location was top secret—that is, until it wasn't. Within a day, there were teenyboppers screaming from the pavement. Both Robinson and photographer Gordon Parks—who had come to London with him—were taken aback at the crowds. People followed him everywhere; he required a police escort. Bobbies circled him as he moved about. Sugar Ray Robinson was a full-fledged international star. Robinson's chauffeur became so agitated that he announced he was going to fling the windows of the castlelike structure open and toot a trumpet to appease the throngs down below. The driver, alas, decided against it.

Robinson hit the London nightclubs, signing autographs, dancing. Tables would be pushed together when his entourage arrived to eat. Diners chuckled when they spotted Jimmy, the midget, sitting on Robinson's lap. Laughter came from all directions. But Gordon Parks was a bit nonplussed by the nonstop gaiety and nonchalance: There was a fight on the horizon! Robinson may not have known much about Randy Turpin, but he did know he held the British middleweight crown. Robinson's camp, when reminded of Turpin's ranking, seemed to yawn and talk about Kid Marcel, the French middleweight champion whom Robinson had all but toyed with in the ring. Parks would remember Robinson in the days leading up to the Turpin bout: "There were no workouts. Sugar Ray played at golf through the days, and at card tables late into the nights." The July weather was indeed beautiful; Robinson golfed at Datchet, a local course, and fans lined up to watch him. Ben Phlagar, an AP reporter, shadowed Robinson one day: "Robinson slept late, amused himself at the piano during the morning and took a long walk this afternoon."

When Robinson returned to his room deep into the night, music—"blues and boogie-woogie"—could be heard from behind the door. Other nights, there were the jumpy voices of card players pitched against the music.

As for Randy Turpin, Robinson's underdog opponent, he had secured a movie projector and as many copies of Robinson fights as he could get his hands on. Randy Turpin watched those fights in darkness. And he altered the speed of the projector because he preferred watching the action in slow motion, believing a slower Robinson—even on screen—just might expose vulnerabilities.

Gamblers and bookies were hardly surprised when the odds for the fight, to take place at Earls Court Arena, were announced: Robinson was a 4–1 favorite.

Gordon Parks predicted that Robinson would "take Turpin apart and return home to even more hero-worship." A columnist for the *Times* of London conceded that the chance of a Turpin victory was just a "forlorn hope" but expressed the desire to see the British fighter at least acquit himself with dignity and pride.

When Lionel Turpin—originally of British Guiana—returned home to London after World War I, where he had fought at the Battle of the Somme, he met Beatrice Whitehouse. He fell in love. The union might have seemed unremarkable—save the fact that Lionel was Negro and Beatrice a white woman. Lionel ignored the racial epithets that flew in their direction, but not Beatrice, who yelled back and shook her fingers at her neighbors. Lionel's death, the result of gas poisoning from the war, left his widow with five children, the youngest being Randy, born in 1928, just shortly after his father's death. The family resided in Leamington Spa, about seventy miles outside London. They were the only "coloured" family in the small town.

Beatrice Turpin's father, Tom, had been a bare-knuckle fighter, and he passed along tips to Beatrice's three boys. Randy was often snickered at by other children, called "Blackie" because of his heritage. He began fighting back, remembering what his grandfather had taught him. In time, the three brothers—Dick and Jackie, in addition to Randy—all learned the skills of boxing, which they honed by following carnivals around and setting up fighting booths for spectators to gawk into and toss coins. All joined the amateur boxing ranks. As a sixteen-year-old, Randy won a national amateur title. He volunteered for the Royal Navy near the end of World War II. He was a cook, but managed to do quite a bit of boxing. His service was marred, however, by a bizarre incident: Following a domestic spat with his girlfriend, Turpin swallowed a poisonous liquid. In order to save his life, doctors had to pump his stomach. Naval officials believed it was an attempted suicide, which, under British law, could put him at risk of a criminal inquiry. Turpin's boxing prowess saved him and the incident was hushed up.

Turpin—honey-skinned, handsome, and broad-shouldered—turned pro in 1946. His first bout was against Gordon Griffiths. Peter Wilson, a boxing writer for the London *Daily Express,* covered the match: "The way Turpin leapt on Griffiths, like a bronze tiger devouring a tethered kid, battering him half-way through the ropes until the referee intervened in the first round," he wrote, "was enough to prove that a new middleweight menace had already arrived . . ." But all of the pro-boxing Turpin brothers were a menace: Dick had his sights on the British Empire championship, a prospect that put British boxing commissioners in a dilemma. The Empire championship was limited to white fighters only. Under mounting pressure, the organization rescinded the rule and Dick Turpin fought his way to the middleweight crown by defeating Vince Hawkins. It seemed a genuine nick in the colonial-era mindset, and England's colored population celebrated wildly. On April 24, 1950, at Nottingham Hall, Dick Turpin lost his crown to Albert Finch, a onetime truck driver, in a fifteen-round contest. Misery didn't last long in the Turpin family. Six months after Dick Turpin's defeat, Randy stepped into the ring in London to face Finch. By the third round, Finch was bloodied; he could not decipher Randy Turpin's up-and-down style, nor did he have any defense against the wicked blows. Randy Turpin was crowned British champion. He had now positioned himself to get the opportunity with Robinson.

Robinson, who had been giving money and purses away as he gallivanted in style across Europe—all on behalf of the Runyon Cancer Fund—began thinking he needed one good payday on his European travels. (He would be paid $84,000, his biggest payday on the Continent, for the Turpin bout; Turpin $24,000.) Neither Robinson nor Gainford, however, would be spending any time watching fight film—slow-motion or otherwise—of Randy Turpin.

It was impossible for Turpin and his followers to miss the hullabaloo around the presence of Sugar Ray Robinson in London. Just as he had done in Paris, Robinson kept the populace in a state of frenzy. Turpin was, indeed, British champ, but that title carried far less cachet than Robinson's world crown. The prospect of Turpin in the ring with Robinson—it had been decreed a world title match—did serve, however, to raise Turpin's profile. Englanders, normally absorbed by their love affair with the less brutal endeavors of cricket and rowing, surrounded his training headquarters—a castle in North Wales—yelling his name while milling around on the grassy lawn below. Sometimes Turpin would appear on the balcony of the castle, staring out across the throngs with a look of wonderment, unaccustomed to this kind of attention. He waved at the crowds, albeit tentatively, as if it all might vanish right before his very eyes.

On July 9—a day before the fight—Turpin, along with his manager, George Middleton, and some family and friends, boarded a train to London. Jack Solomons, the fight promoter, had already announced that all eighteen thousand tickets were sold. When Turpin's train pulled into the station, he was surprised to see that there were upwards of five hundred fans there to greet him. "This is the first time a crowd has bothered to meet me before a fight," he said, glancing around, the train's engine still churning, the crowd closing in on him, "but it does me good. I have never felt better." Middleton whisked the fighter away to a hotel.

Some London writers opined that there hadn't been this much interest in a championship bout since the days of Bob Fitzsimmons, Britain's last world titleholder. The London-born Fitzsimmons became middleweight champion in 1891 and would eventually go on to hold three titles.

The fight was drawing a large contingent of gamblers and bookies into London. The fight odds remained 4–1.

The days in the English countryside suited Robinson—so did the hours-long card games. Edna Mae began to fret. "Why is Ray doing this, not training, playing gin rummy all night?" she asked Gordon Parks. Parks did not know the mysteries of boxers or training, and he had no explanation for her.

"One may smile a little at the size and variety of his entourage," a *Times* of London report offered about Robinson, "but not at his fighting record."

On fight's eve, Sugar Ray hit golf balls.

There were rumors that Robinson's party would travel to Earls Court Arena by way of Windmill Street on the day of the fight. Fans began choking the streets at midday. The appearance of so many bobbies on horseback (crowd control) simply convinced those gathered that their hunches had been correct. Within minutes of its appearance, the much-talked-about pink Cadillac was surrounded by thousands of fans. Inside the automobile, Robinson and Gainford sat surprised once again at the size of the crowd. Faces of excited fans pushed up against the windows. Women blew kisses. Gordon Parks had broken away and hoisted himself above the street, yards in front of the car, so he could get a good photograph. The Cadillac cruised past the London Pavillion—Bert Lahr, one of the stars of *The Wizard of Oz,* and Robert Alda were appearing in a play, their names on the marquee—then past several billiards halls and pubs. The bobbies had to raise their voices over the noise of the crowd in an effort to maintain order. Their horses bridled and turned sideways, scenting the agitation of the crowd. This was yet another reason why Sugar Ray Robinson was bewitched by Europe: He had never received such a reception in America. Here he was the challenger—and being shown such affection! There had been nothing like this in Detroit or Manhattan or Chicago. This is what he and Gainford had witnessed in the heyday of Joe Louis: thousands reaching their hands out; women swooning, men saluting, children scampering with wide grins. Paris had been sweet; London town was even sweeter.

Chauffeur-driven cars pulled up in front of the arena, men alighting from them carrying walking sticks. Young boys swarmed about like fish inside a huge tank. Promoter Jack Solomons looked around the packed Earls Court Arena—diplomats and politicians and entertainers and commoners all in attendance—and lamented that he had not had the foresight to hold the event outdoors, where he imagined he could have drawn more than a hundred thousand. As it was, the eighteen thousand in the sold-out venue sat elbow to elbow. Loud roars greeted both fighters. Robinson's elegant silky blue gown caused one observer to muse that it could "have been designed by Schiaparelli." Turpin's garb did not claim the eye; it was plain and drab. Robinson stayed on his feet during the moments before the bell; Turpin sat on a stool in his corner. There was a preternatural calm about him.

In the first round the fighters felt each other out, trading harmless punches until, with just seconds to go in the round, a Turpin left hook connected and stung Robinson. He wobbled backward; fans roared; Gainford shifted in his corner. The blow seemed a warning to Robinson of Turpin's power. (Even during the weigh-in, Robinson's cornermen marveled at Turpin's physique. He outweighed Robinson, 158 to 154, and appeared all chiseled muscle. And at the age of twenty-three, he was seven years younger.) Many noted, at the beginning of the second round, droplets of blood oozing from Robinson's mouth. It was in the third that Robinson found his natural one-two punch, delivering the combination—he had seemed to jump off the ground while doing so, drawing those long-familiar gasps of shock—right to Turpin's face. Turpin, expressionless, answered with a powerful left hook of his own, which caused a quick puffiness below Robinson's eye. As *The Times* of London correspondent observed, Turpin's "lefts from the start had more sting and weight behind them than Robinson's," a fact clearly noticeable to the fans. At the end of the round, Turpin sat on his stool with the unworried look of a chap waiting for a bus in central London on a sunny day. Watching the bout, Gordon Parks was hardly concerned about Robinson's ring strategy: "No cause to worry, I thought, Ray's just stalling, giving the audience its money's worth."

Turpin was prone to a boxing style of bouncing up and down on his feet as if doing a knee bend. Commentators often described the movements as being like those of an elevator—up and down, up and down. The unorthodox style befuddled Robinson. Turpin would come at Robinson sideways, then start the up-and-down motion—like a lethal gazelle—before unleashing one of his fiery blows. "Turpin was outpunching me," Robinson would later concede. But Sugar Ray, bolstered by some "whiplash lefts and rights," took the sixth round. Gainford nodded heaps of approval; this is what he had been waiting to see all along. Turpin partisans feared it was but a prelude, that the great American fighter was ready for his assault. But then, in the seventh, Robinson suffered a head-butt from Turpin. Some crowd members made gratified sounds, believing the blow had come from a Turpin punch. It appeared accidental. But the gash above Robinson's left eye looked nasty. "His eye! Look at Sugar's eye!" a Turpin partisan cried aloud. "Turpin's opened his eye, I tell you."

"I could tell it was a bad one," Robinson would recall of the wound, "not only from the feel but also from the way Turpin was staring at it and aiming his right hand for it."

Gainford knew as much. "It's bad," he told Robinson in the corner. "Don't let him butt you again."

Turpin hardly needed to. He bore into Robinson with steady rights and jabs. "Hold on, Sugar," Robinson's wife Edna Mae shouted from her seat. Then, in the eleventh, a peculiar thing happened: Robinson himself began moving up and down in an elevatorlike motion, copying Turpin's style. It was the only way he saw to counteract Turpin's ring manner. But Robinson—always a stand-up, dancing fighter—looked awkward. He had never been a fighter to mimic anyone. Gainford did what he could to tend to Robinson's tender facial wounds at the end of the eleventh. But in the twelfth young Turpin slammed another fist into Robinson's nose. More blood. "Get him," Robinson's sister Evelyn cried out, her eyes closed for long periods of time as if she herself began to think the unthinkable. There were murmurs echoing through the crowd now; Robinson's normally sturdy legs looked fragile.

Prognostications aside, it was to the disadvantage of Robinson and George Gainford that they had not seen any of Turpin's three fights leading up to their engagement. One took place on April 16 against Billy Brown. On May 7 he faced Jan de Bruin. And on June 5 it was Jackie Keough. The first two fights ended in second- and sixth-round knockouts; the third was a seventh-round TKO. In each Turpin displayed a ferocious and relentless boxing style with LaMotta-like strength. Anyone seeing those fights, or having studied them, would not have taken Randy Turpin lightly.

At the beginning of the thirteenth—while, again, having looked eerily calm during the break after the previous round—Turpin forcefully attacked an obviously confused Robinson, and, as the UP dispatch noted, "from then on he couldn't be stopped." The English fans, not only unaccustomed to seeing two Negroes in the ring together but feeling now that their Randy Turpin could be victorious, began yelling for blood. When the final bell rang, Randy Turpin—a fighter knows—raised his arm in exuberant triumph. It was the most emotion he had shown the entire evening. He turned to Robinson and put his arm around him and began escorting him to his corner as if he had meant no harm in taking down the older fighter, as if he had merely been fighting for family pride—against all the insults heaped upon the racially mixed Turpin boys their whole lives. Fans rose in their seats; fathers had to yank back sons who wanted to bolt toward the ring. There was the click-clack of typewriters at ringside, some reporters writing furiously as others scurried to find telephones. The pretty nutmeg-brown faces of Edna Mae and Evelyn Robinson had collapsed. Their Sugar Ray had been dethroned.

The AP scorecard was unforgiving: nine rounds for Turpin, four for Robinson, two judged even. Turpin, egged on, stepped toward a microphone and spoke to the crowd. "I hope I'm able to keep this for you for a long time," he said. The applause rose again. Then a boxing official entered the ring and presented Turpin with a silver gilt globe, the representative emblem in England of any world championship. As he was leaving the ring, the arena started singing: "For he's a jolly good fellow . . ." Jack Solomons, the shrewd promoter, had stuffed a victory cigar in his mouth.

Reporters scrambled to get to Turpin's dressing room. They were met by the poised fighter, his brothers, and manager, George Middleton. "I thought I was winning all the way," Turpin told them. "He never hurt me once." Then, as if it were just the right thing to do, Turpin walked over to Robinson's dressing room. "You were a real champion just like they told me," he told the now-former champion. Robinson—suffering only the second defeat of his professional career—was magnanimous. "You were real good," he told Turpin. "Just like they said you were. I have no alibis. I was beaten by a better man." As Turpin departed, Robinson's doctor set to work on the gash above his left eye. It would require ten stitches. The room grew quiet. They were all so unaccustomed to this type of outcome. "Come on, everybody," Evelyn Robinson finally said, breaking the silence, "don't look so sad."

The next day's newspapers, on both sides of the Atlantic, gave big play to the epic story. RAY ROBINSON LOSES TITLE IN BRITAIN, the *New York Times* page-one headline said. "Randy Turpin," the paper's account began, "23-year-old British Negro who never before had fought a bout of more than eight rounds, scored the most amazing upset in twenty-five years of boxing history . . . when he defeated Ray Robinson to win the world's middleweight championship." The *Times* of London report was no less surprised: "Randolph Turpin upset every calculation, even to a great extent perhaps his own, by gaining a boxing victory over the famous Ray Robinson at Earls Court last night." The *Los Angeles Times* headline: TITLE TO TURPIN: BRITISH NEGRO TRIUMPHS IN STUNNING RING UPSET. *Time* magazine weighed in: "It was boxing's biggest upset since 1936, when Max Schmeling knocked out Joe Louis."

What had gone wrong? Blame was laid on Robinson's social calendar and his lack of preparation. All those parties! Those sunny afternoons on those lovely golf courses! A tone of mockery in reference to the entire Robinson European tour threaded its way into some London-based newspaper accounts, with a London *Observer* columnist allowing that Robinson's "triumphal tour [was] more like that of an Oriental potentate than a prizefighter." Gainford had lacked the forcefulness to curtail Robinson's social schedule. And in the aftermath he struck a sanguine note. "This'll do us no harm at all," he insisted. "And the return fight'll be a wow." Those negotiations were under way within hours of the conclusion of the fight.

Robinson was leery of returning to his hotel after the fight. He was never a man to tolerate gloom. There would surely be all those reporters, wanting more and more. His friend Gordon Parks hustled him into his auto and then sped away, determined to find an out-of-the-way hotel for Robinson for the night. As Parks drove along the streets, he was aware of a feeling beyond empathy for Robinson's defeat: He felt such pride. He was not only Robinson's chauffeur right now but his protector. He still called Robinson champ, because always in those witchy moments following a champ's defeat, it was important to keep the glory and aura alive. But he also felt a duty, conscious that they were two Negroes from America, in another land, supping at the high tables of Europe, all the while knowing great shadows still awaited them over their shoulders, back in America. And now, over here, they must watch out for each other—Robinson making sure Parks had all the access he needed; Parks dropping his photographic duties on a night like this to help another American Negro in need. This was a sliver of real freedom, as free as the tales told by all those jazzmen who had come swaying into Robinson's Manhattan club. As far as Gordon Parks was concerned, driving the great Sugar Ray through the night, heading toward some kind of peace was better than being Walker Evans down in Alabama or Dorothea Lange in Georgia or certainly Parks himself enduring insults in those Washington restaurants.

Robinson had sounded the note of grace in defeat, but privately he seethed. "I'll kill him the next time," he vowed to Parks. "So help me I'll kill him." That was a sentiment that echoed throughout the Robinson family: "I don't think I even want to see that fight," Robinson's sister Evelyn said of the pending follow-up match. "Ray will murder him."

Robinson's mother, Leila, had not come to London, remaining in New York City. Fearing that she would worry once she heard news of his injuries, Sugar Ray sent a telegram. MUM—a note of levity struck in using the English word for "Mom"—I LOST ON DECISION BUT I AM OK.

The celebrations for Randy Turpin culminated in his hometown of Leamington Spa. A throng of twenty thousand lined the streets; shops were closed; a jet streaked overhead in honor of the occasion. Many said they hadn't seen such a celebration since the end of World War II.

Perhaps it mattered little to Robinson now, but there remained plenty of Londoners who had been transfixed by his presence in the ring. Writing in the London *Observer* days after the fight, Maurice Richardson conceded that the country's pride and admiration indeed lay deeper with Turpin now: "But there is something really charming and generous about the graceful and fabulous Sugar."

Robinson returned to Paris and allowed the pace and charms of that city to soothe his injuries for a few days. Then it was off to Cannes where he relaxed, whiling away hours at the baccarat table, talking movies with Jack Warner, the Hollywood studio chief who was vacationing there. The dethroned champion looked like a man without a care in the world. Some New Yorkers worried: Where was he? They had anticipated he would return home after the Turpin bout. And when he didn't, there was chatter throughout Manhattan—from Salem Methodist church to City Hall—that perhaps Sugar Ray Robinson had grown morose. There had been no communiqué, save for the telegram to his mother. A group of New Yorkers joined together to write an open letter to the baccarat-playing Robinson that was published in the *Amsterdam News.* The letter was a odd mixture of disbelief at the loss and encouragement for Robinson to pull himself together and return. It ended with a strange bit of gossip, informing Robinson that there were folk back home who believed "you took too many pictures with white women, especially that stuff kissing the big lady of France, and a few remarked that the Communists don't like the way you talk against them and wanted to get revenge." (Robinson had been goaded to take a political stand against American segregation, but refused to do so.) It concluded: "Ray, we don't know what it is, but wherever you are, hurry up and come back and show us that you haven't lost your Sugar. Wherever you are Sugar Ray, Won't You Please Come Home!" It was signed, "Boys on the Block." Anonymous as it was, it had the imprimatur of musicians, actors, Negro political clubhouse leaders—those in Harlem and Manhattan who considered themselves friends of Robinson.

But Sugar Ray, for all his fame and accomplishment on American shores, had fallen prey to something in Europe—freedom. And laughter. And the spirit of ease that he felt surrounded by. He could dally in the southern part of France; the southern part of the United States, even for a world champion, was another matter. Now, sitting in the Parisian cafés—as Duke Ellington, Sidney Bechet, the painter Beauford Delaney, and so many other artistic-minded Negroes had done and were doing—he had become intoxicated. He made decisions willy-nilly; to go here, or not go there. There were no WHITES ONLY signs; no FOR COLORED signs. Many of the black Americans he encountered in France were former military men studying on the GI Bill and jazz musicians in porkpie hats who told him they just couldn't understand why America had had such a strong hand in eliminating Hitler's fascism but was doing little to eliminate bigotry at home. Robinson, who always admired musicians, soaked in the whole scene. When the young novelist James Baldwin had left Sugar Ray's Harlem in 1948 for Paris with a Rosenwald Fellowship to work on a novel, he too was struck by the freedom he found in Paris. Baldwin soon ran out of money, suffered the indignities of being broke—but he laughed. "In some deep, black, stony, and liberating way," Baldwin would write, "my life, in my own eyes, began during that first year in Paris, when it was borne in on me that this laughter is universal and never can be stilled." Gainford and other members of Robinson's entourage told him of the letter that had appeared in the Harlem newspaper, but

Robinson ignored it. He was busy enjoying himself, the air of freedom all around him, the rush of laughter in corner cafés that turned his face and lit his eyes.

It was several weeks before Sugar Ray arrived back in the United States, but when he did, his catty newspaper friend Walter Winchell, along with New York City Mayor Vincent Impellitteri ("I call him Vince," said Robinson), made sure it would be a reception with fanfare. More than a dozen limousines awaited him at the pier. Descending from the ship into the summery sunshine, he still looked—as all could see—like the fabulous Sugar, dressed in a lovely cream-colored suit, white shirt, and dark tie. The fleet of limos cut through the sunshine, making its way toward City Hall. And once there, Robinson was greeted by a boisterous crowd of several thousand. They exploded with applause at the sight of him on the makeshift outdoor dais, and he seemed genuinely touched. Office workers peered from nearby windows; strollers at the back of the crowd stood on tiptoes, many wondering if it was some kind of campaign event. Standing before the throng, Robinson gazed out over the masses, nodding to the faces that were familiar—Salem church members, workers whom he employed in his uptown businesses, and of course the boys from the block. Mayor Impellitteri and Winchell presented Robinson with a scroll saluting his concern for "his fellow human beings" in his efforts abroad raising money for the Runyon Cancer Fund. Winchell had put this in motion, and Robinson knew it. This is what Walter Winchell could do—get the mayor on the phone, lay out his ideas for a Robinson reception, tell the mayor how wise it would be for him to personally attend. Walter Winchell could turn a Robinson ring defeat into a welcome-home salute. The power of the press! Robinson's eyes turned misty looking out over the crowd. He vowed to reclaim the middleweight title and they roared.

There had been much murmuring in that City Hall crowd about the announced date of the Robinson-Turpin rematch. It would take place September 12, at the hallowed Polo Grounds on 155th Street—in Harlem.

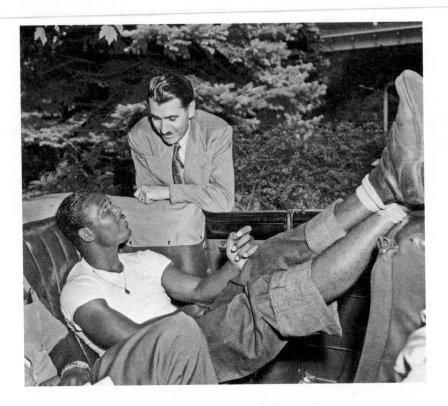

The governing bodies of boxing, realizing the public's fevered anticipation of the match, decreed that there would be no radio broadcasts or TV transmission of the looming fight. Instead, and with Robinson's ready approval since he stood to reap more money, there would be closed circuit viewing on huge theatre screens across the country—in Detroit, Chicago, Philadelphia, and many other cities. The fight was being billed as a must-see cinematic event. It was further proof that Sugar Ray Robinson, as a middleweight, had drawn parity with the decades-long excitement of heavyweight championship battles around the world.

There were few fighters more relaxed than Sugar Ray Robinson during training camp. Here he awaits the rematch with the dangerous Randy Turpin.

Robinson, Gainford, and the rest of the pre-fight assemblage headed for training at Pompton Lakes, New Jersey. A tone of seriousness hung over the camp. Robinson still listened to his boogie-woogie in the evenings, but the sparring sessions were longer. He was ever mindful of Turpin's strength, stamina, and unorthodox fighting style. He put on a few more pounds, believing that his weight loss during his travels in Europe had tested his stamina against Turpin. He seemed determined.

"The title is only lent," Sugar Ray Robinson had warned before leaving London.

Reporters started arriving at Pompton Lakes, more than a dozen at first, then a dozen more—members of the British press. They wanted quotes from Robinson, some kind of insight about the pending battle. "But Ray didn't want to talk," remembers Mel Dick, whom Robinson invited to visit him at the camp. "He could be ornery and cocky." Dick loved waltzing around the grounds, realizing the significance of the bout. One day following his sparring session, Robinson appeared on the front porch of one of the cabins. The reporters quickly huddled together, imagining an impromptu news conference. Gainford stood to Robinson's left, Dick to his right.

"Ray," one of the reporters asked, "what are you gonna do against Turpin?" All eyes went to Robinson. Pencils were gripped.

Gainford and Dick both waited, looking at Robinson and then at each other. "He stood there for ten to fifteen minutes," remembers Dick, "and said nothing. He just looked out over all the reporters. It was something else. I think he was just surveying his turf."

One evening, sitting around, everyone relaxed, Dick asked Robinson if there was anything he could do—perhaps fetch some groceries, run an errand? "Yeah, why don't you go over to Turpin's camp and get some secrets?" They all had a good laugh.

Randy Turpin had left London with a hero's send-off. Hundreds had attended a ballroom event—among them the celebrated actress Margaret Lockwood and well-known English comic Bud Flanagan—to wish him well in defense of his crown. In a blue suit, a beret atop his head, Turpin set sail with a large contingent, among them his brother, Dick and manager, George Middleton.

When his ship docked in Manhattan, the Turpin group was met by host officials and whisked to a midtown hotel. Turpin stared out the car window at the impressive Manhattan skyline as the car sped along. The next day he and his brother insisted on a trip to Harlem, which they had heard so much about. Their eyes widened as they took in the tenements and cacophony of Harlem, at all the bewildering sights. Harlemites were also eager—in homage to the competitive spirit!—to meet the visiting champion who had dethroned their Sugar Ray. A welcoming reception in a private home had been set up for him. Stepping through the doorway, Turpin came up close to the vividness of Harlem—educated men and women, the talk spinning of international affairs and Paris and London, and the mesmerizing fight game. His muscular physique awed many of the guests. Adele Daniels, gorgeous and single, was introduced to the fighter, and soon they were engaged in a low-pitched conversation. Phone numbers were exchanged. George Middleton, Turpin's manager, winced: He did not want his fighter to be distracted before the big fight by a beautiful young woman. But Turpin was entranced.

There was yet another reception, this one at Sugar Ray's nightclub, with the dethroned fighter himself playing the magnanimous host. A huge sign hung over the awning of the club: WELCOME RANDY. The nightclub cooks had prepared fried chicken, collard greens, macaroni salad—and a huge multi-tiered cake. If it was yet another kind of welcoming party for Randy Turpin, it also marked the appearance on the scene of another figure: Walker Smith Sr., Sugar Ray's father, had relocated to New York City. He had been vigilant about avoiding the spotlight. (Even the Harlem reporters could never get him to sit for an interview.) He was also careful not to disrupt the dynamics of Robinson and Gainford, as Robinson had long thought of Gainford as a father figure and his real father knew it. So now Walker Smith Sr.—quiet as a whisper when spotted in public—simply basked in his son's light. Turpin smiled quite a bit inside Robinson's nightclub, and he thanked his host profusely for the affair.

Turpin's party soon left for Grossinger's—site of a rustic resort in the Catskills nearly 150 miles away from Manhattan—where he set up his training camp. Despite the hubbub around him, he seemed, as he had been in London, quite calm. Following his sparring sessions, he would walk the grounds or play table tennis. Sometimes he sat and flipped through his huge assortment of comic books. Other times he thought of Adele Daniels, the woman from Harlem. Soon the tourists began arriving, many from England, wanting a glimpse of their country's hero. British sailors on leave showed up one afternoon, singing songs as they paraded about the grounds. No one paid much attention to the young teenager who was strolling the grounds one afternoon, looking around, nodding, smiling, making small talk. The teenager tried to take in the scene and mood of the training camp, imagining himself a kind of spy. Young Mel Dick had taken Sugar Ray Robinson's challenge about infiltrating the Turpin camp quite seriously. "I had my father take me up there," he recalls. Dick sensed a loose operation, a kind of constant gaiety. He reported his findings back to Robinson, who could only smile at Mel Dick's nerve.

Turpin had, in fact, begun an affair with Adele Daniels, the Harlem beauty, and there were loud arguments within his camp about his disappearances to be with her.

There were chartered flights in the air, heading for America, two days before the bout. British dignitaries and sportsmen—among them the mayor of Turpin's hometown—were en route. Prince Monolulu of Ethiopia by way of St. Croix, as it were, who had been living in London doing business for more than twenty years and had become a fight fan, stepped off one of those planes when it landed in New York City and drew a crowd of gawkers. Plumes of feathers adorned the prince's headdress. "His red vest was adorned with a green shamrock, the six-pointed Jewish Star of David, and other ornaments on the front, while the back had the British and American flags," a reporter noted. Those who arrived on the *Queen Elizabeth* disembarked from the ship, pleading with stewards to rustle up as many tickets to the fight as possible.

Russ J. Cowans, the sports editor of the *Chicago Defender,* could not contain his enthusiasm over the pending battle: "Not since the Marquis of Queensberry laid down the rules of boxing has a fight below the heavyweight division created as much interest of national and international flavor as that between Sugar Ray Robinson and Randy Turpin."

More than 150 workmen assembled at the Polo Grounds, setting up the ring and making preparations for the fight. The ringside seats for Robinson vs. Turpin would stretch back fifteen rows. In the days leading up to the match, tickets were being scalped for $100. Even in the unforgiving and greedy world of scalpers, that was considered astonishing. Radio announcers were billing the fight as the "battle of nations." Sugar Ray felt the enormous buildup. He began to sense it was his "patriotic duty" now to reclaim the title for America. At the International Boxing Club headquarters in Manhattan—sponsors of the bout—secretaries couldn't keep up with the volume of calls inquiring about tickets.

One of the side features of a Sugar Ray Robinson championship bout was the magnetic force with which it pulled in the cream of Negro America—writers, political ward leaders, musicians, Elks members, physicians, dentists, gorgeous fashion models familiar from the pages of Negro publications, big-time Negro funeral home directors, and insurance salesmen. America knew little about them, but among Negro America, they were royalty, (lowercase) kings and queens. Photographers from *Ebony* and *Our World* magazines, and newspapers such as *The Pittsburgh Courier,* the *Chicago Defender,* and the *Amsterdam News* cornered them in hotel lobbies and outside Harlem eateries days before the bout, pleading for a photo—please, please, right over here, that's right, how wonderful, thank you, thank you.

The former champion had spent the night before the fight at his mother's. He had bought her some new jewelry for the occasion. She cooked for him on the day of the fight—he ate lightly. It was late in the day when he climbed into his pink Caddy and rode off toward the Polo Grounds. The air was clear and crisp. Autumn in New York: it was his favorite time of the year—the light, the golden sunshine that turned to velvety darkness.

The gate receipts had already exceeded $700,000; more than sixty-one thousand tickets would eventually be sold. Both figures topped all previous American-set middleweight encounters.

Robinson's Caddy was spotted just outside the Polo Grounds and the yelps erupted into the air; the auto was escorted the remainder of the way. The former champion, given his career achievements, was slightly favored. "Turpin has the youth and strength of a 23-year-old needed to beat a fading veteran," *New York Times* columnist Arthur Daley wrote. But then, hedging his bets: "Robinson has the experience of a 31-year-old campaigner to pin back the ears of a callow youngster." A columnist for *The Times* of London, feeling that Robinson was edging "towards the end of a long career," opined that Turpin had a chance at yet another victory if his confidence held steady: "But if Turpin can feel that, having beaten his man once, he can beat him again, even if the job is now a good deal harder, in fact if he is not thrown out of a stride by a faster tempo, there is the chance that his strength and punching power will pull him through."

Boxing officials were giddy with delight at news of the attendance: The 61,370 attendance figure bested even the heavyweight title bout between Joe Louis and Billy Conn back in 1941.

Before the bell rang in the ring that evening, a trio of heavyweights was introduced, their names skittering out into the open air from the throat of the announcer. They each bent through the ropes to stand at center ring in the twilight, giving nods to Sugar Ray before they turned and squinted against the klieg lights, blurry faces in the distance, and applause from each side of the ring. Joe Louis and Ezzard Charles were former heavyweight titleholders; Jersey Joe Walcott the reigning champion. It was a unique moment in fight annals: The three men and Robinson had all, at differing times, battled the powerful boxing commissions that might have stopped them from integrating the top ranks of their sport. And now they stood together: the four horsemen of the fight world who had crashed through barriers.

The fighters exchanged rudimentary body blows in the first round before Robinson caught Turpin with an uppercut to the face. Turpin countered with a left that connected. It was early, but voices hummed in the overflow crowd anyway. Celebrities and public figures were everywhere in attendance, among them bug-eyed comedian Eddie Cantor, roly-poly magazine writer A. J. Liebling (who was also a gourmand and favored the pork chops at Sugar Ray's nightclub), Yankee Joe DiMaggio, broadcaster Lowell Thomas, the revered Douglas MacArthur, and nightclub owner Toots Shor, hanging with a grinning Walter Winchell, who was doing what he did best, hoarding tidbits and sightings for future columns. Boxing officials had been stunned at the swelling crowd; kids in the farthest reaches of the Polo Grounds tried hopping atop baseball dugouts until they were shooed away.

Turpin, who had so successfully used a clinching tactic in London to either slow Robinson or belt him, found the move harder to pull off this time. Robinson simply shoved him away, a keep-away tactic Gainford had pushed during training. A right from Robinson—quick as a shark's turn—missed Turpin's jaw. But not so the right to Turpin's face just before the bell, which stung him visibly.

In the third Robinson powered shots into Turpin's ribs, the follow-up blow interrupted only by a Turpin clinch, which referee Ruby Goldstein stepped in to break up. Then, deep into the round, there was a solid right-left combination from Turpin that had the visiting British crowd on the edge of their seats, suddenly believing their Turpin was about to make his move. Robinson wobbled a bit before gaining his balance as both fighters heard the bell ring.

During training, Robinson and Gainford had decided that Robinson should try for an early knockout, feeling that the younger Turpin would only gain momentum the longer the fight went on. But the fourth ended with Turpin still on his feet, hardly looking like a candidate for a flattening. By the end of the sixth, Robinson was firing blows to Turpin's well-chiseled body, blows that appeared to stymie him not at all. The fight had seemed remarkably even thus far—if it went on that way it would play to Turpin's favor as the titleholder. Throughout the eighth and ninth rounds, the visiting British crowd had a right to optimism yet again as Turpin unloaded devilish right and left hooks to Robinson's face. Robinson's strategy had betrayed him; it was evident that by the start of the tenth he was "smarting under the terrific blows the Englishman had landed in two previous rounds." Robinson himself realized he was "not really in charge" of the fight.

Just seconds into the tenth, during a clinch, Robinson suffered a head-butt from Turpin. Blood began gushing from above his left eye. Referee Goldstein closed in for a look. Robinson realized that Goldstein might stop the fight at round's end and that a decision would likely be awarded to Turpin: It was always the challenger who had more to prove and the champion given the benefit of the doubt. Robinson pushed himself away from the clinch. Immediately—in the time it takes for a bulb to spill light after a switch has been turned on—he slammed Turpin with a shuddering right hook. Turpin went to the canvas. The fall was almost in slow motion, as if Turpin was trying with everything in his power to will himself against touching the canvas—but he could not. The referee closed in for the nine count. Robinson retreated to his corner, resting his outstretched arms on the ropes like a daydreaming matador. Turpin rose before being called out. With dread swelling in them, the English crowd watched Robinson as he rushed from the ropes. He immediately punched Turpin into the ropes with a shocking fierceness—an uppercut, a right, a left, another left, a right, then a follow-up overhand right. Turpin crouched, doing all he could to keep from flying through the ropes. But Robinson held Turpin up himself with his right hand while he fired away with the left. The punches kept coming—another left, another right, a combination. Blood was still streaking from Robinson's eyes, but no matter; another left, another right—more than thirty punches in less than thirty seconds—and the Polo Grounds exploded. Turpin wheeled and stumbled to the center of the ring as referee Goldstein stepped in; Turpin stared across at Robinson as if he couldn't believe what had gone so wrong so quickly, as if he could continue, but Goldstein put his arms around Turpin's shoulders—as a father might a son who has just heard some painful family news. It was all over. Sugar Ray Robinson had regained the middleweight crown of the world.

A phalanx of New York City police officers jumped up on the canvas, circling the ring to keep fans out. Turpin and Robinson hugged. Those who thought Robinson had become a relic of himself had to contend with his rejuvenated power and dominance. He had done what only two other middleweights—Stanley Ketchel in 1908 and Tony Zale in 1948—had done before him: recaptured a middleweight crown after losing it.

Everyone wanted to see him in his dressing room. A physician hovered around Robinson; the head-butt would need stitches. Mayor Impellitteri was ushered through, followed by other dignitaries. Toots Shor and Walter Winchell were in the flow of bodies angling for entrance. "I paced myself slowly in the seventh, eighth and ninth," Robinson explained, "but when I was cut I went out after him with all I had." George Gainford surveyed the dressing-room scene, nodding at everyone. He was a champion's manager again; a king in Negro America. Turpin sat dejected in his dressing room, still struggling to regain his senses: "Robinson shook me two or three times, but he did not hurt me," he said unconvincingly.

It was a peculiar facet of Sugar Ray Robinson's fight manner that it sometimes took an emotional charge for him to elevate his artistic style to the height of its wicked savagery. He had carefully sought to explain to writers over the years that he was a boxer, a man with a precise craft—trying to draw a distinction between boxing and fighting, the former in his mind an artistic enterprise, the latter the pastime of ruffians and inelegant pugilists. While in the ring, he often tiptoed around, displaying a style beautiful enough to gaze at. But then those emotional challenges appeared: Tommy Bell standing in his way for the championship belt; Jimmy Doyle simply refusing to go down; Jake LaMotta winning for the first time and forever sealing his fate; George Costner robbing him of his name. When Randy Turpin's head bashed into Robinson's, dropping a warm curtain of blood across his face, it was the charge he needed; the savage genie erupted from its elegant bottle. Robinson was, in actuality, a hybrid: a boxer, but also an assassin of his opponent's mind-set. Watching him in slow motion—as Turpin had done— was a bewildering exercise. One moment a caterpillar, the next a butterfly; one moment a boxer, the next a fighter.

The next morning's *New York Times* had the fight story above the fold, at the very top of the paper: ROBINSON KNOCKS OUT TURPIN IN TENTH ROUND OF TITLE BOUT, announced the headline. James Dawson, the *Times*'s boxing writer, referred to Robinson's work as "a savage attack" against Turpin. Peter Wilson, the London *Daily Express* columnist who had long followed Turpin's career and had come across the ocean to see him try to keep his crown, scored Turpin ahead going into the tenth and fateful round. Wilson believed Turpin lost because he "forgot what to do when he was hurt," implying that the young fighter had no strategy to bounce back once stunned by Robinson's brutal explosion.

The newly crowned champion sent out a warning in the aftermath of the bout: He wanted Rocky Graziano next.

In Harlem they were waiting, thousands lining the streets. There was already pandemonium outside his nightclub, joyful noises rising as many gathered there, like guppies circling a huge whale. His club sat less than thirty blocks from the Polo Grounds. A. J. Liebling, the writer, was excited by what he had just witnessed in the ring. He found himself waddling down Eighth Avenue, perspiring in the nighttime humidity, in search of a taxi—the subways were too jammed. "Drive me downtown, past Sugar Ray's," he told the taxi driver whom he had corralled.

He'd stop if there was a clear path to the door; maybe a couple of pork chops, a drink or two.

But it was not a scene that could be easily navigated: "As we approached the Theresa [hotel], the avenue was so jammed up with traffic that we could barely move," Liebling would recall. "People were packed around the safety islands and overflowed onto the street. Somebody was beating an oilcan like a tomtom, and a tall, limber man was dancing in the street. Any idea I may have had of stopping at Sugar Ray's for a nightcap left me when I saw the crowd in front of the door."

The great prizefighter was on his way.

"That was a Cadillac night on Seventh Avenue," Sugar Ray would recall of the aftermath of Turpin and that New York evening. "It looked like an assembly line."

Randy Turpin sailed back to London, wondering aboard ship if he'd have to return to his former job as a bricklayer's assistant.

But Sugar Ray's Harlem was hardly finished with Randy Turpin. The fighter returned to New York City in 1953 for a fight against Bobo Olson. During the visit he resumed his affair with Adele Daniels, the beauty whom he had met shortly after his arrival in New York City to fight Robinson. Daniels soon charged Turpin with assault—later adding a charge of rape. Their relationship had been tempestuous. Turpin's manager scoffed at the charges, as did Turpin, calling it all an attempt to blackmail him. (Turpin's wife in England had told family members he sometimes abused her.) The New York police arrested Turpin at a hotel, preventing him from leaving the country until he posted bond and forcing him to return for trial. The trial got under way in 1955. British tabloids went wild. The Harlem courtroom was packed every day. But the trial didn't last a week— Daniels decided to accept a small monetary settlement.

For Randy Turpin, the brew of adulterous romance melting into celebrity, and the seductive world of the bigtime fight game, was dangerous. Like Jack Johnson, Joe Louis, Henry Armstrong, Jake LaMotta, and other ring stars had before him, Turpin stared bewildered into the glare of shame outside the ring.

Randy Turpin happily sailed away from America after the Daniels trial, having now been bewitched not once but twice in Sugar Ray's Harlem.

For so many of the world-recognized fighters, the arc of victory—
life inside the ring, the circling fame—seems to reach an end, and
then the haunting really begins. This is what happened to the great
Randy Turpin back home in England: He won a couple of British
championships before retiring in 1958. The retirement party was
held at Harringay Arena. Turpin looked resplendent in an evening
suit, his wife, Gwen, and family members in attendance. Some of the
giants of boxing showed up to salute him, among them Max Baer,
Bruce Woodcock, and the great Henry Armstrong. (Sugar Ray sent
his regards.) Turpin was only thirty years old upon retirement—and
he was broke. His business ventures had collapsed. When his earnings were bountiful, he had been quite generous lending others
money. As he sought to borrow money shortly after retiring, no one
helped. He grew embittered. He worked in scrap metal, roaming the
countryside, dragging old abandoned cars back to the yard. It was a
steep fall for a man who had dressed in Savile Row suits. He came out
of retirement and fought once in 1963 and once in 1964. He won
both; the latter fight was held in someplace called Valetta, Malta. No
one cared anymore. He turned to wrestling, crisscrossing the European continent and engaging in farcical bouts. He would tell anyone
who asked that he owed huge back taxes and also had a family to
feed. He wore a hearing aid on account of being deaf in one ear; it was
an old childhood injury that boxing had worsened, and wrestling
only more so. He kept wrestling, vowing his wife and four daughters
would not go hungry. He and Gwen owned a small café in Leamington Spa. They lived in the flat upstairs. It was an unlovely place. He
worked in the kitchen while Gwen worked out front, dealing with
the truckers and stragglers—and the curious who came by to gawk at
the onetime world champ. In December 1965 Turpin journeyed back
to America to attend Sugar Ray Robinson's retirement event, held at
Madison Square Garden. When he bounded beneath the ropes,
embraced by Sugar Ray, the applause was loud. No one in the crowd
realized the torment he was going through. When Turpin returned
to England, he was stunned to find that the tax office was threatening
to take his café. Gwen noticed his mood shifts—agitation one
moment, serenity the next—and told him that it would all work out
some way. On the morning of May 16, 1966, he purposely rammed
his head into a wall inside the café. The next day—just after sending
three of his four daughters off to school—Turpin strolled upstairs,

ostensibly to check on his youngest daughter, Carmen. He pulled a .22 caliber pistol. He shot the seventeen-month-old infant twice, then turned the gun to his heart and pulled the trigger. His wife, Gwen, rushed upstairs and found her daughter curled on the bed and her husband slumped to the floor. She grabbed little Carmen and bolted on foot to a nearby hospital. It was a miracle the child survived—one bullet had entered near her brain, the other near her lungs. Police raced to the house and found Turpin dead.

In the days afterwards, many across England, struggling for clues to such a heinous act, wondered if Randy Turpin had suffered brain damage during his fight career, and if that, along with a mortal fear of losing the means to care for his family, had unhinged him. Psychologists and boxing officials pondered all manner of questions. For years afterwards, Englanders would still talk of Randy Turpin, focusing on those sixty-four days he held the world championship after defeating Sugar Ray Robinson. There was talk through the years of paying some kind of tribute to him, but it came and went. Then, in 2001—exactly a half century after that Robinson victory—an 8'6"-high statue of Randy Turpin was unveiled in Warwick. His daughters appeared at the ceremony. There was a bronze plaque at the base of it, and the words on it echoed the excitement Englanders had held for him in the days leading up to his two bouts with the great Harlem middleweight:

IN PALACE, PUB, AND PARLOUR
THE WHOLE OF BRITAIN HELD ITS BREATH

He is always being hunted. Such is the curse of the champion. There is no place to hide. Champions have always found it difficult to walk away, to take their crown and vanish. In 1952 the great prizefighter had led many to believe he'd had enough of it all. Bright lights shone from another direction in Sugar Ray Robinson's imagination—from the world of entertainment. But then, right in the middle of those dreams, three figures with tantalizing histories—Olson, Graziano, and Maxim— appeared before him. The first two were fearless hunters, and Maxim, a champion already. The public believed in the promise of rare theatre. They knew someone's bones would be left to feast on.

1952

dreams

THERE WERE MORE than a few familiar characters in mid-twentieth-century boxing circles who carried weapons, the small .22 caliber handgun being the most common sidearm. With mischief often lurking in the shadows—owing to the proximity of gangsters and gamblers around the sport—the safety of Sugar Ray Robinson was never far from George Gainford's

Sugar Ray, just retired in 1952, with his wife Edna Mae and Hollywood star Jeff Chandler, along with Sammy Davis Jr., at the Riviera nightclub, in Fort Lee, New Jersey. Robinson dreamed of Broadway; he would eventually get there as technical advisor for the fighter Sammy would play in the acclaimed 1964 production of *Golden Boy*.

mind. While Robinson's sometime driver Chico, the midget, did carry a weapon, few relished the idea of Chico—with his knee-high aim—engaging in a shoot-out with anyone. Gainford, however, had a more potent source of protection in the form of Ellsworth "Bumpy" Johnson. (The bump on the back of Johnson's neck explained the nom de guerre.)

Johnson had become a notorious Manhattan criminal by the 1930s, with dozens of arrests to his name. A well-built man with a menacing look, he gambled and ran numbers. He also engaged in skirmishes with gangster Dutch Schultz over turf in the lucrative Harlem numbers racket. It was Gainford who brought Johnson into the Robinson camp as an ally. (Gainford and Johnson had Charleston, South Carolina, childhoods in common.) Johnson was sometimes seen at Sugar Ray's fights, smiling and nodding like a bronzed potentate, undercover police operatives trailing him. There were many evenings, as well, when he was spotted gliding into Robinson's nightclub; he fancied the fried chicken and cabbage, and was known to leave generous tips. But where Robinson had propelled his life far beyond the confines of Harlem, Johnson's illegal activities left him as a man operating in a social world confined to north of 125th Street. His threatening visage was real, but the range quite limited.

Sugar Ray knew all too well that the waters outside the boxing ring were swampy, so he allowed Gainford to wade into them on his behalf, cutting deals—with Sugar Ray's approval—and analyzing the terrain.

"Ray didn't want people to think George was always in control," says Mel Dick.

Robinson had little to offer shadowy figures such as Johnson, save for a good fight, a welcome at his club, and the smile of a friend. They wanted nothing more.

If Bumpy Johnson was happy to be around the fight game, then Gainford was happy to use Johnson's reputation on Robinson's behalf. Bumpy—in a doorway, unsmiling, bracketed by his minions—was quite a sight. "There was one instance where Gainford was having a back-and-forth with these gangsters—Frankie Carbo and that gang," recalls newspaperman Jimmy Breslin. "Well, Gainford goes down there to meet with them and he's with Bumpy Johnson. And those gangsters fled." (Robinson's personal valet had a name that fit right in with these gangster tête-à-têtes: Bennie Killings had come to the fighter's attention because he seemed adept at interpreting Robinson's sartorial tastes.)

In the first week of June 1952, Johnson had gone to a gambling parlor on 122nd Street. The game seemed to be going well enough, until a fellow gambler rose, pulled a gun, and fired two shots into Bumpy, one lodging in his chest, the other in his abdomen. Johnson was rushed to Sydenham Hospital, operated on, and given the news that he was quite lucky to have survived. "I would have taken that fellow, gun and all, if he had not started shooting when he did," Bumpy said. Bumpy had a private suite and a private nurse. Someone had brought a chessboard up to his room. He whiled away some of the hours staring at kings and queens on the board. Sugar Ray and George Gainford were mindful to send best wishes for Bumpy's recovery.

His record collection was massive, and Sugar Ray Robinson spent hours listening to the likes of Count Basie, Dinah Washington, Duke Ellington, Sinatra, and Billy Eckstine, among others. He adored Sinatra, but dreamily convinced himself he could achieve the allure of Eckstine onstage. As 1952 dawned, Sugar Ray Robinson was thinking more and more of the world of musical entertainment. Joe Louis predicted that 1952 would be Robinson's last year in the ring. And in late 1951 Earl Brown, the *Amsterdam News* columnist, expressed a similar sentiment: "In a year or two, this grand athlete will probably hang up his gloves for good." The talk of retirement was now picking up momentum. Sugar Ray had had long conversations in recent years with bandleader Lionel Hampton and crooner Billy Eckstine about the entertainment world. He continued, as well, to corner musicians entering his nightclub, quizzing them about their work schedule, and insisting on information about nightclubs around the country. In 1951, when he had turned thirty, many observers surmised—with so many great battles and championships already won—that he had earned the right to think of life beyond the ring. But George Gainford thought the talk of a career in entertainment full of folly. He was a manager, and he wished to keep managing the champion he had first laid eyes on in a church basement all those years ago. Gainford reminded Robinson that if he didn't defend his title within certain time limits, he would risk being stripped of it. So the manager lined up two fights. Robinson found himself flying out to San Francisco to face Bobo Olson, a former foe, for the first of those fights. It was a competitive bout and was only stopped in the twelfth when Robinson loosed a combination and a wicked blow into Olson's midsection. (Sometimes Robinson wondered just how many vicious-hitting middleweights were out there in the world, lurking, for they seemed to be all but popping out from behind trees!)

Sugar Ray Robinson's arrival in a city, and the beginning of his training sessions, continued to spark a great deal of interest among the citizenry, especially among Negro athletes from area colleges. To them, Robinson was a figure of great accomplishment who swelled their own pride. When Robinson began his training for the second Olson fight at the Royal Gym in San Francisco, he was so high-spirited—he had had a six-month layoff from the ring—that he invited many locals to come watch his workouts. There were shoeshine men, newspapermen, young local fighters, and members of the University of San Francisco football team, among them Ollie Matson, the great Negro running back. Robinson's pre-fight sessions were lively affairs, with him sometimes frolicking and clowning in the ring.

But Robinson realized in the first round of the bout at Civic Auditorium that Bobo Olson found none of it funny—not Robinson's reported levity during his training sessions, and certainly not the fact that Robinson had already signed for another title defense following the Olson match, as if a victory were a foregone conclusion. Bobo Olson came out swinging and landing blows, and those early flurries saw an eruption of fan support on his behalf. (Hundreds had been turned away at the box office hours before the sold-out encounter, and police braced themselves for a disturbance, which didn't materialize.) Robinson, owing to the long layoff, was missing punch after punch. The hard-hitting Olson "was scoring solidly with a good left to Robinson's chin and an occasional solid right to the ribs." In the seventh, Olson landed a below-the-belt blow, and even though it drew a warning from the referee, the damage was done and Robinson's legs buckled. He looked unsteady, and the tattooed Olson had fire in his eyes. Over in Robinson's corner, a streak of worry crossed Gainford's face. The UP dispatch writer saw it shaping up as a "surprising battle." In the ninth, Olson landed a walloping left to Robinson's chin, then another one in the tenth. Despite the aggressive Olson attack, Robinson seemed unworried. At the end of the tenth, the judges had scored the fight evenly. But in the eleventh, the Sugar Ray of old reappeared: He unleashed roundhouse rights to Olson's body and kidney area, and Olson's head snapped like a puppet's. The joy began to slowly drain from the faces of Olson partisans who had been howling for an upset. It was "cunning" that enabled Robinson's victory, many of the ringside reporters felt. Robinson—who had agreed to the fight for a $1 purse and expenses, donating the prize money to the Runyon Cancer Fund—felt, in the end, it had been too much of a challenge after such a long layoff. "I never fought so hard in my life for $1," he admitted following the bout, sitting in his dressing room draped in a white terry-cloth robe. Gainford tended to him with the gentle satisfaction of someone who had escaped a perilous journey through terrible weather. "Olson is a clean fighter and I hope [he] gets up there after I give up the middleweight title—if I'm still holding it when I retire," Robinson added.

Robinson and Gainford left San Francisco with a month to prepare for the fight in Chicago with Rocky Graziano. But Gainford was feeling uneasy. Not because of Graziano, but because Robinson had again, while in San Francisco, mentioned that word: retirement. The fighter whom he had discovered and trained and invested so much in! Where would that leave George Gainford? He had no intention of returning to the basement of a church on the hard side of Harlem.

The standoff featuring two marquee names was a match for all the dreamers. Sugar Ray Robinson vs. Rocky Graziano was for all the kids who boxed in AAU tournaments; and the men who shadow-boxed in their basements; and the older men on stoops who remembered Henry Armstrong and Jack Dempsey and Gene Tunney and Billy Conn and Marcel Cerdan. It was for all the fans who couldn't forget Lew Jenkins and Charley Burley. And also for all the ladies lucky enough to have beaus who had gotten tickets—April 16, 1952—to the indoor Chicago title fight. Sugar Ray Robinson and

Rocky Graziano were both men with compelling images: Robinson the marcelled-haired, silk-robed gladiator with the pink Cadillac and nightclub, Rocky the street brawler and onetime juvenile delinquent with the humble tastes of a plumber. They were each survivors of the New York City streets in their youth. And each had turned professional in the golden glow before World War II. Also, each had broken through scandalous news accounts—Graziano's prison record, and Robinson's AWOL fugue during the war. It was a wonder they had not met before 1952, except the color bar upheld by the various boxing commissions kept Robinson from the likes of both Graziano and Tony Zale. Both Robinson and Gainford—along with their followers—remembered well what Graziano had howled from the ring in 1945 after his knockout of Billy Arnold: "Now get me Robinson!" By the time of their announced meeting in 1952, boxing fans imagined a turning back of the clock—to a time when both fighters were still fairly new and sensational figures in the world of professional boxing. Fans agreed: It was a fight of extreme interest. Nevertheless, Arthur Daley of *The New York Times* realized it was a match that, with the passage of time, stood "tarnished with age." If Robinson had indeed slipped in his prowess, a point many now began to ponder, "he slipped from so high a peak that he hasn't descended to the timber line," Daley wrote. "He still is in the rarefied atmosphere of true greatness." In 1948, Graziano—who always had a slugger's power but never the guile and cleverness of a Robinson—had lost his belt, and for the next three years he fought a string of forgettable matches. The bright lights of the entertainment world, even as he continued fighting, had dizzied him. "His heart no longer is in his work," Daley of the *Times* believed. "Once . . . he was an uninhibited roughneck who wore no man's collar, including his own. Now he wears a tie and jacket, and combs his hair. Civilization has ruined him."

No matter how stellar Sugar Ray Robinson's achievements, more and more people mused about and predicted the dimming of his fight capabilities. In Chicago for the fight, Joe Nichols of *The New York Times* predicted that Graziano would beat Robinson and regain the title. Joe Bostic of the *Amsterdam News* predicted a Robinson win, but not with much enthusiasm as he also pronounced Robinson "well over the hill" in his fight career.

On the day before what fans hoped would be a fabled match,

Robinson was making his way to his seat at the home opener for the Chicago White Sox. He had the same expression on his face as he often had behind the bar of his nightclub: jovial and relaxed.

Graziano was in a snappy mood. "I'll knock him out," he said of Robinson. "I know I can beat this guy."

And doubtless Rocky Graziano felt reborn standing opposite Sugar Ray Robinson in the ring inside Chicago Stadium during that first round. "He came out of his corner with his curly black hair flopping on his forehead," Robinson would remember, "and with his right hand cocked like a revolver." The 22,264 in attendance—boxing officials had predicted 19,000—was only a thousand less than the world indoor record set in 1932, also in Chicago Stadium, when Jack Dempsey fought King Levinsky. In the first round Graziano caught Robinson with a solid left hook, and many thought to themselves this was the Rocky of yesteryear. But the Robinson answer was quite declarative: a lightning-quick series of punches—delivered "with such breathtaking speed that they hardly could be counted," according to *The New York Times*—that stunned Graziano. In the second round Graziano unloaded "a rocking right" that smashed into Robinson's head. Robinson would admit afterward that had the punch landed "three inches further down my jaw I would have been knocked out."

But then all of it began to unfold in true Robinson fashion: The ghostly-quick Robinson started dancing around Graziano, shifting as he threw his punches, dodging Graziano's blows, then bouncing more punches into Graziano's head. It was as if someone had cranked up a newsreel to high speed. As the third got under way, Graziano knew he was in trouble. Robinson was moving quick about the ring, then dancing in front of Graziano as he unleashed more blows. In one moment, however, Graziano stopped all of it and fired a right into Robinson. Robinson went down—some believed it a slip—but rose up quickly. And when Robinson did, he saw—like a wolf at night peering through trees at prey—the open line into Graziano's unprotected jaw. The Robinson left, delivered as he was backpedaling, was the first salvo of the combination; then came the right, which floored Graziano and sent his mouthpiece flying. Graziano was out cold for five seconds. He then began to stir and struggled up against the ropes, but he was engulfed in a haze. Again he plopped to the canvas. The referee rushed in; Robinson's corner entered the ring to celebrate the victory. It had taken less than eight minutes. The epitaph of Sugar Ray Robinson had been written too soon. He remained a fighter quite far from the timber line of his sport. Robinson turned to Joe Louis in the aftermath: "I'll meet you at the Archway," he said, referring to the local lounge owned by Killer Johnson. (In the minds of Robinson's cornermen, one of the more beguiling things about his personality was how he could go from bruising fighter to post-fight party organizer. He got such joy from directing human traffic, making spontaneous plans, sending word to invite local musicians to the festivities.)

Reporters wanted Robinson's take on the ring proceedings. "I had it tonight; yes sir, I had it tonight when I needed it—thank God," the victor said afterward.

Sugar Ray Robinson had forced the pundits to make reassessments. "Robinson is a cold-blooded machine," Arthur Daley of the *Times* concluded after the fight. Sugar Ray had sent observers from the stadium shaking their heads. But that wave of melancholy about time also surfaced again. Sugar Ray Robinson had a malady known to many great men: He was both a realist and a sentimentalist. The constant drumbeat of one disposition—the realist—without the other was apt to stiffen the mind-set and turn it away from dreams. But too much of the other—the sentimentalist—too often yanked the intellect in directions that left it most vulnerable. The march from Black Bottom to the Waldorf Astoria ballroom had been a mighty one; he could not relinquish the majesty of it so easily. So he allowed degrees of both to settle inside him. "Sooner or later you come to the end of the road and I think two or maybe three more fights and I'll call it a career," he said, much to the dismay of Gainford, and really not sure if he believed it himself.

He shared laughter with Chicago friends before boarding the Twentieth Century Limited train back to Manhattan. Aboard the train, Pullman porters acknowledged Robinson's presence as the sweet laughter flowing from the champion's entourage bounced up and down the aisles. As the train rumbled through the Midwest, Gainford and Robinson broached the subject that had trailed them since arriving in San Francisco months earlier: Joey Maxim. Maxim was the light heavyweight champion of the world. Robinson had been mulling another step up in weight class. In San Francisco he had told reporters he wanted no part of Maxim, and he repeated the assertion in Chicago, but it was all a ruse to gin up interest in the meeting. (Robinson had actually told French reporters while in Paris nearly a year earlier that he very much looked forward to fighting Maxim.)

Back in Manhattan, Robinson was again thinking about his future. Ideas rolled around in his head: He would gather some musicians and hit the road, making a sweep of the country just like Ellington and Billy Eckstine and Count Basie. He would retire. Then, hours later, another decision: No, he would not retire. He would keep fighting, because the public wanted great fighters to keep fighting. Ideas fluctuated day to day. He went to church at Salem Methodist—front pews reserved for the champ and family!—and prayed to the gods for guidance, unsure of what they were trying to tell him. He practiced his tap dancing; he ran his fingers across piano keys in music halls. He would retire. Yes, he would dance and he would focus on his businesses. If only he could approximate the beautiful music of Eckstine and tap like the Nicholas Brothers, Harold or Fayard. He had looked so handsome in white tie and tails. Everyone had told him so. But it was such a mighty dream, perhaps an impossible one. There were as many entertainers who didn't get the right break as there were fighters who didn't get the right break. No, he would keep fighting.

He bewildered reporters, who were trying to figure his next move. Joe Bostic of the *Amsterdam News* was a decade-long acquaintance of Robinson, yet still pronounced the fighter an "enigma." "To fathom Robinson's reasoning quirks is to qualify for election to the world's great geniuses of psychology," Bostic wrote.

Television executives also had a hard time dealing with Robinson's psyche. He always felt that he didn't get enough respect from TV execs when it came to revenues for fight profits, even though, as Sugar Ray knew, he had changed the scope of television boxing, drawing fight fans as well as fans of his style, his artistry. The more viewership, the more revenue. And the more revenue, Robinson figured, the more money in his pockets. In a dirty business, he thought of himself as the closest thing to a Sir Galahad of the fight game. In his mind, when he cancelled a fight, it was akin to workers going on strike: It was done to gain respect and leverage. But he was not always successful in these endeavors—he could not penetrate the various professional boxing organizations, with those Mafia figures in the shadows that sponsored the fights and controlled profits. So he would rebel against them by leaving the ring. After all, he "was the man selling the tickets," he had told one boxing official.

He sat upstairs in his nightclub, the sounds of Harlem traffic sailing through the windows, reading his fan mail. A lot of it came from cancer patients. He slipped down to his business establishments; he had his nails manicured, his hair clipped. Yes, he would leave the ring; he would devote time to answering some of those heartbreaking letters from the cancer patients. "I'm just plain tired of fighting," he had said in San Francisco. "I don't even watch fights anymore, not since Joe Louis and my other friends quit." He would let boxing officials see if they could survive as well as they had without the services of Sugar Ray Robinson, without his marquee pull. At least that was one side of his inner debate. The other side cut to the bone of Sugar Ray's competitive spirit. He began asking Gainford questions about the light heavyweight division, about his chances of taking another crown. And beyond that, he began asking about light heavyweight Joey Maxim. He asked Gainford about Maxim's stance in the ring, the timing of his punches, his stamina. Gainford realized that just as in his Golden Gloves youth, Robinson was pursuing this line of inquiry for a reason. The fighter, who had also been studying Maxim on tape, was clearly plotting. That which Sugar Ray didn't have propelled him forward. The rare fame of a singular Negro simply wasn't enough. Gainford had been caught off guard by Robinson again, and this was what he liked: how Robinson kept him alert, made his cagey assessments seem even more cagey. At times Gainford wondered who was managing whom, but any confusion in their alliance dissipated at the noise Robinson made when he felt unappreciated. He bore in on goals. He wanted desperately to know about life on the road for musicians, so he had cornered Dizzy Gillespie and questioned him all night long. Now he wanted to know everything Gainford thought of Maxim. And it wasn't just Maxim. It was the whole portrait of professional boxing that constantly stayed on Robinson's mind—Armstrong and Joe Louis and Charley Burley and all the Negro fighters who had been wronged. Robinson, the sentimentalist, would avenge their hurts. He also knew—the realist—that the light heavyweight purses were larger than the middleweight purses. Besides, it would prove a comeuppance for boxing officials: He'd yank more money from their tight purses and slippery accounting practices. After some behind-the-scenes negotiations, all mostly orchestrated by Robinson himself, Gainford sent word forth: Sugar Ray Robinson would fight light heavyweight champion Joey Maxim on June 23 at Yankee Stadium.

Sometimes the middleweight champion of the world couldn't keep from dreaming of the multiple titles that his old friend Henry Armstrong had held.

Joey Maxim—he took his ring name after the Maxim machine gun—was raised in the fight-crazed city of Cleveland, Ohio. He turned professional at the age of eighteen. It was against the wishes of his parents, however, who could never bring themselves to see him fight. But plenty of teenyboppers did: Joey Maxim, with his dark hair and smooth skin, had matinee-idol looks and sent girls swooning. He also had his fans in Hollywood: Frank Sinatra counted himself one of the fighter's biggest admirers. In 1950 Maxim won the world light heavyweight title by defeating Freddie Mills in London. "Maxim is as good a fighter as Dempsey, except he can't hit," Maxim's manager, Jack Kearns, once sarcastically said of him. Maxim had also fought heavyweight Ezzard Charles—and lost.

Maxim and Robinson—the latter having gone from welter to middle—had something in common: They were not averse to reaching upward from the mountain they stood on, to test themselves.

By early June, in the days leading up to Robinson-Maxim, the weather in New York City had become unpredictable. Some days came in with normal temperature readings for that time of year; others blistering with heat, and stifling. Those were the days that saw men pushing carts laden with ice for sale up and down the pavement and children skipping around open fire hydrants. On weekends, the well-to-do left town for the Hamptons and Long Island Sound in search of cooler temperatures. People couldn't stop talking about the weather, but the looming title fight generated much conversation too. In downtown Manhattan and in Harlem salons; on barstools and in diners and all the way across Central Park; on rooftops where the breezes blew and down to the bohemian hangouts in Greenwich Village, Manhattan was abuzz about Robinson-Maxim. Fans were lining up at both Madison Square Garden and the Polo Grounds to purchase tickets, priced from $5 to $30. Many offered theories and conjecture about each fighter's chances, about the pitfalls faced by any challenger who was stepping up or down to another weight class. Maxim was stronger; Robinson quicker. Maxim had crafty Jack Kearns, who had managed Jack Dempsey. Robinson had George Gainford, who had led his fighter to two championship titles. Still, many believed Robinson faced the stiffest hill to climb. It was Maxim's caginess and strength—he had already taken on heavyweights—that colored their worries. And yet: "Sugar Ray is no ordinary fighter," Arthur Daley of the *Times* opined before the contest. "He is a boxer who outboxes boxers. He is a slugger who outslugs sluggers."

Robinson, Gainford, and cornerman Harry Wiley—along with the traveling entourage—settled into training camp at Pompton Lakes. But from the start it was tense, with Gainford and Wiley arguing almost daily over which strategy might work best for Robinson in taking on Maxim. Gainford was already feeling uneasy: Rumors had been circulating that Kearns, Maxim's manager, was going to offer Robinson a more lucrative package—utilizing his TV contacts—to manage his career. Robinson assured Gainford he had no interest in Kearns's offer, be it real or imagined. But it hardly seemed to soothe Gainford's worries as he heaved himself about the camp, instructing from the sidelines and all the while arguing with Wiley.

"You let me make the decisions!" Gainford finally roared at Wiley one afternoon, turning heads.

Wiley's eyes bulged. He felt now this was public theatre, with onlookers wondering how he would react. Pride was at stake. "I got as much right to make the decisions as you do," he shouted back. Gainford told Wiley to shut up.

Wiley said he would do no such thing, and seeking an edge against the burly Gainford as he felt a confrontation coming on, pulled a gun. Bystanders began scooting away.

"I can shoot you," he warned Gainford.

Robinson jumped into the fray, demanding that Wiley put the gun away, which he did. Everyone finally relaxed. Through the subsequent days a degree of normalcy returned as tempers cooled. Still, the whole episode left Robinson wondering if his manager and trainer had been focused enough on helping him overtake Maxim.

A gaggle of reporters arrived at the camp—among them roly-poly A. J. Liebling—and began peppering Robinson with questions.

"Have you ever fought a man that heavy?" one reporter wanted to know.

Robinson smiled: "Never a champion that heavy."

"Do you think you can hurt him?" another asked.

"I can hurt anybody," Robinson answered, as Gainford and Wiley nodded in affirmation.

Robinson sparred beneath the arching trees on a makeshift ring. There were old Manhattan acquaintances in attendance; some former boxers. He had had a group of kids from the New York City Police Athletic League brought out and they were knee to knee on bleachers watching him work out and seemed as delighted as if it were Christmas morning. Liebling seemed especially impressed with Robinson's style of jumping rope: "Most fighters jump rope as children do, but infinitely faster. Robinson just swings a length of rope in his right fist and jumps in time to a fast tune whistled by his trainer. He jumps high in the air and twists his joined knees at the top of every bound. When he jumps in double time to 'I'm Just Wild About Harry,' it's something to see."

But once back in Manhattan, Robinson never allowed anyone to sense the strain that had taken place inside his camp. He was seen playing the piano days before the scheduled fight, throwing his head back with wide smiles like Fats Waller.

People arriving in town for the fight—described by one local publication as "big-money men and their womenfolk"—had flooded the city hotels. Bellhops at the Waldorf Astoria, the Edison, the New Yorker, the Commodore, and the Hotel Roosevelt, as well as the Hotel Theresa uptown in Sugar Ray's Harlem, were commenting about the heavy business. But on the day of the fight, not long after the weigh-in at Madison Square Garden, there was an announcement: Because it was an outdoor event, organizers could not ignore the rain in the forecast. "We even referred to the Farmer's Catalogue," said Jim Norris of the International Boxing Club, which was promoting the bout. The fight was postponed for forty-eight hours. Robinson and Maxim maintained a calm demeanor regarding the delay. As Robinson made his way back out to the street, the hubbub intensified, and a crowd materializing behind him. Standing in front of the Garden, dressed in suit pants and wearing a V-neck sweater, he held an umbrella over his head, surrounded by his excitable gallery. Laughing and making light of the weather, he looked like a dandy on holiday.

Going into the weigh-in, oddsmakers had the bout pegged as even. In their thinking, it had simply been too difficult to predict a winner. But the two-day delay shifted opinion and the odds became 7–5 in favor of Sugar Ray—people thought Robinson would better adjust to the postponement than Maxim.

On the evening of the fight, as the skies darkened and the clock showed four hours before the ten p.m. starting time, the Manhattan temperature rested at 96.5 degrees. Already it was a record in the history of the city for June 25. But at Yankee Stadium, the temperature had not yet peaked.

In those charged minutes before the fight, it was difficult to ignore the beautiful people, for they were everywhere, alighting from Cadillacs and Jaguars and chauffeur-driven cars. Some who had toted binoculars were gawking through them like bird-watchers. Eddie Green, a realtor and Sugar Ray acquaintance, had a custom car designed—a "Muntz-Jet automobile"—which made its debut outside Yankee Stadium that night. "The car clips off a smooth 140 mph, is outfitted with a private bar and refrigerator," a reporter would note. "Its lemon-yellow color and out-of-this-world lines caused even the most blasé sportsman to stop and take notice." Betty Granger, a writer for the *Amsterdam News,* couldn't help but notice "the new crop of glamour girls in town from every corner of the country" for the fight. Neither Edna Mae Robinson nor her sister-in-law Evelyn aimed to play second fiddle to any of those girls. Edna Mae turned heads as she sashayed to her Yankee Stadium seat wearing "a full-length coat-dress with graduated hemline over an aqua blue sheath strapless dress." The ensemble was completed by diamond mink cuffs and a black diamond mink stole over her arm. Evelyn Robinson—Bennie Killings, Sugar Ray's high-stepping valet, was her escort—wore a blue Chantilly lace dress. A string of pearls circled her neck, and her blue gloves matched her blue shoes. Evelyn Robinson had, in fact, recently begun designing her own clothing and appearing in fashion shows. In addition, her face was all over advertisements in the New York City subway system: She was seen in promotional ads for Chesterfield cigarettes.

Murmurs across the open air signaled the arrival of the fighters in the ring.

Before the bell, it was hard to dismiss the fifteen-pound weight advantage held by the tall and muscled Maxim. Robinson loosened himself in his corner like an animal shaking off water. The ringing of the bell echoed through the darkness as referee Ruby Goldstein circled the combatants.

Maxim, slow of movement, a plodder even, went right for Robinson's body in the opening round. They were heavy punches delivered with the authority of a light heavyweight. Robinson tossed right jabs to Maxim's upper body. In both the second and third, Maxim continued clinching, offering body blows at the same time; referee Goldstein was forced to break up the hold and warned Maxim about it. Not long into the fourth Robinson landed his most crushing blow yet, a right to Maxim's jaw that shook him. Robinson continued firing, turning Maxim into a huge punching bag. James Dawson of the *Times* felt Robinson was now "giving Maxim a boxing lesson and a battering." Jack Kearns, Maxim's cagey manager-trainer, was seemingly unworried: His fighter looked unfazed even though welts had formed beneath both eyes from the Robinson blows. Maxim continually stepped toward Robinson as if to the cadences of a slow-moving military drill. Every time Maxim clinched, Robinson reacted again by pelting him with left jabs. Plumes of cigarette smoke rose from the press section. The smoke, and the wattage of all the overhead lights, created a saunalike effect: the ring temperature would eventually reach 104 degrees. Cornermen soaked their respective fighters with wet towels in the seconds between rounds. If Maxim had stamina in the first nine rounds, Robinson had points, as all judges had him ahead at that stage in the scheduled fifteen-rounder. "I'm getting sleepy," Robinson had told Gainford at the end of the ninth: it was disorientation from the heat. Still, his left hooks and crosses were delivered crisply. But it was also evident that Robinson's balletic moves—his corner constantly reminded him to keep clear of Maxim's power, so he was really dancing tonight—were tiring him in the heat. (Just before the tenth started, referee Goldstein himself needed some smelling salts.) Both fighters exchanged lefts, then rights, with Maxim connecting on a solid left-right as the bell rang to end the tenth. Goldstein, his white shirt completely soaked, wobbled to the edge of the ring like a sightless man. The ring doctor came to his aid, and after a quick examination, pronounced Goldstein finished for the night. "I thought I was being roasted to death," Goldstein would later say. Referee Ray Miller—one of three substitute referees on hand, and a former boxer himself—climbed into the ring to take Goldstein's place. And now the fight began to turn into a slow-motion minuet, as if a newsreel were broken and droning slowly. The audience was surprised at what they were seeing, something so different from the earlier rounds: Robinson lunging his fists at Maxim as if lifting them through mud; Maxim moving his head as if it weighed a ton; Robinson missing a wild right, his arm moving as if he were waving outward over an expanse of open land; Robinson walking to the wrong corner at the end of the eleventh as if bouncing along a hall of mirrors. Robinson, always so prideful of his hair, looked as if he had just emerged from a swimming pool. In the twelfth Robinson, summoning all of his willpower, let loose with a series of lefts and rights. Maxim stumbled but did not fall. Robinson wilted again, like a wax man torched by the heat; the humidity had him like a giant claw. He was now fighting, he would later admit, without memory of what had happened in the round before or the round before that. In the thirteenth he flung a right and it knocked him to the floor without touching anything save air. It was a rare sight: Sugar Ray Robinson face-first on the canvas. Maxim, aware of victory now, walked to his corner as casually as if walking through the door of the Stork Club. Robinson's corner circled him as he sat on the stool, his head slumped. "Can you stand up?" one of the doctors who had gathered around him asked. Robinson's head went left to right: no. It was over. A thundering noise from many of the more than forty-seven thousand in attendance wafted up and through the darkness. The great Sugar Ray had been defeated.

It was the third defeat of his career, and the first so-called knockout. Gainford and Wiley worried about the effects of the heat on their fighter; thoughts he might die flashed between them. With the help of others, they gingerly got him to the dressing room. Robinson's valet, Bennie Killings, arrived at the door with Edna Mae, who insisted on seeing her husband. Officials at first refused to let her in, not wanting her to see her husband in such a state. Edna Mae prevailed but only for long enough to plant kisses on his face. As she was escorted out, Mayor Impellitteri made his way in. "He didn't knock me out, did he?" Robinson finally asked the mayor, who told him it was the heat and not Maxim. Manny Berardinelli, Maxim's brother, had accompanied Maxim to the fight, working his corner. "The heat didn't get my brother," he would remember, decades later. "It just got Sugar Ray. Joey won that fight and it was the biggest fight of his career."

Robinson was afraid of hospitals and pleaded with doctors in his dressing room not to be taken to one. So he was brought to the home of his mother, Leila. Nearly a dozen people invaded her house, wanting to watch after Sugar Ray. She resented their presence and eventually shooed them away. As the night of her son's mighty defeat deepened—he had dropped more than ten pounds during the encounter—she caressed his lips with ice chips to provide a degree of comfort.

The next morning New Yorkers were greeted with bizarre rumors: Goldstein, the referee, had died; Robinson had been hospitalized—and was on the verge of announcing his retirement from the ring. Reports of Goldstein's death were false; he and his wife only laughed when told about them. Robinson, of course, had never gone to the hospital. As for retirement, he denied it; he said he wanted another shot at Maxim. But Maxim scoffed: "What have I got to gain by fighting him again?" he wondered. He doubted the receipts for another bout would be as remunerative.

Robinson's admirers had given him credit for battling so long and well against Maxim. Many blamed the heat. But such sentiments hardly comforted Robinson. Just a day after the fight he rode into downtown Manhattan and sat in a darkened theatre. Movie theatre owners often showed the big fights a day later on the big screen. Robinson sat like an ordinary fight fan with hundreds of others and watched himself on the screen. He stared. His face grew anguished, as if he couldn't believe he was watching himself fall to defeat. He later harangued Gainford and Wiley for not giving him salt tablets and also for allowing Goldstein to be replaced as the referee. If Goldstein had been given a rest instead, he would have regained his equilibrium. The blame heaped upon them angered Gainford and Wiley, and for the first time ever, they spoke of him with sadness when they were not in his company. Gainford, however, failed to assess the fissures now growing between him and Robinson. It was not a defeat Robinson could let go. He consulted with doctors, listening as they repeated to him, time and time again, that it was the heat that had felled him, that heat could do strange things to the body. And with each reinforcement that it was the heat, Robinson stepped further away from Gainford. In his mind Gainford had spoiled his chance at immortality. It was not a time now for sentimentality. Robinson pleaded for a rematch with Maxim until it became obvious that Maxim and his manager had other plans.

Sugar Ray had wanted to become a triple titleholder like his idol Henry Armstrong, and Bob Fitzsimmons—and that was out of reach now.

He sat in the pew of Salem Methodist on Sunday mornings, seeking divine guidance about the future. Both Gainford and Wiley noticed, following the Maxim defeat, that Robinson had begun talking of God, and intervention; of how God just might have wanted to humble him. They rolled their eyes. They reclined inside his nightclub and imagined he would, in time, stop with the religious jabbering. Strolling away from church, however, Robinson avoided talking about any kind of sports, lest parishioners think him one-dimensional.

The image of old fighters cadging meals in restaurants—in Robinson's own nightclub even—began to haunt him more and more. Joe Louis had looked awful in those last ring moments, his dressing rooms so funereal.

Thirty-year-old Sugar Ray Robinson was still a young man by most standards, but in the world of prizefighting that was the age of most uncertainty, full of hindsight and circumspection. He wanted a future as interesting as his past. For the first time since his teenage years—and his brief Army duty—there were no fights being lined up for him in the weeks following the Maxim bout. He could not abide losing, and being the victim of a knockout—even if classified as a TKO—had always been anathema to him. He had started, in the months before the Maxim bout, to have dreams, and they were dreams about death and dying. Church personnel would come across him at the church during the week, sitting in a pew—praying.

Sugar Ray Robinson found it very difficult to discuss boxing in public. It was a savage sport, but it held a kind of sacredness to him—a mystery. His comments to reporters were always mercifully short; he hid behind musical instruments when away from the ring. So he would not step to a bank of microphones to announce retirement. Because of the Maxim loss, he did not believe he deserved a fancy retirement ceremony. There was no big dinner or farewell event announcing his retirement. He dodged reporters; Gainford and Wiley were dropped from his payroll. It was left to boxing officials in September 1952 to inform the public that the great middleweight champion was leaving the ring. For days and even weeks after, however, stunned fans and watchers debated his career, talked about his major battles in barbershops and diners, in shoeshine parlors and gambling dens. Young fighters talked about his dominance and ring savvy and began collecting magazines that had featured him as keepsakes. Sugar Ray Robinson just slipped away like a ship across dark waves into the night.

He had for so long cherished his independence. While Joe Louis had become entangled with various boxing promotional organizations to keep a steady income, Sugar Ray avoided them. The season had seen him become philosophical, allowing that "any man with two hands can beat you." Now, more than ever, the year 1952 closing around him, he was his own man. His life had played out against a backdrop of wondrous rhythm—buried deep and unseen in those old phonograph records he had hauled around as a young fighter—and in the arc of his fighting career he had showed his epic gifts: Seasoned fighters were vanquished, greatness devoured. He had introduced a new version of pugilist to the world. The French had called him Le Sucre Merveilleux—the marvelous Sugar.

And now, that old dream of entertaining had invaded his senses again. He wanted to do what Lena and Miles were doing. Vaudeville was gone, but cabaret thrived. Every big city had fancy nightclubs, and many of those nightclub denizens had seen his name atop marquees. "Robinson thought he could sing and dance," recalls newspaperman Jimmy Breslin. "I went to a thing one night, a kind of audition of his. It was in an apartment house on Seventh Avenue. Robinson played the piano and he sang. He did this to let the agents see him for the first time. It was okay, but it was street stuff. It wasn't professional."

Entertainment agents are in the business of talent, sure enough, but also smoke and mirrors—why couldn't a world boxing champion who had good legs, looked good in formal wear, and played piano become a success onstage? Other pugilists—Jack Johnson, Max Baer, Rocky Graziano among them—had pushed their way into the realm of entertainment, though not a one with any manner of distinction. Edna Mae Robinson told her husband she knew he could be successful with his own act. Edna Mae, and so many of her lovely girlfriends, had come out of that swinging and sepia world that Sugar Ray Robinson now intended to enter.

Who could know—even among the coast-to-coast newspapermen and fight fans, among the mind readers and tarot card holders of Harlem—that, in time, the flip side of the recording of his life would offer another kind of music? Something to complete the symphony of Sugar Ray Robinson—something as great, bruising, and as heartbreakingly operatic as anything in the annals of the fight game itself?

INTERLUDE **Edna Mae and Those Lovely Sepia Women in the Mirror**

They were beautiful, and they were well practiced at turning— at just the right moment—toward the flashbulbs of the camera. It was the beginning of the 1950s when they started to get noticed. Madison Avenue ignored them, but they strutted on the pages of Negro publications—and also the occasional photo display in special editions of *Life* and *Holiday* magazines. Many were the offspring of strong-willed mothers who encouraged them to have an appreciation of art and music—and their own beauty. They moved from stage to cabaret setting, taking an occasional role in film. Lena Horne was their maiden voyager. But neither Eartha Kitt nor Dorothy Dandridge, Marva Louis nor Hazel Scott nor Edna Mae Robinson felt intimidated by the glow that Horne had cast. Like Horne, all were convinced of their individual sensuality, beauty, and talent. They cast quite a different spell from the darkly hued and heavyset women—Hattie McDaniel, Butterfly McQueen, Louise Beavers—who had been featured in American cinema, often in the role of maid, a decade earlier. This new group aimed to etch a different persona.

Kitt's background had been the most challenging. Born poor in South Carolina, she was given up and reared by foster parents. She detested working in the fields. Eventually, she made her way to Manhattan and found work with the famed Katherine Dunham dance troupe. It led to European travels and her discovery by Orson Welles, who cast her in stage productions. Nightclubs in Paris and London signed her for performances. Back in Manhattan, she was given a significant part in *New Faces of 1952,* a stage musical, and emerged a star. She had an hourglass shape, a theatrical purr to her voice, and a raw sensuality in her walk that upended the senses of men.

Whereas Kitt celebrated an ability to tease and shock, Hazel Scott was seriously refined. A West Indian by birth, she had been a child prodigy at the piano, playing the classics with ease before her tenth birthday. Her piano playing turned heads at the 1939 New York World's Fair. When Charlie Parker recorded his version of Gershwin's "Embraceable You," he sent for Scott to accompany him on piano. Her marriage in 1945 to Adam Clayton Powell Jr.—Sugar Ray's congressman—shocked some in Harlem because Powell had callously divorced his first wife. *Life* magazine showed the wedding over a two-page spread; Scott looked gorgeous in a white Chantilly lace dress. (Langston Hughes and Bill "Bojangles" Robinson were among the many guests at the wedding reception.) Five years later Scott became the first black woman to host a network TV program: *The Hazel Scott Show* premiered on the DuMont network on July 3, 1950. Even though it lasted less than three months, it gave viewers a close-up—albeit on the small screen—of a beautiful and stylish Negro woman.

There was a peek at the gorgeous Dorothy Dandridge in 1951 with the premiere of *The Harlem Globetrotters,* but the movie's success was hobbled by its limited release. The Otto

Preminger–directed *Carmen Jones,* released in 1954 and featuring Dandridge and Harry Belafonte as the leads, received far greater attention: The film garnered Dandridge an Academy Award nomination and she was featured on the cover of *Life* magazine—a first for a Negro actress.

Sometimes Sugar Ray's young friend Mel Dick would drop by his nightclub just to gawk at the movie stars: "And I remember the day I was there and Dorothy Dandridge walked in. Ray just smiled at me." Beauty, in America, suddenly had another dimension. The men who wooed these women were often men of great accomplishments. Nineteen-year-old Marva Trotter was working as a secretary at the *Chicago Defender* when she met Joe Louis in 1934. Louis had a number of women after him, but it was Trotter's attributes—statuesque, raven black hair, cinnamon-colored complexion—that entranced him. Louis married Trotter hours before his September 24, 1935, fight in Manhattan with onetime champion Max Baer. His new bride sat in the audience. Louis mauled Baer, and blood could be seen oozing all over his face. "Here was the coldest concentration ever a man displayed," syndicated columnist Paul Gallico would write. "And I wonder if his new bride's heart beat a little with fear that this terrible thing was hers."

It was a new kind of beauty that was now illuminating the country. It had come floating, seemingly, out of nowhere. But in reality it had sprung from the habits of a thousand mothers prepping their daughters on a thousand evenings for those Negro Cotillion balls in all those American cities where segregation had ruled for so long. Now the beauty had escaped. It was coming out into the world, and it was fascinating to see up close. At different times, Lena Horne, Hazel Scott, Eartha Kitt, Dorothy Dandridge, Marva Louis, and Edna Mae all strolled the length of the bar inside Sugar Ray's nightclub. Their images bounced along the large mirror behind the bar—then out into the world at large: Lena at the White House; Hazel on TV; Eartha on Broadway; Dorothy smoldering across the pages of *Life;* Marva hosting some grand charity event. And Edna Mae walking beside the middleweight champion of the world. Swathed in warm mink, they meant to serve notice to America: They had arrived.

Edna Mae Robinson had never reached the higher levels of show business. The world of solo engagements had eluded her. But now she had a kindred spirit in Sugar Ray. She could travel with him, watch him enter her show business world, enjoy it all over again.

For Sugar Ray, this would be the kind of work that could remind him of his childhood dreams when he had paraded outside Broadway theatres, just staring. And it could also be the very thing to take him away from the bloody business that had consumed him for so much of his life.

His whole life he dreamed of the stage. In 1952
Sugar Ray finally got his chance at the nightclubs.
The audiences were large, until they weren't.

1953–1954

the very thought of you onstage

HE RELISHED EVERY MOMENT of this current undertaking, of creating something new. Whether trying on white tie and tails, or posing while leaning over a piano for a photographer—plenty of publicity shots needed!—or riding through Manhattan with his entertainment agent, Joe Glaser, in Glaser's Rolls and yakking about planned shows, or sitting on a stool watching dancers audition for his act, Sugar Ray was feeling absolutely giddy. He was amazed at how quickly things began to fall into place. Glaser had started making calls around the country, booking Robinson's act even though nightclub owners had not seen it yet.

Robinson shopped for new clothing at Sy Martin's, the stylish haberdashery on Broadway. Robinson would take his nephew, Ken Bristow, with him, to keep watch over the double-parked Caddy. But sometimes Bristow tagged along inside and was entranced as his uncle picked out suits and got fitted. "He'd have suits and sports jackets made," Bristow recalls. "I remember he took Nat King Cole to the same place." Cole told Robinson a little trick he used: He'd have little weights sewn into the lower hem of his suit jacket so that when he raised his arm onstage, the jacket stayed in place. Robinson liked the touch and adopted it as well.

Sugar Ray Robinson was about to try singing for his supper, just as Lena Horne, Langston Hughes, and Miles Davis were doing. Theirs was an America he had long wished to see from the inside.

Miles Davis was off heroin as 1953 ticked into view, then he was back on it: The dope fiend's carousel had claimed him yet again. Playing and getting high; getting high and playing. He played

Miles Davis—who bewitched others—was bewitched by Sugar Ray. Their long friendship revolved around jazz and the mysteries of the fight game.

Birdland in Manhattan that year. He also did some recordings—*Collectors' Items, Blue Haze*—for Prestige. In the fall he found himself in Hermosa Beach, California, working on a live recording. The hipsters and their blonde girlfriends were enraptured. But there was a fight at the club—the bartender had called Davis "a black motherfucking nigger"—and he was carted off to the police station. He threatened NAACP action and was fortunate when the authorities released him without charges. In Detroit, he got work at a place called the Blue Bird. Back in Manhattan, he feared the carousel would only speed up. So he thought of Sugar Ray: "Sugar Ray looked like a socialite when you would see him in the papers getting out of limousines with fine women on his arms, sharp as a tack," Miles would recall. "But when he was training for a fight, he didn't have no women around that anybody knew of, and when he got into the ring with someone to fight, he never smiled like he did in those pictures everybody saw of him . . . I decided that that was the way I was going to be, serious about taking care of my business and disciplined." He started recording again; he laced up the gloves again and got back into shape at Stillman's, the gym. He liked Stillman's: "Sugar Ray used to train there, and when he came in to train, everybody would stop what they were doing and check him out." But of course Sugar Ray wasn't there these days; he was in a rehearsal studio or being fitted at the tailor's with Edna Mae by his side, or down at his nightclub. So Miles found himself hanging around Robinson's club a lot: "That's where a lot of hip people and beautiful women hung out, fighters and big-time hustlers. So they all would be standing there, fat-mouthing and high-signing and styling." The young man with the horn loved being in the club, watching the women, watching Sugar Ray deal with customers, even the occasional belligerent figure: "He'd be standing there," Miles would recall of Sugar Ray, "shoulders squared, feet apart, holding one hand in the other in front of him, rocking back and forth on his heels, cleaner than a motherfucker, grinning, his hair all processed back, smiling that crooked, cocky smile he used to smile when he was daring somebody to say anything out of the way." In the summer of 1954, with Miles in the music world and Robinson new to it, the great prizefighter happily found himself spending as much time as he could with musicians: "He used to come up and tell everyone that I was a great musician who wanted to be a fighter," Miles would recall of Sugar Ray, "and then laugh that high-pitched laugh of his. He liked being around musicians because he liked to play drums."

In the year Sugar Ray Robinson left the ring, Roy DeCarava, a rising Manhattan photographer, began thinking of a photo project that would illuminate life in Harlem—and thus, in his mind, Negro America. DeCarava—who had studied at the Cooper Union school of art—applied for and received a prestigious Guggenheim fellowship. He walked the streets of Harlem with his camera, aiming to capture the Harlem populace in repose. Cumulatively, the resulting pictures cast a light on a world that much of America barely knew existed: a little boy in a window, reading, wearing eyeglasses and a long-sleeved shirt rolled up to his elbows. A paisley-print curtain hangs behind him. Perhaps he sits in the family sitting room, where a little boy—he could have been any Negro boy; he could have been little Walker Smith Jr. in another time—can sit and dream. Here stands a woman, perhaps in her early fifties, dressed in black, outside, resting her defiantly lined hands upon a gate. Maybe she's a washwoman; maybe a schoolteacher. Maybe she is already fretting about next month's rent. But she looks as elegant as Sunday morning. Here walks an old man up out of a subway in a hat that looks as if it has crossed a few state lines. He has that brother-can-you-spare-a-dime stoop. The brim of his hat casts a shadow against a wall. DeCarava liked what he had captured; it was a kind of poetry to him, black-and-white imagery of his landscape—faces plain and innocent, ordinary and beautiful.

He figured he needed someone who could understand it all, someone who could make sense of the light and shadows and depth in the eyes. So he found the poet Langston Hughes and asked him to do something with the photos, put a kind of word-music to the pictures. Hughes proceeded to write imaginary lives for the people, shaping it all around a make-believe narrative. As Hughes saw them, the people—even if economically strapped—are hardly without dreams. Hughes creates Sister Mary, allows her to narrate the story. The whole effect is a kind of prose poem with pictures; faces and poses come alive to the music of the Hughes touch. Sister Mary says: "I done got my feet caught in the sweet flypaper of life and I'll be dogged if I want to get loose." Hughes called his words "a running text." When Simon & Schuster published *The Sweet Flypaper of Life,* it received wonderful reviews. *The New York Times* called it "a delicate and lovely fiction-document of life in Harlem." The *New York Herald Tribune* would write: "Langston Hughes' words and Roy DeCarava's photographs achieve a harmony which is more than poetry or photography alone, but its own kind of art."

Hughes's book title hinted at the fine and gorgeous things—those moments of magic—that filled the Negro world, and that sometimes took white America by surprise.

She felt the cold snubs, felt it in the way her Hollywood agent had no work for her. The jowly senator from Wisconsin, Joe McCarthy, had his subcommittee humming; he began accusing media members, entertainers, and even government officials of having Communist sympathies. Lena Horne had been friendly with Paul Robeson, which was enough to have her caught in those fiery winds. She was reduced to working in nightclubs mostly, whose sometimes Mafia-linked owners were far more liberal than the powers behind movies and television. As Lena's daughter Gail would put it: "Nightclubs were rarely affected by the blacklist—the Mafia did not confuse politics and profits." Horne became one of the biggest nightclub acts in the country, joining the ranks of Dean Martin and Jerry Lewis, Milton Berle, the Will Mastin Trio starring Sammy Davis Jr., Frank Sinatra, Danny Thomas, Peggy Lee, and Tallulah Bankhead, among others. She acquired a loyal following at the Sands Hotel out in Las Vegas. Critics across the country raved.

In 1954 the nine black-robed United States Supreme Court justices issued their decision in *Brown vs. Board of Education,* which outlawed segregation in America's public schools. It opened political fissures across the land. Those were tense times for the American Negro. But it was, conversely, a fine time to be Miles Davis, Langston Hughes, Lena Horne, or Sugar Ray Robinson. Compared to the lot of most Negroes, they had already defined their lives. Their accomplishments were known. They were living on an elevated plateau, awash in the sweet flypaper of life.

Sugar Ray Robinson signed his first nightclub performing contract in October of 1952. (To look as handsome as possible, he had had plastic surgery to repair damage done to his nose while in the ring. Both he and Edna Mae were happy with the results.) The contract-signing event at the French Casino nightclub, the venue where he would debut his act, was attended by reporters from both the entertainment and sports sections of several New York City newspapers. Robinson's new career path caused a clashing of the two reporting disciplines. The signing was full of sequins and feathers and plumes and flashbulbs: background ornamentation was provided by a bevy of beauteous French chorus girls. Naschat Martini, owner of the midtown venue, had personally imported the lovely ladies. This was the appetizing world of before-the-show good times and Robinson relished it. He also shared a bit of news with the gathering: He would soon be headed to the big screen, starring as himself in a major motion picture of his own life. Abner J. Greshler would be the producer. The reporters scribbled away. Robinson, holding up his contract, couldn't keep the lively grin from his face. He would be paid $15,000 a week. (Gainford—vacationing in Paris and conspicuously absent from the affair—had scoffed at the figure, believing it wasn't enough. And Robinson himself, in the days leading up to this moment, had expressed displeasure. He could make $100,000 in just one night as a fighter. He complained to Glaser, his agent, who managed to convince him that once he caught on, his fee would soar.)

To hedge against any type of failure, Robinson surrounded himself with top professionals while preparing his act. He hired Ralph Cooper to manage him. Cooper had cut a dashing figure in a series of Negro films in the early 1940s; he counted both Langston Hughes and Lena Horne among his close acquaintances. He had, in recent years, been a stalwart member of the stage productions at the Apollo Theatre, serving mostly as an emcee. He could also be seen on some nights gliding around Sugar Ray's nightclub. In addition to Cooper, Robinson enlisted Henry Le Tang, a highly respected dance instructor. (Le Tang had sent Robinson outdoors to do roadwork: five miles a day, he told the fighter, would help get Robinson's dancing legs ready. Robinson thought Le Tang was joking; he was not.) And Sugar Ray—with some input from Miles Davis—also secured the services of several musicians from accomplished jazz combos willing to go on the road with him.

The prizefighter was amazed at the grueling work schedule Le Tang put him through in preparation for his November opening. Robinson joked that his boxing training had been no less demanding. Still, it was obvious he was enjoying himself. There was an easy rapport between Robinson and his lovely French chorines. The longer the rehearsals went on, the more Robinson became convinced he had made the right decision in leaving the ring. "A fighter can't go on forever," he said. Pedestrians caught glimpses of Robinson coming from rehearsals; he'd stop to sign autographs. And when they'd begin to pepper him with questions—about the fight game, about rising contenders—he'd feign disinterest, complain about his sore feet, and hustle toward his Caddy.

Martini, the French Casino owner—the club was located near the famed Birdland jazz club—was full of exuberance in the days leading up to Robinson's ballyhooed opening. He sent out personal invitations; he made phone calls; he made sure his radio and newspaper friends would be coming, reminding them of the good seats they would have. He unleashed a blitz of publicity. And it all paid off.

A host of celebrities showed for Sugar Ray's opening night. There was Jackie Robinson and his wife, Rachel; Joe Louis and singer Delores Parker; Deputy Police Commissioner Billy Rowe. There were the comedians Milton Berle, Timmie Rogers, and Nipsey Russell. Hazel Scott and her husband, Congressman Adam Clayton Powell Jr., turned heads as they were led to their seats. The men wore black tie; many of the women were draped in white and silver-blue fur. The glitter of jewelry was everywhere. There was a running gag that owner Martini had a couple of undercover Pinkerton detectives on the premises to keep an eye on the diamonds in the room. (The kids, the swells, were led by young Mel Dick, Robinson's old friend, who had come along with his gang. "We were all underage," he would remember.) Sportswriter Jimmy Cannon showed and took a seat next to the Brown Bomber. International guests from Haiti and France were there. Well-wishers streamed toward Robinson's sisters, Evelyn and Marie, and Edna Mae, all looking gorgeous.

Robinson wrestled with nerves in his dressing room. He didn't like the pancake makeup on his face. He looked elegant—if a little like a riverboat gambler—in his yellow-and-black plaid tuxedo jacket, black satin pants, white shirt, and black bow tie. There were six costume changes to make during the course of the evening. Opening night telegrams poured in. "One thing for sure, Ray, nobody will heckle you," came one from a friend. He chuckled; he looked at himself in the mirror. He checked the damn facial makeup again.

He heard whispering as he neared the stage. (The warm-up act was Dominique, a French magician.) As Robinson was introduced and stepped out before the audience, he was drowned in applause. He opened with a soft-shoe number, trying to mimic Gene Kelly walking along the Seine in the dreamy *An American in Paris.* The chorines kicked up their long legs beside him, their red feathers and plumes swaying against the stage lights to Robinson's obvious pleasure. A reviewer would remember that "the tall, shapely showgirls filled the French Casino stage with color, zest and a certain unmistakable amount of sex." Robinson swayed into another dance number, which he called "Flirtation," and it elicited howls from audience members: Some of his chorines, after a change, were now practically nude, with only large leaves to shield their most private parts. A few of the female audience members blushed; Joe Louis and Jimmy Cannon did not. Robinson himself soon vanished and reemerged in a white Palm Beach dinner jacket and black satin pants.

Joe Scott, a onetime vaudeville performer, played straight man to Robinson in their stage routine.

Sugar Ray: "Do you know the three quickest ways of communication?"

Joe: "No, what?"

Sugar Ray: "Telephone, telegraph, and tell a woman."

It was corny, but they all laughed anyway.

A couple of numbers later, he vanished again, this time returning in a midnight blue formal jacket with matching satin pants. The parade of sartorial surprises delighted his audience. He continued to joke from the stage, but only as prelude to yet another tap routine. For his eleventh and final scene, he appeared dressed in top hat, white tie, and tails. At the end of that number—signaling show's end—he spun about the stage with unalloyed joy. He introduced members of his act. He pumped his fighting fists. His Army buddy Joe Louis was on his feet, soon joined by everyone else in the house. He bowed like a child who had just starred in the school play.

They mobbed him, rushed to his dressing room, told him how marvelous he had been. The critics who were there were mostly boxing writers who had come out of curiosity. They were kind, if cautious, with their remarks. Some of the praise was of the backhanded variety: "The guy is a superb clotheshorse," wrote Lewis Burton in the *New York Journal-American,* "but if you are going in for horses, Native Dancer is a better bet."

But it didn't matter! Smoke and mirrors! The stuff of show business! Robinson's publicity machine went into overdrive, sending out reports of the opening night filled with gushing comments from audience members. But show business—as Ralph Cooper and Henry Le Tang certainly knew—was more than just a crowd of well-wishers inside one Manhattan nightclub; if Robinson was going to succeed as an entertainer he would have to get out and perform across the country. So he hit the road. He made TV appearances on

The Ed Sullivan Show and *The Kate Smith Show,* his hosts fawning over him.

He played the Sahara Hotel in Las Vegas. Jack Benny and Louis Armstrong caught the show. (Wherever Robinson performed, if there were other celebrities in the area, they would try to catch his performance. It was an old show business law: celebrity begat celebrity.) Vegas tourists looked at him bewildered: He was a black entertainer who didn't sing; he tapped, but didn't exactly remind anyone of Bill "Bojangles" Robinson. Some of those tourists wanted to jawbone with Robinson about boxing, but he wanted to hone the show, refine the dance steps. Refinement in Robinson's mind was an elementary thing, however: Quicker movement of the feet, remembering exit left or exit right. The sublime nature of stage shows— where movement and improvisation were second nature, where the comfort level of the performers was never doubted by audience members—had often taken years to reach a level of perfection. Robinson had dreamed of this moment, and he was inside the dream. But dreams so often had a fantastical element. Robinson kept waiting for perfection to come, and night after night, it was evident it was eluding him. He wanted to see the looks on the faces of audience members that he himself had on his own face when watching the likes of the Nicholas Brothers or Buck and Bubbles— serene gratification, unalloyed joy. Ralph Cooper, the impresario, had seen some of the flaws in Robinson's act but kept them to himself. Boxing greats, as he knew, possessed huge egos. (Cooper had cackled at Joe Louis's awkward forays into entertainment as well.) Sugar Ray would retire to his hotel room, dialing up Edna Mae, his sisters, anyone who would listen, imploring them to help him get better quicker. But they were not in his shoes, and they could only offer words of encouragement. In boxing, if Robinson suffered a bad round, he knew he'd recover a round or two later. He had the comfort of strategy and power. Onstage, however, he was showing a mighty small allowance of comfort, and audiences began sensing it.

Robinson moved on to Pittsburgh where he put on four shows during the New Year's Eve celebrations of 1952–1953. *Variety* noted that those shows cost $20,000 to stage, and made only $5,000. Robinson recoiled at the figures. He read the reviews alone in his hotel rooms, taking the harsh critiques like body blows. Suddenly he began to feel smaller. Negro boxing champions were gods of their communities. Sugar Ray hadn't known this type of irrelevance since he had been little Walker Smith Jr. He moved on to the Chicago Theatre in Chicago—on a bill with Louis Armstrong—and there were plenty of old fight fans and Bronzeville residents who came out to see the pair. Among the Chicago guests was Robert Villemain, the French fighter Robinson had beaten in a tough fifteen-rounder back in the summer of 1950. It didn't seem to matter to Sugar Ray that there was more discussion of clothing than act; before long it was announced that Robinson would be going on a national tour with the Count Basie Orchestra and the Dominoes, a much-lauded vocal quintet. It all made him giddy and left him with the false sensation that his act would somehow right itself in the hurly-burly heat of publicity.

Sugar Ray Robinson found himself rolling on a bus with Count Basie, yakking about Duke Ellington and Lena Horne, about juke joints that specialized in barbecued ribs, about hotels that were kind to Negro performers, about drummers and saxophonists. It was a dream come true.

But the great prizefighter was not accustomed to second billing. He imagined perks, the kind he'd gotten used to as a professional fighter. He found himself running his own errands, fetching his own laundry. Show business on the road could be grueling. "Most of the time we were doing one-night stands and when our show ended," Robinson would recall, "we'd jump into the Count's big bus and ride all night to our next stop. We were hot and smelly and trying to sleep on that bus." These caravan shows often involved several groups, and the performances could last well past midnight. Robinson had not had a chance to meet many of the musicians—save the marquee names, many of whom he had met during their forays in and out of Manhattan over the years—until the trip was under way. On his sojourn with Basie, he got into an altercation with one of the traveling valets: The man had been showing up late; Robinson insisted on precision and threatened to dock his pay. While standing in the wings one evening preparing to go out onstage, Robinson turned to find the valet had walked up on him with a .38 pistol. He had tired of Sugar Ray's complaints.

"You not so tough now," the angry valet said. Robinson's face suddenly creased with worry. The tone of the valet's voice convinced him it was no joke.

"Say it again, Robinson, say what you said before and I'll blow your head off."

The music cue came up and Robinson went out onstage, wondering if he would be shot—shot like Abe Lincoln inside a theatre. A stagehand finally got the pistol away from the valet. Robinson was fierce when he finally came offstage. The valet, of course, was quickly fired and also saved from a Robinson pummeling. Sugar Ray was realizing that show business could be as wicked as the shadowy fight game.

One of the benefits of being Sugar Ray Robinson was that heralded groups like the Count Basie Orchestra were inclined to take him on. Additionally, Robinson had the cachet to pluck songwriters and freelance musicians at his whim. There were squabbles about billing—in ads put out by Robinson's people, he would be touted as the main attraction, with his illustrious tour mates mentioned as afterthought. Some musicians wouldn't work with him. But more worrisome than the arguments about billing was the criticism that was picking up speed. It was notable after a return to Manhattan for an engagement at the Band Box. The place was packed that night. In the crowd were crooner Johnny Hartman, and Sammy Davis Jr., a genuine song-and-dance man who had been performing since childhood. Robinson was now, for the most part, handling emceeing chores. It was little surprise that the criticism rattled him: "Even his closest friends saw pretty soon that Sugar was out of character in a nightclub as an entertainer," the *Chicago Defender* opined. "His bag of parlor tricks wasn't heavy enough to keep him going as a $15,000 a week entertainer." Robinson had added Margie McGlory, a drag queen, to his show; she did wicked impersonations of, among others, Nat King Cole and Lena Horne. (Sammy Davis Jr., who also did impersonations, could be heard guffawing at McGlory's verbal technique at the Band Box.) After the show, Sammy rushed backstage like a gaunt bull, showering Robinson with praise. But Robinson didn't escape opening night criticism. Sugar Ray, wrote one reviewer, "fairly dazzles the customers with a flashy tap routine which somehow makes you forgive him for almost boring you to death with constant references to his former fistic triumphs." The reviewer also chided Robinson for what he thought to be lackluster monologues between acts, claiming Robinson needed new writers to "streamline his ante-bellum chatter routine." For now, promoters ignored the weak reviews and kept booking Robinson. Christmas of 1953 saw him and his revue booked into Harlem's famed Apollo ("Worlds Greatest Colored Shows"). "Once I had the act down pat," Robinson claimed, "I didn't have to rehearse too much."

But therein lay the problem and the reason more critics started to pounce: Exact and precise performances depended on rehearsal, and lots of it. Audiences who had seen Robinson had also seen the likes of the Step Brothers and the Will Mastin Trio with young Sammy Davis Jr., just two of the acts soaring during that golden age of tap. But those other groups had honed their dance routines over years and years of being on the road. They were masters at improvisation and the ad lib, but that came in large part from hard work and practice. Though Robinson's fame secured him a position with marquee-name traveling acts—Louis Armstrong, Count Basie—it also gave audiences a chance to compare him to those performers, and he paled next to them. Robinson's act seemed to be in a state of perpetual flux. The machinery never seemed well oiled. Cues were missed. There was indeed a kind of gloss to the act, but it lacked that jaw-dropping authority of movement and precision that the best acts had down cold. Against the backdrop of a mediocre show, Robinson's constant change of wardrobe began to seem a kind of shtick. Edna Mae would watch her husband perform and sometimes shake her head. She had danced at the Cotton Club; she knew timing and movement. The *Chicago Defender* was just one of the publications that began to take aim at Robinson's stage appearances. The paper offered that Robinson "had to be bailed out of trouble in Detroit, and laid whopping eggs in Chicago and Philadelphia." Just twelve months into his show business career, the *Defender* called Robinson "just an average dancer," and insisted he would have to struggle mightily to convince theatergoers otherwise. The criticisms set off speculation that Robinson would soon be running back to the ring. He denied having any such plans. But he did welcome any and all testimonials from fellow entertainers.

Robinson shared a bill with Clyde McPhatter and the Drifters in the late spring of 1954. McPhatter assured the press that Robinson was a "gentleman on and off stage." There had been silly little arguments between Robinson and producers. George Gainford had handled these things in Robinson's boxing life, but Gainford was not around, biding his time instead at Manhattan fight gyms, hoping for another discovery. News of Robinson's tussles with management traveled out along the theatrical grapevine, leaving him with a bruised reputation. Robinson felt he needed a strong rebuke for his critics, so he spoke up himself: While in Chicago for an engagement at the Regal Theatre, Robinson had an assistant fetch him a typewriter. He then wrote an article—"Sugar Ray Punches Back"— answering those who had labeled him "a second rate entertainer." His answer to his critics, published in the *Chicago Defender*, is a defense reflex, exposing a thin-skinned entertainer for the world to see. He wrote that he did not feel at all that his "star in the entertainment world is on the wane." Rather, he argued: "I am making more money in show business today than I was a year ago when I began." He claimed that his crowds had grown bigger in each venue—hardly the analysis of theatre critics across the country— and that he was being well accepted in his new line of work: "I have been very happy to note that, from all indications, in my salary checks and the box office figures, I have finally been accepted not only as Sugar Ray, the champ in the ring, but as an entertainer." One might well pity the entertainer who feels the need to defend his performance in print. And yet, Robinson did have something of a bead on the realities of show business. "One thing I realize is that where there's lots of smoke there is some fire. So maybe the criticism will make me a better person because, while I contend that most of it is untrue, maybe it has opened my eyes to some of the mistakes I've made and am still making."

Sugar Ray continued to dance merrily along. The brightly lit marquees, his name in large lettering, had blinded him to other signs. The planned three-night engagements were amended to one-night affairs; expected sellouts were now shows where there were empty tables. He convinced himself it would all change for the better. He relished the advisers he had access to in choosing gifted singers and musicians to accompany him on the road. He felt like Billy Eckstine, like Nat King Cole, getting agents on the telephone, hiring their singers, promising fine accommodations. This was the world of the *Esquire* men of his youth. While appearing at the Club Oasis in Los Angeles, Robinson chose Patty Ann, a much-talked-about singer in 1954, (her hit was "Midnight") to join his show for a spell. Ann, who had already appeared with the Duke Ellington and Louis Jordan bands, had a fine and tender voice. While in Los Angeles, Robinson desperately wanted to meet with Hollywood executives to talk about his life story coming to the screen. Hollywood had released *The Joe Louis Story* a year earlier, and it doubtless encouraged Robinson in the belief that his saga might be next. The Louis film starred, among others, John Marley, Paul Stewart, James Edwards, and the lovely Hilda Simms. An unknown by the name of Coley Wallace played Louis. Physically, Wallace resembled the young Louis, but the novice simply could not act. The picture was a commercial and critical flop. Little wonder Robinson got the runaround from Hollywood. Soon his movie project faded from view.

By September Robinson was playing abroad in one of his favorite haunts. In Paris the French came out to see him because of his boxing fame, but then they howled with laughter because they considered his show awful. To cut overhead, his act had been pared down; now he was performing solo, backed by a few musicians. Onstage, alone, grappling to keep an audience entranced, he suffered badly. He added new routines—furiously jumping with a rope, as if that were show business. His rudimentary French didn't get across to Parisian audiences; he couldn't compete with the constant clink of glasses and nightclub chatter. Sugar Ray finally hired a translator, but by then it was too late. The critics had mauled him, were still mauling him. "I cannot say I am sore at the press," Robinson said, feeling sore. "Just disappointed. I am sorry I couldn't be understood." He tried a philosophical outlook to assuage his wounds. "I guess they expected me to come out in boxing shorts and beat the bag a few times and things like that." Whatever they expected, one thing was painfully clear to him: "They simply didn't dig my dancing or comedy."

Close observers of Sugar Ray Robinson in Paris would have noticed a familiar figure now keeping company with the fighter. It was George Gainford, seen huddling often with Robinson. The sightings gave rise to a natural question: Was Sugar Ray Robinson now in serious discussions about a ring comeback? Big George Gainford hardly heaved himself all the way across the ocean to take in the sights. Robinson had sent for him to privately discuss fighting again. "He realized his act had no depth outside of spectacle,"

Arthur Barnes says of Robinson. And there was something else, adds Barnes: "He was missing everything about fighting."

Actually, it frightened Sugar Ray Robinson how far he had fallen from being prized and revered. Commoners had threatened him backstage; theatrical critics laughed at him; the sportswriters no longer mentioned him, save in passing. World champion Negro fighters of the 1940s and 1950s were easily the highest-paid Negroes in America. But away from that earning power, it took less than a few steps for the Negro boxer, or professional Negro League baseball player for that matter, to find themselves inching toward the same playing field as the average Negro wage earner. Robinson had seen far too many ex-fighters in Harlem cadging loans from loan sharks. He would play out the remaining dates in his entertainment contract, but he would begin plotting a comeback, using Gainford as his conduit to New York boxing officials. Edna Mae—her lingerie shop right next to her husband's nightclub—had also instructed Gainford to deliver another type of news to Robinson: There was trouble in Sugar Ray's paradise.

While Robinson had been on the road, his businesses in Harlem had suffered. The occasional employee petty theft had ballooned into a consistent activity. Gainford, himself one of Robinson's business associates, had told Robinson what his accountants had told him: Robinson's businesses were hemorrhaging. The nightclub, the hair salon, and Edna Mae's lingerie shop were all losing money. His losses had added up to a staggering quarter of a million dollars. In the past, Robinson's presence, even if sporadic, had ensured the over-sight of his enterprises, but now he was on the road for months, obsessed with song and dance, his businesses being run into the ground. There were, as well, overdue taxes. But those weren't the complete catalogue of Robinson's woes: Augusto Coen, a bartender at Robinson's nightspot who had once fought under the name Gus Levine, was arrested and charged with selling heroin to undercover operatives. Federal authorities announced that none of the sales had taken place at Robinson's club, but, publicity-wise, it was a nasty scar that the club would have to bear. (Coen received a two-year sus-pended sentence.)

Back on American soil, Robinson conferred with his money men.

He began to worry about paying his debts. He went for walks to find places of worship; he'd again sit in churches, pondering his problems—and his future. The denominations of the places where he went to meditate made no difference. "Sometimes mine would be the only black face in the synagogue," he recalled.

He sat in his New York home, not wanting to return to fighting, but seeing no other way to settle his bills, and no way to quiet the drumbeat of what he missed—the recognition, the lights, the acclaim. He would have to put his show business dreams back in the bottle, just as Joe Louis and Henry Armstrong and Rocky Graziano had done. Still he had lived a dream: traveling about the country with his musical heroes, playing to the crowds alongside Louis Armstrong, Cootie Williams, and Count Basie. But the experience had also revealed something else: how cocooned he had been inside the big world of boxing. Out on the road, he had seen firsthand the ongoing day-to-day indignities of the Negro performer. He had come close to being arrested in Georgia after an accident and some testy words with a local sheriff. Luckily he had been recognized and everyone had been let go. He never dreamed how hard musicians and gifted entertainers had to work to make stage life seem effortless. They worked just as hard as he had as a young kid rising into morning darkness and galloping through Central Park and dreaming of a life inside a boxing ring. After a while, playing in front of those small crowds—75, 100, 125 people—began to dismay him. As a fighter, he had played to crowds of 50,000 and more! Upon first entering the entertainment world, Robinson was promised $15,000 a week; now his price was down to less than a third of that figure.

What Sugar Ray Robinson had to face was that in the end, the public wanted him in his earlier incarnation. They didn't much care for the figure in white tie and tails, no matter how handsome he looked. They preferred him when he danced in a boxing ring, stutter-stepping, unleashing frightening bolo combinations, and winning world championships. They wanted Sugar Ray Robinson writ large, the way they remembered him.

He spied himself in the mirror, wondering about his physique and physical condition. He told friends that the dancing had actually kept him in shape. Edna Mae and his two sisters did not want him to return to boxing; they thought he could turn his entertainment fortunes around. When the unlikelihood of that happening became undeniable, they resigned themselves to supporting his decision. Sugar Ray simply did not want to play to near-empty nightclubs.

He found it hard to realize something inside him actually missed the violent sport. It was that rising orchestral applause of a stadium crowd of tens of thousands who had just seen his lightning left hook inflict damage. He conferred with George Gainford first, then Harry Wiley. Gainford wondered how much the passing of time—Robinson had been away from the ring more than two years—would affect his fighter. But he looked at the middleweight landscape—Bobo Olson, Tiger Jones, Carmen Basilio—and, while it was a respectable bunch, he found no reason to fret. There would be something profoundly different this time: Robinson aimed to take even tighter control of his career. And there was one major casualty of his foray out into the stage lights. He would never fully trust Gainford again—the memory of Gainford belittling his show business dream rankled—and aimed to use him as little more than a traveling secretary.

There was a sizeable crowd at the press conference at Sugar Ray's club, though it hardly compared with the crowds that had gathered when there was a big announcement to be made about an upcoming fight. After he announced his comeback, people were seen shadowboxing into thin air on their way out. It was as if their most secret wish had been answered: Sugar Ray would soon be stirring again. Bar patrons toasted one another in Harlem that night.

Shortly thereafter, Wiley, Gainford, and Robinson—along with sparring partners and a cook—vanished into the woods of New York. His Cabin-in-the-Sky training camp at Greenwood Lake had, of course, been named in honor of Lena and her movie. The plan was to stage a few fights after training to gauge the shape Robinson was in and then challenge those fighters who had attempted to fill his absence from the ring.

Robinson ran like a deer through the surroundings of Greenwood Lake. Lovely tunes floated from his phonograph—"Sweet Georgia Brown," "The Very Thought of You." It was autumn. The air was crisp and the leaves golden. Lou Duva—who would come to promote bouts in the 1980s and 1990s featuring stars such as Pernell Whitaker, Thomas Hearns, and Evander Holyfield—had boxed in New Jersey as a youth, gaining some acclaim. During World War II he had taught boxing at Fort Hood in Texas. He found himself hustling up to Robinson's camp—damn an invite—as Robinson began training for his comeback. "You'd watch him jump rope, and it was like watching Astaire dance," Duva recalls. Sugar Ray remained pretty to watch, but Gainford was concerned about his fighter's legs, about stamina, about the former champion's right-left combination. Normally a voluble sort, Robinson was now prone to staring off into the distance, toward the trees. During Robinson's retirement, Gainford had unsuccessfully tried to find the next Sugar Ray Robinson. And now the original left him with doubts, which he mostly kept to himself. Gainford realized that more than two and a half years had passed. In a boxing manager's mind, that means possible speed loss, muscle degeneration, the slowing of natural instinct.

The great prizefighter wouldn't allow the world to see him as a failure. Maybe they could have said that about Walker Smith Jr.— but not the Sugar Ray he had created. He now wanted to make things last; he now wished to endure. He would bleed again, and he would cause others to bleed. History was often on his mind: He had slipped through the curtain that often unfurled around the likes of Joe Louis and Henry Armstrong—where white bewitched black, and black bewitched white—and created the boxer as stylish symbol, inspiring waves of beauty, sepia and otherwise, all about him. He did not look for sympathy, or require it. He just kept running and running, rustling the leaves, as unworried as all great champions must be—and quite happy to be back in his Cabin in the Sky.

They called them comebacks. Won't you come back home, Joe Louis? Won't you please come back home, Henry Armstrong? Rocky Graziano, please come back. Home, of course, being the ring. They all believed in the call of the boxing populace, believed in it so much that it began to sound like a call to civic duty that must be answered. Money, certainly, played a part. But there was something deeper: What if you simply needed to walk back through that door where you knew you'd be admired, touched, and loved again beyond your wildest dreams? Mortals couldn't understand it. Champions made peace with the devil in the afterglow of being given that first belt. They'd retire. And they'd make a comeback. Always hungering for that Great Second Act. Of course it only proved that the gods were always ahead of them, inside the ring.

1954–1956

greatness again

HAVING BEEN AROUND the fight game for much of his adult life, George Gainford realized how unpredictable a comeback could be. He continued to harbor mixed emotions about the entire undertaking, intimating that Robinson's interests were not completely divorced from a return to another venue—that of entertaining. "Sugar and I want to make a tour of the world with our own show, and we figure it will take a quarter of a million dollars to arrange that—hiring singers, dancers and an orches-

The battle outdoors in the heat with Joey Maxim would be talked about for decades.

tra. There is only one way to get the cash and that is for Sugar to fight again."

Gainford was being disingenuous. For Robinson—which meant for Gainford as well, since his income was tied to Robinson's fate—the wolf was at the door.

As soon as he reentered the world of pugilism, Sugar Ray Robinson quickly noticed a change in the boxing landscape. Television executives had gained even more leverage over fight promoters. Boxing officials decided to increase their ranks to contend with the aggressive TV execs. The days of Robinson and Gainford battling alone for his interests in business suites were long gone. Robinson addressed the new realities by increasing his management team. He added two new members: Ernie Braca, a savvy and shrewd fight manager, and Truman Gibson, a Chicago attorney who had handled some business affairs for Joe Louis. He also retained the services of Glaser, his entertainment agent. (It was Braca, sitting over a meal with Robinson at Gallagher's Steak House on Fifty-second Street in Manhattan in 1955, who offered the backing needed to finance Robinson's return to the ring.) Gainford, always protective of his position in the Robinson entourage, did not think the additions necessary but had to concede to Robinson's wishes.

Sugar Ray's intentions were to position himself for a title shot as quickly as possible. There were two reasons for his impatience: He had always lived as a champion. And he also felt that boxing officials had forced him to prematurely give up his middleweight crown as he was pondering a move into the entertainment field. The middleweight crown he had voluntarily given up was now held by Bobo Olson, a fighter he had, of course, already defeated twice. Robinson's team began arranging tune-ups. He traveled to Hamilton, Ontario, where, on November 29 of 1954, he had a bout with the American journeyman Gene Burton. He tussled with Burton for six rounds. ROBINSON FLASHES SKILL, the *New York Times* headline announced. The victory was admirable—Burton had won decisions against both Johnny Bratton and Kid Gavilan, who were estimable punchers—but all the same some of Robinson's more unforgiving fans wondered if the old Sugar Ray knockout punch still existed.

Five weeks later Robinson found himself back in familiar territory: A January 5 bout was the featured attraction at the Olympia in Detroit, and his announced opponent, Joe Rindone, a twenty-eight-year-old ex-Marine from Roxbury, Massachusetts. Boxing actually survived on sinewy and muscled fighters like Rindone. They were good, but mostly beneath the radar; they made few demands on their managers; and they possessed courage enough to climb into the ring with practically anyone. They could pocket upwards of $40,000 a year, a quite attractive income in 1950s America but one that took a drubbing when manager and cornermen fees were subtracted. Rindone's forte was resilience: As Robinson himself said of Rindone, "he had been around."

When Robinson and his team arrived in Detroit, it was like being back home again. Old friends wanted time with him, but he kept his socializing to a minimum, realizing a bad showing could derail his comeback attempt. Onlookers marveled anew at the stylishness of Robinson's entourage. (Outsiders sometimes wondered if the entourage was proof that Robinson had become entranced by stardom. But for the champion Negro boxer, an entourage often served as security protection as they traveled about the country.) Ziggy Johnson, who wrote a column for the *Chicago Defender* from Detroit, thought that Gainford arrived in the city "looking like a gentleman model out of *Esquire.*" Sugar Ray was seen hanging out with jazzman Dizzy Gillespie at the local Gotham Hotel, laughing as his lovely wife Edna Mae beamed nearby.

Even before the bout, some members of Robinson's camp were already shouting that he deserved a shot at titleholder Olson.

Sugar Ray was too seasoned, too long immersed in the chaos of the fight game, to have butterflies, but he was excited as he entered the stadium with nearly twelve thousand fans watching, among them the rising young songstress Sarah Vaughan. "Sugar Ray even has the ladies discussing his comeback," Ziggy Johnson noted. The slashing rain had kept few away. (Noticeably absent, however, were the TV cameras, as the bout was not deemed important enough to televise.) Robinson was accompanied by a half dozen men as he made his way toward the ring. Rindone had an entourage of just two.

Sugar Ray opened the fight with lefts to Rindone's upper body; the quickness of them seemed to stun the former Marine. In the succeeding rounds Robinson alternated between Rindone's upper and lower body, wearing him down. If Rindone seemed steady, he also seemed too cautious, refusing to take advantage of openings Robinson gave him. "When does the fight start?" a fan yelled out during the third round, summing up the audience response to the tepid proceedings. It began—and ended—in the sixth. Just seconds into that round Rindone unwisely dropped his left. Sugar Ray Robinson may not have been the Sugar Ray of the past, but he was about to show everyone he was still Sugar Ray: He unloaded an "explosive right uppercut" that floored Rindone. And then, as *The New York Times* would note, "it was only a matter of seconds before the nimble Negro moved in for the knockout." The fans were on their feet as the referee began the count. Robinson was snorting and Rindone was dazed. Joe Glaser was angling toward the ring. It was all over. Glaser got Robinson's ear first, the lightbulbs throwing off glints of powerful light, Edna Mae Robinson beaming in the stands. "I'm the boss now. I'm going to guide you to the title," the thick-voiced Glaser said to Robinson over the din of noise. Sugar Ray turned to the crowd with his arms raised.

The mood shifted in the locker room, however. Ernie Braca, one of those new members of Robinson's entourage, pronounced himself dissatisfied. He told Sugar Ray he should have floored Rindone far sooner; he told him his timing was far from where it needed to be to face the likes of Bobo Olson. Robinson's showing struck others as lackluster as well. "His misses were wild and many," the *Chicago Defender* concluded of Robinson. "He backed away a great deal and appeared confused each time he was tagged by Rindone." The dissonance unnerved Robinson. Gainford seemed caught between the sensations of the old glory of his fighter, and the reality of Braca's comments.

Little wonder that the Detroit night—and victory—passed quickly. But Truman Gibson, the former adviser to Joe Louis who was another of those new members of Robinson's camp, wished to take advantage of the positive publicity generated by the comeback.

Sugar Ray's negotiators scheduled a televised fight for January 19—just two weeks after Rindone—against Ralph "Tiger" Jones in Chicago.

Jones, a native of Yonkers, New York, was not unlike Rindone in that he was another muscled journeyman. But he was considered more dangerous. That reality caused friction within Robinson's camp. Glaser was wary not only of the swiftness with which Gibson had set up the bout, but the opponent as well. "Jones is a little too tough for Robinson at this point," Glaser told a Chicago reporter. It was the kind of utterance—with its tone of fear and even cowardice—that would never have been allowed in Robinson's boxing past. "We're not looking for soft touches," Glaser added, "but by the same token I'd like to have Ray meet some other middleweight at this time." Gibson felt Robinson couldn't ignore the potent middleweights now fighting, that they were the very fighters who stood in Robinson's path as he eyed Olson. "If Robinson wants to box in Chicago, it'll have to be Ralph 'Tiger' Jones or nobody," Gibson said. He saw everything wrapped in momentum, and a need for a former champion to remind as many fight fans as possible of his skills as quickly as he could. "The fact remains that Robinson will be seen by millions and if he expects to continue fighting and wants the public to turn out at the box office," Gibson argued, "he'll have to meet top opponents."

Gainford was uncharacteristically silent. That wolf at the door now stared across at a Tiger in the ring.

Tiger Jones had a pro record of thirty-five wins and twelve defeats. The fact that he had lost five fights in a row before meeting Sugar Ray did not diminish the respect many had for him. It merely pointed to the crowded and competitive field of middleweight contenders. After all, Jones was ranked third among middleweights.

And in the second round of their bout inside Chicago Stadium, with a national TV audience looking on, Sugar Ray saw why Joe Glaser was wary of Jones: The hard-hitting puncher slammed a blow into Robinson's forehead that drew blood from just above the right eye. Robinson countered with a left hook, but the stealth of Jones shocked him: "When I hit Joe Rindone with that punch," Robinson would recall, "he had gone down. So had maybe fifty other guys through the years." The muscled Jones not only stayed upright, he began bullying Sugar Ray, backing him around the ring. In the third, Jones landed another vicious blow, causing Robinson's nose to bleed. Confusion in Robinson's corner was evident: His cornermen were unable to stanch the flow of blood. Fans gasped. Mel Dick, Robinson's young Brooklyn friend, was in Chicago that night but couldn't bring himself to go see Robinson, so he watched the fight at a local bar. He was among those who thought Sugar Ray should have stayed retired. Sitting on his barstool, looking up at the television, he winced every time Robinson took a hard blow.

Robinson managed to stay even with Jones in the fourth, but

thereafter onlookers noticed how much quicker Jones appeared than Robinson. At the end of the sixth, Gainford leaned over to Robinson in the corner and told him the only way he could salvage the fight was to knock Jones out. It was wishful thinking. From the seventh on, as the UP reporter noted, "Jones landed consistently with both hands to pile up a good margin on points, meanwhile blocking Robinson's wide hooks with both left and right hands." At the end of the ninth, a visibly worried Gainford tended to Sugar Ray's bruised right eye. Parts of the stadium seemed to be in a kind of hushed trance. In the tenth, Robinson staggered about the ring. When the expected victory was announced for Jones—who had come into the fight a 7–2 underdog—onlookers rushed the ring while police officers clamored to keep them out. In his corner, Sugar Ray was slumped over, and he looked like an exhausted man. Cameras flashed as he was led through the throng to his dressing room. Looking around, Tiger Jones suddenly realized that, even in victory, he could not garner as much attention as Robinson in defeat. "Hey, Sugar!" came the cries around the stadium as the former champion disappeared from view. (They were reminiscent of the same cries shouted when Robinson had defeated LaMotta in that same stadium for the middleweight crown.)

His head aching, his nose puffy, Sugar Ray sat bewildered in his dressing room. "The 30-month lay-off was too long," he tried explaining as reporters jostled to get closer to him. Gainford shook his head, and was heard whispering about a possible return to the stage, intimating he and Robinson might shepherd that convoy of stars around the world with Robinson as emcee. He also hinted at the possibility of Robinson linking with Elaine Robinson (widow of Bojangles Robinson) to form a dance act. There was the scent of desperation. Sugar Ray slipped out of wintry Chicago aboard a train with his wife Edna Mae, heading back to Manhattan.

There were those who wondered if Tiger Jones would be a prominent addition to Sugar Ray's epitaph. Wilfred Smith, in the *Chicago Tribune,* had a one-sentence opening paragraph in his story: "Sugar Ray Robinson hasn't got it anymore." Henry Armstrong, the former triple titleholder, had been in the audience that night. "When you're through, you're through," he said of Robinson afterward. Armstrong, usually a quiet man, seemed to enjoy the momentary spotlight, his eyes glinting at the reporters as they flipped the pages of their notebooks before him. Armstrong, of course, might have had his reasons for contributing so enthusiastically to the Robinson epitaph: A young Sugar Ray had beaten the aging Armstrong in that bout at Madison Square Garden in 1943. "Let me tell you, when you get old you don't get young again," he offered by way of personal wisdom. Many, of course, found an opportunity to weigh in. "When a Tiger Jones can lick him, it proves· his comeback is hopeless," Arthur Daley of *The New York Times* said of Robinson, concluding the fighter should retire permanently.

His obituary seemingly written, Sugar Ray announced he would take a week to ponder his comeback commitment.

The once-glorious fighter faced a spiraling of his legacy. He could quit—again—and there would be another run of commentary about his career, about the domination and uniqueness of his fighting style. Such an abrupt move would lack a certain kind of poetry because of the Jones denouement, but the realists would catch up to the significance of his ring contributions. Or he could summon the hungry Walker Smith Jr. and retool himself with the fierce spark and energy of his younger self.

He chose this last path and vanished back to the woods of Greenwood Lake to find the seeds of his youthful rise, when he feared nothing, when he had come out of nowhere.

It was cold at Greenwood Lake, and the wind was howling and the naked tree branches stung as he ran through them. He was heard whistling. "He kept saying, 'I'm gonna do it,' " recalls Mel Dick of Robinson's still-burgeoning triple title dream.

Sugar Ray's team set up a bout for him against a fighter by the name of Georgie Small in Boston. No one was worried about Small; the Robinson contingent didn't even arrive in the city until the day of the fight. Braca and others left Robinson in his hotel room as they went to tend to errands, which always concerned last-minute prefight details. When they returned, Sugar Ray, who had leafed through the newspapers while they were away, was fuming. "How come you didn't tell me this fella killed a man in the ring?" Sugar Ray demanded of Braca. Braca was dumbfounded. Small had killed a fighter by the name of Laverne Roach. Robinson had read about it in the newspapers and the revelation spooked him, turning his mind back to Jimmy Doyle and Cleveland. Sugar Ray told everyone to pack; they were leaving. Braca cried that the fight was to take place that very night, that expense money had already been paid. Sugar Ray instructed Braca to return the $2,500, and everyone departed Boston.

In Cincinnati on March 29, Robinson garnered a victory against Johnny Lombardo. He gained strength as the fight went on, showing some of the old lightning speed toward the end of the ten-rounder. But only 5,124 were in attendance. That figure was almost laughable; he had fought before larger crowds at some of his Golden Gloves bouts. Sugar Ray's stature had now fallen so far that the bout wasn't televised or even broadcast on the radio. He was back fighting in the trenches, clamoring for respect as Walker Smith had once done. He refused to complain. Two weeks later he caught a train to Milwaukee to face Ted Olla. Olla was regarded as a rugged fighter no one was advised to take lightly. Robinson and Olla did little in the first two rounds. Then, in the third, Sugar Ray unleashed a vicious right that stunned Olla, sending him backward. Robinson followed, belting him with eight uninterrupted right punches. He finished him off with a left, which dropped him. Three weeks later—Gainford and Wiley could spot little bits of the old Robinson returning, the speed, the calculation—Robinson was in Detroit, facing Garth Panter. Panter had lost six of his previous seven fights, a fact that gave Sugar Ray little consolation seconds into the first round of their meeting when Panter rocked him with a fierce right. The blow bent Robinson's legs as he briefly lost his balance and was seen grappling for a piece of rope. Robinson had never been on such a slippery slope as he was now, right this moment, in the ring; any loss would almost certainly prevent boxing authorities from granting him a title bout. In the second and third rounds, Robinson went about slugging Panter with abandon, alternating blows to the head and body. Panter held his own until the eighth round, when Robinson treated him to six consecutive blows that had his hometown crowd up out of their seats. That evening he recorded his fourth straight victory.

Sugar Ray turned thirty-four years old while in Detroit. Friends threw him a birthday party. The festive occasion seemed to mark the start of a new confidence on the part of everyone around him. Sugar Ray himself was starting to feel young again. Gainford could not tell if his fighter had worn away all the rust, but he dared wonder if he had somehow managed to beat back the unforgiving clock.

Boxing officials sent word through Robinson's representatives that, with his recent victories, he was indeed a possibility for Olson. But they wanted him to face one more contender and emerge victorious before getting an invitation to face Olson. Robinson's camp settled on Rocky Castellani. (It was noticed by many that he was now turning more often to Braca and Glaser for advice than to Gainford and Wiley; the latter two were viewed more and more by Robinson as relics from his past as opposed to the new thinkers whom he felt he needed.)

Sugar Ray stepped off a train in San Francisco on July 8, and was met with the kind of odds he wasn't accustomed to: Castellani was a 9–5 favorite. Robinson had two weeks to train before their bout at the Cow Palace.

Castellani, a Pennsylvania native, was smart and rangy. He had fought a title bout against Olson in the summer of 1954; Olson had needed all fifteen rounds to hold on to his crown. Even Sugar Ray conceded that Castellani was "a hard hitter."

From the opening round, Robinson's strategy was apparent: He was going to go after Castellani's midsection, hoping to tire him as he sought to deliver targeted blows. But the strategy seemed to wear on Robinson first. (It didn't help that he suffered a head-butt from Castellani in the second that drew blood.) In the fourth, Castellani connected with two hard left hooks to Sugar Ray's face. There was a wave of murmurings from the crowd; the reporters down front winced and scribbled into their notebooks; camera flashes popped. Castellani's corner told him to keep his aggression up and he did so. In the sixth, he threw a trio of punches at Sugar Ray in a span of seconds—a right that slammed into his face, then a left, then another right to the face. That final right was a blow that made Robinson feel as if he had been "whacked with a baseball bat." He slumped to the canvas. Before the eyes of a national TV audience his title shot was slipping away. Referee Jack Downey began his count. Robinson rose just as Downey reached the count of nine, and his supporters breathed a sigh of relief. He held fast in the seventh. Then, in the eighth, Sugar Ray unleashed a volley of blows to Castellani's midsection, which had the 9–5 favorite grimacing. Sugar Ray—was hungry young Walker Smith peeking through his eyes?—now seemed fully energized. He let go with a "bombing right"—as the UP reporter saw it—to Castellani's jaw. He knew then he had Castellani and rushed him to the ropes, firing away at will, lifting the fans from their seats, causing men to wave their cigars in the air, causing the crowd to unleash primal screams.

In the stands, in the aisles, outside in front of the Cow Palace, knots of fight fans were talking about him, about how he looked, about the just-displayed splendor of Sugar Ray. A San Francisco reporter thought it one "of the greatest rallies" of Robinson's career. There had actually been greater rallies in the late 1940s, but one understood the sentiment.

Eight weeks later, International Boxing Club officials announced a middleweight title fight to take place in Chicago: Bobo Olson against Sugar Ray Robinson. It was the matchup Robinson had been waiting for. Even as the blood was being wiped from his face in the aftermath of the Tiger Jones loss—as he had looked into the doubting eyes of Gainford and others—it was the match he dreamed of.

Robinson and Olson met in Chicago in late October to sign contracts before the press. The signing took place on the North Side of the city, at the Cameo club. (The signing venue was odd. It was as if boxing officials were trying to remind Robinson of his nightclub performing days.) Sugar Ray was in a light-colored suit, cuff links peeking, and his hair shone against the constantly snapping camera flashes. Olson—dressed more quietly in a dark suit, sans tie—called Robinson "a great fighter," but allowed as to how he had no intention of giving up his crown.

"The bout will be a good one," Sugar Ray promised, "and we guarantee it will not go more than fifteen rounds."

The reporters chuckled.

Then they enjoyed a buffet provided by boxing officials. As they nibbled and chomped, many of the scribes circled Robinson and began complimenting him on the cut of his suit.

Back in New York, Sugar Ray set off for Greenwood Lake to train. The Olson bout would take place on December 9. He ran miles and miles—through snowstorms even. There was the shriek of wind cutting through the trees, snow billowing over hillsides. George Gainford stared in astonishment. It was as if he, the very man who had discovered Walker Smith Jr., was now seeing something even he couldn't decipher. It was either unimaginable will—or that trick of time. Two of Robinson's sparring partners in camp had been unusually rough. Robinson didn't flinch: "Will we be needing these gorillas anymore?" he asked toward the end of camp. When he was told no, he knocked one out, then the other.

At night, the fireplace in the camp crackled.

Sugar Ray Robinson—getting old, as Henry Armstrong had observed—seemed to be turning into a specimen younger than his years.

"The world was moving for me again" is how Sugar Ray felt.

The Negro men coming in and out of the Conrad Hilton, in long coats and fedoras, with copies of the *Chicago Tribune, Chicago Sun-Times,* and *Chicago Defender* tucked under their arms, blowing the cold from their hands, nodding to staffers: These were Sugar's men. They considered it their duty to watch over him in the days leading up to the title fight. On the day before the fight, they noticed how calm he seemed to be. He played blackjack. After lunch, they all stepped outside; Sugar Ray wanted to go for a walk. They headed off, crunching snow beneath their feet. When Robinson's hat was blown from his head, they all leaned from the sidewalk to retrieve it for him, curls of vapor wafting from their animated mouths. As they continued walking, some were heard huffing and puffing, but not Sugar Ray. They wanted to turn around, kept reminding him of the cold, but he paid them no mind, walking like an explorer. Before they wound up back at the hotel they had walked two miles. In those two miles not one soul had recognized the fighter.

Maybe Bobo Olson should not have spent all that time hunting in the Illinois woods before the fight.

Maybe the challenger—the oddsmakers had him an underdog at 4 to 1—had simply reached back into time, bringing back the best of who he had ever been. And maybe Bobo Olson, eight years younger, could not compete effectively against even a resurrection of the best that Sugar Ray Robinson had ever been. Maybe the national TV audience thrilled Robinson in ways he couldn't imagine. Maybe he was upset at those across the country—and those among the twelve thousand in the arena—who didn't believe in him. Some, he knew, were too young to remember his glory days of the 1940s; he wanted, even after losing to Jones, the benefit of the doubt. Maybe the camera flash and the whistling got to him right from the beginning; and maybe he knew what he planned to do all along, from the moment he left his hotel to the moment he had his Frager gloves slipped onto his delicate hands and his hair smoothed back on his head. Maybe he realized, as never before, the utter aloneness of the fighter—despite the hangers-on, the crowds, the adulation, it was a pitiless profession. Maybe he realized all of that, and the volume of those sensations rang in his ear alongside the roar of the crowd when he slammed a right into Bobo Olson's chest in the first round, stunning the champion. Olson—nearly bald, which always made him look older than his years—began to look like he didn't even belong in a match with Sugar Ray Robinson, began to look, in fact, like a hardware store salesman who had been dropped into the middle of a boxing ring. Two minutes into the second round, with the punches from Sugar Ray coming at a furious clip, he unloaded a right uppercut into Olson. The thudding noise didn't even have time to reverberate before Sugar Ray unfurled a left hook. The one-two combination dropped Olson. He went back with a surprised look on his face, as if blasted by a hurricane-force wind. The moment lifted the fans from their seats, riveted the national TV cameras to Robinson's face, and stopped the popcorn vendors cold in the aisles. Robinson crouched nearer the fallen Olson, as if he were pleading with him to stay down—yet preparing to deliver another wallop. Olson was listless. Sugar Ray had fought, in fact, as if his very dignity had been at stake; as if he considered it a huge intrusion on his time to face, yet again, a fighter he had bested twice in the past. Referee Frank Sikora stood over Olson, counting him out. Sugar Ray Robinson was once again middleweight champion of the world. Gainford draped the white towel around his neck. Fans tried touching him, stretching their arms and hands through the ropes. Robinson had come out of retirement and recaptured his belt. He cried, sobbing like a child as he leaned into the ropes. Gainford and Braca and Glaser looked at him with bewilderment. He was not the type to sob. It was pure joy.

Later that night, they packed the Archway (the Chicago lounge), and drinks flowed as his admirers pumped their fists at one another. Women smudged his cheeks with kisses as jazz tunes floated in the air. This was his world, and he so loved being back in it—the fine and easy thrill of victory swirling around him in whoops and laughter like something lifted from a phonograph; women, willowy and sepia-toned, and the scent of their nutmeg face powder like some kind of sexual language written into the nightclub air; men crowding him like proud and whiny boys. He bought drinks without ever reaching in his pants pockets, noticed that the faces of strangers lit up at the sound of his husky voice as if a switch had been flipped. He noticed faces outside pressed against the windows, peering inside, wanting to get inside just to touch him. This was the joy he had missed—what he called "the sweet sounds" of victory—which he mistakenly thought he had tired of. Deep into the night, however, he began looking around, his eyes resting on certain figures for unusually long amounts of time. He convinced himself he now had to measure those who had believed in him against those who had not.

All his life Sugar Ray had had few close male friends. After his father abandoned him, he would come to find women—his mother, his sisters, the kind ladies at Salem Methodist—more dependable. Men—his father, so many boxing promoters—weren't trustworthy. While he had come close to establishing a rapport with Joe Louis, they simply traveled in different worlds. George Gainford had been around Sugar Ray nearly two decades now, but money was always the glue that held them together—and Sugar Ray was the one who made the money. Peek behind the curtain of his entourage and all its members had specific duties: manicurist, hairstylist, wardrobe attendant. In Sugar Ray's mind, the entourage was business—and his business was style as opposed to bonhomie. He knew, as well as any fighter, that fighters are alone. Little wonder he admired those who pursued solitary endeavors—the jazz trumpeter, the poet, the singer onstage in front of a microphone. To Red Smith, the esteemed sportswriter, Sugar Ray was always an enigma, "a brooding genius, a darkly dedicated soul who walks in a lonely majesty, a prophet without honor, an artist whom nobody, but nobody, understands." Now, at least internally, he was mostly alone. He would strip himself to remake himself. It would comfort him as he went about forging his new identity: a fighter looking for greatness once again.

Sugar Ray Robinson's financial empire, however, was still crumbling. The IRS by now had attached themselves to his life, skimming upwards of three quarters of his take from some fights for back taxes. He refused, however, to allow it to affect his jet-set lifestyle: He flew twenty-two people, all expenses paid, to Los Angeles five months after the last Olson fight for the rematch. The California air was lovely. For training, however, Sugar Ray preferred austere surroundings and set up camp in the desert, near San Jacinto. Then, on the evening of May 18, over at the aging Wrigley Field, he proceeded to knock out Olson again—in round four. The reporters working for the local dailies shook their heads and so did the movie stars who had attended the fight: It was all so mesmerizing.

Sugar Ray Robinson was now forcing columnists and critics everywhere to reassess the depth of their knowledge about him. "It turns out now that we buried Ray before he was dead" is how Russ Cowans of the *Chicago Defender* put it.

He would fight only one more time in 1956, defeating Bob Provizzi in November in a ten-rounder in New Haven. Sugar Ray longed for an opportunity to return "home," to Madison Square Garden, the scene of so much of his glory. He had not fought there in five years. It seemed like, and in some senses was, another lifetime; it also seemed like yesterday to the born-again fighter.

1960–1962

battling

SUGAR RAY LOATHED CARMEN BASILIO, and Carmen Basilio loathed Sugar Ray. The profound mutual dislike bewildered many in their respective camps. No one could quite figure out the roots of the near-hatred. There was, however, a partial explanation: Time had passed, but the old ethnic furies of Robinson-LaMotta couldn't be totally dismissed by the boxing analysts. Also feeding emotions was the fact that both fighters had let it be known what they thought of the other: Robinson

The siren song to come out of retirement snared Robinson. There were still flashes of the indomitable will and brilliance.

deemed Basilio a bully with no style; Basilio believed Robinson more dancer than fighter.

Fighting styles aside, most fighters had one thing in common that linked them beyond the ring—hard backgrounds. Despite the story lines spun by fight managers and publicity mavens, most fighters either sprang from a humble beginning, like Basilio, or a desperate one, like Robinson. In many circumstances, the fighters were also sons of their father's dreams.

Joseph Basilio was an onion farmer in upstate New York. He enjoyed listening to boxing on the radio and later reading the vivid narratives in the newspapers about the nuances and fighting styles of individual champions. He felt compelled to pass these great story-lines of loss and redemption on to his son Carmen. Young Carmen soon caught the fever.

Carmen Basilio—who had helped his father for years on the farm—amassed a distinguished amateur career in the ring before turning pro in 1948. Basilio won the welterweight crown on June 10, 1955, against Tony DeMarco in Syracuse. On March 14, 1956, he lost it to Johnny Saxton in Chicago. But six months later, back in Syracuse, he yanked it back in a match called in his favor after the ninth round. It was all enough to convince Basilio and his manager he was ready to move into middleweight territory and take on Sugar Ray Robinson—the dancer.

Their bout was announced for September 23, 1957, at Yankee Stadium. The air was laden with mutual disrespect. As they stepped toward one another at center ring for the fight's beginning, they cursed each other in low tones—"a muttered exchange of insults," as it was delicately described.

Basilio landed left and right jabs to Sugar Ray's face in the opening round, accompanied by body blows. Robinson answered with punches so rapid they seemed to flicker. By round two Basilio's strategy was obvious: He aimed to play the aggressor. He fired a heavy right into Robinson's head midway through the round, then repeated the blow as the bell rang. Basilio bullied Robinson into the ropes in the third but paid a price: Robinson landed an uppercut to Basilio's chin and a right to his jaw. Blood spurted from Basilio's nose and the crowd—more than thirty-eight thousand in attendance—grunted and shifted. In the fourth Sugar Ray smacked Basilio with another facial punch, this one resulting in a cut over Basilio's left eye. But the onion picker's son, showing a clearly bruised face, seemed impervious to Robinson's blows. "That didn't hurt," he howled at one point, "but just try it again." Gainford had instructed Sugar Ray to conserve his energy against the young fighter and fire away toward the last seconds of each round. (All of Robinson's foes now seemed to be younger—Basilio by six years—as if he himself had emerged from a time machine.) Robinson couldn't escape Basilio's strength and was constantly pulled closer, as Basilio positioned himself to unload punches to Robinson's head. Robinson sensed danger going into round twelve; he had lost the previous three rounds on the judges' cards. Now Basilio was snarling; his grunts could be heard beyond the ring. Sugar Ray stunned Basilio early in round twelve with a right fist to the head, then a torrent of left blows delivered like "machine gun bullets," as Arthur Daley described them. The effectiveness of the blows seemed to energize Robinson. He suddenly looked beautiful: The charcoaled body weaving in and out of the ring lights, reminding one and all who he was, taking them back in time. In rounds thirteen and fourteen Sugar Ray slithered around Basilio and greeted him with a volley of unanswered blows; Basilio shuffled to his corner after round thirteen, like a man willing himself to stand upright. But in the fifteenth—the fans were mesmerized by the grueling evening, and the faces of both fighters were puffy and discolored—Basilio rallied and offered stiff blows to Sugar Ray's midsection. The evening, coming to a close, had showcased two primary emotions within each fighter: contempt and pride. Few could ignore that it had been a close fight. In the excruciating seconds before the announcement of the winner, there was a noticeable hush over Yankee Stadium—"a strange and questioning silence," as one journalist would put it. The victory, in a split decision, went to Basilio. There was immediate outrage among Robinson partisans. Gainford and Wiley cursed into the open air. "Look at what they did to me out there," Sugar Ray cried in the fight's aftermath. "I thought I was ahead." In Basilio's mind, it had all gone perfectly: "I figured my aggressiveness gave me the edge," he allowed. "That's the way I had planned it—to make the fight."

Life magazine called the fifteen-rounder "the grudge fight of the decade." They were not exaggerating. There was immediate talk of a rematch. There was also, from many corners, a sense of marvel at Robinson's showing. "Sugar Ray Robinson tried to fight Carmen

Basilio from memory at Yankee Stadium last night and he came perilously close to getting away with it," Arthur Daley of the *Times* reported.

What went unnoticed in the aftermath of the bout, however, was Robinson's great victory against Jim Norris and the International Boxing Club—the organization that had monopolized the promotion of major fights. In the days leading up to the fight, Sugar Ray had made a personal appearance before the New York State Athletic Commission. Robinson had prepared for his appearance with help from attorney Truman Gibson. Robinson holed up in his office poring over law books, particularly sections on antitrust law. He complained that the IBC monopolized bouts all over the country; that they siphoned off monies that should go to fighters; and that they had long impeded him in his attempt to reap TV revenue from his fights. A dozen New York boxing officials sat at a long heavy table while Sugar Ray stood, gesturing with his hands, giving a lecture that clearly caught the gentlemen off guard. One eyewitness at the proceedings would remark that Robinson had displayed a "fluency and aggressiveness" in stating his case that fighters were often deprived of their just financial rewards when it came to outside revenues. Sugar Ray was well aware of Joe Louis's effort to enter fight promotions. Louis had signed heavyweights Ezzard Charles, Lee Savold, and Jersey Joe Walcott to contracts. But Louis could never get big bouts for his fighters and Norris eventually bought him out for $150,000 and IBC stock. Then Sugar Ray shocked the officials by unloading an ultimatum: Concede to his demands for TV revenue or he would cancel the Basilio fight. The fight had been widely promoted; the boxing officials knew it would be a calamity to cancel the fight. Robinson's public appearance and his charges against the IBC were enough to draw the attention of New York congressman Kenneth Keating, who said boxing needed federal intervention and oversight. Boxing officials all across the country—supported by Nat Fleischer of *Ring* magazine—assailed Keating and Robinson, crying that any oversight of local boxing matters was akin to tampering with states' rights. But those who believed in Robinson's cause immediately began a series of challenges to the IBC in federal court. In 1958 Senator Estes Kefauver of Tennessee began hearings on boxing, which exposed many of the unsavory aspects of the sport. (In 1959 the U.S. Supreme Court upheld a lower court ruling that obliged the IBC to dissolve its operations in New York and Illinois, as well as limiting the number of fights that could take place under IBC auspices. In a way, Sugar Ray Robinson had retaliated against all the promoters and managers and mobsters who had, through the years, taken advantage of the likes of Charley Burley, Henry Armstrong—and Joe Louis.

For his fight against Basilio, Robinson had received $225,000 for TV rights—the largest such payment in his career—as well as nearly half of the gate. It was a grand victory for Sugar Ray and fighters everywhere. Robinson had done what newspaper reporters had been unwilling to do: He had exposed the New York IBC to New York officials in the glare of public scrutiny, which led to government antitrust lawsuits and wide exposure of corruption. The move, tantamount to a kind of emancipation for professional fighters, would continue to bear fruit in later years as fighters negotiated lucrative deals with TV networks such as HBO. Of course Sugar Ray further alienated himself from the business hierarchy of boxing, but he had never been a welcome member of that establishment anyway.

On the very day the bell rang inside Yankee Stadium, sending Robinson and Basilio crashing toward each other, another autumnal set of bells rang hundreds of miles to the west, inside Little Rock's Central High School in Arkansas, summoning nine Negro students to take their seats in the classroom. "The niggers are in our school!" a girl screamed upon sight of the Negro students. Immediately, the white students—their faces contorted into fits of fury that mimicked their mothers and fathers—stalked out. They sang a ditty: "Two, four, six, eight, we ain't gonna integrate." A crowd of about a thousand white protesters—described by one national publication as "white supremacists"—gathered in front of the school. The white supremacists were actually a mix of PTA members, chain-smoking mechanics, goons, soda jerks, Arkansas backwoodsmen, and jobless men in jeans and white T-shirts who simply had nowhere else to be. Once the black children were ferried to safety, the goons—in goose-stepping chorus—began attacking newspapermen, drawing blood. A grim-faced President Eisenhower finally directed federal troops into Little Rock, where they would remain for months.

In a sense, the events in Little Rock seemed to encompass all the past and present: Joe Louis swinging his fists; songstress Lena Horne using her voice during World War II; Langston Hughes giving his verse to freedom rallies; Miles Davis blowing his freedom trumpet; Sugar Ray Robinson battling for the economic rights of pugilists.

It is no fault of Basilio's that his victory against Robinson, won ten hours after the Little Rock clash, resounded rather quietly. In the following days and weeks, the spotlight shone on the Negro schoolchildren, and they were the mightiest warriors.

Decades after that first clash, there remained an enmity between the two fighters. "I went the whole fifteen rounds and kicked his ass," Basilio would say. "But I had to stay up on him, had to keep moving into him." It was the Robinson demeanor, as much as anything, that rankled Basilio: "He was a showboat. Always liked to go first class. He was an egotistical son of a bitch. So I never got close to him. There was no love there at all. It was all business."

Sugar Ray's pronouncements that he might retire yet again after the Basilio defeat were just emotional ruminations of a disappointed prizefighter. He actually couldn't wait to get to Chicago for the March 25 rematch.

A contingent arrived from the West Coast to witness the second meeting—planes swooping into Midway Airport—and among them was Frank Sinatra. Frank was as enamored of certain prizefighters as he was of fellow jazz musicians. In Frank's mind, champion fighters were of the same cultural landscape as himself: lonely and brave artists. (For years rumors had circulated in and out of gossip columns that Sinatra was contemplating entering boxing as a manager. Eventually the rumors died.)

Panic struck the Robinson camp in the hours before the bout— Sugar Ray had come down with a fever. Injections did little to lower it and there was fear the fight might be postponed. Robinson nagged doctors to allow him to fight and followed that with more pleading. Since that 1947 death of Jimmy Doyle—and there had of course been other fatalities as Robinson well knew—boxing commissions had adopted more stringent rules regarding the fitness of a fighter; in the event of a catastrophic injury, it was promised that quick investigations would be carried out. But Sugar Ray Robinson did not figure on being grievously injured by Carmen Basilio. His temperature got down to 101 degrees. There was still reason to worry, but he pleaded with doctors until they assured the local commission he was fit to fight.

By dusk on the evening of the fight, upward of seventeen thousand were making their way into Chicago Stadium. There were movie screens around the country preparing to show the match; seven thousand people had crowded into the fairgrounds in Syracuse, New York, not far from Basilio's hometown. Basilio was a 2–1 favorite. They were the kind of odds he might well have appreciated: In his previous three fights at Chicago Stadium, Basilio had come out the loser. Basilio and his managers had discussed their ring strategy, and it would not veer much from that first meeting: attack, attack, attack.

Stepping into the ring, Sugar Ray's cornermen were worried; not only was their fighter feverish, but he hadn't touched food in twenty hours—the penalty he had to endure to make weight.

The enmity each fighter had for the other was evident as the bell ending the first round sounded and they were still throwing blows. Attack as he might, Basilio could not avoid the fourth-round blow from Robinson's right fist that came like an exclamation point laid in flames. Basilio's head snapped. At the end of the round his left eye was puffed a tomato red and nearly closed. Sugar Ray honed in on the eye, alternating lefts and rights in succeeding rounds. In the eleventh, he "jabbed a string of lefts" to Basilio's face yet again, followed by piercing body punches. When Basilio doubled up as if he wished to scoot into a waiting automobile, it was in an effort to protect himself. But Robinson pelted away. Basilio could not escape his reach. In the stands, a little-known comedian by the name of Redd Foxx—who had often regaled patrons with bawdy one-liners while loitering in Robinson's nightclub and hoping for free food or drink for the impromptu show—was seen gyrating like a puppet. (Foxx was so enamored of Robinson that he had shaved his head, leaving the hair that remained carved into an "S" for Sugar, an act of homage that caused his seatmates to look at him with utter bewilderment.) In the fourteenth, Robinson drove a right, then another right—the red gloves swooping about like robins—then a right uppercut into Basilio. Basilio wobbled but did not fall. In the final round Basilo's frustration showed as he was given a warning for head-butting. Sugar Ray completed the round with two blows into Basilio's midsection as the crowd began to rise, and the comic Foxx started hopping up and down, and the reporters gabbed and flicked ash from their cigars, and the camera flashes went off—because there was no doubt, as there had been at the end of their first meeting, as to the victor. The two combatants embraced, a look of exhaustion upon both. But it was Sugar Ray Robinson with the raised arms. He had avenged defeat. Gainford and Wiley pushed their way to the locker room, having formed a circle with others around Robinson. Edna Mae was close behind, filled with worry. A police officer kept the press from barging into the locker room, but the reporters pounded their fists on the door anyway. Edna Mae got in and emerged after some time, announcing that her husband was "just fine." When he finally showed—in a cream-colored long coat and a porkpie hat—Sugar Ray was whisked to a nearby hotel. "Trying to stop him was like trying to stop a freight train," he told some reporters who had scooted up to his hotel room. "I feel like 10 guys jumped me." It was worse, however, for Basilio. He had been admitted to a nearby hospital for observation so that doctors could attend to his closed eye.

Many were left wordless at Robinson's accomplishment. He had been referred to as an old man, as just a dancer. Daley of *The New York Times* had been one of many columnists who had believed Robinson's heyday had long passed. Now he had to offer another summation: "He's too incredible, too colossal to be true," he said of Robinson.

In and around taking down the onion farmer's son, Sugar Ray Robinson had fight dates with Gene Fullmer, the copper miner's son.

It seems Gene Fullmer's father's dreams for his son were made plain at his birth. Young Fullmer had been named after the fighter Gene Tunney. By age eleven Gene Fullmer, along with his brothers, was already fighting in the amateur ranks in his native Utah, amassing an enviable record. Their father, Lawrence, known as a ferocious street fighter, had a nickname: "Tuff." The Fullmers hailed from a line of copper miners; Gene himself worked in the very same mine as his dad Tuff before turning to professional boxing in 1951. "This boxing is men's business and I don't care too much for it," Gene Fullmer's mother, Dolores, once said. "But our boys have always liked violent exercise and they seem to thrive on it." Fullmer's style as a fighter was rough and hard-charging. His first bout with Sugar Ray Robinson—it would be one of four—was announced for January 2, 1957, at Madison Square Garden. George Gainford worried about Fullmer's rough tactics and sought to deliver a preemptive strike by pleading with the New York State Athletic Commission to make sure the no-head-butting rule was strictly enforced.

In the hours before the contest, Fullmer received a thirty-six-foot-long, two-inch-high telegram from Western Union. It came from well-wishers back in Utah. Madison Square Garden officials would later say it was the longest telegram ever received at the Garden. More than eighteen thousand fans showed at the Garden and arena officials were overjoyed at the turnout: More and more fans were choosing to watch big fights on television and in-person attendance had been steadily declining.

In the early rounds, as Fullmer relentlessly charged, Sugar Ray tried holding him as much as possible. It was an attempt to prevent Fullmer from backing away and charging with raised fists again. The fans did not like Robinson's strategy. "This ain't no Olson, Sugar," someone bellowed. "This one is alive." The early pounding Robinson was taking caused worry in his corner. In the fourth and fifth, Robinson showed savvy, firing short punches to Fullmer that he couldn't thwart. Fullmer had the stoicism of a robot; his facial expression—stony and cold—never altered. Sugar Ray couldn't tell if his punches were having the desired effect. He struck one New York reporter as "the picture book fighter with the beautiful style." But it was a style that the Mormon from Utah treated dismissively: He took the fight into even darker corners.

In the sixth—as they were trading blow for blow—Fullmer made a mighty lunge toward Robinson. Robinson clutched Fullmer and their momentum sent both fighters tumbling against the middle ring rope. The rope snapped; everyone gasped. One could hear the jangled clatter of typewriters as reporters quickly moved to get them out of the way. At the beginning of the thirteenth, Fullmer cracked Robinson with a hard left to the face. In the next round he delivered punishing blows to Robinson's midsection. It would take a knockout on Robinson's part to swing the momentum away from Fullmer, and he did not, on this night, have a knockout punch in him. Sugar Ray took the loss with equanimity. "There's nothing I can say but that the better man won tonight," he said into the glare of TV cameras.

In Chicago for their second bout, champion Fullmer was a 3–1 favorite. Martin Kane of *Sports Illustrated*, who had seen the first encounter, believed Robinson faced an uphill battle: "Instead of thinking his way through 15 rounds he will have to fight his way through a majority of them," he wrote. "It could be not only a better fight but a shorter one, for . . . Gene Fullmer . . . may find the confidence this time to swing from his heels in the early rounds and thus weaken Robinson for a TKO."

Fullmer began their second encounter by once again charging Robinson. Only this time Sugar Ray wasn't surprised; he absorbed every blow. In the second, Fullmer unleashed a torrent of rights and lefts to Robinson's midsection. It was hard not to marvel at Fullmer's stoicism; in the third, Robinson pounded him with left hooks. As Nichols of the *Times* would put it: "There were few indeed who had any hope or confidence that Sugar Ray could 'take out' the hitherto armor-plated Fullmer with a punch." By the end of the fourth round, the judges had split the rounds between the two fighters. Many were twitching, wondering if Sugar Ray would have the stamina to keep going.

Then, 1:27 into the fifth round, there it was, that sweet and blinding and wondrous left hook, coming through the ages and into Fullmer's hour, a silencing to all the doubters and nonbelievers. The crowd roared; Fullmer was collapsing to the canvas; Robinson was dancing with the knowledge that the left had done its damage. The referee began a count, which Fullmer couldn't hear—he was out cold, asleep to the noises of Chicago Stadium and the footsteps of Sugar Ray. At the count of eight, Fullmer did attempt to rise, but he was slow, like a groggy bear, and he collapsed again. "I was just maneuvering him, trying to draw him in with a right," Robinson said afterward. Fullmer came to back in his dressing room.

"What happened?" he demanded to know, staring for an answer from his brother Don.

"He hit you twice and then came up with that left hook," Don explained rather succinctly. "That did it."

Robinson may have been the most stylish of fighters, but Fullmer had come up against another Robinson gift—resilience. "Robinson has to be worked over hard or he will stay with you forever," Fullmer had confided before the match to a Utah reporter.

It was difficult for Sugar Ray Robinson to turn his attentions to the mundane problems of domestic life. Early fame had spoiled him. But he always lavished attention and concern upon his sisters, Evelyn and Marie. In the early spring of 1959 Marie fell ill; it was cancer. She was hospitalized in Manhattan and Sugar Ray rushed to her side. The prognosis delivered by doctors was grim, but Sugar Ray would not accept it. He started making phone calls. He had plenty of contacts—not the least Walter Winchell—in the Damon Runyon Cancer Fund. He had raised all that money for the fund himself, and now he needed that research to save his sister. He told his mother he'd find the best doctors anywhere in the world. He told her that their Marie—lovely and vivacious Marie, who had accompanied her brother on so many out-of-town fights—would recover. Robinson prayed at Salem Methodist, the church where he had learned how to make men bleed. The family brought her to her mother's house in early April. "I'm so sick, I'm so tired," she sighed to her brother. On April 19, 1959, Marie died. Sugar Ray was distraught. He went into a tailspin, believing that his world "would die with her."

By the first week of December 1960, he had landed in Los Angeles. Robinson and Fullmer were stepping into the ring again. The first encounter was judged a draw. The draw created a strange scene inside the ring, with the hands of both Fullmer and Robinson being raised. (The strangeness continued—though it wasn't strange for Hollywood—as a gorgeous Italian beauty, Gina Gianucci, stepped to center ring. Gainford moved to the microphone: "It's fitting now to say that Robinson will be leading man in a feature length movie to be made in Rome next summer and this pretty lady is his leading lady." Gianucci smiled; wolf whistles shot through the air; Sugar Ray smiled. The movie was never realized.) Hack Miller, of the *Deseret News* in Salt Lake City, was at ringside. "I believed Robinson fought the best fight that night," Miller later said. Robinson was old, Fullmer young—and "the mere fact that aging Robinson had held the young slugger from Utah to an unpopular draw was itself a victory for Ray," commented Miller. The two fought a fifteen-rounder in Las Vegas the following year. It was full of brutal hitting, and there were reporters at ringside who wondered how Robinson could withstand the punishment, only, in the fourteenth and fifteenth, to begin wondering how Fullmer could withstand the punishment. There was a thirty-five-second nonstop flurry in the final round, blows greeted with blows, uppercuts followed by right and left hooks, the referee circling furiously. At fight's end, there was blood on each fighter's trunks. That night went to Fullmer; the overall war, many felt, to Robinson.

Sugar Ray had once again played his card—an abrupt pullout if his financial demands weren't met—in negotiations with the Fullmer camp. Fullmer had never seen anything like it: "He was tough on the contract negotiations. He wanted all the money, and everything else in his favor. He wanted everything his way."

As the fifties had closed around him, Sugar Ray could look around and see a kind of golden age of boxing passing. Five middleweight titles lay behind him, in addition to a welterweight title. He had dominated the forties and fifties. He had done what only the greatest in his sport had been able to do: win in a titanic fashion and snatch the rare defeats back with the same style. He was "the miracle man of boxing," according to a 1959 assessment in Nat Fleischer's *Ring* magazine. Fight managers and promoters were always looking for the next great fighter—the next Sugar Ray, the next Joe Louis. Fleischer believed he saw the next great heavyweight a year later, at the Olympics in Rome—the type of fighter whose style and grace made him think of both Robinson and Louis. The fighter was a Kentucky schoolboy and he fascinated Fleischer. The honey-colored and broad-shouldered Cassius Clay, a light heavyweight, had come out of Louisville with a dazzling reputation. In one of the celebrated matches that rocked that summer's Olympics, the Kentuckian bloodied Zbigniew Pietrzykowski, a tough left-handed Polish fighter. "Clay's last-round assault on Pietrzykowski was the outstanding hitting of the tournament," Fleischer proclaimed—and a Fleischer proclamation was not one to take lightly. In Rome three boxers had emerged with gold medals: Eddie Crook, Wilbert McClure, and Clay. And of those three, everyone left talking about Clay.

Shortly before heading off to Rome, Cassius Clay had in fact ventured to Harlem. He wanted to meet Sugar Ray Robinson, whom he idolized as did so many young fighters. Dick Schaap, a man-about-town and the sports editor of *Newsweek* magazine, escorted young Clay. The sights of Harlem entranced the young fighter—street-corner preachers, men and women in colorful attire, big cars. Robinson's Cadillac came into view. Clay, hungry for some possible pointers before heading abroad, thought he might get a sit-down session with Robinson. But Robinson had no interest in the Olympics or Olympians. He offered Clay and Schaap perfunctory hellos and that was pretty much it. His club was failing; he had work to do. "That Sugar Ray, he's something," Clay muttered, hurt. "Someday I'm gonna own two Cadillacs—and a Ford for just getting around in."

The young Cassius Clay couldn't have known it, but the great Sugar Ray Robinson was on the verge of financial ruin. There were catchy names on the doors of his businesses in Harlem—Knockout Productions, Sugar Ray's Entertainment Corporation—but they meant nothing. He signed for a January 22, 1960, fight in Boston against Paul Pender, a former fireman who packed a wallop of a punch. Robinson held sparring sessions on the ground floor inside Filene's, the downtown Boston department store. Huge crowds gathered outside the store to peer in at him through the windows as he skipped rope and shadowboxed. One noontime crowd numbered upward of two thousand. The newspapers often made reference to the thirty-nine-year-old Robinson's age. Some in the crowds had stared at him through the windows with wide-eyed stillness—as if he were a museum piece.

He would receive $49,000 for the Pender fight. (Forty-nine grand used to absorb traveling expenses for European jaunts for his whole entourage—now it was money for bills and old debts and Uncle Sam.) Pender, listless for much of the fight, connected on a volley of blows in the eleventh from which Robinson found it hard to recover. Pender won the fifteen-rounder, thus relieving Sugar Ray of his crown. But the crown itself was only sanctioned by New York, Massachusetts, and Europe. (Gene Fullmer held the National Boxing Association crown, the more legitimate of the two.)

Afterward, the gentlemen from the Fourth Estate crowded around Sugar Ray. Gainford cracked wise, comparing his fighter's loss to the Brink's robbery—a reference to the 1950 Boston heist staged by some local misfits. (It was quite a successful heist, until they were caught.) Losing to the likes of Paul Pender? A fighter who had retired four times from the ring? The reporters wanted to know why; they wondered what had happened to their miracle worker. Robinson laughed. "Man, I'm old," he said.

But on that day in 1960, before he took off for Rome to start his own legend at the 1960 Summer Olympics, the impressionable Cassius Clay saw only the Cadillac, the name atop the outside of the bar, and the glittering aura of his hero.

If he had been one to play and spend more time with his two sons, perhaps Sugar Ray would not have worried so much about his own travails. But fatherhood bewildered him. He thought his sons might simply love him as so many fans did. But a son comes to need a father more than a hero.

Sugar Ray was back to deep brooding, sitting in his office above the nightclub, whistling: "Sweet Georgia Brown," "The Very Thought of You." He still threw some elegant soirees at his nightclub, and his New Year's Eve affairs were the rage. But the flow of champagne was drying up. Even the great Harlem power broker Lloyd Dickens, who had helped usher in the age of the modern Harlem politico by helping to finance campaigns for Adam Clayton Powell Jr. and others, couldn't save Robinson's businesses. He had looked at the books and winced. In 1962, the shuttering began— the barbershop, the lingerie shop, even the fabled nightclub. The community's decline had slowly begun in the late 1940s and early 1950s. Billie Holiday, Ella Fitzgerald, and Count Basie had all abandoned Harlem for fancy homes out in Queens. Minton's Playhouse, Harlem's most notable jazz spot, was struggling, with many of the musicians who had contributed to its fame—Dizzy Gillespie, Thelonious Monk, Kenny Clark—now playing more frequently in Greenwich Village. "The heyday of Negro entertainment is long gone," wrote a Harlem columnist back in 1949. "Nobody seems to care . . . Only a few places offer anything approaching a show, and even so it's nothing like the days when Harlem jumped." After the death of his sister Marie, patrons saw Robinson at the club less and less frequently. Accountants—already worried about the chunks of his income the IRS was siphoning for back taxes—informed him its upkeep was draining his finances. His last New Year's Eve gala at the club was 1961. That night he watched patrons leave, then sat on a stool in front of the long bar. The mirror bounced his reflection back at him: Times were changing. The gyrating and noisy and unpredictable sixties had arrived; it was a whole new era for Sugar Ray.

There were, as well, marital woes. Always a nocturnal figure, he stayed out later and later; sometimes he did not return home. Edna Mae would not have any more of it. He had never really been a family man. Edna Mae liked company in her home—family members, aunts, cousins—and their presence often grated on Sugar Ray. They took her side in arguments, which caused him to flee toward the emotional security of his sisters and mother. He had lived so close to the stars his whole adult life it had given him a certain sense of indomitability. Now his feet were down on the ground and it confused him. The losses seemed almost complete when Edna Mae filed for divorce.

Had there been darker currents at work in the unraveling of the celebrated marriage of Sugar Ray Robinson and Edna Mae? All those smiles, all that glamour! Of course, the curtain that separates any marriage from the public can sway in a tricky and deceptive manner. In the years after Sugar Ray's death, his son, Ray Jr.—who seems to have suffered the not uncommon mixed feelings about a famous father who did not give him the needed attention—charged that his father slapped his mother at times during the marriage. The charges were later mentioned in a cable TV documentary. Robinson's allies—so close to their hero—refused to believe it. "Edna Mae never told me about any abuse," recalls Mel Dick, Robinson's longtime friend. "I'm not saying it didn't happen. Who knows? But Ray Jr. never got along with his father and always had issues with him." Still, there is little doubt that the marriage had moments of volatility. In 1989, a magazine writer visited Edna Mae at her two-bedroom apartment on Manhattan's Upper West Side. Pictures of Sugar Ray were everywhere; the prizefighter had been dead less than a year. Edna Mae was then employed as a personal exercise trainer at a local YWCA. The former dancer had kept herself in shape through the years. She said she was working on a book (never published) about her and Sugar Ray. "He was so different from anything I'd ever known or experienced," she confided to the writer. "We were so opposite to have been attracted [to each other], but they do say that is the way it works." She talked of the multiple miscarriages she had had during the union; she hinted at his womanizing. "No matter what he did—and he could be a rascal—I was always totally his when he fought," she said. The issue of how much money she got in the divorce settlement, a paltry $23,000, still grated on her. Edna Mae, who never remarried, had found it difficult to bring other men into her life. "I tried to have other romances, buy my son was just so unhappy with any relationship that I had." There were hearty men who approached her, but soon they were gone. "They shied away because they felt like they could not walk in his wake. And you know, they may have been right, because there were a lot of things about him that I thought were unique and belonged only to him."

Sugar Ray turned forty-one years old in 1962. What would a forty-one-year-old Negro do? There were no inquiries or job offers from executive suites. Why, the great Henry Armstrong was barely making twenty grand a year working that recreation center job out in St. Louis. Joe Louis had gone through another couple of marriages. To make ends meet, he had turned to refereeing wrestling bouts. He had also turned to snorting cocaine and keeping nefarious company.

Sugar Ray dreamed of options. Hollywood? The only black athlete who had crossed over—and was actually getting work—was former professional football player Woody Strode, who was playing cowboys. The young Cassius Clay, turning pro, had made a pitch to Robinson about becoming his manager. But Robinson thought Clay bewildering and strange; he himself had never been one to engage in braggadocio. And here was Clay, howling from restaurant tables, making knockout predictions, composing poetry in honor of himself.

On top of it all, Clay kept company with the Muslims. When Clay told Robinson that Elijah Muhammad could promise him $700,000 if he converted to Islam, Sugar Ray truly thought the young man insane. He declined the offer to manage Clay.

Sugar Ray fought an undistinguished fighter by the name of Denny Moyer in New York in 1962. He picked up a $20,000 check—though he lost. A year earlier Robinson had beat Moyer in a ten-rounder. The rematch got Robinson on the cover of *Ring* magazine: "Sugar Ray Robinson—Finished?" the headline asked.

In 1963 there was a three-month period when he did not fight at all. He convinced himself he missed the rings, the crowds. George Gainford was still around. So was Harry Wiley. (Braca and his contingent had left over the issue of money they felt Robinson owed them from revenues.) He told them to pack up; they were going back out on the road. There would indeed be more fights. As a matter of fact, they were going to Paris. The French still loved him despite the failure of his cabaret act over there. He knew they did: Le Sucre Merveilleux, the marvelous Sugar.

Suddenly there seemed more of a political bite along the streets of Harlem. Now seemed a time to morph style into action, to channel song and poem and trumpet in the direction of protest. The children of Little Rock had made way for the college kids on Negro campuses. Lena Horne knew it was coming, and she was energized by it: A rolling boulder headed directly for the Kennedy White House. Negro college students had staged sit-ins against segregation in Greensboro, North Carolina; there were threatened boycotts of retail chains in the North. Man had not yet landed on the moon, but the sixties had landed upon America.

In 1960, that building-up year where there would be no turning back, Lena was sitting in Luau, a Hollywood restaurant. A waiter told another customer he'd be right back, kind of bragging that he was serving Lena Horne. "Where is Lena Horne, anyway?" the customer said, in a voice steeped in booze. "She's just another nigger." Horne heard it and popped up from her seat in a rage: "Here I am, you bastard! Here's the nigger you couldn't see." And with that she picked up an ashtray and hurled it at the bigot. There was blood—his—and publicity. The young protesters everywhere now knew where lovely Lena stood. She was soon featured on the cover of an arts periodical, *SHOW* magazine. The cover shows a curtain—white—torn generously at the center with Lena looking through, out onto America. The caption: "Breaking the White Barrier: Lena Horne Speaks on the Artist and the Negro Revolt."

Attorney General Robert Kennedy had asked the writer James

Baldwin—whippet-slender, Baldwin was a seer—to gather a group of Negro artists for a meeting to discuss the protests that were forming in certain pockets of the country. Kennedy feared adverse publicity if the meeting were held at the White House; his father's swank apartment in Manhattan would do. Among others, Baldwin brought along Harry Belafonte, the handsome young movie star; Lorraine Hansberry, whose 1959 play, *A Raisin in the Sun,* about the humanity of a Negro family and their struggle for a home—its title was taken from a Langston Hughes poem—had entranced Broadway; and Lena Horne. Kennedy had never been surrounded by so much Negro genius and beauty—male and female—and his eyes darted about furiously. He reminded those present of the administration's efforts to make life better for Negroes; he also told the gathering that President Kennedy was worried that radical Negroes and Muslims joining together could cause trouble. He seemed to miss the point that the American Negro had been in anguish since slavery. "You don't have no idea what trouble is," a young man at the gathering piped up. "Because I'm close to the moment where I'm ready to take up a gun." His name was Jerome Smith and he had been beaten viciously during the Freedom Rides into Mississippi. His talk resembled a garbled sermon, but it was heartbreaking—jailings, beatings, all for the downtrodden of America. It nearly brought Lena to tears. Afterward, she told Baldwin and Belafonte she'd do anything they needed her to do.

Not many outside Negro America knew about the Spingarn Medal. Inside Negro America, however, it was a kind of Nobel Prize, an annual honor bestowed by the NAACP since 1915 upon a figure who had scaled Olympian heights in America. The list of finalists for the award in 1960 included poet Gwendolyn Brooks, playwright Lorraine Hansberry, the leaders of the Greensboro sit-ins, and Langston Hughes. Hughes was by far the most prolific Negro writer in America—plays, librettos, translations, poetry, short stories, novels; he hit to all corners of the literary playing field. "Have lived longer than any other known Negro solely on writing—from 1925 to now without a regular job!!!" he had reminded a colleague in 1958. The Spingarn Medal went to the fifty-eight-year-old Hughes. He was overwhelmingly delighted. His protest poems had fallen out of favor in the 1950s, viewed as relics. But now, with white and black college kids crisscrossing the nation to protest inequality, carrying paperback copies of his collected poetry, Langston Hughes was in vogue. At the Spingarn ceremony, Hughes said he accepted the honor on behalf of Negro people: "Without them, on my part, there would have been no poems; without their hopes and fears and dreams, no stories; without their struggles, no dramas; without their music, no songs."

In final retirement with wife Millie. They lived quietly in
Los Angeles, uninvolved with the world of boxing.

1963–1966

autumn leaves

HER NAME WAS MILLIE BRUCE, and she was quietly beautiful. She was the kind of woman who slipped into places. Her voice was soft and her stature regal. Edna Mae Robinson had been a noisy beauty, someone who wished to be seen and then fawned over. Millie Bruce's approach was different. She was one of those Negro women in Los Angeles who floated with a certain classiness around the strange jungle of Hollywood, even if Hollywood was mostly unwelcoming to her: But her brother-in-law was Eddie Anderson, Jack Benny's "Rochester" sidekick. Eddie got invited to places and sometimes Millie went along. A woman he knew in San Francisco had told Sugar Ray Robinson to look her friend Millie up in Los Angeles. It was during his two-year whirl in the world of show business. On a dance floor, he tried to make a romantic move. She pushed him away. She would not sleep with a married man, even it was Sugar Ray Robinson. Her pride made him desire her more. As the years rolled by, they kept in intermittent contact. She read about him in the newspapers; he phoned.

In 1962—Sugar Ray and Edna Mae had divorced that year—Millie was in New York City with a girlfriend, seeing the sights. He offered to take them out. It was an old trick of his: Take a woman to a jazz club where, invariably, he knew a member of the band, was invited up onstage to play—drums or piano—and proceeded to wow his date. When his musician friend Curly Hummer called him to the stage at the Spotlight on Fifty-second, Millie and her friend—he'd driven them over in the Cadillac, the top down, the weather lovely—couldn't help but be impressed. He sent yellow roses, gifts. They became an item, and in time she was being referred to as his fiancée.

In 1963, he took Millie to Europe for a string of fights scheduled for the last three months of the year. (Robinson was apolitical most of his life and skipped the historic March on Washington in the late summer of 1963. He simply couldn't bear to tear himself away from the quest to restore his reputation, which he bizarrely felt was falling apart. There was something else: Sugar Ray had never had any links to the political and ministerial world of the South. He had no conduit to connect him with the galvanizing Alabama preacher Martin Luther King Jr., who had, for several years, been knocking at the country's moral conscience. King knew Harry Belafonte, Sammy Davis Jr., Ossie Davis, and Sidney Poitier. Robinson, always an independent, considered such linkages nothing more than cliquishness, a thing he couldn't abide. Hollywood's Negro elite showed at the march: Sammy, Ossie, Harry, Sidney Poitier, as well as Paul Newman, Marlon Brando, James Garner, Charlton Heston, and thousands of others.)

In Europe, with Millie, there were cabarets to attend, there was shopping to be done, music to be heard. Not to mention the myriad receptions held in his honor. As for the fights, they were forgettable. His opponents were unknown on American shores. There was Armand Vanucci, in Paris. (Boxing seemed a pastime for Vanucci. His full-time job was working as a security guard at the Louvre, keeping an eye on the *Mona Lisa.*) There was Fabio Bettini in Lyons; Emile Saerens in Brussels; and Andre Davier in Grenoble. Robinson won them all, save one, a draw against Bettini. He claimed it was part of a master plan to get another title shot. George Gainford wolfed down steak and eggs in the fine hotels and nodded his head. A title shot? Gainford thought otherwise. To avoid a serious injury from one of these fighters who might unload a lucky knockout punch was enough of a challenge. Sugar Ray fought ten times in 1964, which, considering he also turned forty-three that year, was astonishing. But still, his friends—Mel Dick, Miles Davis—pleaded with him to quit. "He kept saying, 'I want to be champion again,' " recalls Mel Dick. Millie offered the blinding love of a fiancée. "He's a wonderful fighter, a wonderful human being," she said, refusing to judge the lackluster competition he now faced. "I've never known a man like him. He's something else." And off they went, all over— Millie and George and Harry and Sugar Ray, first-class airline tickets, George draping the blue silk robe around his shoulders.

(Robinson had recently gotten a $120,000 refund from the IRS, after a lengthy legal battle, because they had wrongfully taken too much of his past earnings.) Then lingering in the dressing room afterward, slipping Robinson's belongings into a bag. They'd been doing this now for more than twenty-five years, a quarter of a century. Greasing the palms of bellhops, commenting on one another's sartorial tastes, laying a little dough and a couple of tickets in the hands of the limo driver.

He surprised Millie in May and swooped her off to Las Vegas. They married in a small chapel. The only witness was the taxi driver, who waited so he could get them back to the airport. If Millie had dreamed of a fancy wedding she didn't complain. "Oh, it's lovely, Ray, it's lovely," she said of the chapel.

There was a June 1965 bout in Hawaii. Millie loved the Hawaiian scenery; inside the ring against hard-hitting Stan Harrington, Sugar Ray took a pummeling. He would remember the night for its sociological lessons. "Man," he told a *Washington Post* reporter, "that Hawaii is crazy. They got all kinds of [racial] mixes. I might spend a month there. They loved me. They kept me bowing for fifteen minutes before and after the bout. I sold the beautiful arena out for the first time." It was left to George Gainford to explain what went wrong in the land of palm trees: "That Harrington in Honolulu bangs Ray's head with his head in the sixth. Ray's no bleeder, but an artery breaks. Only way I can stop it is by using a solution that— well, one drop in the man's eyes and he's blind. Hell, we don't need to win bad enough to go blind. Last four rounds my man sees so much blood he thinks the Red Cross is pumping it."

There was something rather tender about watching the post-fight ministrations of Sugar Ray and Gainford now. They moved slower, they grunted more often from aches and pains, they took their own sweet time in leaving the dressing room. They had spent more than two decades on the road with each other, and often the distrust fell away to simple concern and familiarity. They both claimed they were chasing Joey Giardello, the reigning middleweight champion. The Brooklyn-born Giardello had been fighting professionally since the age of eighteen. He was merciless and fearless. On April 20, 1960, Giardello and Gene Fullmer had waged a savage head-butting contest at the fieldhouse on the Montana State University campus. That had resulted in a draw. Giardello finally took the middleweight crown three years later by defeating Dick Tiger in Atlantic City. Six months earlier he had defeated Sugar Ray Robinson in a ten-rounder in Philadelphia. The loss pained Robinson and stoked his determination. "Nobody has ever been a champion six times," he said, while the sixties churned outside, beyond his concern and own current dreams.

There was a May 24, 1965, fight in Tijuana, Mexico, against Memo Ayon. Both Gainford and Robinson figured they'd scoot into Mexico, whip this nobody Ayon, then maybe catch some rest in Los Angeles, visiting Millie's folks. It didn't work out that way; Ayon won the ten-rounder. Gainford howled it was stolen: "Ray beats this Memo Ayon person down in Tijuana like the United States whipped ol' Hitler," he tried explaining. "Even the Mexican newspapers say we win [sic] eight rounds." But few believed his translation skills. According to Robinson, Ayon "came to me after the fight and said, 'Mister Ray, I sorry.' "

Millie didn't care about the losses. He was a legend and the legend was still beautiful. She liked just watching him move about hotel rooms, swan through airports. She liked how he'd turn, in a small crowd, to glimpse her. They were down in the Dominican Republic, and there he was, in yet another orphanage, in another hospital, talking to the impoverished kids, holding their little hands, slipping dollars here and there, sometimes larger bills. It was easy to see his longtime concern for the downtrodden and oppressed—he came from their class. Now in memory of his sister Marie he seemed to be visiting the sick even more, dropping bills into the hands of nurses and children. "He's a kind man," Millie said. "In Jamaica, the Dominican Republic, Stockholm—he goes to visit hospitals, shut-ins, all kinds of handicapped people. And he asks no credit for it. He does it even when he's not promoting a fight. He tells me, '[Millie], my luck's been good. I got enough to share.' "

In the summer heat of 1965 Robinson landed in Washington, D.C., for a bout. The city hadn't hosted professional boxing in two years; the name Sugar Ray Robinson was great publicity. His mother, Leila, was ailing back in Manhattan; he had gone over to the hospital to visit her before leaving New York. "Jab him. Jab him and follow through," she advised her son.

Sugar Ray and Millie took a suite at the lovely Mayflower Hotel. George was down the hall, and soon ordering room service. Robinson's opponent was "Young" Joe Walcott—no relation to, but managed by, heavyweight Jersey Joe Walcott. Robinson believed fighters like Walcott were his only path to Giardello. Walcott was another nobody. "I want to retire as champion," Sugar Ray said in the nation's capital. "That's the way I think it ought to be. I have faith that's the way it will be." Millie roamed around the city with him in the days leading up to the fight. "Of course Ray's in shape!" she snapped at a question. "He runs every morning in New York. Twice around the reservoir. I know, because I go with him. I don't run, but I go." There was a workout in a small gym at the Washington Jewish Community Center. A few dozen milled around, waiting to be let in. "OK," Gainford instructed when Robinson was in place. "Let the crowd in. He'll skip rope." The crowd numbered less than fifty. In his heyday, hundreds would shove through the doors of the Manhattan gyms just to get a glimpse of him. Gainford admitted he hadn't done much research on Walcott. "Why, ten years ago the commission wouldn't have permitted the match," Gainford told a writer in Washington. "Ray would have beat him on his lunch hour."

It was just a wee bit past the dinner hour when fans started streaming into the Washington Coliseum on the night of June 24, on an evening when city leaders intended to showcase the return of boxing to their city, an evening with the great Sugar Ray Robinson in his dressing room—his name in capital letters on the marquee outside—ready to take center ring. Ed Weaver, the promoter, was hoping for 10,000 paying customers. He fell short by more than half: 3,800 showed. Challenger Walcott arrived at the Coliseum by taxi, wearing sunglasses and sucking on a toothpick. Sugar Ray, Millie, and Gainford arrived by chauffeur-driven car. Alighting, they cut a suave path, Millie in a white-sequined dress, the manager and fighter so easy it seemed they were engaged in a pantomime of footsteps and nods.

Inside, the attendees screamed in unison at the sight of Sugar Ray, the five-time middleweight champion. Millie never saw the forty thousand-plus crowds at Yankee Stadium. She thought the 3,800 in attendance nothing to be ashamed about.

Sugar Ray began pummeling Walcott in the early rounds, uppercuts and hooks. Walcott looked confused, glancing to his corner for advice. At one point Sugar Ray faked a left—he could have delivered it, but there would have been consequences. In days gone by, he wouldn't have cared about the consequences. Those days were locked away in memory and grainy newsreel footage. In the Coliseum, there erupted a strange burst of laughter: Robinson's trunks were slipping down; he yanked them back up with his gloved hands. Then he went back to pounding Walcott. In the seventh, however, Walcott slipped in his first meaningful punches, and he did not let up in the eighth. Sugar Ray looked pained. He was grimacing. Millie began fanning herself with the night's official program, her husband on the cover. "Come on, baby. Come on, love," she cried out, believing somehow he could hear her voice above all the die-hard fans. Robinson held on, if barely, in the final two rounds; but Walcott's late rallies were not enough for a victory. Young Joe seemed content to have survived. A few reporters came by Robinson's dressing room. He didn't want to talk about Walcott, only Giardello. He wanted Giardello, and imagined that tonight's performance against Walcott would keep his momentum going in that direction. "I'd like it here in Washington," Sugar Ray said, alluding to a championship bout with Giardello.

The reporters shot glances at one another.

"Outdoors in that big ballpark, maybe," he went on. "It ain't too cold here in September, is it?"

The reporters left; Robinson showered; and, as always, Gainford waited. He didn't let just anybody into the dressing room anymore. Too many shadowy figures had slipped in in the past. "He had started saying, 'You can't come in here unless you show that you're on Social Security,'" remembers Jimmy Breslin. The sound of whooshing shower spray was heard. Then Robinson's voice shot from the showers: "Hey, George! What was that cat's name I fought tonight?"

After Walcott, Sugar Ray fought twice in July, once in August, twice more in September, and twice in October. They were not pushover fighters, but none would prove valuable on the road to Giardello. Robinson lost two of those contests. The national press had, for the most part, stopped paying attention. Then Giardello said he had absolutely no interest in fighting Sugar Ray Robinson again. Robinson scoffed, believing Giardello was bluffing, angling for a larger purse.

Reporters wanted Sugar Ray to sit down with them so they could write long and nuanced profiles. But he rebuffed them. "Something fascinates me about second acts in American life," says Larry L.

King, a young writer for *Sports Illustrated* at the time, who pleaded and pleaded with Robinson to spend time with him. Millie convinced Robinson to relent. King was excited, then realized Sugar Ray was on to him. "He was smart enough to know I was not there to talk about the glory days of his career," recalls King. "I was not going to write a piece about how great he was. It was going to be a downhill piece. He was hiding from me even when he was around."

Sugar Ray landed in Pittsburgh for a November 10 fight against Joey Archer. This time, the reporters showed up, but seemingly only to pounce. They asked why he was still fighting; what was he trying to prove; they asked him about his age, and the tone implied they thought he was too old. "To win the title again," Sugar Ray said, in answer to questions of why he was still in the ring. "The beautiful end of a beautiful story."

Joey Archer was a dangerous foe. In nearly fifty fights, he had suffered just one defeat, a record that positioned him as a legitimate middleweight contender. Sugar Ray and Millie, and George and his wife, Hazel—Hazel rarely traveled with George; did she sense she was needed now?—checked into rooms at the swanky downtown Carlton House. And there was someone else in the entourage, Sugar Ray's old trumpet-blowing friend: Miles Davis. Like many of Robinson's musician friends, Miles had become worried about his continued fighting. Of them all, it was Miles who knew addiction, the way it could hold and grip. And Sugar Ray Robinson—on these wanderings that had taken him through the stifling heat of Mexico, now into the cold of Pittsburgh, pocketing no more than $700 a fight—was addicted to gallantry, to the fighter's pride. Robinson had last fought in Pittsburgh in the winter of 1961. His foe that night had been Wilf Greaves. Greaves never saw the eighth-round hook coming; his eyes shut before he hit the canvas as voices whipped and whooshed atop one another. But that was 1961, and this was 1965.

Archer swung hard and relentlessly in the early rounds. A Robinson punch here, there—lightning-quick—made some believe he would make a fight of it. But when Archer floored him in the eighth, heads shook in wonder, fans asking themselves if this was it, if the great Sugar Ray would get up. The referee count stopped at eight. But it was a telltale sign; Archer bore down in the final two rounds. Then there stood the referee, raising the arm of Joey Archer.

George draped the silk robe over Sugar Ray's shoulders. The same way he used to do in the small upstate towns of New York in the Golden Gloves days. Robinson had intimated—in the days leading up to his arrival in Pittsburgh—that if he lost to Archer, he would leave the ring for good. Now, in the dressing room after the fight, Millie was worried about how her husband would take this loss that put another title shot out of reach. The reporters were quiet. Fans lingered outside the dressing room, wanting to chat a bit with the legend. Sugar Ray was not up to it. Inside the dressing room, Miles strolled over to the great prizefighter. "Sugar, it's time, man," he whispered into Robinson's puffed-up face. And so it ended there, with George and Millie and the trumpeter at his side. He would never fight again.

He showered and dressed. Millie wrapped her arms around him. The small entourage strolled through the dark Pittsburgh cold to a waiting car.

"I hate to go on too long campaigning for another chance," he said the next day to the press, with George nodding by his side.

"I had hopes of fighting for the championship again if I had beaten Archer," he said, with Millie looking on. Those hopes were over. Sugar Ray had left the ring.

Back in Manhattan, his boxing life behind him, Sugar Ray and Millie moved into a $365-a-month apartment on Riverside Drive. They liked the way the sun set over the Hudson River in the evenings. But he had to figure out a means to make money. The IRS payment had been spent and there was little to show for the recent bouts. He found himself having to borrow money. Vincent Impellitteri, the former mayor, loaned him a few thousand. Millie found a secretarial job over at NBC; she never complained about having to work, but Sugar Ray wasn't happy about it. He dropped the names of movie and theatrical figures who he said were eager to work with him. He was, for the most part, exaggerating: He did chat up John Huston in Rome, but there was no offer of movie work. Richard Rodgers talked to him about a planned stage production of *Pal Joey,* but nothing came of it. There was a role as technical consultant for Sammy Davis Jr.'s kinetic Broadway musical *Golden Boy*—an adaptation of Clifford Odets's play about a tormented boxer—which opened in 1964. Robinson enjoyed getting over to the theatre for rehearsals, walking the same

Broadway streets he used to romp along as a kid when he thought he might end up beneath stage lights. He announced to the press—trying to revive publicity for a long-dormant project—that he'd like to see a movie biopic of his life. (In the early sixties, Robinson favored the choice of Sam Cooke to portray him. Cooke was shot by a hotel clerk in Los Angeles in 1964.)

Millie figured he was growing despondent. There were no more fights, and there were no job offers coming in. She surprised him with a piano. He played "The Very Thought of You" over and over.

Madison Square Garden officials hatched a plan to honor Robinson. When they phoned, he was quite touched. The event was to take place on December 11, a prelude to an Emile Griffith–Manny Gonzalez bout at the Garden. His old foes, onetime champions themselves, were there: Gene Fullmer, Bobo Olson, Paul Pender, Carmen Basilio, Rocky Graziano. The organizers even paid Randy Turpin to come over from London; Robinson personally requested Turpin's presence. Cassius Clay—now Muhammad Ali—was there. The Garden was jammed. Manhattan businessmen, Harlem hepcats, socialites and their husbands, jazzmen, young amateur fighters in the cheap seats. When the announcer called Sugar Ray Robinson's name, roars went up. The great prizefighter stepped into the ring and did a little Japanese bow. He was wearing a short terry-cloth robe. Now Millie saw: He had done things that would never be forgotten. Her eyes were lit. He walked to each corner of the ring and waved. They were the very corners between which he had tangled with the best of his time, where he had defended his championship titles. He was handed a huge and gleaming trophy. At the end of his brief comments, he said, "*A tout à l'heure*"—I'll see you later. There was a dinner at Mama Leone's, a renowned Italian restaurant near Broadway. The thick-shouldered fighters sat around a table together. Champagne and heaps of food arrived. Muhammad Ali spoke, and his words had a sweetness about them. "When I was a little kid I watched Sugar Ray Robinson on the TV, and when I started fighting I copied his moves, and I still do. When I go into the ring now he's on my mind."

And yet, someone was missing. Where was the Bull—Jake LaMotta? It wasn't as if Garden officials would have had a hard time locating him. He lived only ten blocks away. He never got an invitation. The thrown Billy Fox fight, among other things, had stuck to him, sullied his reputation. He was livid: "I was only the first fighter to lick him when he was on top! I was the only guy he defeated for the middleweight title, and I was also the guy he waltzed with in six slambang wars, and—what the hell—I was the only former champ who could have walked to the Garden!"

Every fighter leaves the game with his own haunting memories of loss.

Sugar Ray loved the jazz clubs. He now had time to go whenever he wanted to. On July 17, 1967, John Coltrane died out on Long Island. There were all manner of tributes in Manhattan. Miles Davis and Dizzy Gillespie set up camp at the Village Gate for a whole month, in honor of Trane. The lines were long; many nights sold out. Miles was playing with great touch, melodies—"Milestones," "Stella by Starlight," "Autumn Leaves," "All of You"—with such verve. One night, he spotted the fighters. "Sugar Ray Robinson came by along with Archie Moore, the great old champion from St. Louis," Miles would recall. "I remember when they came down I asked Dizzy to introduce them from the stage and he told me I was the fight fan, so why didn't I do it." But Miles just stared out into the audience, pointing his instrument; it was as if words were caught in his throat. He nodded as Dizzy finally introduced Sugar Ray Robinson and Archie Moore to the gathering.

In 1966 Sugar Ray had signed a contract with Viking for his autobiography. He got $50,000, money he sorely needed. As cowriter, Robinson suggested David Anderson, who had been a sportswriter for the *New York Journal-American* and was now writing for *The New York Times.* Anderson was excited about the project. When David Anderson had been a teenager, his father had taken him to some of Sugar Ray's fights.

In preparing to interview Robinson for the book, Anderson bought a heap of blank tapes and a tape recorder. But the sessions at Sugar Ray's apartment were brief, which annoyed the writer. "He had no endurance with the tape recorder," recalls Anderson. "He would say he was tired. I'd say, 'Ray, you went fifteen rounds with Jake LaMotta, you can go another hour with the tape recorder.'" But Robinson would shoo him away. Back again, switching on the tape recorder, Millie busying herself in another room, Anderson asked about Robinson's Army service, about those stories about desertion. It was a topic that always caused Robinson to tense up. He wished to change the subject, but Anderson bore on, saying he needed to properly record what happened. "His lawyers finally came up with some Army papers saying he was supposed to have fallen down some stairs and woke up in a Staten Island hospital," says Anderson.

The publishers were happy with the finished book. A lavish coast-to-coast book tour was planned. An appearance had been scheduled for the Johnny Carson show. "He said, 'I gotta get paid for that,' " recalls Anderson. It was awkard; authors did not get paid for book tours. "[His publisher] said, 'Ray, you don't get paid for that.' He said, 'I don't get paid, I ain't doing it.' " The publicists implored Anderson to talk to Sugar Ray. But the fighter, who had always believed people—fight promoters mainly—were manipulating him when it came to financial dealings, would not budge. "You couldn't reason with him," says Anderson. Viking published *Sugar Ray* in 1970. The cover art—a painting of Robinson in fighting pose colored in blues and greens—had been done by LeRoy Neiman. The autobiography, with no public appearances on the part of its subject, did only modest business. Soon after the book's publication, both Gainford and Harry Wiley got word to Robinson that they did not like the book, claiming their roles in Robinson's success had been greatly minimized. A nuisance lawsuit was quickly dismissed. Neither man ever spoke to Robinson again.

Sugar Ray may have been apolitical, but the presidential candidacy of Robert F. Kennedy excited him. Kennedy invited him to Hickory Hill, his estate in McLean, Virginia, where they talked about the problems of urban America. Robinson would have liked Kennedy's independent streak—he had stood up to labor racketeers as U.S. attorney general, and now he was connecting with blacks in an unusually soulful manner. But then came the assassination, and that took the breath out of so many.

Millie started to miss home. So Sugar Ray convinced himself he could make a living out in Hollywood. In 1967, Sugar Ray Robinson and his wife quietly slipped out of New York City for good, bound for California.

He'd see them while looking out the living room window. Or while strolling the neighborhood. Some looked lost, some desperate. The great prizefighter would tap Millie on the shoulder, imploring her to look at all the children. She didn't quite realize he was pointing to himself, gazing back through the looking glass, seeing his own hardscrabble childhood. No, he really never knew his father, just as his two sons never really knew him. If only he could save the children from unforeseen calamities. Just like all those church members had reached out to him. He'd be enlarging that mythical version of fatherhood. He'd be reaching out far, far beyond himself.

Sometimes he'd stare at them and it seemed as if he were on the verge of tears. Little Walker Smiths. Little Marie Smiths. Look, Millie, he'd say. Just look at them.

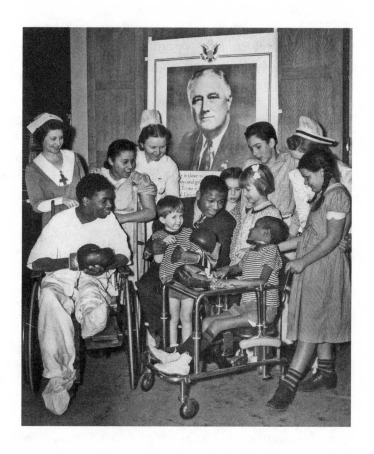

1967–1989

saving all those Walker Smith Juniors

MILLIE AND SUGAR RAY MOVED into a house on West Adams Boulevard in Los Angeles. Wright Fillmore, who lived downstairs, owned the property. He knew Millie's family well. And he was quite happy to help a family friend who happened to be married to a world-champion prizefighter. Located in a leafy, middle-class neighborhood of mostly black families, it was a comfortable, two-bedroom house with a balcony. They would never live anyplace else.

Sugar Ray got busy trying to break into Hollywood. He didn't have much difficulty getting

He saw Walker Smith Juniors in the faces of children everywhere.

meetings with directors. Most, however, once beyond the pleasantries of introduction, just wanted to talk about fighting. Conversation over, they'd pat him on the back, tell him they'd be in touch. He expected the phone to start ringing, and it did, but not on any regular basis. The transition was painful. There were some roles offered in TV dramas—*Car 54, Where Are You?, Lost in Space, Mission Impossible*—but they were minor parts. There seemed to be a bit of a spark between him and Diahann Carroll in her TV show, *Julia,* in which she played a single nurse raising her son. But the producers did not keep Robinson around; there were other suitors for Julia, among them Fred Williamson, a former professional football player. Nothing if not a positive thinker, Robinson began wondering if his real future lay on the big screen. He played a New York police officer in *The Detective,* a major motion picture starring Frank Sinatra. He told Millie that Sinatra insisted his role be enlarged. Most of it ended up on the cutting room floor—in the end, he had less than a dozen words of dialogue. He appeared in *Candy,* the Richard Burton farce. "I play my part just as Ray Robinson would," he said, in summing up his screen persona—and the folly of his approach.

His landing in Hollywood was somewhat fortuitous: It was in the late sixties that Hollywood really started to notice black actors and actresses. And there were examples of the black athlete turned actor getting opportunities. At the top of that list was Jim Brown, the former Cleveland Browns running back. In 1967 Brown had appeared in *The Dirty Dozen* alongside Lee Marvin, then got a starring role in the 1969 Western *100 Rifles.* In the latter he played opposite Raquel Welch; their on-screen affair had cracked a big-screen taboo against sexual relationships between black and white. On screen Robinson lacked what Brown had—nuance and depth.

Sugar Ray would tell friends that he just didn't understand Hollywood; that they didn't know how to use him. Then he started bemoaning the violence in movies—as if he were suddenly made queasy by the make-believe of the brutality he had thrived in. The Hollywood producers and casting agents stopped calling. He tried radio. He and Pearl Bailey—it was an age when broadcast producers took risks—did some on-air commentary for the closed-circuit telecast of the 1973 Joe Frazier–George Foreman fight. The broadcasters didn't call back.

Boxing, of course, hadn't forgotten him. The promoters continued to invite him to widely publicized fights, just as they always did former champions. He'd always arrive late on purpose, getting there just as they were about to introduce the other gathered champions— Willie Pep, Bobo Olson, Gene Fullmer, Rocky Graziano, Joe Louis. Then he'd let it be known he was there—but only after everyone else had been introduced and seated. When his name was finally announced, he would emerge, like sunlight around the side of a mountain, and the crowd would roar. Every time he flew over to Las Vegas, he'd look in on his old Army pal Joe. Joe Louis had begun working for Caesars Palace in 1970. The casino got his name—he was a greeter, a public relations figure, a great curiosity—and he got a paycheck. They'd dine over prawns and asparagus and sip wine, all compliments of Caesar's. They were a sight gliding through the casinos—proud black champions. Champions *before* the civil rights movement. A deep aura surrounded them as they walked, Sugar Ray grinning and Joe nodding his head.

In Los Angeles, he and Millie enjoyed quiet dinners. They played cards out on the balcony, blackjack, which had been the game he played while waiting to get over to Yankee Stadium for those big fights. They drove over to Central Avenue on weekends to listen to some good jazz. Sometimes he got invited to schools and talked to the children about education and physical fitness. (He shot a TV pilot for a program about physical fitness, the ex-fighter going through workout routines. But none of the networks picked it up.)

Since Millie had surprised him with that piano, one day he surprised her with an invitation: They were going to London. He had been personally invited to attend a birthday party for Queen Elizabeth in 1969. Millie was beside herself—London, Buckingham Palace. As they flew away from America, the cities were still on fire, the protests on college campuses raging. There was much talk in London about the unrest on American streets and campuses. Prince Philip, the queen's husband, pulled Robinson aside and wanted to talk to him about the turmoil in America. Then Prince Philip suggested to Robinson that he get engaged. "Sugar," he said, "I believe you could help that." He told Robinson that youngsters looked up to him, that his popularity would make him a role model. Back at their hotel, Sugar Ray couldn't stop talking to Millie about the conversation he'd had with the prince. Even if he couldn't quite figure exactly what he was going to do about it.

And then, it came to him. All those children running by him back in Los Angeles—around his home, over on Central Avenue, over in Watts. Many of them, he knew, were impoverished; many of them had a desperate look in their eyes, wore ill-fitting clothes; so many of them were out late at night. His own country was engulfed in riots; leaders had been assassinated; but the children were still running, and the vulnerable ones were in need of direction and guidance. On so many afternoons at home, when he had gone for walks—he put in five miles a day—those children had begun to remind him of his own childhood, when he ran the streets of Detroit and then the streets of Harlem, when he could have vanished into the world of juvenile delinquency but didn't because he got pulled down into a church basement. From London he sent telegrams to acquaintances back in California; he was coming home with an idea.

Back in Los Angeles, he became determined to start a youth foundation. "My heart cries," Sugar Ray said, "when I read of the problems we are having with narcotics and dope pushers in our schools." He went to Wright Fillmore, Millie's family friend. Fillmore, a natty dresser, partial to sunglasses, was in his seventies, retired, and one of those Los Angeles Negroes who had contacts, who had earned respect as part of the backbone of the community. Sugar Ray told him about his idea; Fillmore loved it. But he quickly reminded Robinson that he was retired. "No," Robinson told him. "You have just started working." Fillmore was amused, this relative newcomer to Los Angeles—his city!—laying out this grand plan. But then he found himself getting caught up in the idea. (He would eventually become the foundation president.) He set chairs out in his backyard for meetings and got some others to join in. They sat listening to Sugar Ray's plan: There'd be ballet, tap dance, drama, soccer, volleyball, a whole range of youth activities; there'd be fashion modeling, lessons in etiquette. There would, however, be no emphasis on boxing. He did not wish to see the children hitting one another under any circumstances. Another day they'd all gather in Millie's kitchen, and Millie, who would become a member of the organization's board, coming up with a list of volunteers she knew she could count on, the sun setting against the windows with the chatter still going at a fever-pitch. "If you can get the money, I can get the children," Fillmore finally said to Sugar Ray.

They needed seed money, funds to get them going. Fillmore and Robinson found themselves sitting before deacons and ministers of the local Council of Churches. Church leaders had no problem listening to a pitch from a world boxing champion. And after listening, after hearing the exuberance in Sugar Ray's voice, they were more than happy to sign on, offering funds to begin putting the plan into action. "I honestly believe," Sugar Ray announced to the media, "a competitive sports program would cut crime in half and also would give youngsters an incentive, as it did for me."

Fillmore knew of an empty one-story building at 1905 Tenth Avenue. They purchased it. Sugar Ray wrote state officials asking for more money. He wrote the TV and film stars he knew. Bob Hope would drop by, and so would Muhammad Ali, who lived in Los Angeles. He'd hit them up for financial contributions. "Everybody wanted to come by and just be around Sugar Ray," recalls Ken Bristow, Robinson's nephew. Millie would claim she had never seen him so happy.

In 1969, the Sugar Ray Robinson Youth Foundation received its charter. By 1972, when it received state funding, it had implemented year-round programs drawing youth from elementary and junior high schools throughout the Los Angeles area. Bob Hope joined the board of directors and was named honorary chairman of the foundation. Carroll Rosenbloom, owner of the Los Angeles Rams, also became a board member. Former California governor Edmund G. Brown became legal counsel. Actor Glenn Ford and his wife, Cynthia, were big supporters. The annual teen pageants began in 1974, hundreds of teens gathering in honor of their accomplishments. It was as if Sugar Ray Robinson—and all those hired to work at the foundation—wished to impart a semblance of style and class and etiquette to each of the children. The 1975 teen pageant took place at the Hollywood Palladium. (Hope and Sugar Ray used their contacts to secure the venue.) Lee Meriwether, a former Miss America, served as mistress of ceremonies. Hope cracked some one-liners from the stage. Toward the end of that night's program, there was a fashion tribute to Sugar Ray; he and Millie looked resplendent. The presentation was called "A Touch of Class." At its conclusion, applause washed over them. Nancy Sinatra and O. C. Smith were the featured entertainers at the 1977 Miss Sugar Ray Teen Pageant. For the 1978 pageant, Sugar Ray called in Howard Bingham—the great photographer who took so many scintillating shots of Muhammad Ali—to take the pictures.

The teens who participated in the program became noticeably more poised and confident. Their teachers complimented them. They were grateful. "I've always felt withdrawn from everyone else, but when I joined Sugar Ray's and associated with other girls," recalled thirteen-year-old Teri Ogata, "it proved to me that I was just as good as the next person."

"Sugar Ray understands us and our needs for fun, character building, entertainment and the need for someone to care about us kids," said twelve-year-old Geraldine Manuel.

"The foundation provides a lot of love, friendship, and kindness," said fifteen-year-old Florence Griffith. Griffith would go on to run in the 1988 Olympics—as Florence Griffith-Joyner—and win three gold medals. Her style—colorful outfits, long and lovely hair— seemed as captivating to the watching world as her speed.

"I thought only the wealthy had the opportunity to take advantage of special programs," said thirteen-year-old Anita Trevino. "With Sugar Ray's, anyone and everyone is welcome."

On many afternoons, a not-so-old prizefighter would join the kids on the playground of his foundation headquarters, his husky laugh floating over them. They'd rush up to him, tugging at him. The littlest ones hopped right up into his arms. The kids wore T-shirts that said "Sugar Ray's Youth Foundation." They were white kids and black kids and Latino kids. They came from the barrios and they came from Watts and they came from Pasadena. Standing there, he would look around at the kids and feel proud. "It meant so much to him because of his own youth and how the church had saved him," says Ken Bristow, who visited the foundation when in Los Angeles.

Fighters often see themselves in children, keenly feeling the echoes of who they were. Sugar Ray's growing-up idol, Henry Armstrong, also devoted his post-fight life to helping children. Two world champion sluggers, young again and at peace.

By the late 1970s there were more than two thousand kids involved with the program on a yearly basis. Every year there seemed to be challenges meeting the program budget, but Sugar Ray would just start making his rounds, hat in hand: He'd go to Motown, to Capitol Records, to Warner Brothers; he'd glide by the stores on Rodeo Drive, throw a little shadowboxing, give them his spiel about the kids; he'd go over to UCLA and to USC asking for contributions. There were those who felt such glad-handing was beneath him, but he said anything he did for the kids made him feel larger. Somehow he always managed to make up for the budget shortfall. And he kept going, year to year, the kids going off to high school or college, then coming back over to the foundation, looking for Mr. Robinson, looking for Mrs. Robinson, wrapping their arms around both of them all over again. It was like having a large, extended family.

Life often intruded. Robinson's father, Walker Smith, died in 1969. He flew back East in 1981 for the funeral of George Gainford. George had spent his last years traveling up and down the East Coast, looking for another great prizefighter. He'd cough and wheeze in small hotel rooms, then in the morning get himself over to the local fight gym. His long association with Sugar Ray Robinson still netted him respect and entrée—but he never found another Sugar Ray. Robinson's mother, Leila, died in 1987.

He never complained, but Sugar Ray Robinson was fairly broke. There never was enough money to move into one of the more upscale neighborhoods of Los Angeles, like Hancock Park. He told people he felt richer than ever: the kids, the youth work. "I've got friends" is how he explained his financial survival. "I borrow five grand, I pay back three. I borrow three, and pay two. Then something drops in, and I pay everybody." The days of the pink Cadillac with the "RR" license plates were gone. He now drove a little red Pinto. He damn near had to squeeze himself into the thing. Every Sunday, though, he'd take Mrs. Robinson out to dinner at Mateo's, in Westwood. Movie stars, lovely china, white cloth napkins, soft conversation.

In 1979, Sugar Ray Robinson traveled to Washington, D.C., where he received an award from the Congressional Black Caucus for his work with youth. He felt mighty proud, regaling the politicians with stories of the kids in his program. It wasn't until 1982 that he dropped in on Manhattan. He and Millie took a room at the St. Regis. Autumn in New York; he used to drive it with the top down. Dave Anderson, his cowriter on the autobiography, threw a party for him. The guests swirled around the champion.

"Where the fuck is everybody?" he asked *New York Post* reporter Pete Hamill. (Millie had politely asked the reporters to refrain from trying to do long interviews.)

Many had moved to the warmer climes in Florida. For every Manhattan fight gym that had closed, there was another one that had opened in Philadelphia, in Detroit, and some of the young fighters and managers had gone where the opportunities were. He went up to Harlem and shook his head: a lot of decay, a lot of misery. No lasting memory of what he had done in the community; no reminders of the days when he was bringing home Golden Gloves trophies, winning all those world championships. An apartment building had replaced his nightclub and barbershop. They were calling it urban renewal. He flew back home to Los Angeles.

Millie was after him about his blood pressure medication, about the hypertension. His ailments all seemed to worsen beginning in the early 1980s. He didn't want her to worry so much. He was put on various medications, but he loathed having to pop pills of any kind. Just as he abhorred visits to the hospital. It was a fear, rooted in his fight psyche: If he had been hurt in the ring, he'd plead with a doctor to follow him to his house and take care of him there. He feared being stuck in a hospital, being given bad news. Neighbors would still see him walking around the neighborhood, trying to get in his five miles; they turned to four miles, then three. He'd go get his out-of-town newspapers. Did he ever think, on those long walks, of Jimmy Doyle, the boxer he had killed, the young fighter who hailed from Los Angeles, who'd lived just a few miles away?

His old friend Mel Dick sensed something amiss on a visit. "I went to look for him over at the youth foundation," he recalls. "They told me he was shopping with Millie, over at Ralph's Market. He was down an aisle, and he was wearing a red satin jacket. He said, 'Hey, Mel,' soon as he saw me. But he was slurring the words. And I knew something was up. But no one let on."

Millie certainly wouldn't let on; it was as if his strong pride had settled inside of her. He had been diagnosed with Alzheimer's in 1984. Mel was worried enough that he came back a few months later with Bobbi, his wife. They all went to dinner at Mateo's. "He asked me, three times,'Hey, Mel, what are you doing now?' " says Dick. Millie asked Mel to persuade Sugar Ray to go to the hospital. He kept complaining about the foundation—that they needed him. "When we tried to get him to go into the hospital, he wouldn't listen," says Mel.

He finally relented, and was in and out of the hospital several times in 1987. Kids from the foundation came by, dropping off little get-well notes. Dave Anderson was out in Los Angeles in 1987 to cover the Super Bowl. He phoned and Millie invited him over. "As I came in, Ray was sitting in a chair," Anderson recalls. "And Millie leaned over to him and said, 'Ray, Ray, it's Dave.' He bounced up. He looked at me. Then he sat right back down.' It was one of the saddest things I'd ever seen." Still, Millie cooked dinner; she had invited a few guests to meet Anderson. "Every now and then someone would say something, and Ray would look up. But then, just like that, he'd go right back into a cocoon," says Anderson.

Reporters would come by the house, trying to get interviews, having heard word that the great prizefighter was ailing. Greg Moore was a young journalist with the Cleveland *Plain Dealer.* He'd been an amateur fighter in his youth, and Sugar Ray was an idol. He found himself out in California, on vacation, so he went over to West Adams, having found out Sugar Ray's address. He went up and knocked. Millie opened the door. He introduced himself and asked if he could meet Sugar Ray; he wanted to do a story. "She said she'd have to charge money for the interview, and I told her I couldn't do that," recalls Moore. He left without his story, but he did get some souvenir brochures and a few pictures.

Sugar Ray spent much of January through April in bed, a sick man. Then Millie noticed something; it had begun in April. He would fold his arms across his chest and his fists would be balled. Every night, those charcoal-colored fists laid across his chest. She couldn't bear to open them.

On the morning of April 12, she heard some labored breathing. She checked on him, then found herself trying to revive him. Unable to, she rushed for the phone. The ambulance arrived within minutes. He was taken to the Brotman Medical Center in Culver City. But there was nothing they could do, and fifteen minutes after his arrival, the great prizefighter died. It was 10:09 in the morning, Pacific time. The final autopsy would show he died of heart failure. There was also the Alzheimer's and the hypertension. He was sixty-seven years old.

By early afternoon of the day he died, a great many of the children from his foundation were seen out on their porches in the neighborhoods of Los Angeles, openly weeping.

Tributes came from all over the world. The great fighters, his foes, sent condolences. Photo spreads in newspapers provided a cumulative portrait, a figure both dazzling and ferocious: in high hat and tails, in tailored gabardine suit; or in the ring, firing a muscled left hook into Bobo Olson. The obituary writers strained to find comparisons for his sartorial splendor, his fighting prowess, but they came up short no matter how they turned their memories inside out. He had been an original—at once vintage and new.

"Let's sing a song for Sugar Ray Robinson," Pete Hamill wrote on the front page of the *New York Post.* "Get Miles on the horn and Max on drums, and play it in all the night places of the world."

How many children, in the end, had he saved? How many dreams had his foundation set loose? He'd wondered about such things on his daily walks. Sometimes he would knock on Wright Fillmore's door with another idea, something for the kids. "The best," Sugar Ray Robinson had started saying toward the end of his life, "is always fragile."

The funeral took place at the West Angeles Church of God and Christ in Los Angeles. The limos were parked deep; among the two thousand in attendance were former governor Edmund G. Brown, Motown founder Berry Gordy, California Assembly Speaker Willie Brown, singer Lou Rawls, and actresses Elizabeth Taylor and Barbara McNair. The sun was shining. The former fight champions Bobo Olson, Archie Moore, and Ken Norton were easily recognized.

Inside the ornate church, flowers covered the sides of the beige coffin. Children from Robinson's youth foundation wept some more. Many wondered if the foundation would continue. (It would.) Elizabeth Taylor—there had always been a good seat for her and Richard Burton at Sugar Ray's nightclub—walked down the aisle holding Millie's hand. "Elizabeth loved Ray," says Mel Dick. Mel tried to find Edna Mae; he knew she was there somewhere. Then someone told him she was indeed there, sitting toward the back. She was wearing a blonde wig, trying to disguise herself. Lou Rawls picked up a microphone during Jesse Jackson's eulogy and started singing "My Buddy," a plaintive ballad.

In the months and years to come—she died in 1995—an elegant lady was often spotted crossing the grounds of the Evergreen Cemetery. She had a lovely little sway to her stride, as if she were listening to some jazz melody playing in the recesses of her mind. It was Millie Robinson, flowers in hand, going to meet her prizefighter.

Langston Hughes died May 22, 1967, without ever having been able to get Sugar Ray to appear in one of his musical plays. (He thought Robinson would have been perfect for *Tambourines to Glory.*) His poetry and prose had swept across oceans, explaining a sepia world in such jubilant and expressive tones. Miles continued to struggle mightily with drugs. Still, in his later years, he could be spotted at boxing gyms from Manhattan to San Francisco, going a couple rounds with some young pugilists. He'd regale them afterward with tales of Sugar Ray. One of his last recordings was with Shirley Horn: *You Won't Forget Me.* Miles, like Sugar Ray, had fallen in love with the West Coast; he died in Santa Monica in 1991. Lena Horne opened on Broadway in 1981 in a one-woman show. She looked luminous, her voice shatteringly strong. She won many honors for the engagement, among them a Tony. In 2008 she celebrated her ninety-first birthday in Manhattan. Call them all—Sugar Ray coming out of retirement to reclaim a championship belt—great Second Acts that possessed magic and made their America take notice.

Imagine them, once again, in front of that long mirror inside the great prizefighter's nightclub, setting off on their unknown journeys.

epilogue

I AM DRIVING into Sugar Ray's Detroit, around some of the very streets he knew as a child. Another world champion prizefighter lives here. His name is Hilmer Kenty. In 1980 he became world lightweight champion by defeating Ernesto España. Kenty first arrived in Detroit from Columbus, Ohio, on New Year's Eve, 1979. He was raised by a single mother; his Black Bottom in Columbus was the Windsor Terrace housing project. When he landed in Detroit he had five hundred bucks to his name and a run-down automobile. "They used to talk about the Brewster Recreation Center and Sugar Ray and Joe when I first got here. All the old-timers remembered them," he says, sitting in his television room. He still looks fit. His red championship belt is in a nearby glass case. He fought a lot of his early fights at the old Olympia, the venue where Sugar Ray fought so many times. Hilmer Kenty was such an underdog in his championship bout that bettors out in Las Vegas didn't even draw odds. Howard Cosell called the Kenty-España fight and seemed stunned like everyone else. "One of my trainers had said to me, 'All you can do for a fighter is teach him the basics, then you have to let him go.'" He says in big fights the world, the audience, tends to go silent. "You don't hear anything but your cornerman because you're used to hearing his voice a lot." Over the next couple of hours we sit watching Sugar Ray on a screen, studying some of the old fights in their glorious black-and-white texture. Sugar Ray is going after Basilio just now. "You see how Robinson throws the combination? That's what Ali got from Robinson. Robinson got power from each of his punches. I'd have power maybe behind four of my punches. Robinson had power behind each punch." (There is a story that, in Kenty's mind, explains the power of the middleweight. One day during training, with his manager away on the road, he itched to get some work in. There was no one at the gym but a middleweight. A manager would never allow a lightweight to spar with a middleweight. "He threw a punch and broke my collar-bone," Kenty says of that middleweight.) He says a key to Robinson was his legs. "If you don't have legs, you don't have anything. There is nothing like having a guy come at you with punches and your legs are gone. Take a look at his legs. They're bent. That's why he can punch with movement, because he's in a good boxer's position. His legs are underneath him. Plus, he looks *pretty* doing it. It's a different thing to win and look pretty doing it. You gonna get paid more." Before he turned pro, Hilmer had an amateur fight out in Las Vegas. After one victory, he got to shake the great prizefighter's hand. He just stared at Sugar Ray. Another video: Robinson and Rocky Graziano. "You can't teach people how to put themselves in the right position to land that kind of uppercut," he says of a just-delivered blow. For years Kenty wondered how Sugar Ray could knock someone out while backing away from them. "I really can't explain that." Hilmer stands up, takes a fighter's position. "I guess he had his foot planted just right. You think someone taught him that? Didn't nobody teach him that." He also says: "One of the things Sugar Ray was so successful at is he put a lot of punches together. Punches in bunches. A lot of times the guy never saw the punch that knocked him out. One of the mistakes I made is that I didn't watch his filmed fights while I was training. That's a big regret of mine." A not-so-old world champion stands in the driveway, waving goodbye.

It is not just the boxing, of course, that has made so many fighters—from Joe Louis to Muhammad Ali to Tommy Hearns to Hilmer Kenty to Sugar Ray Leonard (the genesis of his nom de guerre obvious) to Oscar De La Hoya—believe Sugar Ray was the best ever. It was the aura and greatness he forged through his own will. And yet, the question of his greatness has to take in more than just the ring. Sugar Ray Robinson was the cool narrator of boxing's history. He seemed to say, from the earliest: This is where the sport came from, and this is where I plan to take it. He pushed boxing in a new direction, giving it something it had never had—a ballast of music and style. Boxing ruined men because they never tamed the sport; he tamed it to fit his own emotions and resolve, and this is why artists and poets found in him more than they found in the average champion. He made them feel he understood the recesses from which their own art sprang. They sensed an originality, the celebration of discipline and genius. He was beyond fads and possessed a certain hauteur. Poseurs assaulted his pride and vulgarity angered him. The Speed Graphic camera tried to catch his quickness but he seemed faster than the flash: a dark ghost of the ring. He made calculations in the ring that took him beyond vengeance, and the citizenry realized it, which is why so many clamored to see him when his fights were first being broadcast on TV. He was like something ferocious that had been let out of an enclosure, and he made the action resemble a fast and dazzlingly tight Broadway musical. This was boxing, but it was something else: a cultural force being unleashed and witnessed. Before him, fighters who wished to entertain in the ring took on a clownish air; he was the boxer as entertainer, but relentlessly serious while entertaining. He studied the sport like an archaeologist, digging up secrets that only abetted his demonic gifts. No fighter ever knocked him out. Maxim had dropped him, of course, but it was in the heat and considered a TKO as opposed to an uncontested knockout. What he had was greatness; it is why he has become such a touchstone, a point of reference in the vaunted history of the sport. The final record stands at 173 wins, 19 losses, and 6 draws against a backdrop of a quarter century spent in the ring. It is easy and far too simple to keep making the pound-for-pound claim; the arc of his fighting career demands a deeper consideration. He lives because he lies beyond imitation. He is, as Stravinsky was to music, a wonder, a mystery, a piece of time.

Two of Sugar Ray's contemporaries, Rocky Graziano (*Somebody Up There Likes Me*) and Jake LaMotta (*Raging Bull*), were both subjects of Hollywood movies. With his epic life, continental style, championship belts, riveting comeback, supple intelligence, race-defying posture—not to mention the debt all fighters owe him because of his battles on behalf of income inequality with TV and radio revenues—it seems a missed opportunity that Robinson's life has yet to be added to that medium. Upon the anniversary rerelease of Martin Scorsese's *Raging Bull*, the film critic David Thomson observed that "to miss Sugar and fall on LaMotta suggests something very different on Scorsese's mind, and something tricky to spell out." Sugar Ray had less than five minutes in the LaMotta biopic.

Just weeks after his death, officials at Salem Methodist Episcopal Church—where it had all begun for him with the Salem Crescent Athletic Club—announced plans for a gala tribute in honor of the prizefighter. And on a Sunday afternoon in June, they gathered in Harlem. There was Evelyn, his sole surviving sister. She looked beautiful in a black dress, pearls, white heels, white hat, white gloves: that Robinson style. There was former champion Floyd Patterson; attorney and future mayor of New York City David Dinkins. The low-pitched voices were broken by louder voices: The Bull. Madison Square Garden officials may have ignored Jake LaMotta, but not the ministers of Salem. There was Honi Coles, the tap dancer, and Ralph Cooper, the old impresario from Sugar Ray's nightclub act. There were members of the Copasetics, a smooth dance ensemble. There were some still-lovely ladies who used to dance in the Harlem nightclubs of the thirties and forties. Five hundred people showed up. The organizers had expected more but were happy with the crowd.

Inside the church, at the pulpit, there were memories of Walker Smith Jr., as he was when he first burst upon the scene—the scrawny kid from Detroit who had seemed so devoted and relentless. There were memories of the great fights at the Garden: LaMotta was asked to rise, and that still tough-looking man seemed softened by the reverential applause. "It's about the things he stood for," said Rev. Robert Royal, one of the event's organizers, speaking of Robinson. "We have brought together today people who haven't seen each other for years." Bodies were gently swaying in seats. Heads rocked into amens. It was as if that pink Cadillac were still parked right outside. Rev. Thomas Grissom, a member of the Salem ministry, pointed out the pew where Sugar would sit on Sunday mornings. "He always had an entourage of no less than twelve," he recalled. "They'd sit down and we'd say, 'Well, we can have church now.' "

Afterwards, Evelyn Robinson led the assembled group up Seventh Avenue. They were carrying a fifteen-foot-long banner with the words "Salem Crescent Athletic Club" printed on it. City officials had provided a police escort during the walk. Over at the site of his old nightclub, they unveiled a plaque:

WALKER SMITH JR.
Sugar Ray Robinson

CHAMPION OF CHAMPIONS
May 3, 1921–April 12, 1989

A sepia-toned picture of the fighter appeared in the plaque's center.

The following weekend, there were salutes and toasts to Sugar Ray Robinson at the Showman's Café, at the Casablanca Café, at 22 West Restaurant, at many of the bars and nightclubs up and down the streets of Harlem. He was yet again, as he had always dreamed, a part of the soliloquies sweeping around town as men and women discussed him: Swirling beneath the ring light of Madison Square Garden as a Golden Glover; taking the welterweight crown from Tommy Bell in that tough fifteen-rounder; cackling with Duke Ellington and Miles inside his nightclub; gliding into a eatery with Army buddy Joe Louis and forking into slices of sweet potato pie; sitting in the back of his top-down convertible during the parade after he won the first of those five middleweight crowns; cutting a dance step at the Savoy; catching the boat for Paris and returning with gifts for his barmaids and doormen; walking Lena to the front door of his club; sharing a low-pitched conversation with Langston Hughes out in front of the Hotel Theresa; turning in the winter light on the street corner, his trench coat wrapped just so, the black fedora in his hand; having a manicure at his barbershop and seeing the faces of children pressed against the window, watching him with their moon-wide eyes; climbing into the Cadillac with Chico the midget behind the wheel. And rolling away, waving to all the sweethearts, off to take on the very best while the world shuddered with anticipation. Who is to say that, in the harsh and terrifying world he sprang from, it wasn't the beautiful end of a beautiful story?

acknowledgments

MY FIRST EXPERIENCE with professional boxing came as a cub reporter in Columbus, Ohio, in the late 1970s. I worked for a weekly publication, sent over to the fairgrounds coliseum to cover bouts. (Sugar Ray Robinson fought in Columbus once—in 1950, before I was born—and he dispatched someone by the name of Cliff Beckett in three rounds.) Even as a young reporter, I was transfixed by the sport, its silhouetted figures—our coliseum was so huge it doubled as a rodeo site—beneath the glow of light and coming right into my widening gaze. Even then, traveling around with some of those fighters, among them Bill Douglas, whose son Buster would grow up to become heavyweight champion of the world, I knew this: A fighter's life was often as fascinating outside the ring as inside it. Bill, a fearsome middleweight, was never less than warm and generous toward me and my questions about the boxing business. I can't help but think that something between my curiosity and this mysterious sport was lit back then.

As to the middleweight who dominates this chronicle, the first individual I ever met who had known Sugar Ray, who, in fact, as a kid played bumper pool with him in his Los Angeles home, was Peter Gethers. Peter grew up to become an esteemed book editor at Knopf. Who knows if something had been lit for him back when he met the great prizefighter? I'm inclined to think so. Peter listened to my passion for Sugar Ray, read the proposal, and confided to me: "I've been waiting on someone to come to me wanting to write the Sugar Ray biography." This book marks the third in a trilogy—Adam Clayton Powell Jr., Sammy Davis Jr., now Sugar Ray—of enigmatic American lives that have deeply fascinated me. Peter has given his gifts to the latter two, and I'm hugely fortunate.

Every time Claudia Herr, the brilliant Knopf editor, laid her eyes and pencil upon this book, it got better. Her questions were shrewd and her insights bountiful. She obliged my deep curiosity about the cultural swirl around Sugar Ray and then offered suggestions on how to make it all— Lena's voice, Miles's music, Langston's prose—work around the main figure. I simply could not have done better than the Gethers-Herr dynamic. Also at Knopf I thank Sonny Mehta, Kathy Zuckerman, Brady Emerson, Christina Malach, Abby Weintraub, Maggie Hinders, Victoria Pearson, and Holly Webber.

My agent, Esther Newberg, grew up in Connecticut hearing stories of the great Willie Pep (boon buddy to Sugar Ray) from her father. This experience would come to pique her interest in Robinson himself. She understood the scope of this project and championed it every step of the way. She is fearlessly unique.

A writer worries, wondering if friends care to hear just one more conversation about their biographical subject, then one more after that. I feel blessed. These friends never doubted: Sabrina Goodwin Monday, Steve Flannigan (who delved into his archives and sent fight tapes), Carol Tyler, Cindy Bitterman, Serena Williams, Professor Valerie Boyd (whose invite to the University of Georgia as Visiting Writer provided a welcome break), Dick Rhodes, Tom Mulvoy, Larry Young, Peggy King, Tina Moody, Dave Lieber, my nephew Tony Stigger, and the folks at Politics and Prose. I also thank Mary Jo Green, Warren Tyler, Marty Anderson, and Jerry Hammond for the roundtable discussions and four-star in-house dining.

Larry James, Michael Coleman, and Jerry Saunders have my gratitude.

Lynn Peterson—whom I first met in a bookstore some years back—took time to find the obscure boxing book and send it my way, not to mention the wonderful music of Miles. She is special.

This book is dedicated to three longtime allies. I've known Phil Bennett for two decades now, beginning in Boston, when we were young reporters awash in newspapering, where we used to hang out at the Brattle Theatre ("Forget it Jake. It's Chinatown") watching movies, then at the *Washington Post,* where he served as managing editor before joining Duke University as professor of journalism and public policy. Peter Guralnick, fellow biographer (Elvis, Sam Cooke), has been a years-long model to me of discipline, focus, and graciousness. Listening to him discuss Sugar Ray delighted and inspired me. Greg Moore used to be an amateur boxer; now he's editor of the *Denver Post.* It was in Colorado at his gorgeous hacienda beside the mountains where I first started talking to him about Sugar Ray. His enthusiasm was infectious. Later he sent me some Sugar Ray files he had collected over the years that proved extremely helpful.

It was Deb Heard, formerly of the *Washington Post,* who extended a leave of absence to complete this book, and I thank her. Len Downie, former editor of the *Post* and now a teacher and novelist, brought me to the newspaper. The preternaturally cool Steve Reiss, my story editor at the *Post,* has taught me things about the craft of writing I shall not forget. Also at the

Post I would like to thank the inspiring Kevin Merida, as well as publisher Katharine Weymouth, Don Graham, Anton Ramkissoon, Lisa Frazier Page, Aimee Sanders, Frank Rose, Michael Cotterman, Julia Ewan, Jill Grisco, Cheryl Rucker, and Shirley Carswell. The graciousness of each has been unforgettable.

source notes

A BIOGRAPHY is a journey along a particular road. The navigation of this four-year odyssey was made so much more pleasant by individuals who took a special interest in the destination. Steve Lott of Bigfights sent every video of Sugar Ray Robinson in the ring that I requested. Then he sent tapes of other fighters from Robinson's era that he insisted I study. Jeff Brophy, of the Boxing Hall of Fame in Canastota, New York, never failed to answer a question, or provide materials. Brett Snyder found copies of vintage magazines. Bruce Martin and Betty Culpepper of the Library of Congress gave me office space in that wondrous institution to do research. I shall not forget an evening program—"The Great Punch-Out"—sponsored by the library, which took place, fortuitously, during my study there. I sat in a darkened theatre and watched Sugar Ray battle Jake LaMotta, then Randy Turpin. Even the moody black-and-white newsreel footage advertising the fights was rewarding to see. I like to think I experienced the same sensation watching those fights as fans felt in the days when they rushed to a theatre—on Broadway or in Kansas City—in the aftermath of a Robinson fight and watched it replayed on the big screen.

I am exceedingly grateful to those who welcomed me into their homes to talk about not only Sugar Ray but in many instances, Lena, Langston, and Miles as well. They are listed below, but five individuals truly stand out: Rev. Robert Royal and Jimmy Booker shared their memories of Sugar Ray's nightclub, as well as his last years in Harlem. Congressman Charlie Rangel helped me understand the Sugar Ray–Joe Louis dynamic. Emile Milne, a Rangel aide, was also helpful with Harlem sources. And Mel Dick, who knew Robinson for five decades—who seemed to sense the sensation that swept through me as I fingered the Robinson championship belt in his possession—sat with me for hours in Miami answering my endless questions. Others who were interviewed include: Hilmer Kenty, Jack Winchester, Carmen Basilio, David Dinkins, Billie Allen, Edward Peeks, Nat Hentoff, Dave Anderson, Jake LaMotta, Edward Allen, Richard Berardinelli (Joey Maxim's brother), Louis Stokes, Arthur Barnes, Jimmy Bivens, Jess Rand, Arthur Mercante, Ken Bristow, Lou

Duva, Artie Levine, Angelo Dundee, Gene Fullmer, Karen Fullmer, Budd Schulberg, Albert Murray, Evelyn Cunningham, Jimmy Breslin, Marty Plax, and Larry L. King.

(Note: All citations of win-loss records and dates of professional bouts are taken from *The Boxing Register* [4th edition], long considered the bible of fight data.)

selected bibliography

Anderson, Jervis. *This Was Harlem: A Cultural Portrait, 1900–1950.*
New York: Farrar Straus Giroux, 1983.

Armstrong, Henry. *Gloves, Glory and God: An Autobiography.*
Westwood, N.J.: Fleming H. Revell Company, 1956.

Baker, Jean-Claude, and Chris Chase. *Josephine: The Hungry Heart.* New
York: Cooper Square Press, 2001.

Beevor, Antony, and Artemis Cooper. *Paris After the Liberation:
1944–1949.* New York: Penguin Books, 2004.

Bernard, Emily, ed. *Remember Me to Harlem: The Letters of Langston
Hughes and Carl Van Vechten, 1925–1964.* New York: Knopf, 2001.

Birtley, Jack. *The Tragedy of Randolph Turpin.* London: New English
Library, 1976.

Blumenthal, Ralph. *Stork Club: America's Most Famous Nightspot and the
Lost World of Café Society.* Boston: Little, Brown and Company, 2000.

Boyle, Kevin. *Arc of Justice: A Saga of Race, Civil Rights and Murder in
the Jazz Age.* New York: Henry Holt, 2004.

Branch, Taylor. *Parting the Waters: America in the King Years: 1954–63.*
New York: Simon & Schuster, 1988.

Buckley, Lumet Gail. *The Hornes: An American Family.* New York:
Knopf, 1986.

Cavanaugh, Jack. *Tunney: Boxing's Brainiest Champ and His Upset of the
Great Jack Dempsey.* New York: Random House, 2006.

Cook, Richard. *It's About that Time: Miles Davis On and Off Record.* New York: Oxford University Press, 2007.

Cramer, Ben Richard. *Joe DiMaggio: The Hero's Life.* New York: Simon & Schuster, 2000.

Crouch, Stanley. *Considering Genius: Writings On Jazz.* New York: Basic Civitas Books, 2006.

Davis, Miles, with Quincy Troupe. *Miles: The Autobiography.* New York: Simon & Schuster, 1989.

Erenberg, Lewis. *Louis vs. Schmeling: The Greatest Fight of Our Generation.* New York: Oxford University Press, 2006.

Evans, Harold. *The American Century.* New York: Knopf, 2000.

Farrell, Bill. *Cradle of Champions: 60 Years of New York Daily News Golden Gloves.* Champaign, Ill.: Sports Publishing L.L.C., 2006.

Friedrich, Otto. *City of Nets: A Portrait of Hollywood in the 1940's.* New York: Harper & Row, 1986.

Fried, Ronald K. *Corner Men: Great Boxing Trainers.* New York: Four Walls Eight Windows, 1991.

Gabler, Neal. *Winchell: Gossip, Power and the Culture of Celebrity.* New York: Knopf, 1994.

Gingrich, Arnold. *Nothing but People: The Early Years at Esquire.* New York: Crown, 1971.

Goodwin, Doris Kearns. *No Ordinary Time: Franklin & Eleanor Roosevelt: The Home Front in World War II.* New York: Simon & Schuster, 1994.

Hajdu, David. *Lush Life: A Biography of Billy Strayhorn.* New York: Farrar Straus Giroux, 1996.

Halberstam, David. *The Fifties.* New York: Fawcett Columbine, 1993.

————. *What a Time It Was: The Best of W. C. Heinz on Sports.* San Francisco: Da Capo, 2001.

Hoff, Charles. *The Fights.* San Francisco: Chronicle Books, 1996.

Karnow, Stanley. *Paris in the Fifties.* New York: Times Books, 1997.

Kitt, Eartha. *Thursday's Child.* New York: Duell, Sloan and Pearce, 1956.

LaGumina, Salvatore. *WOP: A Documentary History of Anti-Italian Discrimination in the United States.* San Francisco: Straight Arrow Books, 1973.

LaMotta, Jake. *Raging Bull: My Story.* Englewood Cliffs, N.J.: Da Capo, 1970.

LaMotta, Vikki, and Thomas Hauser. *Knockout: The Sexy, Violent, Extraordinary Life of Vikki LaMotta.* Toronto: Sports Media Publishing, 2006.

Lemann, Nicholas. *The Promised Land: The Great Black Migration and How It Changed America.* New York: Knopf, 1991.

Lewis, David Levering. *When Harlem Was in Vogue.* New York: Knopf, 1981.

————. *W. E. B. DuBois: The Fight for Equality and the American Century, 1919–1963.* New York: Henry Holt, 2000.

Liebling, A. J. *The Sweet Science.* New York: North Point Press, 2004.

Litwack, Leon F. *Trouble In Mind: Black Southerners in the Age of Jim Crow.* New York: Knopf, 1998.

Manning, Frankie, and Cynthia R. Millman. *Frankie Manning: Ambassador of Lindy Hop.* Philadelphia: Temple University Press, 2007.

Maraniss, David. *Rome 1960: The Olympics that Changed the World.* New York: Simon & Schuster, 2008.

Margolick, David. *Beyond Glory: Joe Louis vs. Max Schmeling, and a World on the Brink.* New York: Vintage, 2006.

Mead, Chris. *Champion: Joe Louis, Black Hero in White America.* New York: Scribner's, 1985.

Meier, August, and Elliott Rudwick. *Black Detroit and the Rise of the UAW.* Ann Arbor: The University of Michigan Press, 2007.

Mercante, Arthur, with Phil Guarnieri. *Inside the Ropes.* Ithaca, N.Y.: McBooks Press, 2006.

Milford, Nancy. *Savage Beauty: The Life of Edna St. Vincent Millay.* New York: Random House, 2001.

Miller, Hack, and Gene Fullmer. *The Story of Gene Fullmer.* Unpublished manuscript, 1994.

Murray, Albert, and John F. Callahan. *Trading Twelves: The Selected Letters of Ralph Ellison and Albert Murray.* New York: Vintage, 2001.

Nichols, Charles H. *Arna Bontemps–Langston Hughes Letters, 1925–1967.* New York: Dodd, Mead & Company, 1980.

Parks, Gordon. *Voices in the Mirror: An Autobiography.* New York: Harlem Moon, 2005.

Rangel, Charles B., with Leon Wynter. *And I Haven't Had a Bad Day Since: From the Streets of Harlem to the Halls of Congress.* New York: St. Martin's Press, 2007.

Remnick, David. *King of the World.* New York: Random House, 1998.

Robinson, Sugar Ray, with Dave Anderson. *Sugar Ray.* New York: Viking, 1969.

Roberts, James B., and Alexander G. Skutt. *The Boxing Register,* 4th edition. Ithaca, N.Y.: McBooks Press, Inc., 2004.

Silverman, Jeff. *The Greatest Boxing Stories Ever Told.* Guilford, Conn.: Lyons Press, 2002.

Stovall, Tyler. *Paris Noir: African Americans in the City of Light.* Boston: Houghton Mifflin, 1996.

Szwed, John. *So What: The Life of Miles Davis.* New York: Simon & Schuster, 2004.

Ward, Geoffrey C., and Ken Burns. *Jazz: A History of America's Music.* New York: Knopf, 2000.

———. *Unforgivable Blackness: The Rise and Fall of Jack Johnson.* New York: Knopf, 2004.

Newspapers:

AN: *Amsterdam News*
CD: *Chicago Defender*
CPD: Cleveland *Plain Dealer*
CT: *Chicago Tribune*
DFP: *Detroit Free Press*
NYHT: *New York Herald Tribune*
NYT: *The New York Times*
WP: *The Washington Post*

notes

Prologue: Round Midnight

5 This fight isn't on TV: Nat Hentoff interview by author.

Say Goodbye to Walker Smith Jr.

11 The Flight out of Egypt: Lemann, *The Promised Land,* 16.

11 I am Sick of the South: Litwack, *Trouble In Mind,* 491.

12 I'm goin' to Detroit: Meier, *Black Detroit,* 5.

12 good salaries: Robinson, *Sugar Ray,* 7.

13 A city which is built: Boyle, *Arc of Justice,* 103.

14 He was a good dresser: Robinson, *Sugar Ray,* 9.

14 One time I hid in the rumble seat: ibid., 7.

15 Here I am: Boyle, *Arc of Justice,* 123.

17 The heroic defense of their homes: ibid., 221.

17 The law in America: ibid., 242.

17 I realized that defending [N]egros: ibid., 230.

18 Prejudices have burned: ibid., 333.

18 I ask you, gentlemen: ibid., 334.

18 We ate well: Robinson, *Sugar Ray,* 12.

19 The gray of winter: ibid., 13.

20 Sometimes we'd make a couple dollars: ibid., 26.

21 She'd give you a fucking beating: Breslin interview by author.

21 hot dogs and beans: Robinson, *Sugar Ray,* 24.

21 This nation asks for action: Evans, *The American Century,* 246.

23 A blue haze descended: Lewis, *When Harlem Was in Vogue,* 103.

23 Send it, and send it damn quick: ibid., 110.

23 Mom really had a time: Robinson, *Sugar Ray,* 24.

23 In Harlem he is called upon: Anderson, *This Was Harlem,* 319.

24 Harlem in those days: Royal interview by author.

25 St. Phillips was known: Barnes interview by author.

25 Salem Crescent was one of the top: Royal interview by author.

26 a strange perfume: Robinson, *Sugar Ray,* 37.

26 Sugar Ray had a nickname: Bristow interview by author.

27 You're only as good: Fried, *Corner Men,* xiii.

27 You got good moves: Robinson, *Sugar Ray,* 39.

29 Smitty, you gonna get killed: ibid., 42.

29 At first he didn't look: *Saturday Evening Post,* 12-9-1950.

31 Here's my flyweight: Robinson, *Sugar Ray,* 43.

31 As scared as I was: ibid., 46.

35 at top speed: *Watertown Daily Times,* 1-5-1939.

35 tossed leather with reckless abandon: ibid.

35 The little Negro: ibid.

35 That's a sweet fighter: Robinson, *Sugar Ray,* 53.

35 As sweet as sugar: ibid.

36 Sugar Robinson: *Watertown Daily Times,* 1-6-1939.

36 RAYMOND SCORES WIN: ibid.

36 born in Virginia: brochure, Mel Dick collection.

36 Walker Smith Jr.: Robinson, *Sugar Ray,* 61.

37 Ray's going to be world's champion: *Watertown Daily Times,* 4-13-1989.

39 unearth some unknown: Farrell, *Cradle of Champions,* 2.

41 It was a very depressed period: Mercante interview by author.

42 Among the more impressive youths: NYT, 3-7-1939.

42 Robinson took the fancy: ibid.

42 a roar of applause: Robinson, *Sugar Ray,* 69.

43 The greatest thrill: *Saturday Evening Post,* 12-9-1950.

43 the best showing: NYT, 2-20-1940.

43 He gamely made for his foe: "a spectacular knockout": NYT, 3-5-1940.

43 With a terrific right: ibid.

44 set the standard: ibid., 26.

44 Robinson never has lost: Robinson, *Sugar Ray,* 72.

45 His family is wealthy enough: WP, 2-20-1942.

46 He can come up with: Robinson, *Sugar Ray,* 74.

48 I moved out: *Sport* magazine, 8-1958.

48 of superb handling: WP, 2-20-1942.

48 In another era: ibid.

49 rates among the welters: *Ring,* 6-1942.

49 Speed to burn: ibid.

49 In order to achieve the greatness: ibid.

50 I had learned: Robinson, *Sugar Ray,* 73.

50 Robinson is a comparative novice: CD, 11-1-1941.

Sugar Ray's Uniform

56 Labor in America wants no war: Lewis. *W. E. B. DuBois,* Vol. 2, 462.

57 If you'd see both of them: Rangel interview by author.

58 I laid it solid: Erenberg, *The Greatest Fight,* 125.

59 For the benefit of: Anderson, *This Was Harlem,* 286.

59 We're going to do our part: ibid., 185.

60 Why Ma?: Otto Friedrich, *City of Nets,* 107.

60 Draft dodger!: ibid., 160.

61 Everything's over: Buckley, *The Hornes,* 151.

62 Lena Horne, a singer from the Downtown: ibid., 152.

62 And well, who is Lena Horne?: ibid., 159.

63 Now we have someone: ibid., 178.

65 superman: CD, 6-6-1942.

65 Anyone Jackie Wilson can hit: ibid.

65 It may seem odd: NYT, 2-19-1943.

66 Corp. Ray Robinson: *Ring,* 9-1943.

67 [t]he world's greatest boxing show: AN, 9-11-1943.

68 a quiet parable: *Life,* 9-13-1943.

68 RAY ROBINSON BOXES: CD, 4-24-1943.

68 JOE LOUIS SIGNS: ibid.

69 I turned to a friend: Allen interview by author.

69 It was a tremendous thing: Dundee interview by author.

71 Come on and fight: Ward, *Unforgivable Blackness,* 123.

71 You Niggers are getting beside yourselves: Litwack, *Trouble In Mind,* 442.

71 [W]e wanted to see Joe and you: Robinson, *Sugar Ray,* 120.

72 Is it true that the Negro troops: ibid.

72 I understand that you are giving orders: ibid., 121.

72 under orders: ibid.

73 crazy: ibid., 122.

73 When you complained: ibid.

75 Picking up tabs: ibid., 126.

75 [W]e knew there was more money: ibid., 126.

75 JOE DIMAGGIO SLAMS: Cramer, *Joe DiMaggio,* 208.

75 We'd congregate: Peeks interview by author.

77 Sugar had the same effect: Murray interview by author.

77 the heirs and continuators: Murray, *Trading Twelves,* xxiii.

78 The domestic scene: Goodwin, *No Ordinary Time,* 444.

78 Here is an historic town: ibid.

78 If these 'poor whites': ibid.

79 We realize the fact: ibid.

79 No nigger is goin' to join iron: ibid.

79 No use standin' round: Robinson, *Sugar Ray,* 123.

80 Soldier . . . your color: ibid.

81 That's Joe Louis: ibid.

82 If I was just an average G.I.: Erenberg, *The Greatest Fight,* 195.

83 Joe and I had a few laughs: Robinson, *Sugar Ray,* 124.

83 How a girl from Brooklyn: Buckley, *The Hornes,* 173.

83 Unlike most Negro chanteuses: ibid.

85 He was growing out of this world: Szwed, *So What,* 25.

86 Man, could that motherfucker: Davis, *Autobiography,* 44.

86 I thought I could play the trumpet: ibid., 50.

87 I wish to register herewith: Bernard, *Remember Me to Harlem,* 215.

87 if I did not wander: Nichols, *Bontemps-Hughes Letters,* 127.

88 I'm getting wonderful fan letters: ibid., 133.

88 Good news comes in: Goodwin, *No Ordinary Time,* 470.

88 If ever there was a time: ibid., 484.

89 [t]o put the touch: Robinson, *Sugar Ray,* 126.

90 I'd like to fight again: WP, 1-28-1943.

91 Four jacks: Robinson, *Sugar Ray,* 126.

92 Nurse . . . Nurse!: ibid., 127.

92 He was unable to give any information: ibid., 128.

94 So I just wrote it: Anderson interview by author.

94 conflicting versions: Halberstam, *What a Time It Was,* 90.

94 I'm sorry, but I just can't: ibid., 90.

94 He was a guy: Heinz interview by author.

95 I arrived in New York City: Davis, *Autobiography,* 51.

Esquire Men

99 He was, like them, an entertainer: Schulberg interview by author.

100 I would say: Royal interview by author.

101 In Harlem Sugar Ray hung around: Murray interview by author.

102 He had a great flair: Gingrich, *Nothing but People,* 23.

102 That was the Cadillac page: ibid., 93.

103 the color line: ibid., 95.

103 He knew that this kid: ibid.

104 I wanted to yell Eureka: ibid.

104 To analyze its name: ibid., 102.

104 Conceived during the Bank Holiday: ibid., 142.

104 All these guys were influenced: Murray interview by author.

105 become my cup of tea: ibid., 290.

105 The most important influences: Barnes interview by author.

106 for a justifiable place: *Esquire Jazz Book,* 1944 edition, 7.

106 By 1932 Joe Marsala: ibid., 9.

106 Sugar Ray wasn't the type: Breslin interview by author.

107 Over and above the beat: ibid., 87.

107 Featured as vocalist: ibid., 67.

107 A one-time lawyer: ibid., 66.

109 He was the unofficial ambassador: Royal interview by author.

110 the prettiest pair: Robinson, *Sugar Ray,* 90.

110 She walked with: Mel Dick interview by author.

110 Ray took Edna Mae: Robert Royal interview by author.

111 He really admired her: Allen interview by author.

111 You cannot steal: CD, 12-18-1943.

111 Edna Mae and Sugar: Billie Allen interview by author.

111 My business was: Robinson, *Sugar Ray,* 151.

112 Ray Robinson has class: AN, 10-10-1942.

112 The ungracious grumpy Mr. Parker's: ibid.

113 Robinson is impossible; I didn't need: Robinson, *Sugar Ray,* 131.

114 And the prices: AN, 1-18-1947.

116 The structure is a three-story: Anderson, *This Was Harlem,* 96–97.

117 nose trouble: *Newsweek,* 5-6-1946.

117 just where he has been: ibid.

117 He plays too rough: NYT, 12-20-1946.

117 Nobody wanted to fight Bell: Dundee interview by author.

118 I was taking Tommy Bell: Robinson, *Sugar Ray,* 134.

118 Will they stand up?: AN, 12-21-1946.

120 Gainford was brilliant: Royal interview by author.

121 That I, an American Negro: Bernard, *Remember Me to Harlem,* 241.

122 They were some country motherfuckers: Davis, *Autobiography,* 92.

122 *Esquire* magazine had voted me: ibid., 97.

122 one of the great welterweights: AN, 12-21-1946.

123 Tommy Bell's Right: ibid.

123 a sizzling left: AN, 12-28-1946.

123 like a cobra striking: NYT, 12-21-1946.

124 My face was on the floor: Robinson, *Sugar Ray,* 135.

124 The Harlemite was hurt: NYT, 12-21-1946.

124 staggered Robinson: ibid.

124 For Bell made a fight: NYT, ibid.

125 Clear that aisle: Robinson, *Sugar Ray,* 136; New York *Daily News,* 12-21-1946.

125 From the beginning: AN, 12-28-1946.

126 The stringy colored sensation: *Ring,* 6-1942.

126 We heard him and knew: Ward, *Jazz,* 306.

127 Nothing like it in town: AN, 12-28-1946.

127 Sugar Ray Robinson's cleverly designed bar: AN, 1-11-1947.

127 They didn't have Sugar Ray: Rangel interview by author.

128 He was a wonderful person: Royal interview by author.

128 **You'd ask yourself:** Barnes interview by author.

129 **And now the lights:** Robinson, *Sugar Ray,* 137.

130 **Outstanding Male Dressers:** AN, 1-4-1947.

130 **Bar hopping was so important:** Rangel interview by author.

131 **Duke Ellington used to come:** Allen interview by author.

132 **Outside on the sidewalk:** ibid.

132 **Sugar had gone down to Miami:** Manning interview by author.

132 **That car was the Hope Diamond:** Robinson, *Sugar Ray,* 155.

132 **A poem compresses much:** *Holiday* magazine, 4-1949.

133 **Golden girl:** ibid.

134 **He was generous:** Royal interview by author.

A Lovely Setup for the Old Man

137 **my boyhood idol:** Robinson, *Sugar Ray,* 114.

138 **being led across a river:** Armstrong, *Gloves, Glory and God,* 20.

139 **Oranges falling like manna:** ibid., 78–79.

139 **They weren't friendly:** ibid., 84.

140 **It was neither jab nor hook:** ibid., 127.

140 **I lived in Los Angeles:** Schulberg interview by author.

141 **Armstrong hooked two lefts:** NYT, 6-1-1938.

141 **Like a human tornado:** ibid.

141 **It was the easiest fight:** ibid.

141 **This was my last fight:** ibid.

143 *Shhh . . .* **be quiet:** Robinson, *Sugar Ray,* 113.

143 **He's trying to put a touch:** ibid., 114.

144 **Did you see what Mike Jacobs:** ibid.

145 **I'll never fight Armstrong:** ibid.

145 **Ray Robinson definitely does not want:** CD, 12-12-1942.

145 **promoters would be blowing:** AN, 10-3-1942.

145 **That's something few real fans:** ibid.

146 **You remember his first Golden Gloves:** Robinson, *Sugar Ray,* 115.

146 **God Forbid:** CD, 12-12-1942.

146 **[N]ever before has he met:** *St. Louis Post-Dispatch,* 8-26-1943.

147 **near capacity:** NYT, 8-27-1943.

147 **Rooster Hammond of Detroit:** CD, 10-9-1943.

147 **never a champion:** NYHT, 8-28-1943.

147 **merely pecked away:** NYT, 8-28-1943.

148 **Armstrong would snort:** ibid.

148 **The man who rose to fistic fame:** NYHT, 8-28-1943.

148 **spectacle:** NYT, 8-28-1943.

148 ROBINSON OUTPOINTS ARMSTRONG: NYHT, 8-28-1943.

148 OLD MASTER TAKES BEATIN': AN, 9-4-1943.

148 **I'm through:** *St. Louis Post-Dispatch,* 8-28-1943.

149 **I know it looked bad:** ibid.

149 **the greatest I ever; I never could:** ibid.

149 **At times Ray, failing to take:** ibid.

149 **The New York press was pretty bitter:** NYHT, 8-29-1943.

149 **It was highway robbery:** ibid.

149 **The boxing clients for years:** ibid.

150 **I couldn't hurt an old man:** Robinson, *Sugar Ray,* 115–116.

150 **The old speed was gone:** Armstrong, *Gloves, Glory and God,* 239.

151 **You're letting a million boys down:** ibid., 246.

151 **He had films of his fights:** *St. Louis Post-Dispatch,* 10-25-1988.

151 **To think that two guys:** ibid.

152 He had a lot of fantastic friends: ibid.

152 He'd charge a rhinoceros: *Los Angeles Times,* 10-25-1988.

Killer

158 I was Jack's press agent: CPD, 7-25-1981.

160 now that Ray is in training: *Cleveland Call & Post,* 6-14-1947.

160 New York's crack Negro boxer: NYT, 6-24-1947.

161 Don't know what all the fuss: ibid., 6-21-1947.

161 Not that I ever suspected: ibid.

162 Doyle could fight: Bivens interview by author.

162 He wasn't afraid of nothing: ibid.

163 Once again . . . has Johnson sent down: Silverman, *Greatest Boxing Stories,* 54.

164 A right to the body: NYT, 1-13-1945.

164 rugged: ibid., 1-31-1945.

164 Jimmy Doyle last night: ibid.

164 He was a good little fighter: Schulberg interview by author.

165 We hope to put Doyle away: CPD, 6-24-1947.

165 They insist the Californian: NYT, 6-24-1947.

166 rallied from way behind: CPD, 6-21-1947.

167 You see, Levine had hit me: *Cleveland Press,* 6-27-1947.

167 All's we gotta say: CPD, 6-24-1947.

168 A solid right cross: *Cleveland Call & Post,* 6-28-1947.

168 Man, . . . I threw everything at him: CPD, 6-25-1947.

169 GOOD LUCK, JIMMY: CPD, 6-25-1947.

169 The left hook that lifted Doyle: Los Angeles *Herald Express,* 6-25-1947.

171 I never seen anybody leave: Bertinelli interview by author.

171 I didn't think I hit him: CPD, 6-25-1947.

171 anything serious: *Cleveland Press,* 6-25-1947.

172 extensive damage: ibid.

172 I'm sure sorry: ibid.

172 He told me after the Levine fight: *Cleveland Press,* ibid.

172 unholy pressure: NYT, 6-26-1947.

172 no power whatsoever: ibid.

173 Why not consider this: *Cleveland Press,* 6-26-1947.

173 I will not identify him: ibid.

174 tip-top: NYT, 6-27-1947.

175 Did you personally rank Doyle: *Cleveland Press,* 6-26-1947.

175 Well, . . . Doyle had a very impressive record: ibid.

175 I'm not a physician, sir: ibid.

175 smart . . . evasive: *Cleveland Call & Post,* 7-5-1947.

175 If there are any manslaughter charges: *Chicago Daily Tribune,* 6-27-1947.

175 The rugged business of fisticuffs: *Cleveland Press,* 6-25-1947.

176 absolutely blameless: WP, 7-1-1947.

176 should not be considered negligent: ibid.

177 I don't know how it will affect: *Cleveland Call & Post,* 7-5-1947.

178 Well, did you notice: CPD, 6-26-1947.

178 Getting him in trouble: ibid.

179 You killed a man: NYT, 8-25-2006.

179 You don't have to tell everybody: ibid.

An Opera in Six Brutal Acts

183 I fought like I didn't deserve: LaMotta, *Raging Bull,* xi.

183 On the streets, it was the 'nigger': Royal interview by author.

187 A fight . . . is all of a piece: LaMotta, *Raging Bull*, 68.

187 The Italians who come: LaGumina, *WOP*, 63–64.

187 the dagoes: ibid., 75.

188 I cry to you with a million voices: Milford, *Savage Beauty*, 298.

188 "Justice Denied in Massachusetts": ibid., 299.

189 It was the first time: LaMotta, *Raging Bull*, 4.

190 nuts: ibid., 45.

190 goddam moron: ibid., 51.

191 home relief and boxing: ibid., 83.

191 LA MOTTA WINS FOURTH STRAIGHT: ibid., 83.

191 Many of those colored six-round fighters: ibid., 87.

191 You would just about have to kill: ibid.

193 a lot of shaking of the head: AN, 10-3-1942.

193 Robinson has an alarming tendency: ibid.

193 Sugar Ray was the boss: LaMotta interview by author.

193 Sugar Ray took on LaMotta: Dundee interview by author.

194 A fighter who performs in the windmill style: AN, 10-3-1942.

194 A surprisingly large number of boxing experts: CD, 10-3-1942.

194 The welterweights, you know, are tricky: LaMotta, *Raging Bull*, 87.

194 favored: ibid., 112.

194 hard puncher: ibid.

195 a flood of nerve-jarring right and left hooks: AN, 10-10-1942.

195 The Harlem fighter worked: NYT, 10-3-1942.

195 victim: ibid.

195 with the grace and artistry: AN, 10-10-1942.

195 There's a lot things: ibid.

196 Beating middleweights is among them: ibid.

196 He hit me one left hook: ibid.

196 a poor ignorant Italian: LaMotta, *Raging Bull*, 112.

197 I'm his good luck charm: *Detroit News*, 2-3-1943.

198 Not much space: ibid.

198 There's where you learned: ibid.

198 Oh, oh, I wonder how that gal: ibid.

199 I used to carry Joe Louis's gloves: ibid.

199 Yep . . . there's gonna be a jam session: ibid.

199 People pay too much attention: DFP, 2-3-1943.

200 Often one good punch: ibid.

200 When Ray defeated Jake: DFP, 2-2-1943.

200 It's His Big Night: DFP, 2-5-1943.

200 the gallery gods: ibid.

201 Jake stomped me: Robinson, *Sugar Ray*, 109.

201 The crowd let out a roar: DFP, 2-6-1943.

203 When Jacob LaMotta brought the Sugar Man: DFP, 2-9-1943.

203 When I met Ray in the Garden: *Detroit News*, 2-7-1943.

204 JAKE IS CITY'S CINDERELLA: DFP, 2-7-1943.

204 I still think I can defeat: CD, 2-13-1943.

204 END OF ROBINSON STRING: NYT, 2-7-1943.

204 had given Detroit a brand: DFP, 2-26-1943.

204 That's the biggest check: *Detroit News*, 2-7-1943.

206 This boxer is in unusually good condition: DFP, 2-25-1943.

206 Sugar Ray's Dynamite Knobs: ibid.

206 Ray is a boxer: *Detroit News*, 2-25-1943.

206 He'll have a tough time: ibid.

207 For a long time . . . Jake was a $25: ibid., 2-23-1943.

207 The crowd didn't like that: ibid., 2-27-1943.

207 and two jarring uppercuts: ibid.

208 trying for a knockout: ibid.

208 So deafening and so prolonged: ibid., 2-27-1943.

209 If they say I lost: ibid.

209 He really hurt me with a left: DFP, 2-27-1943.

209 I didn't lose it: LaMotta, *Raging Bull,* 119.

209 That's when I began to think: ibid.

210 Watching those guys: Dinkins interview by author.

211 and moves about the ring: CD, 1-27-1945.

211 This bout is a natural: ibid., 2-3-1945.

211 We never had such an advance sale: ibid.

211 If he does [win]: ibid.

212 Not since Joe Louis fought: ibid., 2-24-1945.

212 [A]ll you had to do was drop in: ibid., 2-24-1945.

215 All the rumors and suspicions: NYHT, 2-21-1945.

215 Every one likes Joe Louis: ibid.

216 They were out to kill: Mercante interview by author.

217 a definite legend: *New York Daily Mirror,* 2-14-1945.

217 There are only three or four pounds: NYHT, 2-22-1945.

218 pawing away at the body: *New York Daily Mirror,* 2-24-1945.

218 slow-thinking: ibid.

218 a murderous left hook: NYHT, 2-24-1945.

219 His left was a classic: ibid.

219 right crosses, upper cuts: AN, 3-3-1945.

219 one of the slickest bits: ibid.

220 Class . . . told against bull-like strength: NYT, 2-24-1945.

220 How LaMotta stood up: AN, 3-3-1945.

220 You don't keep fighting: LaMotta interview by author.

221 I was getting a little tired: AN, 3-3-1945.

221 There was a time: LaMotta, *Raging Bull,* 79.

222 I knew what I wanted: LaMotta interview by author.

224 What makes Robinson doubly anxious: CD, 8-25-1945.

225 the best money match: *Chicago Daily Tribune,* 9-25-1945.

225 We'll wager the best fists: CD, 9-8-1945.

225 ultimate goal is a fight: CT, 9-25-1945.

225 I still was no nearer a crack: LaMotta, *Raging Bull,* 121.

227 inspiring: *Chicago Daily Tribune,* 9-27-1945.

227 visibly tired: ibid.

227 out from nowhere: ibid.

228 close victory: ibid.

228 unpopular decision: ibid., 9-28-1945.

228 last ditch stand: AN, 10-6-1945.

228 And as in the others: PM (Marshall Field's newspaper), 9-27-1945.

228 LaMotta is the toughest man: CD, 10-6-1945.

228 I thought I won: CT, 9-28-1945.

229 The only thing I really wanted: LaMotta, *Raging Bull,* 151.

229–232 All quotes in "Interlude: Dreaming Sugar": Dick interview by author.

232 We actually left home: Buckley, *The Hornes,* 213.

233 dripping ermine: ibid.

234 It was a special club: Stovall, *Paris Noir,* 149.

234 quadruple pearl choker: Buckley, *The Hornes,* 214.

234 I wanted the instruments: Davis, *Autobiography,* 118.

234 Even the band and the music: ibid., 126.

235 Miles didn't go there: Szwed, *So What,* 197.

236 Practically everybody is going: Nichols, *Bontemps-Hughes Letters,* 272.

236 the mark of a true professional: Video/Bigfights, 11-8-1950.

237 It wasn't usual for nine Negroes: Robinson, *Sugar Ray,* 169.

237 The boxer, Sugar Ray Robinson: ibid.

237 captured Paris more completely: CT, 3-20-1951.

238 Yet here I was, fifteen years old: LaMotta, *Knockout,* 48.

238 She looked like a beauty-contest winner: LaMotta, *Raging Bull,* 119.

239 He was jealous of other men: LaMotta, *Knockout,* 64.

239 I remember one of the Robinson fights: LaMotta, *Raging Bull,* 148.

239 be trying his rushing: NYT, 11-14-1947.

240 Then he backed across the ring: ibid., 11-15-1947.

240 numerous lefts and rights: ibid.

240 Stop the fight!: ibid.

240 FOX KNOCKS OUT LAMOTTA: ibid.

241 The popularity of LaMotta here: NYT, 6-15-1949.

242 I want an authentic world middleweight: ibid.

242 And it was a thing of beauty: LaMotta, *Knockout,* 76.

243 against a huskier stronger: NYT, 6-17-1949.

243 white silk stockings: LaMotta, *Knockout,* 76.

243 That was Jake's moment: ibid., 76.

244 With all my strength: NYT, 10-29-1949.

244 Having accomplished first part: ibid.

244 had plunged the nation: ibid.

244 What did you expect?: LaMotta, *Knockout,* 77.

246 SEE YOU FEBRUARY 14: Robinson, *Sugar Ray,* 179.

246 This exclusive DuMont picture: NYT, 2-14-1951.

246 Davega Will Take Any Size: ibid., 2-15-1951.

247 Keep it: Robinson, *Sugar Ray,* 183.

247 You look too cool: ibid., 184.

247 This broadcast tonight: Video/Bigfights, 2-14-1951.

247 The bout the world's been waiting for: ibid.

248 Ray's lean ribs: CT, 2-15-1951.

248 A right obviously hurt: Husing, Video/Bigfights, 2-14-1951.

248 I just couldn't level away: WP, 2-15-1951.

248 . . . the more I kept punching: ibid.

249 a dying swan gesture: ibid.

249 Then he pulled the switch: ibid.

249 No man can endure: Husing, Video/Bigfights, 2-14-1951.

249 I'm here with you: WP, 2-15-1951.

250 ROBINSON TKO'S LAMOTTA: ibid., 2-15-1951.

250 spectacular: NYT, 2-16-1951.

250 At least a million Hoosiers: WP, 2-16-1951.

251 Physically and psychologically: LaMotta, *Knockout,* 83.

254 W.W., I did the best: Video/Bigfights, 2-14-1951.

255 He had always scoffed: Gabler, *Winchell,* 348.

255 Now, sensing his: ibid., 348.

256 When I die, if I had: ibid., 350.

256 Winchell really wanted Sugar Ray: Rand interview by author.

256 You're with me: Robinson, *Sugar Ray,* 152.

257 Extraordinary Limited Engagement!: Baker, *Josephine,* 305.

258 It was like the revelation: ibid., 6.

258 Well . . . last night after the show: ibid., 116.

258 Who the fuck let her in?: Blumenthal, *The Stork Club,* 164.

260 I wish you wouldn't, champ: Gabler, *Winchell,* 414.

260 I can't tell you how: ibid., 416.

260 Why are you here?: Baker, *Josephine,* 310.

261 I will not go to the Stork Club: Blumenthal, *Stork Club,* 179.

261 a radio trial: ibid., 172.

261 to defend the honor: Baker, *Josephine,* 313.

261 The suspect list: Blumenthal, *Stork Club,* 178.

261 But of all those things: ibid., 174.

262 an ally of black people: Baker, *Josephine,* 313.

262 Winchell's valet: Gabler, *Winchell,* 429.

262 blood would flow: ibid.

264 it was like trying to console: Robinson, *Sugar Ray,* 211.

264 What's the use: Mead, *Champion,* 259.

264 I didn't want to make the same mistake: Robinson, *Sugar Ray,* 211.

264 It seemed a terrible punishment: Mead, *Champion,* 265.

Around (a Part of) the World in Fifty Days

268 I will pay the shipping charge: Robinson, *Sugar Ray,* 186.

270 They were of migrant workers: Parks, *Voices,* 87.

270 You have to get at the source: ibid., 106.

271 Chico was a badass dude: Brown interview by author.

272 The return of Napoleon Bonaparte: Parks, *Voices,* 188.

272 I loved to drive around Paris: Robinson, *Sugar Ray,* 188.

272 On the Champs-Elysées: *Life,* 7-23-1951.

273 Paris' No. 1 celebrity: *Time,* 6-25-1951.

274 Sure, if she wants to: *Life,* 7-23-1951.

274 about Detroit and Georgia: Robinson, *Sugar Ray,* 193.

274 at his feet: Parks, *Voices,* 193.

275 But even this blow: NYT, 5-27-1951.

275 You are too good: Robinson, *Sugar Ray,* 194.

275 a combination of smashing blows: WP, 6-25-1951.

276 Foul! Foul! Foul!: ibid.; "Just like": ibid.

278 There were no workouts: Parks, *Voices,* 193.

278 Robinson slept late: WP, 7-10-1951.

278 blues and boogie-woogie: *Life,* 7-10-1951.

279 take Turpin apart: Parks, *Voices,* 193.

279 forlorn hope: *Times* of London, 7-10-1951.

280 The way Turpin leapt: Birtley, *The Tragedy of Randolph Turpin,* 27.

281 This is the first time: WP, 7-10-1951.

281 Why is Ray doing this: Parks, *Voices,* 194.

281 One may smile a little: *Times* of London, 7-10-1951.

282 have been designed: London *Observer,* 7-15-1951.

283 lefts from the start: *Times* of London, 7-11-1951.

283 No cause to worry: Parks, *Voices,* 194.

283 Turpin was outpunching me: Robinson, *Sugar Ray,* 202.

283 whiplash lefts and rights: *Times* of London, 7-11-1951.

283 His eye!: London *Observer,* 7-15-1951.

284 I could tell it was: Robinson, *Sugar Ray,* 201.

284 It's bad: ibid., 202.

284 Hold on, Sugar: *Life,* 7-23-1951.

284 Get him: ibid.

284 from then on he couldn't: NYT, 7-11-1951.

285 I hope I'm able to keep this: *Los Angeles Times,* 7-11-1951.

285 I thought I was winning: NYT, 7-11-1951.

285 You were a real champion: ibid.

285 Come on, everybody: London *Observer,* 7-15-1951.

285 RAY ROBINSON LOSES: *New York Times,* 7-11-1951.

285–286 Randolph Turpin upset: *Times* of London, 7-11-1951.

286 TITLE TO TURPIN: *Los Angeles Times,* 7-11-1951.

286 It was boxing's biggest upset: *Current Biography,* Turpin entry, 1951.

286 triumphal tour: London *Observer,* 7-15-1951.

286 This'll do us no harm: ibid.

287 I'll kill him: Parks, *Voices,* 194.

287 I don't think I even want to see: *Life,* 7-23-1951.

287 MUM . . . I LOST ON DECISION: AN, 7-14-1951.

287 But there is something really charming: London *Observer,* 7-15-1951.

288 you took too many pictures: AN, 7-14-1951.

288 Ray, we don't know: ibid.

288 In some deep, black, stony: Baldwin, James, *Notes of a Native Son,* (Boston: Beacon Press, 1957), 158.

289 I call him Vince: NYT, 6-25-1951.

289 his fellow human beings: CD, 8-11-1951.

291 The title is only lent: NYT, 7-12-1951.

291 But Ray didn't want: Dick interview by author.

291 Ray . . . what are you gonna do: ibid.

291 He stood there: ibid.

291 Yeah, why don't you go over: ibid.

293 I had my father: ibid.

293 His red vest was adorned: NYT, 9-12-1951.

293 Not since the Marquis: CD, 9-15-1951.

294 patriotic duty: Robinson, *Sugar Ray,* 208.

294 Turpin has the youth: NYT, 9-12-1951.

294 towards the end of a long career: *Times* of London, 9-11-1951.

296 smarting under the terrific blows: NYT, 9-13-1951.

297 I paced myself slowly: ibid.

297 Robinson shook me: ibid., 9-15-1951.

298 ROBINSON KNOCKS OUT TURPIN: ibid., 9-13-1951.

298 a savage attack: ibid., 9-13-1951.

298 forgot what to do: ibid.

298 Drive me downtown: Liebling, *The Sweet Science,* 61.

299 As we approached the Theresa: ibid.

299 That was a Cadillac night: Robinson, *Sugar Ray,* 210.

Dreams

306 Ray didn't want people to think: Dick interview by author.

306 There was one instance: Breslin interview by author.

307 I would have taken that fellow: AN, 6-21-1952.

307 In a year or two: ibid., 9-22-1951.

308 was scoring solidly: NYT, 3-14-1952.

309 surprising battle: ibid.

309 cunning: ibid., 3-14-1952.

309 I never fought so hard: *San Francisco Chronicle,* 3-14-1952.

309 Olson is a clean fighter: ibid.

310 Now get me Robinson!: NYT, 4-16-1952.

310 tarnished with: ibid., 4-14-1952.

310 he slipped from so high: ibid.

310 His heart no longer: ibid.

310 well over the hill: AN, 4-12-1952.

311 I'll knock him out: NYT, 4-16-1952.

311 He came out of his corner: Robinson, *Sugar Ray,* 216.

311 with such breathtaking speed: NYT, 4-18-1952.

311 a rocking right: AN, 4-19-1952.

311 three inches further: ibid.

312 I'll meet you at the Archway: Dick interview by author.

312 I had it tonight: NYT, 4-17-1952.

312 Robinson is a cold-blooded machine: ibid., 4-18-1952.

312 Sooner or later you come: NYT, 4-17-1952.

313 enigma: AN, 7-5-1952.

314 was the man selling the tickets: Robinson, *Sugar Ray,* 218.

314 I'm just plain tired: AN, 3-22-1952.

315 Maxim is as good a fighter: Liebling, *Sweet Science,* 63.

316 Sugar Ray is no ordinary fighter: NYT, 6-23-1952.

316 You let me make: Robinson, *Sugar Ray,* 218.

316 I got as much right: ibid.

316 I can shoot you: ibid.

317 Have you ever fought a man: Liebling, *Sweet Science,* 67.

317 Most fighters jump rope: ibid., 68.

317 big-money men: AN, 6-28-1952.

317 We even referred to: NYT, 6-24-1952.

318 The car clips off: AN, 6-28-1952.

318 the new crop of glamour girls: ibid.

318 a full length coat-dress: ibid.

319 giving Maxim a boxing lesson: NYT, 6-26-1952.

319 I'm getting sleepy: Robinson, *Sugar Ray,* 221.

320 I thought I was being roasted: *Life,* 7-7-1952.

320 Can you stand up?: ibid.

321 He didn't knock me out: NYT, 6-27-1952.

321 The heat didn't get my brother: Berardinelli interview by author.

321 What have I got to gain: AN, 6-28-1952.

323 any man with two hands: *Time,* 6-25-1951.

323 Robinson thought he could sing: Breslin interview by author.

326 And I remember the day: Dick interview by author.

326 Here was the coldest concentration: Mead, *Champion,* 72.

The Very Thought of You Onstage

329 He'd have suits and sports jackets: Bristow interview by author.

330 a black motherfucking nigger: Davis, *Autobiography,* 169.

330 Sugar Ray looked like a socialite: ibid., 174.

331 Sugar Ray used to train there: ibid., 180.

331 That's where a lot of hip people: ibid., 182.

331 He'd be standing there: ibid.

331 He used to come up and tell everyone: ibid., 183.

332 I done got my feet caught: Bernard, *Remember Me to Harlem,* 282.

332 a running text: ibid.

332 a delicate and lovely fiction-document: ibid.

332 Langston Hughes' words: ibid.

333 Nightclubs were rarely affected: Buckley, *The Hornes,* 222.

334 A fighter can't go on forever: *Life,* 11-10-1952.

335 We were all underage: Dick interview by author.

335 One thing for sure, Ray: AN, 11-15-1952.

335 the tall, shapely showgirls: ibid.

336 Do you know the three quickest: Robinson, *Sugar Ray,* 229.

336 The guy is a superb clotheshorse: ibid., 228–229.

338 Most of the time: ibid., 231.

338 You not so tough: ibid., 229–230.

339 Even his closest friends: CD, 12-6-1952.

339 fairly dazzles the customers: AN, 10-17-1953.

340 Once I had the act down: Robinson, *Sugar Ray,* 231.

340 had to be bailed out: CD, 12-19-1953.

340 just an average dancer: ibid.

340 gentleman on and off stage: ibid., 5-15-1954.

341 a second rate entertainer: ibid., 5-8-1954.

341 star in the entertainment world: ibid.

341 I have been very happy: ibid.

341 One thing I realize: ibid.

342 I cannot say I am sore: ibid., 9-11-1954.

342 I guess they expected me: ibid.

342 He realized his act: Barnes interview by author.

344 Sometimes mine would be the only black face: *Life,* 12-19-1955.

346 You'd watch him jump rope: Duva interview by author.

Greatness Again

349 Sugar and I want to make a tour: NYT, 10-8-1954.

350 ROBINSON FLASHES SKILL: ibid., 11-30-1954.

351 he had been around: Robinson, *Sugar Ray,* 241.

351 looking like a gentleman: CD, 5-21-1955.

351 Sugar Ray even has the ladies: ibid., 2-5-1955.

351 When does the fight start?: ibid., 1-5-1955.

352 explosive right uppercut: NYT, 1-6-1955.

352 it was only a matter: ibid.

352 I'm the boss now: Robinson, *Sugar Ray,* 241.

352 His misses were wild: CD, 1-15-1955.

352 Jones is a little too tough: ibid.

353 We're not looking for soft touches: ibid.

353 If Robinson wants to box: ibid.

353 The fact remains that Robinson: ibid.

353 When I hit Joe Rindone: Robinson, *Sugar Ray,* 244.

354 Jones landed consistently: NYT, 1-20-1955.

354 Hey, Sugar!: CD, 1-29-1955.

354 The 30-month lay-off: ibid.

354 Sugar Ray Robinson hasn't got it: CT, 1-20-1955.

354 When you're through: CD, 1-29-1955.

355 When a Tiger Jones can lick him: NYT, 1-21-1955.

355 He kept saying: Dick interview by author.

355 How come you didn't: *Sport* magazine, 8-1958.

357 a hard hitter: Robinson, *Sugar Ray,* 259.

357 whacked with a baseball bat: ibid.

358 bombing right: NYT, 7-23-1955.

358 of the greatest rallies: ibid.

358 a great fighter: CD, 10-22-1955.

358 The bout will be a good one: ibid.

359 Will we be needing these gorillas: *Life,* 12-19-1955.

359 The world was moving: Robinson, *Sugar Ray,* 259.

361 the sweet sounds: ibid., 266.

361 a brooding genius: *Sport* magazine, 8-1958.

362 It turns out now: CD, 1-7-1956.

Battling

364 a muttered exchange: *Life*, 10-7-1957.
365 That didn't hurt: ibid.
365 machine gun bullets: NYT, 9-24-1957.
365 a strange and questioning silence: ibid.
365 Look at what they did to me: ibid.
365 I figured my aggressiveness: ibid.
365 the grudge fight: *Life*, 10-7-1957.
365 Sugar Ray tried to fight: NYT, 9-24-1957.
366 fluency and aggressiveness: *Ring*, 11-1957.
367 The niggers are in our school!: *Life*, 10-7-1957.
367 Two, four, six, eight: NYT, 9-24-1957.
367 white supremacists: ibid.
368 I went the whole fifteen rounds: Basilio interview by author.
368 He was a showboat: ibid.
369 jabbed a string of lefts: NYT, 3-26-1958.
370 just fine: ibid.
370 Trying to stop him: *Life*, 4-7-1958.
370 He's too incredible: NYT, 3-27-1958.
370 This boxing is men's business: ibid., 1-3-1957.
371 This ain't no Olson: ibid.
371 the picture-book fighter: ibid.
371 There's nothing I can say: ibid.
372 Instead of thinking his way: *Sports Illustrated*, 4-29-1957.
372 There were few indeed: NYT, 5-2-1957.
372 I was just maneuvering him: ibid.
372 What happened?: ibid.
372 Robinson has to be worked over hard: Unpublished Fullmer manuscript, 7.
373 I'm so sick: Robinson, *Sugar Ray*, 291.

373 It's fitting now to say: ibid., 10.
373 I believed Robinson fought: ibid., 6.
374 He was tough: Fullmer interview by author.
374 the miracle man of boxing: *Ring*, 2-1959.
374 Clay's last-round assault: Maraniss, *Rome 1960*, 282.
375 That Sugar Ray, he's something: Remnick, *King of the World*, 101.
376 Man, I'm old: *Newsweek*, 2-1-1960.
376 The heyday of Negro entertainment: Anderson, *This Was Harlem*, 349.
379 Sugar Ray Robinson—Finished?: *Ring*, 12-1960.
379 Where is Lena Horne?: Buckley, *The Hornes*, 242.
379 Here I am: ibid.
379 Breaking the White Barrier: *SHOW* magazine, 9-1969.
380 You don't have no idea: Branch, *Parting the Waters*, 810.
380 Have lived longer: Nichols, *Bontemps-Hughes Letters*, 376.
381 Without them, on my part: Bernard, *Remember Me to Harlem*, 310.

Autumn Leaves

384 He kept saying: Dick interview by author.
384 He's a wonderful fighter: *Sports Illustrated*, 9-6-1965.
385 Oh, it's lovely: Robinson, *Sugar Ray*, 353.
385 Man . . . that Hawaii: WP, 6-13-1965.
385 That Harrington in Honolulu: *Sports Illustrated*, 9-6-1965.
386 Nobody has ever been a champion: ibid.
386 Ray beats this Memo Ayon: WP, 6-13-1965.
386 came to me after the fight: ibid.

386 He's a kind man: *Sports Illustrated,* 9-6-1965.
386 Jab him. Jab him: *Sports Illustrated,* 9-6-1965.
387 I want to retire as champion: WP, 6-23-1965.
387 Of course Ray's in shape!: *Sports Illustrated,* 9-6-1965.
387 OK, . . . let the crowd in: ibid.
387 Why, ten years ago: ibid.
388 Come on, baby: ibid.
388 I'd like it here: ibid.
388 He had started saying: Breslin interview by author.
388 Hey, George!: *Sports Illustrated,* 9-6-1965.
388 Something fascinates me about second acts: King interview by author.
389 To win the title again: Robinson, *Sugar Ray,* 357.
390 Sugar, its time, man: Dick interview by author.
390 I hate to go on too long: WP, 11-12-1965.
390 I had hopes: ibid.
391 When I was a little kid: WP, 12-12-1965.
392 I was only the first fighter: LaMotta, *Raging Bull,* 214.
392 Sugar Ray Robinson came: Davis, *Autobiography,* 287.
392 He had no endurance: Anderson interview by author.
393 His lawyers finally came up with: ibid.
393 He said, 'I gotta get paid': ibid.

Saving All Those Walker Smith Juniors

398 I play my part: WP, 8-2-1966.
399 Sugar . . . I believe you could help: Halberstam, *What a Time it Was,* 93.
400 My heart cries: WP, 6-9-1969.
400 No . . . You have just started: Halberstam, *What a Time it Was,* 99.

401 I honestly believe: ibid.
401 Everybody wanted to come by: Bristow interview by author.
401–402 I've always felt; Sugar Ray understands; The foundation; I thought only: All quotes from 1978 Sugar Ray Foundation Awards Banquet program, author possession.
402 It meant so much to him: Bristow interview by author.
403 I've got friends: Halberstam, *What a Time it Was,* 101.
403 Where the fuck is everybody?: Hamill interview by author.
404 I went to look for him: Dick interview by author.
404 He asked me, three times: ibid.
404–405 As I came in: Anderson interview by author.
405 Every now and then: ibid.
405 She said she'd have to charge: Moore interview by author.
406 Let's sing a song: *New York Post,* 4-13-1989.
406 The best . . . is always fragile: Souvenir booklet, Sugar Ray Foundation, author possession.
406 Elizabeth loved Ray: Dick interview by author.

Epilogue

409 They used to talk: Kilmer interview by author.
409 One of my trainers: ibid.
409 You don't hear anything: ibid.
409 You see how Robinson: ibid.
410 He threw a punch: ibid.
410 If you don't have legs: ibid.
410 You can't teach people: ibid.
410 I really can't explain: ibid.
411 to miss Sugar: *The Guardian,* 8-10-2007.
412 It's about the things: New York *Daily News,* 6-6-1989.
412 He always had an entourage: ibid.

Index

Golden Gloves victories of, 41–5, 123, 146, 178, 181, 224, 228, 314, 356, 390, 404

Gordon Parks and, 272, 273, 274, 278, 279, 281, 282, 283, 286, 287

Graziano's title bout with, 309–12

greatness and originality of, 409–12

Harlem childhood of, 20–1, 22, 23, 400

Hollywood and, 342, 393, 397–8

Horrmann's financial backing of, 45–6, 48, 49–51

hospitals feared by, 321, 404

illegal kidney punch charged to, 275–6

injuries to, 159, 171, 179, 283–4, 285, 296, 297, 385

International Boxing Club challenged by, 366–7, 368

jazz, jazzmen and, 37, 75, 90, 99, 100–1, 106–7, 108, 111–12, 113, 115, 127–8, 130–2, 392, 399

Keesler Field incident, 71–3

LaMotta's bouts with, 193–6, 200–3, 201, 206–9, 217–22, 224–5, 226–8, 247–50, 252, 253, 354

marital problems of, 377–8

Maxim's bout with, 317–18, 319–22, 323, 349

Mel Dick's friendship with, 229–32, 290–1, 293, 303, 326, 335, 353, 355, 377, 384, 404, 406

Miles Davis's friendship with, 69, 105, 235, 330–1, 330, 334, 384, 389, 390, 392

in military discharge controversy, 93–4, 214–15

Millie Bruce and, 382, 383–5, 386–8, 389, 390, 391, 393, 399, 400, 401, 403, 404–6

name changed by, 31, 35–6

as nightclub owner, 3–4, 6, 7, 113, 114, 127–8, 130–1, 133, 134, 262–3, 269, 376–7

Olson's title bout with, 359–60

in Paris, 237, 272–4, 273, 342

pink Cadillac of, 102–3, 132, 152, 231, 260, 264, 268, 269, 272, 282, 294, 310, 329, 375, 383, 403, 412, 413

racism and, 15–16, 68, 71–3, 74, 79–81, 82, 344

reaction of women to, 82, 83, 90, 360–1

retirement of, from boxing, 305, 307, 309, 313, 314, 323, 390–3

Salem Crescent Athletic Club and, 24–5, 26, 27–9, 30

show business criticism of, 337, 339–41, 342, 343

sportswriters on, 36, 42, 48–9, 112, 117, 125, 126, 149–50, 169, 203–4, 285–6, 290, 298, 313, 375–6, 388–9

Tiger Jones's bout with, 352–5, 358, 360

Turpin's London bout with, 281–6

Turpin's rematch with, 289, 293–4, 295–8

Walter Winchell and, 254–5, 256–7, 260–1, 262, 289, 295, 373

weight division change by, 192–3, 237–8, 245, 313

in welterweight title bout, 117–18, 123–6, 127

youth foundation started by, 397, 399–403, 404, 406

Rodgers, Richard, 390

Rogers, Timmie, 335

Roosevelt, Eleanor, 64, 67, 77, 78, 93, 95

Roosevelt, Franklin D., 21–2, 23, 24, 64, 69, 88, 183, 214, 222, 270

Rosenbloom, Carroll, 401

Rosenwald Fellowship, 288

Ross, Barney, 141–2, 151

Rothstein, Arthur, 270

Rowe, Billy, 81, 92

Rowland, Dick, 15

Roxborough, John, 19, 53

Royal, Robert, 24, 25, 100, 109, 110, 128, 134, 183, 412

Royal Gym, San Francisco, 308

Rubio, Norman, 49, 116, 126

Runyon, Damon, 214, 217, 255–6, 257

Rushing, Jimmy, 105

Russell, Nipsey, 335

Ruth, Babe, 51

S

Sacco, Nicola, 188

Saerens, Emile, 384

Sahara Hotel, 337

St. James Presbyterian Church, 22

St. Louis Post-Dispatch, 146, 149

St. Philip's Protestant Episcopal Church, 22, 25

St. Regis Hotel, 403

ABOUT THE AUTHOR

WIL HAYGOOD began his writing career on a small weekly in his hometown of Columbus, Ohio. He went on to work for *The Charleston Gazette,* the *Pittsburgh Post-Gazette, The Boston Globe,* and currently *The Washington Post.* A celebrated journalist, he has received wide acclaim as well for his nonfiction books. His *In Black and White: The Life of Sammy Davis, Jr.,* won the Zora Neale Hurston–Richard Wright Legacy Award, the ASCAP–Deems Taylor Outstanding Music Biography Award, and the Nonfiction Book of the Year award from the Black Caucus of the American Library Association. His *King of the Cats: The Life and Times of Adam Clayton Powell, Jr.,* was a New York Times Notable Book. The author's family memoir, *The Haygoods of Columbus*—which critic David Nicholson wrote should be placed "squarely in the kingdom of literature"—received the Great Lakes Book Award. Haygood's journalism honors include the National Headliner Award, the New England Associated Press Award, the Sunday Magazine Editors award, the Paul L. Myhre Single Story award, and five first-place writing awards from the National Association of Black Journalists. Haygood has been an Alicia Patterson Foundation fellow and a Pulitzer Prize finalist, and also a visiting writer at the University of Georgia, Vanderbilt University, Colorado College, and his alma mater, Miami University, in Oxford, Ohio. He resides in Washington, D.C.

A NOTE ON THE TYPE

The text of this book was set in Garamond No. 3. It is not a true copy of any of the designs of Claude Garamond (ca. 1480–1561), but an adaptation of his types, which set the European standard for two centuries. It probably owes as much to the designs of Jean Jannon, a Protestant printer working in Sedan in the early seventeenth century, who had worked with Garamond's romans earlier, in Paris, but who was denied their use because of Catholic censorship. Jannon's matrices came into the possession of the Imprimerie nationale, where they were thought to be by Garamond himself, and were so described when the Imprimerie revived the type in 1900. This particular version is based on an adaptation by Morris Fuller Benton.

Composed by North Market Street Graphics, Lancaster, Pennsylvania
Printed and bound by Berryville Graphics, Berryville, Virginia
Designed by Maggie Hinders